SOPHONISBA
BRECKINRIDGE

Sophonisba Breckinridge

CHAMPIONING WOMEN'S ACTIVISM IN MODERN AMERICA

Anya Jabour

UNIVERSITY OF
ILLINOIS PRESS
Urbana, Chicago, and Springfield

Publication of this book was supported in part by a grant from the Baldridge Book Subvention Fund through the Humanities Institute of the College of Humanities and Sciences at the University of Montana.

Manufactured in the United States of America
1 2 3 4 5 C P 5 4 3 2 1
⊚ This book is printed on acid-free paper.

Library of Congress Cataloging-in-Publication Data
Names: Jabour, Anya, author.
Title: Sophonisba Breckinridge: championing women's
   activism in modern America / Anya Jabour.
Description: [Urbana, Illinois] : University of Illinois, [2019]
   | Series: Women, gender, and sexuality in American
   history | Includes bibliographical references and index.
Identifiers: LCCN 2019005786 (print) | LCCN 2019009631
   (ebook) | ISBN 9780252051524 (ebook) | ISBN
   9780252042676 (cloth : alk. paper) | ISBN 9780252084515
   (pbk. : alk. paper)
Subjects: LCSH: Breckinridge, Sophonisba P. (Sophonisba
   Preston), 1866–1948. | Feminists—United States—
   Biography. | Feminism—United States—History—
   19th century. | Feminism—United States—History—
   20th century. | Women social workers—United
   States—Biography. | Women social reformers—
   United States—Biography.
Classification: LCC HV40.32.B73 (ebook) | LCC HV40.32.B73
   J33 2019 (print) | DDC 305.42092 [B]—dc23
LC record available at https://lccn.loc.gov/2019005786

Contents

PREFACE

Forgotten Feminist

In 1933, Sophonisba Preston Breckinridge responded to a young woman's request for career advice by suggesting that she contact Democratic Party insider Mary W. Dewson, known as "More Women Dewson" for her success in placing women in New Deal positions. "She is a good feminist," commented Breckinridge, "which simply means that she wants good women to have their chance." Breckinridge, too, was "a good feminist" throughout her long life, from 1866 to 1948. Nationally and internationally renowned in her lifetime, since her death in 1948 Breckinridge has been largely forgotten. This book—the first comprehensive biography of this "forgotten feminist"—reclaims Breckinridge from historical amnesia and offers fresh insights into women's activism in modern America.[1]

I didn't set out to write a biography of Breckinridge. I have a longstanding interest in exploring personal lives in historical context: My first book was a case study of a married couple; my second and third books included "cameos" of individuals; and I have published numerous articles featuring case studies of individuals, families, and circles of friends. Nonetheless, when I discovered Breckinridge, it was by chance. In 2009, in the course of conducting background research for a planned book project on women teachers in the Victorian South, I came across a short biographical profile of Breckinridge. I was immediately intrigued to learn that, despite earning advanced degrees in politics, economics, and law, she was unable to find an academic position in any of her fields of specialty.[2]

As I learned more about Breckinridge, I was intrigued to find that she responded to the limited professional opportunities available to women by pioneering a new, female-friendly profession: social work. This discovery prompted me to reexamine my assumptions about "feminized" occupations, especially when

I learned that, in 1905, Breckinridge taught what was arguably the first women's studies class in the United States—in a Department of Household Administration! Who was this woman who persisted despite sex discrimination and transformed gender ghettos into feminist strongholds?[3]

Breckinridge's background as well as her accomplishments interested me. How had this privileged daughter of one of the leading families of the Southern Confederacy come to be an outspoken advocate for African Americans, immigrants, and the working class? What family influences and childhood experiences had paved the way for an elite white woman to become, as one laudatory profile in the *Woman's Journal* put it, "a champion of the championless"?[4]

Breckinridge's personal relationships with other professionally successful and politically powerful women—Alice Freeman Palmer, president of Wellesley College; Marion Talbot, dean of women at the University of Chicago; Jane Addams, head of Hull House; Julia Lathrop, chief of the U.S. Children's Bureau; and Edith Abbott, dean of the University of Chicago's School of Social Service Administration, among many others—also caught my attention. What role did female friendship play in defining Breckinridge's life's course?

My curiosity was piqued. I wanted to know more about this remarkable woman, but I found myself frustrated by a lack of scholarship about her. Sociologists and social workers had written a handful of articles about her, and historians occasionally included her in broader discussions of social reform and social work education, but nobody had attempted a comprehensive study of her life and work. I found that, despite her long association with Jane Addams and Progressive reform, books on these subjects routinely omitted Breckinridge—or, if they included her, they misspelled her name. In addition, I discovered that while Breckinridge reached the height of her influence in the 1920s and 1930s, extant treatments of her career—like studies of progressivism and feminism more generally—usually concluded in 1920.[5]

At this point, my research began in earnest. Wondering if a lack of source material accounted for this neglect, I investigated further. To my delight, I discovered that the Library of Congress held a thirty-seven-reel set of microfilmed papers, representing thirty-nine boxes of manuscript material, available via interlibrary loan. I immediately ordered the first four reels, the maximum permissible quantity. I anxiously awaited their arrival, eager to see what I might find in the approximately fourteen thousand items included in the Sophonisba P. Breckinridge Papers. When my order at last arrived, I wasted no time in taking my precious reels of microfilm and my laptop computer to the little-used microfilm readers located in the basement of the University of Montana's Mansfield Library. I was not disappointed. Indeed, I soon realized that Breckinridge's papers were a treasure trove of information about women's activism in modern America.

Breckinridge was involved in virtually every reform of the Progressive and New Deal eras. Her early correspondence documented all the women's activism I had been teaching about in my U.S. women's history classes for the preceding fifteen years. As I read further, into the 1920s and 1930s, I found that Breckinridge was involved in still other reform movements that were new to me. In order to keep track of her many activities, I created a timeline on sheets of butcher paper affixed to my study wall. To organize copies of her voluminous correspondence, reams of memoranda, and draft publications, I began a growing collection of three-ring binders, organized by date and topic. To find space for all the material I was collecting, I had to build additional bookcases and reorganize my study. Soon, I had an entire room dedicated to Breckinridge.

As my excitement grew, I could hardly bear the wait between batches of microfilm. I whiled away the intervening weeks by conducting repeated searches for even glancing references to Breckinridge in published sources and tracking footnotes to the original sources. I discovered that she had begun an autobiography and that more than one hundred pages of her memoirs, in disorganized, frequently emended manuscript pages, could be read at the Special Collections Research Center at the University of Chicago's Regenstein Library. Having identified numerous individuals and organizations in Breckinridge's microfilmed papers, I expanded my search to include those collections as well. Online finding aids helped me to identify pertinent materials, both in microfilm and manuscript, held at various repositories around the country.[6]

With the financial support of my mother, Jane Cress Edgar; the University of Montana; and the National Endowment for the Humanities, I spent my summer and winter breaks examining personal collections, organizational records, and family papers in Chicago, Washington, D.C., and Lexington, Kentucky. I discovered a collection of oral histories with early social workers and traveled to New York City to read the transcripts. I went to Lincoln, Nebraska, to examine the papers of Breckinridge's closest companion, Edith Abbott. I spent time in Minneapolis, Minnesota, to find Breckinridge's comments recorded in the transcripts, held at the Social Welfare History Archives, of professional social work conference proceedings. I made repeated trips to Chicago to examine not only Breckinridge's own papers but also those of her colleagues—and rivals—at both the University of Chicago and the Chicago School of Civics and Philanthropy. I spent rainy days at the Library of Congress reading material in the Breckinridge family papers not included in the microfilmed edition of Breckinridge's papers, including her correspondence with her mother while she was attending Wellesley College, files related to her father's trial for breach-of-promise, and an intriguing collection of family snapshots. I learned to navigate the D.C. Metro in order to visit the National Archives, where I sifted through memoranda detailing the political maneuvering surrounding Breckinridge's appointment as an official U.S. delegate to the Seventh Pan-American Conference in Montevideo, Uruguay, in 1933.

I immersed myself in Breckinridge's milieu. In Chicago, I roamed the University of Chicago campus, exploring Green Hall, the graduate women's residence hall she presided over for more than forty years, and Cobb Hall, where she studied and worked for more than fifty years. I made repeated visits to the Hull House Museum, where the original house and dining hall—although not, alas, the third floor where Breckinridge had her living quarters—are preserved and open to the public. In Kentucky, I made a pilgrimage to Breckinridge's grave in the Lexington Cemetery and contemplated her tombstone, designed by life partner Edith Abbott, which described her simply as a scholar, teacher, and humanitarian.

When teaching and administrative responsibilities kept me in Missoula, I continued my quest from afar. I conducted database research in periodicals, finding articles by Breckinridge in publications ranging from the *Journal of Political Economy* to the *Journal of Home Economics* and reading back issues of the *Social Service Review*, the first professional social work journal, which Breckinridge and Abbott established in 1927. I scoured the digitized back issues of the *Chicago Tribune* and the *New York Times* for references to Breckinridge. I delighted in the Smithsonian Institution's "Chronicling America" online collection of digitized newspapers, where I found reports on Breckinridge's professional accomplishments and political views sandwiched between fashion columns and literary reviews on the women's pages of small-town newspapers. I wandered the Government Documents stacks to find congressional hearings and government reports featuring Breckinridge. I ordered additional reels of microfilm from the *Jane Addams Papers Project* to find correspondence with and references to Breckinridge, as well as microfilmed papers from the Women's International League for Peace and Freedom and the American Association for Labor Legislation, among other organizations. I consulted maps, charts, and photos detailing daily life in the neighborhood surrounding Hull House, where Breckinridge spent all her vacations between 1907 and 1921, available on the "Urban Experience in Chicago" website. And I read contemporary novels, short stories, poetry, and magazines, seeking to see Breckinridge's world through her eyes.

Librarians and archivists were valuable allies. Interlibrary loan officers at the University of Montana and at a plethora of other libraries around the country allowed me to obtain remote access to multiple microfilmed collections. A helpful archivist at Wellesley College responded to my queries by sending photocopies and scans of materials about Breckinridge's graduating class. An equally helpful archivist at the Schlesinger Library agreed to photocopy selected materials from several collections of suffrage correspondence, including the papers of National

Woman's Party member Doris Stevens, Breckinridge's archenemy. The archivist at the University of Montana obtained access to the digitized papers of the National Woman's Party and the League of Women Voters, which contained vast quantities of information about Breckinridge's opposition to the Equal Rights Amendment, her work on the League of Women Voters' Committee on the Legal Status of Women, and her role as the United States' first female delegate to an international convention at the Pan-American Congress of 1933. Fellow scholars and research assistants also provided essential assistance by sharing photocopies and scans of materials from far-flung repositories around the country—and even from abroad.

As I worked with the materials I had collected, constructed an organizational framework, and drafted chapters, the question of why Breckinridge had been forgotten continued to haunt me. Eventually, not only did I identify explanations for scholars' neglect, but I also realized that, in resurrecting the story of this forgotten feminist, I had the opportunity to revise the history of American feminism. By telling the story of what the *Woman's Journal* dubbed "her many-sided work," I intend both to reclaim Breckinridge as an important figure in U.S. women's history and to retrace the contours of women's activism in modern America.[7]

Acknowledgments

Like Breckinridge, I have been blessed with the good fortune of conducting my work as part of a supportive community. Fellow scholars passed on useful references and copies of original materials. Bari Burke shared the link to a fascinating interview with Breckinridge about her work as a lawyer; Teresa Marques sent materials from the Bertha Lutz papers in Brazil; Nancy Cooper alerted me to a report on "Un-American Activities" that included Breckinridge; Richard Drake provided a citation from the Robert LaFollette Papers; Melanie Beals Goan sent me a photocopy of Breckinridge's memoirs; Joan Marie Johnson provided me with excerpts from the M. Carey Thomas Papers relating to Breckinridge's suffrage work; Anne Meis Knupfer sent copies of correspondence documenting a job offer Breckinridge received from the Western College for Women in Oxford, Ohio; and Anthony Todd pointed me to a student's reminiscences and sent scans of materials about the Chicago School of Civics and Philanthropy.

Librarians and archivists also helped me identify and acquire materials both on site and from afar. While I am indebted to every staff member who provided assistance at every repository consulted, special thanks are due to Linnea Anderson at the Social Welfare History Archives; Jennifer Brathvode at the Library of Congress; Jane Callahan at the Wellesley College Archives; David M. Hays at the University of Colorado; Lynda Leahy at the Schlesinger Library; Pam Marek at the University of Montana's Mansfield Library's Interlibrary Loan Department; Daniel Meyer at the University of Chicago's Special Collections Research Center; Donna McCrea at Archives and Special Collections at the University of Montana; Lynn Niedermeier at Western Kentucky University's Special Collections; Kathleen Banks Nutter at the Sophia Smith Collection; Mariana Oller from Wellesley College's Special Collections; Laura Reiner at Wellesley College Archives; and Robin Wallace of the Filson Historical Society. In addition, Kayla Blackman, Laura Baines-Walsh, and Hillary Zulli provided essential research services at the Schlesinger Library, Wellesley College Archives, and the Library of Congress, respectively.

Colleagues near and far also have helped me develop my analysis of Breckinridge's life and work. At the University of Montana, participants in the History Department's Lockridge Workshops—especially Richard Drake, Rachel Gross, Paul Lauren, Patrick O'Connor, Jody Pavilack, Tobin Miller Shearer, and Kyle Volk—not only offered useful suggestions on the structure of the book as a whole but also provided valuable feedback on Breckinridge's work on both foreign and domestic policy. Conversations with the students who enrolled in my graduate seminar on "Gender, Politics, and Society" helped me clarify my thinking about the "difference versus equality" binary. Guest lectures in Janet Finn's courses on the history of social policy in the School of Social Work gave me the opportunity to discuss my ongoing research and refine my analysis of Breckinridge's contributions to the social work profession. Bari Burke and Nancy Cooper, fellow biographers from the School of Law and the School of Music, respectively, offered useful insight on many draft chapters as well as unflagging support and unstinting encouragement.

Further afield, the members of the Newberry Seminar on Women and Gender challenged me to examine the multiple meanings of feminism in U.S. history. Both the editors of the *Journal of Women's History* and the anonymous reviewers for the journal pushed me to refine my ideas about women's activism in modern America. Two Summer Institutes sponsored by the National Endowment for the Humanities—one on Progressive-era Chicago and another on Suffrage in the Americas—deepened my understanding of Breckinridge's activism at both the local and the global level. I am especially appreciative of the helpful suggestions and probing questions offered by Katherine Marino, Caroline Merithew, Teresa Marques, and Megan Threlkeld, all of whom took time away from their own scholarship to read and respond to mine. I also received valuable insights from fellow panelists and audience members at meetings of the American Historical Association, the Berkshire Conference on the History of Women and Gender, the Organization of American Historians, the Society for Historians of American Foreign Policy, the Society for the History of Children and Youth, the Southern Area Women Historians, and the Western Area Women Historians, among others. Special thanks to Pamela Stewart and Evelyn Blackwood for stimulating conversations about women's relationships in historical perspective and to Lorri Glover and Joan Marie Johnson for pushing me to think seriously about how both family relationships and female friendships shaped Breckinridge's life.

Family and friends offered unstinting support throughout this project. My mother, Jane Cress Edgar, not only subsidized my first research trip to Chicago but also accompanied me on a self-guided, Breckinridge-themed tour of the University of Chicago campus. Sara Hayden has been a sounding board from the very beginning, never complaining about the many e-mails I sent her with variations on the subject line, "Nisba is so cool!" Tammy Whitlock hosted me during a research trip to Lexington, Kentucky, and helped me locate Breckinridge's grave. Finally, Maren Christensen believed that I would finish this book even when I did not. I am grateful for her unwavering faith in me.

Institutional support was vital as well. A summer stipend from the National Endowment for the Humanities provided essential funding for travel to archives, as did both the History Department and the Faculty Professional Enhancement Program at the University of Montana. UM's Women's, Gender, and Sexuality Studies Program's sponsorship of annual writing retreats offered me both time and space to write and congenial company in which to discuss my work. Finally, publication of this book was supported in part by a grant from the Baldridge Book Subvention Fund through the Humanities Institute of the College of Humanities and Sciences at the University of Montana.

Portions of chapter 1 previously appeared in another form in Anya Jabour, "Autobiography of an Activist: Sophonisba Breckinridge, 'Champion of the Championless,'" in Delphine Letort and Benaouda Lebdai, eds., *Women Activists and Civil Rights Leaders in Auto/Biographical Literature and Films* (Cham, Switzerland: Palgrave MacMillan, 2018), 45–63. Portions of chapters 1, 2, and 3 previously appeared in another form in Anya Jabour, "Duty and Destiny: A Progressive Reformer's Coming of Age in the Gilded Age," in James Marten, ed., *Children and Youth during the Gilded Age and Progressive Era* (New York: New York University Press, 2014), 230–51, and in Anya Jabour, "Sophonisba Breckinridge (1866–1948): Homegrown Heroine," in Melissa A. McEuen and Thomas H. Appleton, eds., *Kentucky Women: Their Lives and Times* (Athens: University of Georgia Press, 2015), 140–67. Portions of chapters 4, 5, and 10 previously appeared in another form in Anya Jabour, "Relationship and Leadership: Sophonisba Breckinridge and Women in Social Work," *Affilia: Journal of Women and Social Work* 27, no. 1 (Spring 2012): 22–37. Thanks to these publishers for permission to republish this work.

SOPHONISBA BRECKINRIDGE

Sophonisba Breckinridge was one of the most influential Americans
of her generation. In her lifetime, which extended from the Civil War
to the Cold War, she played an important role in movements for
women's rights, immigrant welfare, civil rights, labor legislation, and
world peace. This image of her striding boldly across the campus of
the University of Chicago captures her attitude of fearless advocacy
and her commitment to advancing social justice. For Breckinridge, "a
woman's work" was "the work of the world."

Courtesy Special Collections Research Center, University of Chicago Library

INTRODUCTION

"A Woman's Work" and
"The Work of the World"

"The work of the world," pioneering social work educator Sophonisba Preston Breckinridge (1866–1948) reportedly admonished her students, "is not done by giving up when you get tired." Apocryphal or not, this oft-repeated anecdote captures Breckinridge's lifelong commitment to social justice. Although she briefly considered taking religious vows, by the time she reached adulthood, Breckinridge had exchanged the "simple faith" of her childhood for a more secular sense of social responsibility. However, she remained convinced that "the Lord has planned a woman's work for me," as she explained to one would-be suitor. That work, however, entailed not a cloistered life but rather a lifelong commitment to social justice.[1]

Breckinridge dedicated her entire life to being "a woman who helps," as one contemporary account put it. Born and raised in Kentucky, she spent her adult life in Chicago, where she earned advanced degrees in economics, political science, and law; joined the community of women reformers based at Hull House; and established the University of Chicago's School of Social Service Administration, the first school of social work affiliated with a major research university. Thereafter, Breckinridge used her position at the university to engage in social and political reform both in the United States and abroad, ranging from the antilynching movement to the labor movement, from the slums of Chicago to the capitals of Europe. Nationally and internationally renowned in her own time, Breckinridge has, since her death in 1948, been largely forgotten. Yet her story deserves to be told, because her insistence on doing "the work of the world" illuminates American women's participation in the struggle for social justice both in the United

States and beyond its borders. Throughout her long life, Breckinridge worked to advance the rights and welfare of all disadvantaged groups and to foster a peaceful and just social order that protected fundamental human rights.[2]

Breckinridge's lifelong commitment to social justice sheds new light on women's activism in modern America. Breckinridge was involved in virtually every reform—including legal aid for immigrants, civil rights for blacks, labor legislation for workers, and juvenile courts for youth—of the Progressive and New Deal eras. She also demanded safe working conditions, a minimum wage, and full citizenship rights for women. With her partner, Edith Abbott, Breckinridge made the School of Social Service Administration a feminist "think tank" that addressed all of these issues and made women key players in policymaking.

Through the alchemy of social scientific research, Breckinridge translated the social reforms envisioned by women's voluntary groups into public policies enacted in government agencies. An indefatigable advocate for the nation's dispossessed, Breckinridge pressured local, state, and federal officials to fund programs and pass legislation to benefit women, workers, and children, as well as the poor, the elderly, and the disabled. As a member of an advisory committee for programs established by the Social Security Act of 1935, the basis for the modern welfare state, Breckinridge literally set the standards for professional education and civil service for the first generation of public welfare workers.

Breckinridge's influence extended beyond national boundaries. A co-founder of the U.S. chapter of the Women's International League for Peace and Freedom, Breckinridge called on European governments to establish an international community, uphold national self-determination, enforce international law, defend human rights, and ensure lasting peace—a set of goals that ultimately informed both the League of Nations and the United Nations. As the first American woman to represent the United States at an international diplomatic conference, she promoted the "Good Neighbor Policy," which established a new framework for U.S.–Latin American relations in the 1930s, and she helped lay the groundwork for the idea that "women's rights are human rights."

Despite Breckinridge's many accomplishments—and the extensive records that document her life and work—she has been overlooked by subsequent generations. This has been the case for many women, of course. Even though U.S. women's history has enjoyed a renaissance of sorts since the 1970s, historians and journalists alike continue to engage in the important work of recovering the lost stories of women like the "hidden figures" who worked at NASA and the "immortal life" of the woman whose cells revolutionized science.[3]

These women were black; the lives of educated white women who engaged in professional work and political activism, like Breckinridge, have, on balance, received considerably more attention. Yet not Breckinridge. Whereas scholars have produced numerous biographies of Breckinridge's collaborator and contemporary Jane Addams, as historian James Klotter remarked in his 1986 study, *The Breckinridges of Kentucky*, Breckinridge still "awaits a biographer."[4]

One reason for this collective amnesia may be Breckinridge's penchant for collaborative projects. While she played an important role in many major developments and movements, she did not act alone but in concert with other women professionals and feminist activists. She thus has not drawn the sort of sustained attention that acknowledged leaders, such as Jane Addams, have gained. As Emily Nussbaum observed in a 2012 *New York Times* article about feminist superstars, "We often have a cultural fantasy about individuals. But collaboration is just as frequently the source of great things, and it's less rarely recognized."[5]

In addition, Breckinridge usually worked behind the scenes to influence policy. She also based her influence on her demonstrable professional competence rather than on supposedly innate feminine characteristics. According to Jill Conway, whereas women like Addams, who presented themselves as feminine prophetesses, had "great resonance for American popular culture" and became cultural heroines, the "woman as expert . . . did not capture the popular imagination in the same way or remain widely known beyond her generation."[6]

The duration and scope of Breckinridge's life work also pose obstacles. Because her work spanned several decades and encompassed multiple issues, she does not fit neatly into broader studies of particular eras or movements. Although several histories of social welfare and the Progressive era include her, studies of women's activism and of later periods usually exclude her. In this, Breckinridge's near-invisibility reflects historians' lack of attention to feminism in the postsuffrage era; for instance, in her 2010 history of American feminism, Christine Stansell characterizes the interwar period as "the lost years" between "first wave feminism" (the suffrage struggle, concluding in 1920) and "second wave feminism" (the modern women's movement, commencing in the 1960s).[7]

Although Nancy A. Hewitt and others urged scholars to rethink the history and periodization of feminism in the 2010 anthology *No Permanent Waves: Recasting Histories of U.S. Feminism,* most U.S. women's historians continue to work within the "wave" framework. Perhaps for this reason, scholars have not mined the majority of Breckinridge's extensive personal papers, instead relying principally on Breckinridge's incomplete autobiography and her comparatively scant pre-1920 correspondence—and thereby missing the most productive and best documented decades of Breckinridge's life, the 1920s and 1930s.[8]

Breckinridge's vocal denunciation of the Equal Rights Amendment (on the grounds that it would invalidate gender-specific labor and health legislation) also may have played a role in some feminist scholars' lack of interest in her later career. Indeed, Breckinridge's simultaneous commitment to equal rights and protective legislation prevents her from fitting neatly into scholarly categories such as "radical" or "social" feminist, typically differentiated by the "difference versus equality" binary.[9]

In addition, the wide range of Breckinridge's interests—which included internationalism, civil rights, and pacifism as well as social welfare and women's rights—make it difficult to categorize her and, paradoxically, probably contributed to her omission from studies on these individual movements. As Mary Trigg observes in her 2014 book, we are only beginning to understand "feminism as life's work" rather than as a discrete movement.[10]

Breckinridge's life merits attention not only because Breckinridge was an important figure in early-twentieth-century reform but also because examining her life work offers new insight into feminist activism in twentieth-century America. Indeed, it is precisely the characteristics of Breckinridge's career that make her easy to overlook that shed light on previously underappreciated aspects of women's activism in modern America.

Breckinridge's collaboration with others highlights the cooperative nature of women's activism. Breckinridge's contemporaries often spoke of her as part of a cohort of women working together to achieve common aims, what one admirer called "a whole epoch of great American women." Breckinridge was part of a close-knit circle of women reformers who met at Hull House and went on to play important roles on the national and international stage. "The Great Ladies of Hull-House," as one account described them, included Jane Addams, Edith and Grace Abbott, Florence Kelley, and Julia Lathrop, among others. These "strong-minded women" drew their strength from one another. As one contemporary explained it, this "extraordinary and delightful Chicago group" was so effective, in part, because its members shared values, divided responsibilities, and encouraged one another. Recalling the early years when Breckinridge's "little group of social leaders" struggled to establish social welfare services, one acquaintance perceptively noted: "I have often thought that those fine spirits, through their close association, must have strengthened and stimulated one another more than even they realized."[11] Personal relationships enhanced women's political power in early-twentieth-century America. Collaboration, rather than leadership, defined women's activism in modern America.

In addition, Breckinridge's behind-the-scenes work calls attention to the connections between research and reform in modern America. Breckinridge was one of the foremost intellectuals of her generation at a time when scholars were standard-bearers for social policy as well as for intellectual life. In 1945, when *Life* magazine published a laudatory account of the University of Chicago's "new pattern for U.S. education"—one that included both Platonic philosophy and policy papers—Breckinridge, along with Abbott, was one of just two women included in a group photo of "fifty of Chicago's most brilliant professors."[12] Breckinridge regarded scholarship as the basis for social reform. She built her professional career and reputation during the Progressive era, when public intellectuals played a prominent role in shaping public policy. She reached the height of her influence in the 1930s, when she used her professional expertise to promote new approaches to both domestic programs and foreign relations. For Breckinridge, as for many of her contemporaries, academia represented not a refuge from the real world but a power base from which to change the world for the better. Breckinridge's long career as a public scholar highlights women's role in crafting the intellectual foundation for social reform.

Tracing Breckinridge's involvement in multiple reform activities also indicates the interrelatedness of social reforms that are usually treated in isolation from one another. As a biographical profile of her put it in 1912, "Miss Breckinridge's activities are manifold." Breckinridge, like many of her contemporaries, was no single-issue advocate. Rather, because she understood the multiple sources of injustice, Breckinridge insisted on promoting justice in multiple ways. Her simultaneous commitments to women's rights and child welfare, civil rights and social welfare, and domestic policy and international relations—to name a few of her many interests—reflected her belief that only the protection of the rights and the promotion of the welfare of all people could ensure a just and peaceful world. As she explained to the *Woman's Journal*, her mission was "to help and protect 'all those who are desolate and oppressed.'"[13]

Following Breckinridge's lifelong commitment to women's rights challenges received wisdom that the first wave of feminism receded after the achievement of woman suffrage. After gaining professional success and political rights, Breckinridge used her hard-won advantages to promote social justice. While she took up new causes, Breckinridge never abandoned organized feminism; rather, she supported women's rights for the rest of her long life. In 1943, at age seventy-seven, she attended a "Women's Rights demonstration" and suffrage exhibit at Radcliffe College, noting that she did so "in memory of the old suffragists."[14] Decades after participating in the suffrage struggle, Breckinridge remained identified with "the march of women's progress."[15]

Breckinridge's commitment to demanding equality while acknowledging difference also offers insight into the central dilemma of modern feminism. Throughout her life, Breckinridge advocated for what she called "the rights of women," although she insisted these must be obtained "the right way." For Breckinridge, the right way to achieve rights was to provide women with both equal opportunities and special protections. Only by addressing women's particular needs as women, she insisted, could women take their place as men's equals. Fair treatment, not identical treatment, was the key to true equality.[16]

Finally, examining the full range of Breckinridge's activities calls attention to the wide scope of women's activism in modern America. For Breckinridge, as for other women reformers, women's activism encompassed women's rights, but it was by no means limited to women's interests. During the summer of 1935, Breckinridge wrote a series of letters to her mentor, Marion Talbot, detailing meetings regarding civil service exams for Chicago's Woman's Court, background research related to the final details of the Social Security Act, and preparation for the Pan American Child Congress to be held in Mexico later that year. "Life is a little complicated," she remarked with considerable understatement.[17] Breckinridge's insistence on working on all these issues simultaneously and in the stifling heat of a Chicago summer testifies to her conviction that achieving social justice was neither simple nor easy but required unremitting effort on multiple fronts. Her work also reveals the wide range and the long duration of women's activism in modern America. Breckinridge considered her activities—which included protecting women's civil rights, providing public welfare, and promoting world peace—as essential to the "woman's work" she undertook at the height of the suffrage struggle. For women activists in modern America, "a woman's work" was "the work of the world."

A careful study of Breckinridge's life and work significantly reshapes our understanding of both the chronology and the contours of U.S. feminism, requiring us to acknowledge the continuity of feminist activism, rethink the notion of feminist leadership, reevaluate academic endeavors as central to American activism, and recognize the diversity and the interrelatedness of the many issues that women have considered "feminist." By foregrounding the life and work of this forgotten feminist, my biography of Breckinridge presents a more complete—and more complex—story of women's activism in modern America.

Although in the largest sense this is a conventional "cradle-to-grave" biography, this story generally proceeds thematically rather than according to strict chronology. The first three chapters, which address Breckinridge's formative years and her long years of preparation for her life's work, appear chronologically.

Chapter 1 examines how Breckinridge's Kentucky childhood shaped her adult career. Breckinridge achieved national and international prominence in her lifetime, but when she sat down in 1945 to record her life, she began by situating herself in the context of her family of origin. As she recognized, both Breckinridge's family legacy and her relationships with other family members would have a profound impact on her future work. This chapter combines Breckinridge's unfinished and unpublished memoirs with family records to suggest the ways in which her family heritage and youthful experiences foreshadowed her future career.[18]

Chapter 2 details Breckinridge's brilliant career at Wellesley College, an all-female institution with rigorous academic requirements. When Breckinridge left Kentucky to attend school, her father urged her to use her time away from home to learn to "be your own mistress." Exposure to both a demanding liberal arts curriculum and alternative models of womanhood gave Breckinridge the tools she would need to become an independent woman. Family correspondence, augmented by materials from Wellesley College, demonstrate that Breckinridge's college experience prepared her for a future as a self-supporting professional and a social justice activist.[19]

Chapter 3 highlights the challenges faced by "New Women" like Breckinridge while also demonstrating the role of higher education in determining Breckinridge's future life course. After graduating from Wellesley in 1888, Breckinridge struggled to reconcile her duty to her family with her desire to be independent. Breckinridge's personal correspondence and her later memoirs alike reveal that she, like other college-educated New Women in turn-of-the-century America, found it nearly impossible to reconcile what her contemporary Jane Addams called "the family claim" with her professional goals. But while Breckinridge's postcollegiate difficulties postponed her career, they also further defined the form it would eventually take. Ultimately, Breckinridge found her path to personal fulfillment and professional success by pursuing higher education at the University of Chicago, where—with the help of Marion Talbot, the dean of women, and the guidance of Ernst Freund, an iconoclastic legal scholar—she earned advanced degrees in political science and political economy and went on to become the top-ranked member of the first graduating class of the University of Chicago's new law school.[20]

While the opening chapters of this book trace Breckinridge's life in chronological order, subsequent chapters offer a more thematic approach. As Breckinridge became established in her career, she adopted a busy—often hectic—schedule in which she divided her time among an ever-increasing number of causes. As she expressed it, her "multiplicity of jobs" made life "one grand futile rush" and meant that her days were often "broken bits."[21] A thematic approach slows down this "futile rush" and allows for a fuller examination of each of the "broken bits." Presented as a sort of kaleidoscope of the many causes to which Breckinridge dedicated her life, the ensuing chapters overlap chronologically, offering related but distinct views of Breckinridge's work on behalf of human welfare.

Chapter 4 examines Breckinridge's participation in progressive reform in her adopted home, Chicago. At the same time that she engaged in teaching and research at the Chicago School of Civics and Philanthropy, Breckinridge joined a community of women activists at Hull House and became a key player in Progressive reform in the Second City. Supplementing Breckinridge's personal correspondence and published scholarship with records from the many institutions and organizations with which she was affiliated, this chapter demonstrates how Breckinridge's participation in Progressive reform laid the groundwork for her subsequent activities as an "activist academic" committed to establishing what she called a "national minimum" standard of living.[22]

Chapter 5 details Breckinridge's collaboration with Edith Abbott at the University of Chicago's School of Social Service Administration during what one correspondent called "the most exciting period in the development of social work," exploring the pair's distinctive approach to the professionalization of social work and their consistent emphasis on public welfare programs. Institutional records, professional correspondence, oral histories, and scholarly publications illuminate what students called "the Abbott-Breckinridge point of view" and reveal how Breckinridge and Abbott used their professional status and scholarly expertise to advance social reform and shape public policy.[23]

Chapter 6 explores Breckinridge's work in the national suffrage organization, the National American Woman Suffrage Association, and its successor organization, the League of Women Voters. Organizational records and personal correspondence document Breckinridge's determination to reconcile gender-specific legislation with equal citizenship rights in a quest for fairness, Breckinridge's measure of what she called "true equality." By exploring Breckinridge's work with national feminist organizations both during and after the suffrage struggle, this chapter highlights women's continuous activism as well as their ideological differences, shedding new light on the so-called "lost years" after the Susan B. Anthony Amendment and providing a reexamination of the "difference versus equality" debate.[24]

Chapter 7 focuses on Breckinridge's involvement in an international women's movement dedicated to feminism, pacifism, and justice that flourished in the United States and Europe during and after World War I. While scholars have long recognized peace as a "women's issue," Breckinridge's participation in the Women's International League for Peace and Freedom and in international social work circles reveals new dimensions of feminist-pacifism. Institutional records and Breckinridge's papers alike reveal that a shared commitment to social justice fueled women's continued commitment to internationalism even during the isolationist decades following World War I.[25]

Chapter 8 follows Breckinridge to the Seventh Pan-American Conference in Montevideo, Uruguay, where she and other women activists from the United States and Latin America vigorously debated the meaning of women's equality. Breckinridge's personal correspondence and public speeches, together with official records and others' memoirs, reveal sharp disagreements among Pan-American feminists at the same time that they illuminate how women in the Americas laid the groundwork for the idea that "women's rights are human rights."[26]

Chapter 9 traces Breckinridge's contributions to the nascent welfare state. During the Great Depression, Breckinridge and other activist women, building on the programs they had established at the state level during the Progressive era, made it their mission to address widespread poverty by crafting a federal welfare state. Breckinridge's personal correspondence with fellow New Dealers—especially those associated with the U.S. Children's Bureau—reveals her behind-the-scenes work on behalf of New Deal policies that advanced Breckinridge's long-standing goal of providing a "national minimum" for all Americans.

Chapter 10 focuses on Breckinridge's lifelong partnership with Edith Abbott, which facilitated her life's work on behalf of social justice. This concluding chapter, like the opening chapter, also offers a more intimate view of Breckinridge, whose professional persona, public statements, and published writings often obscured her personal life. Personal letters—especially those Breckinridge and Abbott exchanged during their infrequent separations and those Abbott received after Breckinridge's death—provide a different perspective, revealing Breckinridge's inner life and documenting her most intimate relationship. By coming full circle from her family of origin to her family of choice, this chapter demonstrates that Breckinridge's professional success and political efficacy were grounded in her personal relationships.

Finally, an Epilogue offers reflections on Breckinridge's philosophy of "passionate patience" and the lasting legacy of her lifelong dedication to social justice. After Breckinridge's death, one of her admirers wondered whether "a new generation of American women" would continue the work Breckinridge and her compatriots had begun. Another assured Abbott that "her life and labors were germinal rather than terminal."[27] Noting the striking parallels between the issues that concerned Breckinridge and those that confront Americans today, this book concludes with the lessons that Breckinridge's life might impart to the current generation of American activists.

CHAPTER ONE

Becoming a Breckinridge
A Kentucky Childhood

"Peace baby"

Easter Sunday 1866 in Lexington, Kentucky, was a dark, damp, and altogether "disagreeable" day. While a storm raged outside, a "frail" infant fought her way into the "blustering" world. The newborn's mother, who suffered from poor health, was relieved at the safe delivery, if disappointed at not having a son. Issa Desha Breckinridge regarded the arrival of another daughter as a bit of an "April Fool" hoax when her second child came into the world on April 1, 1866. After all, the Desha-Breckinridge kinship network represented one of Kentucky's greatest dynasties. One of the newborn's great-grandfathers, Joseph Desha, had been the governor of Kentucky, while the other, John Breckinridge, had drafted the Kentucky Resolutions of 1798. In an era in which most Americans regarded politics as outside "woman's sphere," it is no wonder that Issa hoped for a son to carry on the family legacy. However, her husband, whose service in the Confederate Army had prevented him from spending time with the couple's first child, was overjoyed. Dubbing the newborn his "peace baby," William Campbell Preston Breckinridge regarded her as his special charge from the moment of her birth. It was fortunate that he did so, for the newborn's life hung in the balance. Over the next several months, as W.C.P. paced to and fro with his infant daughter in his arms, the young father allowed himself to dream about her future, vowing to give the child he named for his "sainted mother" extraordinary opportunities and constant encouragement—if she lived. Sophonisba Preston Breckinridge did survive, demonstrating in the first year of her life a remarkable perseverance in the face of adversity that would prove indispensable for the rest of her long and productive life.[1]

Sophonisba Breckinridge was the second of seven children. Although the Civil War resulted in a gap of four years between the birth of the first, Eleanor (known as Ella), and the second, Sophonisba (known as Nisba), there were still "babies and babies" to come: Desha, Campbell, "Little Issa," Robert, and Mary Curry (known as Curry). Campbell and "Little Issa" both died in early childhood. Here, Nisba (marked with an "X") is shown with her mother, Issa Desha Breckinridge, and her two youngest siblings.

Courtesy Edith and Grace Abbott Papers, Archives and Special Collections, University of Nebraska-Lincoln Libraries.

"Who I am"

In her lifetime, Sophonisba Breckinridge would achieve both national and international recognition for her work as a social work educator and social justice reformer. Yet near the end of her life, when sat down to record her memoirs, she explained "Who I am" by situating herself in the context of her family of origin. As she recognized, both Breckinridge's family legacy and her relationships with other family members would have a profound impact on her future career as an educator and a reformer.[2]

W.C.P. and Issa Desha Breckinridge reinforced the importance of family ties by naming all their children for ancestors on both sides of the family, dating back four generations. They christened their second child Sophonisba after her paternal grandmother, but they called her Nisba, a nickname that she continued to use with intimates for the rest of her life.[3]

The importance of family was one lesson Nisba learned in her childhood that she never forgot. Near the end of her life, when she attempted to record her life story, she devoted a significant portion of the unorganized, incomplete, and much-amended pages to her family. Indeed, in one draft table of contents, she labeled the first chapter "My Ancestry." Nisba knew from an early age that she would have to work hard to live up to the example set by illustrious relatives on both sides of the family. But if Nisba recognized the importance of the family tradition of intellectual achievement and public service, she also understood the importance of family relationships in shaping her own future. Explaining her rationale in beginning her own life story with her family heritage, she noted, "I do this because they meant so much not only in the way of my inheritance but because they meant so much in my conscious experience."[4]

Nisba grew up surrounded by family. Like many other elite white families struggling to adapt to the harsh realities of life in the postwar South, the Breckinridges shared their household with numerous kinfolk. Initially, when W.C.P. completed his four years of service in the Confederate Army and returned home in 1865, he had a house built next door to his wife's parents' home in downtown Lexington. Located at the northwest intersection of High and Upper Streets, this house probably was financed by Issa's father, "Dada" John R. Desha, a successful physician. However, economic reversals soon changed both the family fortunes and their household composition. In 1872, at the beginning of a period of prolonged financial woes later known as the Panic of 1873, a creditor defaulted on a debt, "Dada" Desha lost his fortune, and he, "Grandmother" Mary Curry Desha, and their adult daughter, schoolteacher Mary Desha, combined households with the Breckinridges on nearby Short Street. That same year, after a self-imposed exile in Cuba, England, and Canada, Nisba's uncle and Confederate sympathizer John

Nisba grew up surrounded by family. Her extended household included not only her parents, W.C.P. and Issa Breckinridge, and her six siblings, but also her maternal grandparents, "Dada" Desha and "Grandmother" Mary, and her schoolteacher aunt, Mary Desha. Members of the Breckinridge kinship network also made extended visits. Here, the family is shown picnicking at their ancestral home, Cabell's Dale, in 1884.

Courtesy Issa Desha Breckinridge Collection, Filson Historical Society, Louisville, Kentucky

Cabell Breckinridge and his wife and children returned to Lexington and stayed with Nisba's family "until they could find a modest home of their own." In addition to sharing a household with these kin for economic reasons, the Breckinridges also frequently hosted other relatives. W.C.P.'s sister Marie Breckinridge Handy, her minister husband, and their children came for extended visits of several months. W.C.P.'s brother Robert Jefferson Breckinridge Jr.'s children, who lived nearby, also visited often. Nisba thus grew up with assorted grandparents, aunts and uncles, and cousins, as well as with members of her immediate family.[5]

"I loved my father"

Of all of the members of the extended Breckinridge household, Nisba had the most significant relationship with her father, lawyer and politician W.C.P. Breckinridge. Although Nisba was the second-born, in many ways her relationship with her father was more typical of first-born children. W.C.P.'s first wife, Lucretia Clay, had died in childbirth less than a year after their marriage, and their infant son died just two months later. Although W.C.P. quickly remarried, and he and his second wife, Issa Desha, began a family immediately, he left home to serve in the Confederate Army when their first child, Ella, was only a month old. W.C.P. was not reunited with his wife and child until the end of the war, in 1865.[6]

After this series of tragic losses and missed opportunities, W.C.P. Breckinridge, like many men who served in the Confederate Army, was eager to embrace the role of involved father, and he claimed Nisba as his own. "You were my baby from the hour of your birth," he asserted, backing up his claim with a detailed account of his early care for his favorite child: "I put you to sleep; I walked you when you were sick." Like many other future feminists of her generation, Nisba enjoyed a close relationship with her father. In her autobiography Nisba described her father as closely involved in her upbringing; it was her father who taught her how to tie her shoes, and it was her father who taught her the alphabet by pointing the letters out in his law books, imbuing her with a lifelong reverence for learning and law.[7]

By contrast, Nisba had an attenuated relationship with her mother, Issa. As Breckinridge recorded in numerous drafts of her unfinished autobiography, her mother's health was poor, largely as a result of her constant childbearing. "There was no doctrine of birth control or spaced child bearing prevalent at that time," she explained, and after her parents were reunited after the Civil War, repeated pregnancies "came in swift succession." Although a gap of four years separated the eldest, Ella, from the second-born, Nisba, the next three children—Desha, Campbell, and "Little Issa"—were born at intervals of only fifteen months, and there were still more "babies and babies to come": Robert and Curry. The illness and death of two children—Campbell in 1870 and Little Issa in 1872—also consumed Issa's attention and sapped her strength. Although she fostered a close relationship with Ella, building on the strong bond the two forged during W.C.P.'s wartime absence, Issa had little time or energy to devote to her younger children. Instead, she relied on African American servants to perform basic domestic tasks, from preparing meals to bathing and dressing the children.[8]

Although mother and daughter would later develop a close and mutually supportive relationship, as a child, Nisba seems to have found it difficult to connect with her mother. In her later memoirs, she wistfully recalled that while her younger brother Desha could alleviate his mother's severe headaches by rubbing her head, when Nisba herself attempted this, she tangled her fingers in her mother's hair "and rather caused her distress than brought her relief." Perhaps it was because of her distant relationship with her mother that Nisba retrospectively "had less self-respect" than her siblings. According to Nisba's later accounts, "Ella was clever and lovely to look at," "Desha was gentle and skilful," and Curry was "a lovely baby with big blue eyes," but she herself was "dull" and humorless, frequently missing the point of jokes told by other family members.[9]

As she quickly pointed out, however, Nisba was "not stupid, just dull." If she could not compete for her mother's attention, she reveled in her father's love. In multiple drafts of her autobiography, Nisba linked statements about her mother's ill health and lack of availability to comments about her father's close attention to his children, especially Nisba. Because "Mama was far from strong, Papa helped in many ways," she explained. It was because of her father's attention and encouragement that Nisba described herself not only as "dull" and "common" but also as "attractive" and intelligent. Reflecting on her low self-esteem and her humorless outlook as a child, Breckinridge later reflected: "Two things saved me, in a way. I loved my father and wanted to please him."[10]

Indeed, Nisba idolized her father and identified with him to such an extent that when she attempted to write her own autobiography, she confessed, "I cannot speak of myself without speaking at length of him." As a child, she would do anything to please him. She described herself as "a good child," obedient and well-behaved, because "I was so anxious to please my father."[11]

Most of all, Nisba pleased her father by excelling in her studies. W.C.P., who had been the one to choose a name that meant "a woman who conserves wisdom" for his second child, also encouraged her to acquire wisdom for herself. Nisba was always a bookish child. As an adult, she would develop a close relationship with her brother Desha and her sister Curry, but as a child, she was not particularly close to any of her siblings. Rather, Nisba was a solitary child who spent a great deal of time reading. As her father later recalled, "Books were her playthings before she knew her letters, and as she grew they became her companions, then her friends."[12]

Although Nisba always emphasized her father's role in promoting her intellectual development, the Deshas also shaped Nisba's early education in important ways. Nisba's maternal grandmother, Mary Curry Desha, who lived either next door to or with the Breckinridges throughout Nisba's childhood, read classical poetry and Victorian moral tales aloud to the children, including Rev. Charles Kingsley's *Water Babies*. Suggestively, *Water Babies* offers critiques of class inequity and child labor, issues Breckinridge would address as an adult. Nisba's early exposure to Homer laid the groundwork for her study of the classics in college. *Tales from Shakespeare* also made a lasting impression; as an adult, Breckinridge joined the Chicago Shakespeare Society, and theater became one of her few leisure

Nisba was always a serious and solitary child. Rarely joining her siblings in their play, she preferred to spend her time reading. Her father
later recalled: "Books were her playthings before she knew her letters,
and as she grew they became her companions, then her friends."

Courtesy Edith and Grace Abbott Papers, Archives and Special Collections,
University of Nebraska-Lincoln Libraries.

activities. Grandmother Mary also required the children to memorize long passages of poetry and recite them aloud, providing early training in public speaking.[13]

Nisba's "Auntie," Mary Desha, who also lived with the Breckinridges, was an
equally important influence—and a still more important role model. Nisba,
whose family had strong ties to the Presbyterian church, initially attended an
"old Presbyterian school," possibly the all-girls Sayre School, where her sister Ella
studied. However, she later enrolled in the public school system, where her aunt
"gallantly" took a job after financial reversals associated with the Panic of 1873, as
Nisba later recalled. Never marrying, Mary Desha continued to earn wages as a
schoolteacher and as a government employee until her death. Her example as an
unmarried career woman encouraged Nisba to envision an independent future;
she also rounded out her niece's early childhood education by introducing her
to the study of arithmetic, helping to pave the way for Nisba's later interest in
statistical research.[14]

Young Nisba took advantage of all the opportunities available to improve her
mind and prove herself to her father—and perhaps to herself as well. If Nisba
could not compete for her mother's affection, her siblings could not compete with
her for her father's approval. W.C.P. urged all of his children to work hard in school
by offering them rewards for perfect reports. Nisba easily outperformed all her
siblings. Ella was more interested in boys than books; Desha was an indifferent
student; Robert was a wayward adolescent; and Curry suffered from dyslexia. In
her earliest preserved school report, dated January 24, 1873 (and signed by "Miss
Desha"), six-year-old Nisba earned perfect scores in every category: attendance,
deportment, neatness, spelling, reading, writing, geography, arithmetic, mental
arithmetic, composition, and poetry. Small wonder, then, that Issa once remarked,
"I fear you [are] Papa's sole [and] only hope for an educated daughter."[15]

"An educated daughter"

Eager for his favorite daughter to continue her education, W.C.P. convinced the
trustees of Kentucky Agricultural and Mechanical College, or A&M (now the
University of Kentucky), to admit women to its new teacher-training program.
In 1880, fourteen-year-old Nisba entered A&M along with forty-one other female
students, who were outnumbered by male students nearly five to one. Although
A&M allowed women to attend classes, it by no means treated them as equals.
Female students could only earn certificates, not diplomas, and there was significant resistance to their presence on campus. Although Nisba excelled in her
classes, even after four years of college-level work she did not obtain a degree
from the future University of Kentucky.[16]

Nisba's experience at A&M made her a determined advocate for women's equality. While she always had "cared a great deal about grades," Nisba now had an additional reason to do well in her coursework: to prove women's intellectual capacity. "I cared about grades because it pleased my Father to have me make good grades and justified his position with reference to the treatment of women," she explained, but her account of her competition with the men in her class for top grades, and even more, her account of an altercation with an instructor "who did not like girls in his class," indicated that Nisba also had something to prove.[17]

In her later memoirs, Breckinridge related, with relish, an occasion on which she turned the tables on the sexist instructor. The math professor attempted to "humiliate" his lone female student by giving her particularly difficult problems to solve. One day he succeeded in stumping her in front of the class, but she figured out the solution in the middle of the night. The next day, she said nothing to him, suspecting that "he would try again to humiliate me," and also knowing that "that was a day when the trustees were likely to drop in." As she gleefully recounted the event:

> Sure enough, the committee of trustees dropped in and sure enough he gave me the unsolved problem of the day before. I was so pleased that I probably looked a little triumphant and put my problem on the board and then explained to the visitors about the equation. I was maliciously complacent and he was really quite upset. He knew that nobody could have helped me, and at last he said, "How did you do it[?]" And I said politely[,] "I suppose I knew that you thought I couldn't do it . . . at any rate it came to me in my sleep. I am glad you gave me another chance."[18]

While Nisba was demonstrating women's intellectual capacity, feminists were demanding political equality. A souvenir in her personal papers indicates that Nisba was both aware and supportive of the women's rights movement from an early age. Among her papers is a picture of the Smith sisters of Glastonbury, Connecticut, dated 1877. A handwritten notation on the reverse identifies them as refusing to pay "tax without representation." Because the notation also references the *History of Woman Suffrage*, a six-volume work published by women's rights pioneers beginning in 1881, Nisba's earliest knowledge of the suffrage movement can be dated to her teens with reasonable certainty. (Nisba's selection of two northern abolitionists as role models also foreshadowed her later commitment to African American equality.)[19] Her simultaneous introduction to the suffrage movement and to institutionalized sexism inspired a lifelong commitment to women's rights. As an adult, she would become one of the most well-known feminists of the early twentieth century.

Although neither of Nisba's parents supported the suffrage movement, both influenced her in her commitment to women's rights, broadly defined. Issa's example probably inspired Breckinridge's later concern with women's control over their own bodies. Having, as a child, observed her mother's delicate health and her siblings' early deaths, Breckinridge would become, as an adult, an ardent advocate of family planning, birth control, and prenatal and postnatal care for mothers and infants. W.C.P.'s insistence on giving his daughter's mind "a fair chance to show its power" not only increased Nisba's awareness of gender discrimination but also gave her the tools with which to challenge it.[20]

The emphasis W.C.P. Breckinridge placed on education—including education for girls—was increasingly common in the postwar South. Nisba was a member of a rising generation of southern white women who grew up with—and helped to create—a new image of southern womanhood. Unlike antebellum elite women, who expected to marry well and manage slaves, or Civil War wives like Issa Desha Breckinridge, who reluctantly adapted to the transition from slavery to free labor, the generation born after the Civil War had no memories of either slavery or the gender system it supported, in which white women, like black slaves, were expected to be dependent on—and submissive to—white male heads of households. While older generations both resisted and accommodated changing household economies and gender relations, women of Nisba's generation, who grew up with the expectation that they would become self-supporting or at least contribute to their family's financial welfare, adopted an ethic of self-reliance that set them apart from earlier generations of southern white women and aligned their expectations and experiences much more closely with those of northern white women. Women from both regions, then, constituted the "New Women" who attained higher education and sought financial independence and public influence as female professionals and clubwomen. Ultimately, this generation would revitalize the antebellum women's rights movement in a successful twentieth-century campaign for the right to vote.[21]

Although Nisba would become the most widely known Breckinridge woman of her generation, the illustrious careers of other family members demonstrate that a profound generational change in gender roles was occurring. In the Breckinridge kinship network, a family tradition of personal achievement and public service combined with a generational shift in gender roles and female opportunity to produce a remarkable cohort of women professionals and reformers. Reflecting family traditions of public service as well as shifting expectations for "new women," several of Nisba's contemporary kinswomen would pursue careers as teachers and reformers.[22]

Financial uncertainty also encouraged the younger generation of Breckinridge women to join the cohort of New Women who came of age between the Civil War and the turn of the century and pursued higher education, paid work, professional careers, and public roles. Like other southern girls of her generation, Nisba grew up with the expectation that she would need to make her own living. W.C.P., like many elite but impoverished whites in the uncertain economy of the Reconstruction era, hoped that higher education and "honest toil" would enable his daughter to support herself rather than depend on either her father or a husband.[23]

Although the Breckinridges were relatively prosperous, they were not wealthy, and their fortunes were in decline rather than on the rise. In 1870 Nisba's family had five live-in domestic servants; by 1880, they had none. The dramatic reversal in the family's fortunes came in 1872, when one of John R. Desha's creditors defaulted on a loan in the midst of a severe economic downturn. "Dada" Desha's downfall became a cautionary tale, reminding Nisba that the future was uncertain. It also convinced her that circumstances, not character, were the cause of financial failure. As an adult, Nisba would become a staunch supporter of public welfare programs for people who fell on hard times due to economic fluctuations and family members' deaths.[24]

Nisba's Grandmother Mary also shaped her ideas about class differences, although not in the ways the older woman might have wished. A stern, autocratic woman who prided herself on her ancestry and vigorously enforced social hierarchies, Grandmother Mary "was truly an aristocrat," recalled Nisba. Much to her grandmother's chagrin, Nisba was a "common" child who "liked all kinds of people and was not particular in [her] choice of amusement or companionship." Although she had been a frail infant, Nisba grew to become a "sturdy" girl who enjoyed outdoor play with neighborhood boys. She also had what to her grandmother was an unacceptable fascination with street traffic. In several different versions of her draft autobiography, Nisba included the account of her grandmother's finding Nisba sitting on the curb outside the house, "watching the world pass by." Scandalized at the sight of her granddaughter's proximity to the gutter (and perhaps to African Americans and poor whites), Grandmother Mary seized Nisba by the ear and forced her inside, scolding her for being "a common child." Although Ella had fond memories of listening to their grandmother's bedtime stories, for Nisba, Grandmother Mary's harsh discipline undermined her authority. As an adult, Breckinridge recalled her grandmother's "very vigorous methods" of enforcing rules, which included not only boxing ears but also submerging Nisba's head in a basin of water. Young Nisba's "real terror" of her grandmother inspired her to rebel against her. As she later recalled, although, as a child, she worked hard at her lessons to please her father, she somehow was unable to "make a decent buttonhole"—her grandmother's measure of "good breeding." As an adult, Breckinridge would become a champion for the poor, closely allying herself with the "common" people that her grandmother so despised.[25]

Although she was a "frail" infant, Nisba developed into a "sturdy" youngster who enjoyed spending time outdoors. She also became a keen observer of urban life, developing what her grandmother considered an unacceptable fascination with street traffic in downtown Lexington. When she found her sitting on the curb "watching the world pass by," Grandmother Mary scolded Nisba for being "a common child." As an adult, Breckinridge would dedicate her life to urban reform and to serving the "common" people her aristocratic grandmother so despised.

Courtesy Edith and Grace Abbott Papers, Archives and Special Collections, University of Nebraska-Lincoln Libraries.

In her early teens, however, Nisba apparently responded to her grandmother's harsh discipline with a brief teenage rebellion. After Mary Curry Desha died in 1884, eighteen-year-old Nisba reflected on her early teen years, when she "began to feel grown up and hateful." She confessed, "I know that for these last four years I have been selfish and inconsiderate." It was probably at this time that Nisba became "a leader in the gayeties of young people, and especially fond of horses, horse-back riding and races," as a college friend later described her.[26]

Even though the shy child had matured into a popular teenager, becoming "a belle of the Blue Grass," according to one later account, by the time Nisba reached adolescence, the Breckinridges seem to have come to the conclusion that she would never marry.[27] Observing her mother's nonstop childbearing and chronic health problems may well have led Nisba to reject marriage and motherhood at an early age. Her young siblings' deaths, which occurred when Nisba was four and five years old, surely had a profound effect on her. Awareness of her parents' marital difficulties also may have contributed to Nisba's apparent resolution to remain single for life. Issa and W.C.P., while both from prominent Kentucky families, were otherwise ill-matched. After Issa's death in 1893, W.C.P.'s long-term affair with another woman came to light. Although she later claimed to have been entirely ignorant of the affair until the scandal became public, Nisba probably had some intimations of problems in her parents' marriage well before that time. Whatever her reasons, Nisba never seriously considered marriage.[28]

While attending the University of Kentucky, Nisba had two serious suitors. Although in her memoirs she claimed to have "really loved them," she quickly dismissed the possibility of marrying either, noting, "neither really loved me though each for the moment thought he did." She concluded this extremely brief discussion of her suitors: "Both [men] married women who were cleverer than I was and both made happy gracious homes." In her reflections on her life, Breckinridge displayed little emotion in her discussion of her suitors—indeed, she did not even bother to name them. In the years to come, instead of seeking a suitable husband, she would spend her life in the company of other women.[29]

"Noble things"

If Nisba was keenly aware of the potential drawbacks of domestic life, she was also well versed in the family ethic of public achievement. In the Bluegrass State, the Breckinridge name was synonymous with public service and political leadership. As one admirer wrote to her father, "The name of *Breckinridge* seems to fill the minds of the people." W.C.P. encouraged Nisba to seek alternatives to what he called the "aimless life" of the southern belle and to carry on the family tradition of higher learning and public service. "The [Breckinridge] name has been connected with good intellectual work for some generations—for over a century," he counseled. "You must preserve this connection for the next generation."[30] Issa, too, believed that her daughter was destined to do "noble things."[31]

The Breckinridges' high expectations for their second daughter, coupled with their assumption that she would remain single for life, suggest that they, like many other patrician families in late-nineteenth-century America, regarded Nisba as their "designated daughter," in whom they invested their highest hopes for public achievement.[32] Like similarly prominent families in both the North and the South, the Breckinridges—who were repeatedly disappointed in their sons—looked to a particularly gifted daughter to carry on the family name and advance the family reputation. While first-born children more commonly filled this role, Nisba, who had early demonstrated her intellectual capacity, was the logical choice for this position in the Breckinridge family.

Both Nisba's intellectual bent and her leanings in the direction of public service were apparent at a young age. As she detailed in her autobiography, her father offered Nisba and Ella their choice of either a dollar or a party as a reward for good marks. While fashionable and popular Ella chose the party, intellectual and serious Nisba chose the dollar. But she did not use the money for herself. Nisba had "quite a little sum saved" when a female visitor, a missionary to China, gave such a stirring account of Chinese children's dire poverty that Nisba promptly donated all her savings to alleviate their suffering. Breckinridge doubtless included this story in her autobiography because it so succinctly established her early interest in assisting the poor, and perhaps also because it hinted at her participation in international welfare movements as an adult.[33]

When she was "quite a big girl," Nisba had another lesson in helping the less fortunate—and avoiding snap judgments. While walking with her father in Lexington's business district, she watched "a forlorn looking man" approach her father and was surprised when her father handed a five dollar bill to "the beggar, as I thought the stranger to be." When she asked for an explanation, her father explained that "this apparently down-and-out man was an ex-confederate soldier," an intelligent man from a respected family, who had become addicted to morphine after being wounded in battle. Nisba learned from this experience to consider each individual's circumstances, rather than blaming the poor for their plight. The encounter also opened her eyes to the negative consequences of there being "no psychiatric treatment" and no "occupational provision" for physically or mentally incapacitated people. Both of these insights would inform her later work on behalf of the poor and the disabled.[34]

"Not the enemy but war itself is the source of wrong!"

Breckinridge's childhood experiences and her family legacy predisposed her to a life of public service. They also, perhaps paradoxically, fostered her incipient pacifism and paved the way for her to become an advocate of racial equality. Nisba grew up hearing stories about her ancestors' political leadership and distinguished bloodlines. Many of these stories revolved around the secession crisis and "the bitter cleavages of opinion characteristic of many families of the border states." On her mother's side, both the Currys and the Deshas—who owned slaves—were "ardent advocate[s] of the Confederate Cause," but the Civil War had divided the Breckinridge clan.[35]

While keenly aware of sectional divisions, in her retelling of the family stories Nisba emphasized her ancestors' shared commitment to the nation and their record of distinguished leadership. Breckinridges had long been opposed to slavery but supportive of states' rights. John Breckinridge, Nisba's great-grandfather, drafted the Kentucky Resolutions of 1798, but he also attempted to preserve free blacks' right to vote in the new state of Kentucky. His son, Nisba's grandfather, Robert Jefferson Breckinridge, was a Presbyterian minister and an outspoken antislavery advocate. In her memoirs, Nisba noted with pride that her grandfather "not only supported the Union but gave to Lincoln the doctrine regarding the perpetuity of the Union enunciated in his, Lincoln's, first presidential message." However, a member of another branch of the family, W.C.P.'s cousin, John Cabell Breckinridge, cast his loyalties with the Confederacy. In an interesting twist, Breckinridge claimed in her autobiography that his nomination "by the extreme southern group as candidate for the presidency" assured Lincoln's victory.[36]

Nisba's own branch of the Breckinridge family tree also split when the secession crisis reached a fever pitch. Robert Jefferson Breckinridge supported the Union; two of his sons served in the Union Army, while two others, including Nisba's father, joined the Confederate Army. "It is difficult to imagine the family strains in the face of such varied and difficult problems," Breckinridge reflected in her autobiography.[37] Although she did not include these details in her memoirs, the war also created a serious rift between her mother, Issa, and her paternal grandfather, Robert Jefferson Breckinridge. During the war, unwilling to reside with her Unionist in-laws, Issa first moved in with her parents and then fled to Canada in order to find congenial company among fellow Confederates. For two years after the war, she refused to allow R. J. Breckinridge to see the Breckinridge children.[38]

Breckinridge later claimed that it was her intimate knowledge of war's destructiveness that inspired her lifelong pacifism. Witnessing firsthand the "resentment," "confusion," "hatred," "domestic tragedy," "deprivation," and "distorted social relationships" created by the Civil War, she recalled, convinced her early on of the "futility" of war. Although, like most Confederate children, she originally learned that "the object of resentment and hatred was the enemy," she soon became convinced "that not the enemy but war itself is the source of wrong!" Instead of defending "states' rights," as so many southern whites did, Breckinridge instead, as an adult, came to advocate international cooperation as a route to world peace and equal rights.[39]

Breckinridge's pacifism also shaped her adult understanding of her father's military service. While many children of Confederate veterans grew up learning to revere the Lost Cause and its fallen soldiers, in her autobiography, she chose to interpret the Civil War differently. She recalled that at the end of the war, her father gracefully conceded the Confederacy's defeat and committed himself to "a new union which the arbitrament [sic] of war had determined was 'one and indissoluble.' Being both brave and honest," she concluded, "he accepted the verdict of the Confederate failure and made his contribution to the building of a new nation."[40]

Other evidence suggests that Nisba's parents were more enthusiastic supporters of the Confederacy than she chose to record for posterity. Her mother was an officer of the local chapter of the United Daughters of the Confederacy, a group that produced textbooks and erected monuments celebrating the Lost Cause; her father, who held periodic reunions of his old unit and described military service as a valuable lesson about "the wrestle of life," also was a sought-out speaker at dedication ceremonies for Confederate monuments.[41] The Breckinridges' loyalty to the Lost Cause complicates the story, which Breckinridge herself promoted and often told in contemporary newspapers, that she imbibed racial liberalism from her father. W.C.P. Breckinridge was certainly more liberal than many of his fellow southern Democrats where race relations were concerned, but he also was a stalwart defender of white superiority. Issa Breckinridge also accepted white dominance and black submission as both natural and desirable. Before she could become an advocate for African Americans, Breckinridge would have to overcome much of her childhood training.[42]

"Fairness, justice and protection"

Although she fondly recalled the African American women who helped run the household and care for the children, Breckinridge did not comment in her autobiography on either local race relations or her parents' views on race. This is a telling omission. Nisba was born in the heyday of Radical Reconstruction, when the Republican-dominated U.S. Congress passed constitutional amendments freeing slaves, granting African American civil rights, and guaranteeing black men's right to vote. Southern whites, who faced disfranchisement if they refused to accede to these measures, nonetheless fought to maintain white supremacy in both legal and extralegal ways. As W.C.P. Breckinridge himself put it: "We want a white man's State and we intend to have it."[43]

In Nisba's own hometown, the city council, at her father's suggestion, held elections early, before the Fifteenth Amendment went into effect, to preempt blacks from participating. W.C.P. later defended local officials who prevented African Americans from casting a ballot on the basis that new laws required all voters to pay a "capitation tax," Kentucky's version of the notorious "poll tax" that robbed newly enfranchised blacks of their potential political power. In public speeches, the "silver tongued orator from Kentucky" defended the South's right to self-rule and allied himself with the "Redeemers," who reclaimed white Democrats' political dominance beginning in 1877. Nisba's father also defended suspected Klansmen accused of brutalizing local blacks.[44]

Although, given her silence on the matter, it is impossible to know how much young Nisba knew about these events at the time, it stretches credulity to assume that she was entirely ignorant of the tense race relations that prevailed in her hometown during her childhood. Certainly, she was well acquainted with the dynamics of white supremacy. Her sister Ella later claimed of her childhood: "There was no race problem in Lexington in the days of which I write." She went on to detail the "pleasant relations" between the Breckinridge family and their African American servants. Ella recalled with special fondness the children's nurse, Clacy, a former slave who, Ella explained, had been awarded to Issa "as a first present to the hour-old baby" and subsequently "nursed my Mother through every illness, received every one of her children into her arms, loved, scolded, and disciplined every one of us, . . . and would gladly have died for any one of us."[45]

Ella's memoir not only celebrates slavery even after emancipation, but it also makes clear that the Breckinridge family abided by a code of conduct intended to reinforce white supremacy. In the postbellum South, white and black children alike learned "racial etiquette" from their elders, with blacks learning to defer to whites with whom they came into contact and whites learning to be polite while maintaining social distance. While formal segregation, or "Jim Crow," did not fully take hold until the turn of the century, informally segregated residential patterns meant that white children usually encountered African Americans only as servants in their own homes. Although white family members and black domestic workers necessarily shared household space, white parents also taught their children to maintain physical and thereby social separation in a variety of ways, especially by taking meals separately from African Americans. White parents also trained their offspring to display their own racial superiority and reinforce blacks' servility by referring to adult African Americans by their given names, rather than by a title and surname, while at the same time requiring blacks to use titles when referring or speaking to whites of any age. This pattern is clear in Ella's reminiscences; Nisba also displayed this linguistic hierarchy in fragmentary, handwritten autobiographical notes (not included in later drafts of her autobiography), in which she referred to the younger African American women who worked in her household by their first names and called the elderly household manager "Aunt Polly"—"Aunt" and "Uncle" being the most honorable terms that a southern white could bestow on a black person.[46]

It would not be until 1884, when eighteen-year-old Nisba left Kentucky to attend Wellesley College, that she began to question her childhood acceptance of racial hierarchies. However, her early exposure to competing views on slavery may have encouraged her to question the validity of racial hierarchies. Most important, the conflict between her father's insistence on "fair play" and his commitment to white supremacy helped lay the groundwork for Breckinridge's adult commitment to African American rights. Nisba received mixed messages about race from her father, whose emphasis on reason and fairness ran counter to his beliefs in racism and segregation. Although W.C.P. characterized African Americans as "savages" incapable of self-government, he also supported African American education in his home state, even sharing the speaker's podium with black civil rights advocates at times, because he believed that since African Americans paid taxes, those taxes should be used to fund African American schools. Although he helped orchestrate and defend laws that denied African American men the right to vote, he also insisted that blacks be allowed to give testimony against whites in Kentucky courts, even when this unpopular stance lost him a race for district attorney of the tenth circuit court. And although he believed that the "Teutonic race" was destined to "dominate the world," he also asserted that African Americans were entitled to "fairness, justice and protection," if not to equal rights.[47]

Nisba's childhood thus predisposed her, if not toward racial liberalism, at least toward questioning received wisdom about race, especially where white supremacy threatened basic fairness or ran counter to simple logic. As she grew older, interacted with African Americans, and studied the sources of social inequality, Nisba ultimately would conclude that white supremacy was entirely incompatible with either justice or reason and would go much further in the direction of racial liberalism than her father ever had. As a child, Nisba admired her father's sense of "fair play"; as an adult, she would become an advocate of racial equality.

Although W.C.P.'s influence on his daughter's future commitment to African American rights was equivocal, his views on immigration helped prepare her for a lifetime of service to the foreign-born. W.C.P. was unquestionably a racist, but he was no nativist. While he steadfastly defended the Lost Cause of the Confederacy, he also decried sectional divisions and hoped that a "new generation" of Americans—northerners who felt no need to criticize slavery, and southerners who felt no need to defend it—would create "the public of the future," a "joint product of not only the North and South, but the West and those hosts of immigrants [who] yearly seek homes in our midst," which would deal effectively with remaining and new social questions while also respecting "the controlling force of law." Breckinridge, who as an adult marked her typed copy of this speech "use as illustration of his early eloquence," was destined to become part of that "new generation" that abandoned old rivalries and welcomed new immigrants.[48]

Sophonisba Breckinridge's social activism had its genesis in her Kentucky childhood. Her family's legacy of public service; her relationships with family members; her membership in a rising generation of New Women; her status as the Breckinridges' "designated daughter"; her youthful exposure to inequities of class, race, and gender; and her understanding of her father's sense of "fair play" all shaped her career trajectory and her commitment to reform. Attending Wellesley would strengthen her sense of mission, provide her with additional role models of female achievement, give her the tools to support herself, challenge her assumptions about race, and provide further clues to the direction her life would take.

CHAPTER TWO

Preparation for Citizenship

An "All-Around Girl" at Wellesley College

"Made . . . for the likes of me"

In 1890 Katharine Coman, professor of history and political economy at Wellesley College, published an essay on "Preparation for Citizenship at Wellesley College" containing several bold statements. "No one interested in the subject can have failed to notice that a remarkable transformation of the woman question has taken place in the past twenty years," she declared. "Woman's sphere of usefulness," she asserted, "is enlarging every year," with women assuming new responsibilities in industry, politics, education, religion, society, and philanthropy. Under these circumstances, she claimed, "What needs doing now is not to proclaim the wrongs of woman, nor to demand larger scope for her wasted powers, but to fit her to meet the heavy responsibilities that are pressing upon her." Fortunately, Coman assured her readers, higher education was the path to this preparation for citizenship. "The function of the college is not to produce a book-worm, nor a pedagogue, nor a society belle," Coman explained, "but an all-round woman—strong in physique, able in mind, intelligent in all that concerns the well-being of humanity, and fitted to act with vigor and discretion in behalf of any interest committed to her charge." "A college course, no longer a strange and dubious venture for a woman, is recognized to be the essential preparation for a strong and useful life," Coman concluded, "and every woman's college is full to overflowing with girls eager to fit themselves for active service in the world." Wellesley College—an elite New England school with a rigorous curriculum that encompassed the classics, advanced scientific study, and, of course, Coman's own specialties in history, political science, and economics—was ideally suited to prepare a woman "to comprehend her social and political obligations" and "to master the perplexing problems" of modern life.[1]

It was in accordance with these high aims that eighteen-year-old Nisba Breck-inridge enrolled at Wellesley College in 1884. In later years, Breckinridge aptly observed: "The great charm that Wellesley had for me was that it was made or established for me or the likes of me."[2] Indeed, Wellesley College was an ideal place for an intelligent woman in Victorian America to develop confidence in her abilities and find a context for her ambitions. Alice Freeman, who assumed the presidency of Wellesley College in 1881, guided a group of extraordinarily talented women faculty and students in a unique experiment in higher education for women. In this "Adamless Eden," a women's college with an all-female faculty, students and teachers alike forged strong personal and professional bonds that fostered female achievement and social reform. Breckinridge did not exaggerate when she described Wellesley as her "natural sphere."[3]

Although she later questioned her decision to attend Wellesley because her coursework there did not prepare her for a "useful" or "practical" career path, Breckinridge's four years at the liberal arts college provided her with precisely the "preparation for citizenship" that she would utilize for the rest of her long life. She benefited tremendously from the comprehensive curriculum at Welles-ley College, which honed her skills in critical thinking, clear writing, and public speaking and provided her with a breadth of knowledge that would allow her to take advantage of emerging fields of expertise, especially in the then-nascent social science disciplines. Just as Coman predicted, Breckinridge gained a deeper understanding of social problems and developed an intense determination to pro-mote social welfare. She also reveled in the women's world at Wellesley, where she found a supportive community in which scholarship, service, and social activities intermingled. Finally, while she remained close to her family of origin, she also acquired new role models who challenged her childhood beliefs and provided her with alternatives to conventional womanhood. By the time Breckinridge gradu-ated from Wellesley at age twenty-two, she not only was "the most popular girl at Wellesley," according to one observer, but also was poised to become one of the school's most notable graduates.[4]

"Preparing for a professional life"

By the time she arrived on campus in fall 1884, Breckinridge had waged an ex-tended campaign to convince her parents to allow her to leave home to attend Wellesley College. She did not spell out her reasons for choosing Wellesley over other options. Perhaps after her experience at A&M she was reluctant to attend one of the other state universities then conducting the "dangerous experiment" of coeducation. She may well have understood that, like A&M, the other schools she considered—the University of Michigan and Cornell University—offered only an illusion of equality.[5]

Having already encountered the truth behind "the myth of equal education," it is not surprising that Breckinridge would set her sights on one of the Seven Sisters schools. Other enterprising southern women also chose the elite New England women's colleges for their higher education. Students from the Upper South were especially likely to go north for college, favoring Wellesley and Vassar; at least one other Lexingtonian had attended (although not graduated from) Wellesley before Breckinridge matriculated there. While each school had its own unique features, all of the Seven Sisters colleges were residential schools where the faculty acted in loco parentis, which probably reassured southern parents sending their precocious daughters away from home. All also emphasized a gender-specific form of higher education, enforcing proper feminine conduct as well as rigorous academic standards. Wellesley president Alice Freeman's assertion that "much stress is laid upon assisting girl students to attain balanced characters, charming manners, and ambitions that are not unwomanly" may well have reassured Breckinridge's parents. The college's relatively low cost, with subsidized annual tuition of $300 and inexpensive room and board of $250 per year, was also likely an inducement for Breckinridge and her parents. The religious bent of both the founder and the president of the college also may have made the Breckinridges—members of Lexington's Mt. Horeb Presbyterian Church—more comfortable. Finally, the southern origins of the founder's wife, Pauline Durant, may have helped reconcile the Breckinridges to sending their daughter north to school.[6]

More than anything else, however, given her single-minded focus on intellectual development and her early determination to support herself, it was probably Wellesley's reputation for academic rigor and the school's penchant for producing professional women that attracted the intelligent and ambitious Kentuckian. Breckinridge entered college with a firm resolve to prepare for meaningful work and self-support. "I am fairly pining to get to work,—to do something, somehow—somewhere," she confided to her mother in an oft-repeated refrain.[7] Although she was uncertain of exactly what professional career she might pursue, she was equally certain that attending college would help her to do so. "My life will be much braver and better for having had the time here," she predicted. "I do love the College," she wrote at the conclusion of her junior year, adding, "I know I am better for having been here."[8]

Her parents, similarly, were sure that college would prepare their daughter to "make [her] own living" and to do "noble things." Even when they were vague about the details, the Breckinridges were confident that higher education would enable their talented daughter to determine her future course in life. Expressing relief that Nisba was "not a genius"—probably because he associated genius with madness, not because he doubted his daughter's intellectual capacity—W.C.P. praised her "hard-working, dutiful, trained intellect" and predicted that she would be "capable of doing anything because willing to undergo the necessary labor and submit to the regular discipline." Accordingly, he urged his daughter to use her time away from home to cultivate "habits of self-reliance, self-dependence & definite purpose" and to envision a future devoted to "honest toil." "You ought to look squarely in the face that if I die, you will have to make your own living; and if I live, you may have to do so anyhow," he reminded her. Unable to provide ongoing financial support and unimpressed by the frivolous lives of his neighbors' daughters, he encouraged her to become both financially independent and self-directed. "God preserve you . . . from the aimless, worse than aimless life" of the southern belle, he exclaimed.[9]

Determined to avoid an "aimless life," Nisba Breckinridge nonetheless lacked a clear career goal. This was a common situation for many New Women, members of the first generation of female college graduates, whose educational opportunities far outstripped their career options. Thus, although Breckinridge was universally acknowledged to be "preparing for a professional life," the precise nature of her future profession remained a mystery.[10]

Teaching was the most obvious option. Whether in private homes as governesses, in a growing public-school system, or in women's academies and colleges, teaching was the field that offered the most opportunities for women seeking careers in Victorian America. In addition, Wellesley especially emphasized the career possibilities of teaching. The *Wellesley Courant* published the names of Wellesley alumnae who joined "the noble army of teachers," and fully a third of Wellesley graduates in Breckinridge's class became teachers. Not surprisingly then, Breckinridge also considered teaching as a possible future profession. "One path at least is open to me," she commented when one of her Latin instructors encouraged her to continue her studies in that subject and assured her that there was a demand for Latin teachers. Breckinridge was reassured that at least one avenue for self-support was virtually guaranteed. "I was very very glad to have her speak as if it were not only possible but [al]most probable for me to make my own way," she noted.[11]

Although aware that teaching was the most viable option, Breckinridge preferred to envision herself following in her father's footsteps by practicing law. In later recollections of her college years, she insisted that her goal always was to study law; in correspondence written while she was in college, as well, she constantly returned to the subject of law. However, because most law schools were closed to women and because most lawyers continued to prepare for the bar by assisting established lawyers in their practice, she assumed that she would read law in her father's office rather than attend law school. "You will let me work for you, won[']t you?" she demanded in one letter to her father.[12]

While determined to pursue a professional career after graduation, as a college student Breckinridge avoided strictly vocational courses, preferring to focus on academic subjects. Even though her schoolteacher aunt, Mary Desha, urged her to investigate the "special" courses for teachers, she did not undertake this specialized curriculum, probably because it was less rigorous than the regular Wellesley coursework. She briefly studied shorthand at her father's suggestion. However, she soon asked for permission to drop shorthand so that she could focus on her academic subjects.[13] As she later explained, "I selected my studies . . . from the point of view of a person who intended to use her college course for cultural purposes and obtain the professional training afterwards."[14]

Rather than focusing on job preparation, Breckinridge attended Wellesley to "learn to live," as she expressed it an 1887 letter to her father.[15] As her future course would demonstrate, the broad training that she received at Wellesley would prove to be ideally suited to prepare her for a rapidly changing world—and to become an agent of change. Indeed, in later life, Breckinridge would counsel other aspiring professional women to undertake a broad-based, liberal-arts curriculum as the best possible preparation for graduate study and professional pursuits. "I feel very strongly that when possible there should be a wide range of interests open to the college student," she responded to a query from the Intercollegiate Bureau of Occupations in 1914, "in order that she may be free to choose from the whole realm of knowledge, when she is ready to make a choice."[16] As Breckinridge's own experience had taught her by the time she penned these words, her varied course of study in college gave her the flexibility she would need to finesse the limited options for women that she confronted after graduation, as well as the tools to increase those options by pioneering the new, female-friendly field of social work.

"The whole realm of knowledge"

As one of the nation's first liberal arts colleges, Wellesley was the perfect choice for a New Woman coming of age at the turn of the century. Wellesley's founder, Henry Durant, originally envisioned the college as a training ground for Christian teachers, and the existence of a preparatory school, the requirement of Bible classes, and mandatory attendance at chapel during Breckinridge's tenure there testified to these original purposes.[17] But by the time Breckinridge arrived on campus, a new president, the young and dynamic Alice Freeman, had begun to transform Wellesley into a modern liberal arts college. In addition to classical courses traditionally required in men's colleges, such as Latin, rhetoric, and philosophy, Wellesley's required curriculum in the 1880s included chemistry, physics, mathematics, literature, and history. Electives included modern languages such as German and French; laboratory-based science courses in botany and geology; advanced math courses such as geometry and trigonometry; and courses in the emerging field of social science, such as political economy. Indeed, with the exception of the required religion courses and the absence of required Greek coursework, Wellesley's curriculum was comparable, if not superior, to that of the most elite men's colleges.[18] Breckinridge chose a rigorous curriculum with a dual emphasis on mathematics and Latin, supplemented by coursework in rhetoric, literature, history, and philosophy.[19]

Breckinridge thoroughly enjoyed her college coursework, frequently writing home to express her satisfaction with her studies and with Wellesley. "I am ever so happy now and my studies go very smoothly," she glowed in one early letter home, "so think of me as being in a very blissful state." Similarly, midway through her junior year, she announced: "My work is going beautifully . . . in fact every thing is lovely and I am happy as the day is long." Unlike some students, who dreaded the examinations held thrice-yearly in the first year and twice-yearly thereafter, Breckinridge enjoyed the opportunity to display her learning. In 1886 she remarked to her father, "I hope you will never hear another word of complaint from me about examinations or anything else. I think after this, my chief desire will be to have the examinations come back again. They have been so very lovely and I have enjoyed every one."[20]

Breckinridge excelled in all of her coursework. She studied the classics—"those old Pagans"—throughout her time at Wellesley, as well as reading Latin for pleasure.[21] She found experimental science "fascinating" despite numerous laboratory mishaps, including an occasion on which she spilled nitric acid on her hand.[22] Most of all, however, she was enthralled with her mathematics coursework, describing herself as "literally intoxicated" by Conic Sections and "breathless at the infinite curves to which I was introduced in Calculus."[23] She enjoyed the intellectual challenge of her courses in advanced mathematics, especially the difficult problems that the mathematics professor, Helen Shafer, presented to her students. Although Breckinridge described herself as "constantly on the rack till the problems are done," she also enjoyed the "delicious" feeling of completing her math homework correctly. Just as she had at A&M, she thought about Shafer's "very pretty problems" day and night until she solved them. When presented with one particularly difficult problem, she found herself unable to solve it before bedtime. "But in the night," she later recalled, "my roommate found me in my nightclothes, bare feet and all sitting at the door and calling 'Oh Miss Shafer I've got it! I've got it!'"[24]

Although she had no way of knowing it at the time, advanced mathematic study provided Breckinridge with a proficiency with numbers that would serve her well in later years, when the emergence of social science as a new field of study would allow her to use her skill with numbers to conduct pioneering statistical studies of social conditions in industrializing America. Math classes with Helen

Shafer also reinforced Nisba's penchant for persistence and problem solving—qualities that would prove absolutely indispensable in the years to come. "After all, my heart's best affection is bestowed on Mathematics," she reflected on the eve of her twenty-first birthday. "Sometimes I think if the Lord wants to make me perfectly content in Heaven he will give hard problems that I can at last solve."[25]

While she gave math first place in both her head and her heart during her time at Wellesley, Breckinridge took advantage of the full range of the liberal arts curriculum. Taken as a whole, her coursework at Wellesley prompted her to develop habits of critical thinking and provided her with a heightened awareness of social injustice. They also foreshadowed elements of her adult life as an educator and reformer in Progressive-era Chicago.

In addition to providing a broad-based curriculum and challenging courses, Wellesley's faculty demanded careful analysis and critical thinking. For instance, Breckinridge's "very charming" literature professor, Katharine Lee Bates, emphasized social commentary as well as close analysis of assigned texts. Like many Wellesley professors, Bates did not use a textbook; unlike most, rather than relying on lecture, she practiced the Socratic method—with such success that enthusiastic students in her seminars prolonged class discussions from the required three hours to four or five.[26] In later years, Breckinridge's own classroom instruction, based on lively discussions of carefully assembled primary sources, would exhibit many of the hallmarks of the Wellesley educational system as practiced by Bates and others.

Wellesley faculty members also pushed their students to consider the social implications of their intellectual pursuits. When Vida Dutton Scudder joined the faculty during Breckinridge's senior year, she strengthened the English Department's emphasis on both literary analysis and social concerns by treating novels as primary sources and calling attention to women's status in literature and life. Scudder also shared her enthusiasm for the settlement-house movement, the labor movement, and the suffrage movement with her students—thereby familiarizing Breckinridge with what would become her future milieu.[27]

Similarly, Breckinridge's history teacher, Katharine Coman, emphasized classroom instruction and independent research rather than relying on textbooks, and her courses gave equal attention to historical context and contemporary applications. In all of her courses, Coman emphasized women's role in creating social change, explaining: "We propose to enable our students to discover the causes of vice and misery and to estimate the wisdom of the various schemes for reform."[28] Coman's statement was an apt one, given that Breckinridge would devote much of her adult life to understanding the sources of poverty and injustice and finding ways to prevent human misery.

Women's rights as well as women's responsibilities permeated the Wellesley curriculum. Breckinridge raved about philosophy instructor Anne Morgan, who taught philosophy and logic, insisting that with the exception of President Freeman, Morgan was "the most brilliant woman in the college." The daughter of an abolitionist philosophy professor at Oberlin College, Morgan earned her BA and MA there before joining the Wellesley faculty in 1878. At Wellesley she actively promoted temperance and women's rights. Her commitment to feminism infused her classroom instruction, leading the Wellesley annalist for Breckinridge's senior year to comment that she was responsible for ensuring that Wellesley students made a "proper study of *woman*, as well as *man*-kind."[29] Morgan's emphasis on clear thinking and her commitment to women's equality would inform Breckinridge's future scholarship and activism.

Wellesley pushed students to engage in intellectual exchange, scholarly production, and social commentary. Regular debates in the required rhetoric and elocution classes offered Wellesley students the opportunity to apply critical thinking to social issues and to conduct individual research on subjects ranging from protective tariffs to attorney–client privilege. Some rhetoric assignments, echoing the feminist themes of other coursework, addressed women's role in society. In January 1886 Breckinridge informed her father that she and her classmates debated the proposition, "Women should speak in Religious meetings." Not surprisingly, she added, "Almost all the girls said they should."[30] Judging from the frequency with which she mentioned debates in letters home, Breckinridge found this to be one of the most interesting and rewarding aspects of her education at Wellesley. She prepared carefully for debates by reading political theorists, including Daniel Webster, John C. Calhoun, and James Madison. She often asked her father for reading suggestions, the texts of his speeches, and copies of legislation.[31] Rhetoric and elocution prepared Breckinridge for the legal studies she intended to undertake; the practice in crafting compelling arguments and public speaking also would serve her well in a long career as both a social justice advocate and a public policy analyst.

Across the board, Wellesley's curriculum emphasized writing. Frequent composition assignments, like debates, required students to conduct independent research and craft arguments on a wide range of topics. Breckinridge initially struggled with her writing assignments at Wellesley, explaining that "the ones I wrote at home were written according to very little law and order." However, she soon became accustomed to the more rigorous expectations she encountered at Wellesley and began to receive compliments on her written work. "I have had seven written reviews in two weeks," she confided to her mother during her sophomore year, "and was getting so much used to them that they seemed the proper manner of things." Although students sometimes had the latitude to choose their own topics and design their own format—Breckinridge wrote one purely descriptive piece about her native state—most compositions required students to make and support an argument. In spring 1886 her essay assignment was to take the form of an editorial. "My subject is should women join the professions," she informed her mother.[32] Writings assignments like this one not only provided the would-be career woman with an opportunity to envision her future but also gave her the tools necessary to pursue any profession.

"Important social problems"

Breckinridge's educational experience was not confined to the classroom. At Wellesley, extracurricular activities were a vital part of the college experience. Wellesley's faculty prided themselves on the school's academic rigor; President Freeman emphasized the importance of producing balanced, well-rounded individuals; and the college's founder wished above all to create good Christians. These goals merged to produce a busy campus with many out-of-classroom opportunities to delve into a wide variety of subjects.[33]

A list of activities Breckinridge kept during her first term demonstrated how extracurricular events were built in to the campus schedule and suggested the wide range of subjects covered in campus-wide activities. All Wellesley students were required to attend Sunday chapel services, where they heard a rotating assortment of ministers preach, mostly on texts taken from the New Testament, followed by a concert by piano instructor and organist Henrietta Middlekauff, which Breckinridge described as her favorite hour of the week. Classes were suspended on Mondays, which allowed students extra time to prepare for their lessons and to attend lectures on a variety of topics. Lectures and concerts were also held on campus on Friday evenings. Visiting lecturers shared the podium with Wellesley faculty; students might hear an address by President Alice Freeman, a reading of the *Odyssey* by Harvard's Professor George Herbert Palmer, a music recital from Wellesley's students and faculty, or a concert from Boston's Beethoven Club. Lecture topics were divided roughly equally between religious or moral subjects; intellectual or artistic study; and politics and current events. For instance, Breckinridge attended a temperance lecture and a missionary meeting; learned about the "sol fa" method of singing notes and Leif Erickson's explorations in Norway; and attended lectures on the "political situation in France" and the education of deaf students at Gallaudet University.[34]

While the subject matter of campus events was diverse, social justice was the dominant theme. During Breckinridge's time at Wellesley, a "Social Science craze" swept the campus, and many visiting speakers focused on "important social problems." Issues of labor and poverty were at the forefront of discourse, as were discussions of social inequality and civil rights.[35] On one occasion, escaped slave and former abolitionist Frederick Douglass spoke about his experiences in slavery, his acquisition of literacy, and his escape to freedom. Confessing that it made her uncomfortable to hear her northern classmates discuss slavery, Breckinridge also noted that she found Douglass's account "a pitiful story."[36] Several speakers addressed "Indian civilization, religion, and thought," prompting Breckinridge to query her father about citizenship rights and educational opportunities for Native Americans.[37] She also attended a series of lectures on women's citizenship and common law. This series, which informed students about the legal framework of the "covered woman," whereby a married woman's legal identity was subsumed by her husband's and she became incapable of holding property or making contracts, attracted keen interest on campus.[38] Visiting lecturers thus echoed many of the themes addressed in Breckinridge's courses, not only deepening her concern for social welfare but also providing her with concrete information about the ways that class, race, ethnicity, and gender structured society.

Breckinridge was profoundly affected by the constant emphasis on social responsibility. One winter, she told her father, she was unable to enjoy the heavy snowfall because President Freeman's prayers for the "poor and needy" rang in her ears. "Do you suppose someday I will be called to do something for them?" she pondered.[39] Both in her coursework and at chapel, as a college student, Breckinridge found herself constantly reminded of the need for social reform and inspired to find a profession dedicated to promoting a more just society.

"My day has been so very pleasant"

Neither a focus on scholarship nor concerns about social malaise prevented Breckinridge from enjoying a rich social life at Wellesley. On a campus where student life revolved around scholarship, service, and socializing, she soon achieved the contemporary ideal of the "all-around girl," one who easily combined success in the classroom with participation in campus life. After the isolation she had experienced at A&M, it must have been especially satisfying for her to find her niche at Wellesley, where she quickly became a universally popular student and an acknowledged leader. As her mother observed, "I never saw a girl commanded the respect & affection she does."[40] Decades later, her classmates continued to comment on the impression she had made on them with her "luminous personality."[41]

At Wellesley, Breckinridge—who had been an outsider both at home and at school—could at last enjoy "a happy sense of being in the midst of congenial minds."[42] Wellesley students regarded intellectual achievement as a badge of honor. Thus, when her classmates praised her as "the most brilliant student in the class," they also expressed their admiration for her. The mostly northern-born student body also was attracted by what they saw as Breckinridge's southern charm, especially her gracious manners and her soft accent. Many were impressed, as well,

Nisba Breckenridge

PACH BRO'S   841 B'WAY. N. Y.   PACH BRO'S   841 B'WAY, N. Y.

Nisba Breckinridge, who had been an outsider first in her own family and then at Kentucky Agricultural and Mechanical College, found her niche at Wellesley College, where her classmates celebrated her for her keen intelligence, "luminous personality," and gracious manners—as well as her good looks. These photos from her college years highlight what her admirers called her "crown of dark hair," her "fine aristocratic features," and her "wonderful dark eyes."

Courtesy Wellesley College Archives

by her illustrious heritage, especially by "the great distinction" of her well-known father's political career. She also gained a reputation as a beauty, with classmates remarking upon her "crown of dark hair," her fair complexion, her "fine aristocratic features," and her "wonderful dark eyes." Finally, her classmates identified her as a natural leader, electing her class president during her first year.[43]

Breckinridge's selection as class president suggests that she had quickly impressed her fellow students as the right person to lead an extraordinary group of women. Wellesley fostered a strong sense of class identity and class loyalty, and Breckinridge's class was no exception. The class of 1888 history celebrated the group as dignified, attractive, independent, and resilient ("cheerful under difficulties"). With all these qualities, the group's future success seemed assured. As the class annalist expounded, "'88 need have no fears for her future fate, if we may judge from her Freshman year. As a class, the girls came in well-prepared, wide-awake, and ready to make the most of everything."[44]

As these descriptions suggest, Breckinridge and the other members of the class of '88 quickly established a reputation for high standards of scholarship and a strong sense of social responsibility. These inclinations were evident in the elaborate rituals that marked Tree Day, a campus tradition that formally welcomed the incoming class by charging them with planting a class tree during their first year. Breckinridge was an enthusiastic participant in this event, appealing to her mother to provide the tree, a southern elm, and to order a seal of the class motto, "Not for Us," from Tiffany's. While the class motto was intended to convey the class of 1888's commitment to service, other aspects of their Tree Day highlighted academic achievement. Breckinridge chaired the committee on costumes for the event, working closely with math instructor Ellen Hayes to design "an extraordinary and glittering array of head-dresses and robes covered with mathematical signs and figures" in the class colors, blue and silver. From Breckinridge's perspective, "Tree Day was perfect." She expressed satisfaction that she and her classmates "immortalized themselves" as exemplars of both high achievement and humble service.[45]

Throughout her time at Wellesley, Breckinridge continued to enjoy student activities, which often blended socializing with scholarship, service, or both. Not surprisingly, given her predilection for social service, Breckinridge was especially active in benevolent activities. She served on the board of the Christian Association, founded her first year. Dedicated to "all branches of Christian work," including missionary work and temperance, the Christian Association also engaged in philanthropic activities. For instance, the club raised money for a "hospital for colored people" in Virginia and an Indian mission school in the Dakotas.[46] Breckinridge herself engaged in benevolent work on her own as well as under the auspices of the Christian Association. In letters home, she mentioned visiting women in prison, putting together "a big box" of items for "the poor," and organizing "a Thanksgiving entertainment at an Asylum for women." She also taught a Sunday School class for millworkers in the nearby factory town of Needham.[47]

While service to others was important to Breckinridge, she also enjoyed social events with other students. At Wellesley many student gatherings revolved around literary or historic themes and had a theatrical flair. While at Wellesley, Breckinridge received an invitation to "an author's party" in which she was requested to adopt the character of Ralph Waldo Emerson and accompany another girl in the guise of Thomas Carlyle; participated in a "Chaucer affair," in which the seniors

At Wellesley, Breckinridge and the other members of the class of '88 quickly established a reputation for both high standards of scholarship and a strong sense of social responsibility. These inclinations were evident in Breckinridge's leadership role in planning the elaborate rituals that marked Tree Day, a campus tradition that formally welcomed the incoming class by charging them with planting a class tree during their first year. While the class motto, "Not for Us," emphasized commitment to others, other aspects of Tree Day highlighted academic achievement. Breckinridge chaired the committee on costumes for the event, working closely with math instructor Ellen Hayes to design "an extraordinary and glittering array of head-dresses and robes covered with mathematical signs and figures" in the class colors, blue and silver, depicted in this 1884 photo. Breckinridge is in the center of the second row from the front.

Courtesy Wellesley College Archives

performed the Knight's tale and she and her fellow sophomores presented them with flowers; and attended a "Martha Washington style" dinner in which students and faculty alike dressed for the occasion. Breckinridge herself organized a class social with a classical theme, in which the students dined on ambrosia and dressed as characters from Greek and Roman mythology. Club activities, as well, brought literature and culture out of the classroom and concert hall and into mainstream student life. The Shakespeare Society, the Dickens Club, and the Beethoven Club all held regular entertainments, acting out scenes and playing music. Breckinridge also enjoyed informal gatherings in the college dormitories, where she and her fellow students had "quite a jolly time."[48]

Although she was universally popular, unlike many women who attended boarding schools and women's colleges in the nineteenth century, Breckinridge apparently formed no particular friendship. Initially, her closest companions at Wellesley were her roommate, Helen Clark, and Mary Meddick. However, both girls left Wellesley after Breckinridge's freshman year, Clark intermittently, to care for her dying mother and to recover from her own repeated illnesses, and Meddick after graduating in 1885. "Helen left this afternoon," Breckinridge regretfully remarked in a letter to her mother. "When she and Miss Meddick leave they take about all I care for in the College away." She maintained a close relationship with both of her absent friends, corresponding with Clark, who lived in New Haven, and visiting Meddick, who lived nearby. She also expanded her social circle. After Clark's departure, Breckinridge had a single room, although she often played host to younger students seeking her advice. "I don't go very much to the girls' rooms," she explained to her father in fall 1886, "but a good many, [come] to mine, & I can't help feeling that I do help a little to make things easier, and I know I shall be glad to think when I go out of College that I have made some freshman's life easier." Her guidance to other students, especially first-year students, foreshadowed a lifetime dedicated to advancing women's educational opportunities and professional achievements. Decades later, Josephine Simrall, a fellow southerner and future schoolteacher, described herself as one of Breckinridge's "devoted little Wellesley freshmen." At her father's insistence, Breckinridge made a point of introducing herself to her fellow southern students, but she confessed to her mother that she had very little to do with "the Kentucky girls" during her time at Wellesley. Instead, most of her closest associates were non-southerners whom she met through shared interests, such as fellow crew member Marion Ely and fellow class officer May Estelle Cook, both from the Chicago area. In part because Cook was the corresponding secretary for the class of '88, Breckinridge would remain in touch with her for the rest of her life. Although she does not appear to have had any particularly close friendships for the remainder of her college years, Breckinridge never had any difficulty finding "one of the girls" to keep her company, whether reading quietly in College Hall, attending a lecture in the chapel, or gathering wildflowers in the woods.[49]

Breckinridge enjoyed the company of other women throughout her college years. Her newfound enjoyment of female companionship—so different from her lonely childhood in Lexington and her outsider status at A&M—would help define the rest of her life.

"Never in my life before did I feel or do so much in the same space of time"

Female friendship and outdoor activities alike helped to counterbalance Breckinridge's rigorous coursework and strong sense of social responsibility. For her, one of the chief attractions of Wellesley was the expansive, park-like campus. "Don't be afraid of my working too hard," she reassured her mother. "I could not in this lovely place." Indeed, Wellesley's three hundred acres, offering a choice of "rolling hills," picturesque woods, "lovely meadows," Lake Waban, and "clear streams," provided ample incentives for exploring the outdoor environs of the "College Beautiful." Breckinridge frequently mentioned going on long walks, or "tramps," either on her own or with other students. She also took up rowing, briefly joining the crew team in an effort, she commented whimsically, "to learn to row and get strong in my arms or die in the attempt." Although she dropped crew midway through the spring of her freshman year, she continued to boat for pleasure, especially enjoying one "moon-light row" with May Estelle Cook. While other Wellesley students engaged in sleigh riding and sledding, southern-born Nisba, who did not enjoy being outdoors in wintry weather, chose not to participate in these activities. She did, however, continue to exercise year-round thanks to the college's gymnastics requirement, which encouraged students to play basketball and use rowing machines as well as making use of dumbbells, chin-up bars, and other athletic equipment.[50]

Breckinridge so enjoyed vigorous physical activity, in fact, that she became an ardent advocate of dress reform. Inspired by the example of Greek instructor and dress-reform advocate Caroline Soule, who "goes any distance without feeling it," she contemplated going so far as to adopt "divided skirts" but eventually abandoned this idea in favor of wearing either "corded underwaists or just nothing in place of corsets" under a loose-fitting "shirtwaist" blouse. In addition to asking her mother to remake her clothing to allow for more freedom of movement, she urged Issa to adopt the new system for herself. "It would pay, if there were no more backaches or headaches," she urged, "and you could skim over the ground because all of you worked at it."[51]

Breckinridge's enthusiasm for physical exertion and dress reform had special significance for New Women in Victorian America, when discussions about women's physical health doubled as debates over women's proper role. Just as well-to-do white women began to gain greater educational opportunities and explore alternatives to conventional family life, some physicians, wary of mounting challenges to prevailing gender roles, began to advance the argument that higher education and professional careers imperiled women's health, curbed their reproductive capacity, and even endangered their lives. Supporters of the New Woman countered that it was precisely the constraints and demands of traditional domesticity—a homebound existence, restrictive corsets, and unceasing childbearing—that accounted for women's poor health. President Freeman, who also was president of the Association of Collegiate Alumnae (later the American Association of University Women), used one chapel meeting to assure Wellesley students that the educational organization's longitudinal statistical study revealed that the vast majority of college graduates were in good health, that only a handful of women attributed ill health to overwork, and that some reported that college actually improved their health.[52]

In this context, Breckinridge's parents' constant concern about her health reflected their uncertainty about the advisability of higher education for women at the same time that their financial, practical, and emotional support made it possible for her to attend college. Both parents expressed anxiety about her health in the northern climate; Issa sent a new coat, warm undergarments, and flannel nightgowns, while W.C.P. recommended that she request a room with a southern exposure and avoid excessive exercise in cold weather.[53]

Issa, however, expressed more specific concerns about her daughter's menstrual cycle, peppering her with queries about the onset of her menses and advising extra rest during the menstrual period. Issa's own health problems, including extreme lassitude and mysterious aches, were precisely the sort of vague symptoms that Victorian physicians usually interpreted as "hysteria," an affliction of the womb that, according to conservative commentators, was especially likely to plague college-educated women. Her letters to her daughter thus reflected her own health problems as well as prevailing concerns about women's higher education. When she learned that her daughter's menses had ceased during her first year at Wellesley, Issa's counsel to leave her books alone and "make no exertion for at least four days" echoed the recommendations of those Victorian physicians who warned against the health threats allegedly posed by higher education and recommended the "rest cure" as a remedy.[54]

Breckinridge worked hard to persuade her parents—especially her mother—that her studies did not endanger her health. "Please Mama don't get anxious over me," she begged. "I am not overworking," she assured her. Rather, "I am as well as I ever was in my life," she asserted, pointing out that she was "really very much fatter" than she had ever been before (at the time, fleshiness was associated with health rather than with obesity). After all, she noted, she was surrounded by exemplars of both female achievement and excellent health. Pointing to the example of Caroline Soule, she informed her mother, "She is so jolly and happy & such fun, that she would knock all your theories about college girls being overworked & that kind of thing."[55]

Rather than limiting her intellectual pursuits, then, Breckinridge determined to promote her health by engaging in regular exercise and wearing unrestrictive clothing. Indeed, one of her reasons for abandoning corsets was to prepare for professional work. "I don't see why if I am going to be a working woman I should keep on in any thing that can hinder my work," she explained. "These girls that wear clothes like these . . . have no back[ache]s nor ill days," she argued. "Why can't I be as well?" After speaking with Caroline Soule and obtaining a clothing catalog from yet another dress-reform advocate, Breckinridge was determined to make the experiment. Her exemplars had "worked out their own Salvations," she argued. "I may as well do all I can to make my work good and easy too."[56]

The health regimen Breckinridge adopted as a college student served her well in college and throughout the rest of her long life. "I confess to you that never in my life before did I feel or do so much in the same space of time," she confided to her mother, "but never did I realize before the great value of good health."[57] Although she had been a sickly child, Breckinridge enjoyed remarkably good health as an adult. Moreover, just as she predicted, her good health made it possible for her to keep pace with the demands of a busy career. In years to come, students and colleagues would marvel at Breckinridge's remarkable stamina. Even near the end of her life, as one profile pointed out, despite her "frail appearance" and diminutive figure—she was barely five feet tall and weighed only ninety pounds—she had a "strong constitution," scoffed at offers of help with heavy loads, and scorned vacations as "the invention of the devil."[58]

"Other mothers"

Attending Wellesley helped Breckinridge balance work and play; it also enclosed her in a community of women, providing her with important role models and an alternative to her family of origin. Her father was keenly aware of the possibility that these new associations might "weaken if not destroy those tender ties" of home and family. During the fall of his daughter's first year, he admitted, "at times it is a little gloomy" to realize that while away at school, Nisba and her siblings were "forming new ties that are absolutely dissimilar" from their childhood relationships. "I know that it is inevitable that you will drift away from me, & I will make no complaint at it," he wrote the following spring. "I will be satisfied if you keep steadily in view that life is real & earnest & dutiful; that duty is the noblest pursuit & compatible with the highest attainments."[59]

While the theme of duty remained constant in Breckinridge's life and helped bridge the gap between her childhood and her college years—Wellesley's motto, after all, was "Not To Be Served but To Serve"—her father's "gloomy" reflections proved prescient.[60] While at Wellesley, she, like her fellow students, was deeply impressed both by individual faculty members and by the female-centered community they fostered.

Wellesley students understood that their instructors provided them not only with a superior education but also with an alternative model of womanhood. As the class of 1888's Tree Day Oration declared: "As life architects we must have our models."[61] Wellesley's faculty, who dedicated their lives to intellectual development, social reform, and a female community rather than to marriage, childrearing, and domestic tasks, were those models. Wellesley's faculty members took their job as mentors seriously. Soon after arriving on campus, Breckinridge was "quite surprised" when her Latin instructor, Emily Clark, invited the student to her room for a discussion of future careers; in the same letter, Breckinridge commented that another Latin teacher, Frances Ellen Lord, "has in a certain way taken me under her protection."[62]

Breckinridge soon found that close faculty-student relationships were commonplace at Wellesley. Conscious of their importance as mentors, Wellesley faculty members made a point of interacting with students outside the classroom by hosting social occasions, encouraging individual students to visit them in their homes, and accompanying students on long walks and carriage rides. Breckinridge, like other Wellesley students, sought out the company of her instructors and developed close bonds with them. Her relationships with her instructors strengthened her ambitions, reinforced her misgivings about marriage, and provided her with an attractive alternative to conventional womanhood. They also prompted her to question received knowledge about regionalism, race, and religion and, ultimately, to adopt "absolutely dissimilar" ideas about these topics, distancing her from her family of origin and her childhood teachings.[63]

The contrast between conventional femininity and new womanhood must have been especially apparent for Breckinridge at Wellesley, where she observed dramatic differences between her mother's life and that of the college faculty. As she pointed out in her later memoirs, Issa's schooling ended before her marriage at the early age of seventeen; she suffered from poor health resulting from excessive childbearing; and she was troubled by as-yet-unconfirmed suspicions that her husband was unfaithful to her.[64]

Breckinridge's correspondence with her mother during her college years served to highlight the differences between them even as it demonstrated that they had—after a rocky start—developed a relationship characterized by mutual care and concern. When Breckinridge first arrived at Wellesley, she suffered from terrible homesickness. Assuring her daughter that she could return home if she really wished to do so, Issa also encouraged her to remember why she had been so eager to leave home to attend Wellesley in the first place. Issa's unhappiness with her own life—"I am absolutely no account to my self or any one else," she sighed—reinforced her admonitions that her daughter should make the most of her opportunities. Issa described home as "dull" and "stupid," characterized married life as full of "pain—sorrow—& anxiety," and depicted herself as "never satisfied," even "desperate." Contrasting her situation to her daughter's, she urged her to make the most of her opportunities. "If your health is spared you can do any thing a woman can do—& more than most," she wrote.[65] Loving as they were, Issa's letters must have reinforced Breckinridge's quest for role models at Wellesley College.

Indeed, while at Wellesley, Breckinridge found an alternative to the natal family in the community of women faculty, becoming particularly close to the college president, Alice Freeman. "I love Miss Freeman," she enthused in her junior year. While Wellesley students universally idolized the college president, Breckinridge enjoyed an especially close relationship with Freeman. When she remained on campus during breaks, she sat at Freeman's table for meals, which made her "very happy." Breckinridge and Freeman also visited one another and took walks together, times prized for the "lovely thoughts" the older woman shared with the younger one. Indeed, Freeman even came to regard Breckinridge almost as an adopted child, calling her "My dearest Child" and "My dear Child-Nisba" and signing her letters from her "other mother."[66]

As a leader in the movement for women's higher education, Breckinridge's "other mother" offered a dramatic contrast to her birth mother. However, Freeman's decision to marry—and her related departure from Wellesley—also served as a reminder of the stark choices that confronted women in turn-of-the-century America. Breckinridge's relationship with Freeman thus powerfully—if inadvertently—reinforced the prevailing notion that women had to choose between marriage and a career.[67]

When she arrived at Wellesley, Breckinridge already possessed a strong predisposition to prioritize her own intellectual development over romantic relationships. During her first year, she dismissed a would-be suitor in favor of preparing for a debate. Responding to a letter from her mother in which Issa hinted that former A&M schoolmate Tom Shackelford wished to correspond with her, Breckinridge replied in haste: "I will write to Tom when I have time. Just at present all my time and attention are given to Tariff." However, there is no evidence that she ever found time to pursue a relationship with Shackelford. Nor did she maintain contact with her other suitor from her A&M years, also named Tom, who had faithfully carried her books for her on the Kentucky campus.[68] Witnessing Freeman's difficult—and long-delayed—decision to marry may have helped to convince Breckinridge that marriage and career were incompatible.

Midway through Breckinridge's junior year, Alice Freeman married Harvard professor George Herbert Palmer and—at his insistence—resigned her post as Wellesley's president, although she continued to play a key role in guiding the college as a member of the board of trustees. Breckinridge, who previously had held a long conversation with Freeman about the situation, was acutely aware of her mentor's ambivalence. The new Mrs. Palmer assured her "dearest Child" that she was happy with her decision to "make a home together" with her new husband and insisted that her move to Harvard would not interfere with her commitment to "dear Wellesley." Nonetheless, her departure probably reinforced Breckinridge's conviction that pursuing a professional career was incompatible with making a "charming happy home," as she expressed the idea in her later reflections on the outcome of her own courtships.[69]

Next to Freeman, Breckinridge's favorite faculty member was Helen Shafer, who not only was the head of the Mathematics Department but also succeeded Freeman as president in 1887. Breckinridge counted herself "fortunate to go to Wellesley where Miss Shafer who was a great teacher of mathematics opened my mind to the vistas of Conic Sections, Calculus and other forms of equations with which I became intoxicated." Shafer, a graduate of one of the nation's first coeducational schools, Oberlin College, was an innovative instructor who raised Wellesley's entrance requirements in mathematics to the highest level in the country. As Freeman's successor as president, Shafer continued the trend toward emphasizing the liberal arts, hiring young faculty, and deemphasizing religious instruction. Breckinridge thoroughly approved of her selection as Freeman's successor, writing, "she is charming & the only one here fitted for the place."[70]

Shafer, who never married, presented Breckinridge with the other side of the marriage-versus-career coin. Because the vast majority of Wellesley's illustrious female faculty remained unmarried, the school provided plentiful examples of unmarried professional women, perhaps predisposing its graduates to abjure marriage. In the class of 1888, fewer than half of Wellesley graduates—45 percent— ever married, compared with a national marriage rate of 90 percent.[71] Breckinridge's admiration for Shafer probably reinforced both her desire to pursue a career and her belief that the way to do so was to avoid marriage.

Although unmarried, Wellesley's professors were far from alone. Most faculty members lived and dined communally on campus, thriving in an atmosphere in which personal relationships and professional commitments reinforced one another. When Wellesley's faculty did live off campus, they usually chose to live with fellow faculty members, female family members, or both. Moreover, many Wellesley instructors formed long-term romantic relationships. Indeed, such domestic partnerships were so common on campus that instead of using the better-known phrase "Boston marriages" to describe them, Wellesley faculty and students referred to women's committed relationships as "Wellesley marriages." Women in "Wellesley marriages" shared domestic responsibilities, pooled finances, vacationed together, and supported one another in their careers. Wellesley faculty who formed such partnerships resolved the seeming contradiction between love and career.[72]

Wellesley's faculty thus offered the student body encouragement to avoid matrimony and pursue professional careers along with examples of satisfying single life and loving partnerships. For Breckinridge, who did not wish to follow her mother's life course, the women's community of scholars and friends at Wellesley College must have been a revelation. Although the most well-known Wellesley marriages—those of Katharine Lee Bates and Katharine Coman, Margaret Sherwood and Martha Shackford, and Vida Scudder and Florence Converse—probably postdated Breckinridge's time on campus, she spent ample time with another faculty twosome, philosophy professor Anne Morgan and her assistant, ethics instructor Estelle Hurll. Attracted both by the women's intellectual gifts and by their reform sensibilities—Morgan was one of Wellesley's leading feminists, while Hurll, a former teacher at the Carlisle School, was an advocate for American Indians—Breckinridge spent a great deal of time with them, joining the informal book club they organized and visiting with them in their (apparently shared) quarters on campus. After enjoying "a charming call on Miss Morgan & Miss Hurl[l]," she enthused, "Miss Morgan & Miss Hurl[l] are both so lovely, and they have been as kind as they could to me." Breckinridge's obvious admiration for these women foreshadowed her own future, in which she formed personal and professional partnerships with fellow female academics.[73]

Breckinridge's exposure to "Wellesley marriages" offered examples of relationships that—unlike the marriages of either her own mother, Issa, or her "other mother," Alice Freeman Palmer—helped to sustain women's professional pursuits. As Vida Scudder explained: "The women's colleges have helped to develop such friendships, which . . . can and do supply a great need."[74]

"Working through the problem of racial relationships"

Breckinridge's relationships with fellow students fostered a lifelong tendency to seek companionship and pursue collaboration with other women, while her faculty mentors provided her with inspirational role models who demonstrated that it was possible for women to "work out their own salvations" and find personal fulfillment and professional success as unmarried—but not lonely—women. Relationships with faculty and students alike also prompted Breckinridge to reevaluate her ideas about race, challenging the regional values that the southern-born student had brought with her to the northern school.

As the daughter of loyal Confederates, Breckinridge arrived at Wellesley well versed in a regional interpretation of the Civil War that defended slavery as a positive good, insisted that secession was necessary to defend states' rights, and critiqued Radical Reconstruction as a disastrous period in southern (white) history. Both Issa and W.C.P. Breckinridge were strong advocates of "redemption," by which white Democrats reclaimed political dominance from black Republicans and their northern allies. Indeed, W.C.P. owed his political success as a long-time member of the House of Congress (1885–1895) to southern whites' desire to regain their former superiority. When W.C.P. first gained office in 1884, during his daughter's first year at Wellesley, Issa rejoiced at the return of "home rule" by southern whites.[75]

Thus, when Breckinridge enrolled in Katharine Coman's upper-division elective on the social and political history of England and the United States, the U.S. portion of which addressed abolitionism, the Civil War, and Reconstruction, she was exposed to alternative interpretations of recent events that profoundly challenged her parents' teachings. According to Coman, "Northern and Southern girls debate . . . the vexed questions of state rights, negro suffrage and reconstruction policy . . . with great good temper, and gain broader and juster views of national policy."[76]

Although this course must have been difficult for Breckinridge, she rose to the occasion. Unlike some southern students at the Seven Sisters colleges, who joined Southern Clubs and fiercely defended their Confederate heritage, Breckinridge—who later celebrated both her father's sense of "fair play" and her forefathers' support for African American rights—evidently welcomed the opportunity to explore alternative interpretations of southern history.[77] She sought out opportunities to have conversations with Coman about history and politics, even soliciting copies of her father's speeches and other materials from her father for Coman's use in her course in parliamentary history.[78] She also voluntarily undertook an independent study of the Civil War. Asking her parents to help her to select books, she explained, "I want to read the history telling of the causes, and circumstances leading up to the Civil War, and the orations made before."[79]

Breckinridge's exposure to competing interpretations of southern history helped to lay the groundwork for her later work as an advocate for African American equality. Attending the only one of the Seven Sisters women's colleges to admit

African Americans also provided her with what she later called "the occasion of my working through the problem of racial relationships."[80]

While she had grown up in close proximity to African Americans, prior to attending Wellesley, Breckinridge had never encountered black people as equals, only as subordinates. Staunch defenders of white supremacy, her parents expressed considerable concern about the presence of African American students on campus at the same time that they hoped that their daughter would have limited contact with them. The Breckinridges' comments on the situation suggested how entrenched their beliefs in racial inequality were even as they offered suggestions on how to navigate race relations on the northern campus. Issa reflected: "It is a hard thing for people raised with our prejudices to ever treat them as equals—but they can do you no harm. & I can trust you to treat them properly—I suppose Papa wrote you how." For his part, W.C.P. counseled "forbearance." Although he opined that it would impossible to regard African Americans as equals, he remarked: "To a gentleman or lady there need be no personal embarrassment." As to the larger question "of what ought to be done with the race," he confessed that "the problem of the colored race in America is a very troublesome one" but need not affect interpersonal relationships. In short, the Breckinridges expected their daughter to abide by the racial etiquette she had learned at home, maintaining her "dignity" and her status as "a lady" by treating African Americans with polite distance.[81]

Breckinridge's cultural conditioning was evident in her early letters home from college, in which she expressed discomfort at encountering African Americans as fellow students rather than as family servants. "There are three negro girls here," she wrote in one of her earliest letters home, one of them a "Greek scholar." She added, "I have only seen one, a 'Miss' Smith, and she is very nice looking." Despite her praise of the black student's appearance and intelligence, Breckinridge's racial socialization was evident in her uncomfortable use of the title "Miss," which she enclosed in quotation marks.[82]

Initially, her childhood socialization held fast; Issa was relieved to learn that she saw "nothing of the colored girls." Ultimately, however, college would become the key to unlocking the chains of cultural conditioning forged in Breckinridge's childhood. Her close relationship with and admiration for Alice Freeman, together with what her father called the college president's "fanaticism" on the issue of racial equality, forced her to reexamine her views on race.[83]

In her unpublished autobiography, Breckinridge relates several incidents that challenged her southern upbringing. Both the effectiveness of her childhood training and the ways that college challenged familiar beliefs are suggested by Breckinridge's account of the first time she shared a meal with African Americans. When an African American choir from Fisk University performed at Wellesley during Breckinridge's first term at the school, President Freeman invited the singers to dine with the students and faculty. Sharing a meal was a potent symbol of equality. Although white family members and black domestic workers necessarily shared household space, white southern parents taught their children to maintain physical and thereby social separation in a variety of ways, especially by taking meals separately from African Americans. For Breckinridge, encountering African Americans at the dinner table amounted to an existential crisis. Caught between her childhood training and her desire to please the college president, she served the black women seated at her table but was unable to eat her own meal.[84]

The situation she described in the college's dining hall was a familiar one to other southern whites at northern colleges, who either shunned or ignored their black classmates. Accustomed to encountering African Americans only in subservient roles, many southern whites found that attending college in the North required them to acknowledge their deeply held beliefs about white supremacy and black inferiority for the first time. Many resisted any serious reexamination of these beliefs; some openly engaged in racial bullying. Breckinridge, like a handful of other future civil rights activists, responded by rejecting, rather than by reaffirming, the racial teachings of childhood.[85]

Two years after the dining room incident—after Breckinridge had begun studying history with Coman—the Junior Promenade proved to be a test case for Breckinridge's evolving attitudes about racial equality. In her time at Wellesley, she had become well acquainted with fellow classics student Ella Smith—the same "Miss" Smith she had mentioned in an early letter home. Breckinridge had been selected to help organize the Junior Promenade, which she described as "our chief event of college life." Smith wanted to invite guests to attend the Junior Promenade, but some of her white classmates objected. Using an argument that Breckinridge would have been familiar with from her own upbringing, they argued that educational equality did not necessitate social equality. With President Freeman's backing, however, Breckinridge convinced her classmates that "every experience at Wellesley was educational," and Smith's guests attended the event. Breckinridge entered Wellesley College skeptical about African American equality; she left the school committed to advancing African American rights.[86]

"Simple faith"

Breckinridge carefully omitted any mention of her changing beliefs about racial equality from her letters home, so her parents remained, at least for the time being, unaware of how far their daughter had drifted from her childhood teachings on white supremacy. Instead, her parents worried that her time at Wellesley would undermine her religious faith.

On the surface, it might seem as if the Breckinridges had little reason to worry that their daughter might abandon her religious upbringing. After all, Bible was a required subject at Wellesley, as was regular attendance at the college chapel. Moreover, even though President Freeman took steps to secularize the school's curriculum, she also founded its Christian Association. In addition to being active in the Christian Association, in her senior year Breckinridge organized and served as president of the Chapel Fund Association. In addition, she cultivated close relationships with several devout faculty members. Two of her favorite instructors, Helen Shafer and Katharine Coman, took turns leading the Christian Association.[87] President Freeman, who conducted daily chapel services and led Sunday services in the absence of visiting ministers, also encouraged personal faith among her acolytes on the "semi-secular" college campus.[88] And Breckinridge greatly admired her philosophy teacher, Anne Morgan, whom she described as an exemplar of Christian faith. Despite Morgan's losing several family members in a short period, Breckinridge reflected, "she teaches & lives the Love of God."[89]

Nonetheless, Breckinridge rarely discussed her required Bible studies, except to comment on her "ignorance" on the subject, and her parents expressed concern about the increasingly secular cast of the northern school and signs of their daughter's inattention to spiritual matters. "My precious child it would give us great delight to know that you were studying your bible with the same zeal you do your Geometry," her father wrote, urging his classically trained daughter to read the books of the Bible with the same care and attention "as you would a letter of Plato" and to connect her studies of ethics with religion. Both parents urged her to read the Bible on her own and to attend prayer meetings as a "safe-guard" for "simple faith."[90]

Breckinridge did in fact attend prayer meetings, and she did not abandon religion during her college years. When her maternal grandmother died, for instance, she turned to religion for support. "You know, Mama, how very seriously one has to think here about everything," she wrote home, "and this winter has made me love my Bible as I ought if it has not done any thing else for me."[91] Despite her parents' concerns, Breckinridge learned her Bible well, frequently including biblical quotations in public speeches she delivered decades later. In addition, at certain difficult passages in her life—such as the years following college, addressed in the next chapter—Breckinridge also turned to religion as a source of comfort. For the rest of her life, she would look to Christianity both as a source of personal support and as a spur to social activism.

"It is good to feel that something you
set out to do is done"

Thoughts of the future dominated Breckinridge's senior year at Wellesley. As she finished her junior year, she reflected that although she was sad to think that her time at Wellesley was coming to an end, "it is good to feel that something you set out to do is done. I shall be glad when I graduate, for I want to go to work."[92] By June 1888, when Breckinridge graduated from Wellesley College with a BS degree, she was ready to launch the next phase of her life.[93]

Her priorities were reflected in the class of '88's Tree Day oration. Breckinridge was mistress of ceremonies for this event, which was held two weeks prior to graduation and challenged the graduating seniors to take "busy women" as their models for female achievement, honor "the strong, heroic faces which shine on us through the ages," and prove their own ability by surpassing the achievements of their predecessors. Recognizing that this would be no easy task, the speaker, class president Christabel Lee, also emphasized the strength of mind that the senior class had achieved at Wellesley. "We have learned independence," Lee pronounced, "the power to trust our work, to stand alone. Through our failures we have learned resolution—the power not merely to stand alone, but to walk alone over whatever obstacles may be placed in our pathway."[94]

The themes of high aspirations and firm resolve were evident, as well, in the class of '88's commencement exercises. On graduation day the commencement speaker—none other than W.C.P. Breckinridge—urged the graduating class to seriously consider the "solemn" question: "What am I to do?" Adjuring his listeners to "be reverent to the teachings of your fathers," he also reminded them to "be cautious in believing what by common consensus is accepted as true. Above all, be true to your intellects and to your consciences." In short, W.C.P. urged the graduating class to think for themselves, to question received wisdom, and to make their own decisions. At the dinner following commencement, he expanded on these points in an address on "Woman's Education and the Nation." Echoing Katharine Coman's words on "education for citizenship," he insisted that it was up to educated women "to advance the interests of our great Nation."[95]

Commencement ceremonies even indicated how individual graduates might take up this important task. The class prophecy, presented in the form of an imaginary women's convention held twenty years in the future, described the illustrious careers of the class of 1888. The class sibyl predicted that Nisba Breckinridge would found a settlement house, become a legal advocate for women, and build a reputation as "the great friend of the people." As it turned out, this was a remarkably accurate prediction; Breckinridge would indeed live and work at a settlement house for many years; she went on to earn a law degree; and she devoted her career to serving women, the poor, immigrants, African Americans, and other disfranchised and dispossessed members of society.[96]

Ambition, independence, determination, and service—as Breckinridge left college behind to return to her hometown, these ideas must have echoed in her mind. Not only were these traits hallmarks of the class of '88's official record of Breckinridge's senior year, but they also would be recurring themes throughout her long life. Yet as the class of 1888's official historian pointed out, the Wellesley experience was both unique and fleeting. "Books, art, nature, all these wait for our appreciation everywhere," she acknowledged, "but where and when again can we have the surroundings and the emotions which were ours on the quiet Sunday evenings at Wellesley?"[97] When they graduated, Wellesley's alumnae traded an all-female space dedicated to self-improvement for a male-dominated world defined by strict gender roles. College may indeed have been preparation for citizenship, but the immediate postcollege years posed a predicament for many female college graduates of Breckinridge's generation.

CHAPTER THREE

Striving for the Ideal

Female Achievement and the Family Claim

By the promise of noon's blue splendor in the dawn's first silvery gleam,
By the song of the sea that compelleth the path of the rock-cleaving stream,
I summon thee, recreant dreamer, to rise and follow thy dream.

At the inmost core of thy being I am a burning fire
From thine own altar-flame kindled, in the hour when souls aspire;
For know that men's prayers shall be answered, and guard thy spirit's desire.

That which thou wouldst be thou must be, that which thou shalt be thou art;
As the oak, astir in the acorn, the dull earth rendeth apart,
Lo, thou, the seed of thy longing, that breaketh and waketh the heart!

Mine is the cry of the night wind, startling thy traitorous sleep;
Moaning I echo thy music, and e'en while thou boastest to reap
Alien harvests, my anger resounds from the vehement deep.

I am the solitude folding thy soul in a sudden embrace;
Faint waxes the voice of thy fellow, wan the light on his face;
Life is as cloud-drift about thee alone in shelterless space.

I am the drawn sword barring the lanes thy mutinous feet
Vainly covet for greenness. Loitering pace or fleet,
Thine is the crag-path chosen. On the crest shall rest be sweet.

I am thy strong consoler, when the desolate human pain
Darkens upon thee, the azure out-blotted by rush of the rain.
All thou dost cherish may perish; still shall thy quest remain.

Call me thy foe in thy passion; claim me in peace for thy friend;
Yet bethink thee by lowland or upland, wherever thou willest to wend,
I am thine Angel of Judgment; mine eyes thou must meet in the end.

—Katharine Lee Bates, "The Ideal," *Century Illustrated Magazine,* 1890

"The Ideal"

On Easter Sunday 1893—her twenty-seventh birthday—Nisba Breckinridge penned a heartfelt letter to her former literature professor, Katharine Lee Bates, to express her "delight and admiration" for "The Ideal," a poem Bates had published three years previously. "If you had written only that, it would be worth while to have lived," enthused Nisba, adding, "I read it and was affected as by a magnificent peal of an organ, and feel it to have been a distinct gain to me to have found it."[1]

Why was Breckinridge so moved by this poem? The answer lies in her experiences following her graduation from Wellesley. By the time she ran across this poem in an old bound volume of the *Century Illustrated Magazine*, seemingly by chance, she had been struggling for five years to find a way to express the "burning fire" of her ambition, but she had found that the "crag-path" from college to career, as the poem put it, was a difficult one. "We all meet with so many discouragements," she confided to her former teacher, and yet the words of the poem, simultaneously consoling and challenging, gave her fresh resolve by reminding her: "That which thou wouldst be thou must be, that which thou shalt be thou art." After a period of "traitorous sleep," during which she had allowed herself to drift from her appointed path and doubt her destiny, she once again felt the "longing" and "passion" to rejoin the "quest" and seek her "spirit's desire" once more. On her birthday, a time to reflect on the past and make plans for the future, Breckinridge thrilled to the call to action expressed in the poem: "I summon thee, recreant dreamer, to rise and follow thy dream."[2]

When Breckinridge graduated from Wellesley in 1888, her future seemed bright. Yet, like so many other pioneering women college graduates, she struggled with the question of "After college, what?"[3] For nearly ten years, she searched for a meaningful vocation. She taught school, kept house, and traveled abroad, but none of these activities fully satisfied her. She studied law, qualified for the bar, and worked in her father's law office, but she found it impossible to establish a rewarding practice. Meanwhile, family difficulties increased her domestic responsibilities and combined with a spell of serious illness to produce severe depression. Finally, her mother's untimely death in 1892 and the subsequent revelation of her father's infidelity shook the very foundations of her world. Many decades later, when she looked back on her first decade of postcollegiate life, Breckinridge blurred painful details and obscured the passage of time, writing: "My own life during the years after Wellesley was a confused life."[4]

While some of Breckinridge's difficulties—particularly her father's scandalous affair with a much younger woman and its long-lasting aftereffects—were unique, many women of her generation experienced a similarly "confused life" after college. After graduation, Breckinridge encountered the dilemma of the New

After graduating from Wellesley, Breckinridge struggled to find a
suitable outlet for her talents, but her high ambitions were repeatedly
frustrated by family responsibilities. In her memoirs, she described
herself as "miserable." Her facial expression in this full-length portrait
suggests the melancholy that plagued her during this difficult decade.
She later wrote that she found a temporary respite from depression in
her favorite subject, mathematics. Indeed, intellectual pursuits would
prove to be her salvation.

*Courtesy Edith and Grace Abbott Papers, Archives and Special Collections,
University of Nebraska-Lincoln Libraries.*

Woman, for whom a wide gap separated expectations and realities. While high ambitions and higher education seemingly paved the way to individual achievement, family obligations and limited opportunities presented almost insuperable obstacles to professional goals. When Breckinridge encountered the disparity between her girlhood hopes and her adult options, she confronted the combination of choice and constraint that characterized the generation of women who came of age in turn-of-the-century America. In particular, the pattern she established of repeatedly deferring her own goals to cope with family crises dramatically illustrates what her fellow college graduate and future colleague, Jane Addams, called "the family claim": the assumption that unmarried women were perennially "on call" for their family of origin. Caught between her own lofty ambitions and her family's demands, for nearly a decade Breckinridge attempted, in fits and starts, to find a route to useful independence. While professional work and higher education provided a respite from domestic responsibilities, she never fully succeeded in reconciling female achievement with the family claim. It was not until 1905, after both parents' deaths, that she was able to prioritize her goals over her family's demands and begin to fulfill her vast potential.[5]

"A confused life"

After graduating from Wellesley, Breckinridge hoped to study and practice law in her father's office. However, W.C.P. Breckinridge, who had won a seat in Congress in 1884, had little time or inclination to tutor his daughter. W.C.P. was a favorite of the Democratic Party, and he easily gained reelection until 1894, when his political career would be destroyed by scandal. Unable to support his large family on his congressional salary alone, he eagerly accepted invitations to speak around the country on diverse topics ranging from tariff reform to race relations. Although he also continued to practice law, he devoted most of his limited time at the office to training his eldest son, Desha, as his partner and successor. W.C.P.'s behavior reflected as well as reinforced the barriers that confronted would-be women professionals in Victorian America.[6]

W.C.P.'s decision to focus his attentions on a son who showed no particular interest in or aptitude for law rather than on a daughter who yearned to pursue a legal career and had used her college years to prepare for legal study must have been a terrible disappointment for Nisba Breckinridge, although she never commented on this irony in her memoirs. Instead, she blamed herself for her "stupid" reasoning in pursuing a liberal arts education and her "foolish" decision to attend Wellesley College rather than the University of Michigan, which had begun "the dangerous experiment" of admitting women in 1870, offering a handful of intrepid women the opportunity to earn a law degree. "It is pitiful to recall how my college work had failed in every way to help me toward a profession," she reflected painfully. "I was no nearer earning my living when I came back from college than when I had left home fo[u]r years before."[7]

In point of fact, however, social constraints and family demands, more than individual decisions, limited educated women's options in turn-of-the-century America. In 1920, in response to a study conducted by the Bureau of Vocational Information, an independent agency founded by the alumnae of the Seven Sisters colleges to promote women's professional work, Breckinridge pointed to gender discrimination as the primary barrier to women's success in the legal profession. Shut out from the more lucrative and prestigious careers in corporate law, many female lawyers resorted to employment in legal aid societies or struggled to find enough clients to maintain a private practice; in both cases, "the remunerative returns are not large." Small wonder, then, that Breckinridge concluded that "the reason that women have not gone into the law in great numbers nor forged forward in it is very evident."[8]

In addition to outright discrimination, domestic duties also thwarted many women's ambitions. The "family claim" frustrated many female college graduates at the time, but it may have been especially powerful for southern women, whose workforce participation rates lagged behind those of their northern counterparts.[9] Certainly Breckinridge's sense of duty to her family combined with the limited options for women to prevent her from pursuing legal studies. As she later explained: "At that time there were not many law schools open to women. My mother's health was frail, and the family expenses were high. The only law school open to women in Washington had classes in the evening and that was when I could be of service at home."[10]

Unable either to study law in her father's law office or to attend law school, Breckinridge cast about for alternatives. Teaching school was the most obvious option. Over the course of the nineteenth century, as more and more women attained higher education and sought professional careers, an expanding system of public and private schools staffed classrooms affordably by hiring women, who typically earned just half of what their male counterparts were paid. Although not a lucrative profession, teaching school was a respectable occupation for women because it could be described as a logical extension of women's domestic responsibilities, especially caring for children, and therefore could be understood as consistent with conventional femininity. Finally, Wellesley College prepared its graduates for teaching and provided them with role models, as fully half of the college's faculty members had previously worked as schoolteachers.[11]

Nonetheless, teaching was far from Breckinridge's first choice. "I had promised myself to be a lawyer and had never thought of teaching," she insisted in her autobiography. Even though she had earlier acknowledged the possibility that teaching might be her best avenue to self-support, she still hoped to realize her lifelong dream of practicing law alongside her father. However, teaching seemed to be the only route open to her, particularly since her father, unwilling to help his daughter realize her legal ambitions, was willing to use his connections to secure a teaching post for her at Washington High School, one of the capital city's first coeducational public schools. "My father tried to make it clear that he wanted me appointed because of my qualifications, not as a favor to him," emphasized Breckinridge in her memoirs, "and I did earn my salary."[12]

Although teaching was not her dream job, she dedicated herself wholeheartedly to the task, buoyed by congratulations from Alice Freeman Palmer, who encouraged her former student to see her teaching post as the beginning of a successful career. Impressing her students with her calm demeanor when an inquisitive mouse interrupted class, "Miss Nisba Breckinridge" taught algebra and geometry for two school years, 1888–89 and 1889–90. According to one former student, she was "a most excellent teacher, and all the girls loved her."[13]

Although teaching school was a respectable profession for an unmarried woman, the low pay, combined with "the family claim," also meant that it could be incompatible with female liberation. Teaching at Washington High School allowed Breckinridge to reside with her parents and younger siblings, who accompanied W.C.P. to the capital when Congress was in session.[14] Like many unmarried daughters living at home, she made practical as well as financial contributions to the household. "The salary was certainly a real contribution to the family income," she later recalled, "and I greatly enjoyed my first earnings which I gave to Mama." She also "did a good deal of the housekeeping" in the family's rented quarters on East Capitol Street.[15] Ultimately, Breckinridge's first job reinforced the family claim instead of promoting female independence.

Many single women in nineteenth-century America, especially in the South, dedicated their entire lives to their families of origin. They contributed their earnings, if any, to their parents; educated younger siblings and cared for the children of older married siblings; and engaged in charitable and civic work in their hometowns. Combining poorly paid work in a feminized profession with unpaid domestic labor in the family home, Breckinridge seemed to have resigned herself to the role of "dutiful daughter" by 1890. That year, however, marked the beginning of a series of jarring events that, while extremely difficult and emotionally painful at the time, ultimately freed her from family obligations and created new opportunities for further education.[16]

During Breckinridge's second year at Washington High School, an outbreak of typhoid fever struck the city. Several of her fellow teachers contracted the disease, leaving the remaining staff with an increased workload. In hindsight, Breckinridge reflected, "I think that I worked myself into a state of panic." On top of these problems at work, contagious disease also affected life at home. When her father became ill during "a bad epidemic of influenza," she contracted the virus as well. Still carrying the dual burden of schoolwork and housework, she fainted while doing the family shopping and had to be carried out of the marketplace. Influenza was a serious and sometimes deadly ailment in early-twentieth-century America. During the "Spanish flu" (H1N1) pandemic of 1918–1920, nearly one-third of the world's population was infected, and at least one out of ten sufferers died as a result. Although the 1890 outbreak was less severe, Breckinridge was "quite ill for some time," and she remained a "semi-invalid" for months afterward.[17]

Breckinridge's illness prevented her from accepting an invitation to teach a third year at Washington High School; instead, she devoted her limited energies to keeping house and tutoring her younger sister, Curry. This exclusively domestic life did not agree with her. Responding to a request for information about Wellesley alumnae, she wrote with some asperity:

> There was a cruel touch of sarcasm in the secretary's statement that the class letters this time were to be limited to one hundred words. One word suffices abundantly to tell what I am doing. Nothing, nothing, nothing.[18]

Although she complained of doing "nothing," Breckinridge continued to put her college education to good use. In 1890, she helped her aunt establish the Daughters of the American Revolution, using her experience in student government at Wellesley to draft the new organization's constitution and bylaws. Although she would later downplay her involvement with the conservative group, in her autobiography Breckinridge described the organization as having sprung from feminist principles. "The men had organized the Sons of the American Revolution," she explained, "and Auntie [Mary Desha] was determined that the contribution of women should not be ignored."[19]

Breckinridge also continued to dream of a different future. In 1890 she had been inspired by a chance meeting with suffrage leader Susan B. Anthony, who stayed at the Breckinridges' boardinghouse while engaged in a renewed effort to pass a federal woman suffrage amendment. A later *New York Times* article indicated that in addition to "vigorously" attempting to "indoctrinate" Breckinridge with "woman's rights principles," the septuagenarian suffragist encouraged the younger woman in her "penchant for a professional career."[20]

"I do want to do something with myself"

Clearly, Breckinridge had not yet relinquished her dream of pursuing a legal career, and she soon had a new opportunity to study law. In May 1891 the Breckinridges sent Nisba abroad in charge of her younger sister, fifteen-year-old Curry, hoping

After completing her studies at Wellesley, Breckinridge returned to
the family home, where she assumed responsibility for managing
the household and for tutoring her younger sister, Curry. After the
intellectually stimulating atmosphere of Wellesley, she found home
life stultifying. Summarizing her situation for the alumnae newsletter,
she wrote: "One word suffices abundantly to tell what I am doing.
Nothing, nothing, nothing."

*Courtesy Edith and Grace Abbott Papers, Archives and Special Collections,
University of Nebraska-Lincoln Libraries.*

that the trip would allow the girls to rejuvenate their health and refresh their spirits. Spending time in Belgium, Switzerland, and France, Nisba and Curry reveled in European art, architecture, history, music, and landscape.[21]

A year in Europe was a rite of passage for elite Americans. For many well-to-do young women, time abroad served as a final year of "finishing" between school and marriage. However, a sojourn abroad also offered intelligent and ambitious young women an opportunity to pursue their individual desires away from parental oversight and domestic responsibilities. Not surprisingly, then, many pioneering professionals in Victorian America found their true calling during extended European travels.[22]

For the Breckinridge girls, as for other New Women, a trip to Europe was intended as a prelude to self-support rather than an interlude between school and marriage. W.C.P., who struggled to meet his day-to-day expenses, anticipated that his children would have to marry well or support themselves, and he considered the latter the more likely option for both Nisba and Curry. (Their older sister, Ella, had married in 1889.) Moreover, the wayward careers of the Breckinridge sons—Desha interrupted his desultory study of the law to supervise a lumber company in West Virginia, and Robert led a dissipated life before boarding a ship apparently bound for Calcutta—prompted the Breckinridges to encourage their unmarried daughters to pursue the success that eluded their brothers. "If God gave our girls more purpose than our boys," pronounced Issa, "He intended they should do more."[23]

Thus, in addition to sightseeing, Curry and Nisba also studied during their European sojourn. Curry attended local schools to learn French and German; her parents hoped that studying languages abroad would make learning easier for Curry, whose dyslexia sometimes made school a trial. Meanwhile, following in the footsteps of other American women who responded to limited opportunities at home by pursuing higher education overseas, Nisba found a professor in Europe who was willing to instruct her and undertook private tutoring in French and Roman law.[24]

Perhaps because they understood the link between Nisba's professional disappointments and her poor health, the Breckinridges encouraged Nisba in her legal studies. "I am glad that you are studying law," her father wrote in January 1892. "You can succeed at anything you undertake & if you enjoy it, go ahead." Issa also cheered her daughter on: "I am glad you love law & are going to study & make it your profession." With her parents' blessing, Nisba regained her earlier sense of mission. "I will try to do something," she vowed. "I do want to do something with myself."[25]

A renewed commitment to the legal professional coincided with—and may have contributed to—Breckinridge's continued determination to remain single.

During her time in Europe, she corresponded with Gerald Stanley Lee, a suitor who took a unique approach to courtship by discussing ideas and politics. He also supported Breckinridge's plans for studying the law, although he was uncertain what she planned to do with the knowledge. "I have often wondered just what you anticipated at one time in the study of law," he wrote, assuring her that "I am very much attracted too by all strenuous ideals in a woman's life—and I have wondered often, as to what you meant by an expression of yours in one of your letters 'The Lord has planned a woman's work for me.'" Exactly what that "woman's work" might be was unclear, but it evidently did not include marriage, as Breckinridge rejected Lee's proposal.[26]

It was during her time in Europe that Breckinridge became, by her own recollection, "wickedly pious." While living in Washington, D.C., she had strayed from her Presbyterian roots, worshipped in a local Episcopal church, and been "tempted by the prospect of a sisterhood, Episcopal but demanding the vows of poverty, chastity and obedience." Still "concerned for my soul" while in Europe, every Sunday she insisted on attending church services rather than enjoying cultural opportunities. She may still have been considering a cloistered life. While she ultimately rejected this option, contemplating taking religious vows must have discouraged her from considering marriage even as her spiritual crisis deepened her conviction that she was destined to undertake "a woman's work."[27]

Indirectly, Issa's comments about her own marriage probably reinforced her daughter's decision to remain single. Complaining frequently of the "neuralgia" and ennui that made her "good for nothing" and of the unsettled life she led as the wife of a congressman, Issa insisted that W.C.P. was an attentive and loving husband but also remarked, "I am sorry for every girl who marries—it takes a lot of love to make life happy." Encouraging both girls to prolong their stay in Europe, Issa commented that travel was more important than study, because "you can study all your lives (provided you do not get married)." By reminding her of both the daily difficulties of married life and the obstacles that marriage posed to continued intellectual development, Issa provided her daughter with ample reasons to seek other options.[28]

Breckinridge's continued contact with college friends also kept her plans for a professional career at the forefront of her mind. While in Europe, she corresponded with several Wellesley classmates, who affectionately recalled her reputation for studiousness, chided her for her tendencies toward "self-deprecation" and insomnia, informed her about other alumnae's continued studies and teaching careers, and requested updates on her career. "That you are working some good I feel sure, and the Wellesley motto is still your guide for each day," one classmate wrote. May Estelle Cook no doubt reinforced the Wellesley commitment to public service when she informed Breckinridge that four of their classmates were living and working at Hull House, the Chicago settlement house that so closely resembled the fictional one that the class of '88 sibyl had predicted Breckinridge herself would establish.[29]

Freed from domestic responsibilities and encouraged by family and friends to pursue her goals, Breckinridge began to investigate the possibility of attending law school at the University of Michigan upon her return to the United States. However, even when separated from her parents by an ocean, she could not help but wonder if they would approve. Like so many women of her generation who felt compelled to answer the "family claim," she worried that while her dream was to pursue law, her duty was to serve her family. "She is quite undecided wheather [sic] it is her duty to stay at home or learn law," Curry explained.[30]

How the Breckinridges might have responded to Nisba's latest plan for continued education remains a mystery, however. Shortly after Curry confided in them on the subject, Issa contracted dysentery, and W.C.P. sent funds to permit the Breckinridge girls to return home immediately. Hastily boarding a ship for America, Nisba and Curry arrived home only to find that their mother had already expired.[31]

"A sad home-coming"

Issa's sudden death was a terrible shock. It also struck a devastating blow to Nisba's plans for the future. "Poor girls what a sad home-coming for you," Desha commiserated before resuming his education at the University of Virginia and assigning his unmarried sisters responsibility for comforting their bereaved father. "I hated to leave papa but I was worthless there & he seemed to prefer that I come [back to school] so I am trying to make myself of some account," he excused himself. "You & Curry can do him great good I think, he will be so glad to see you & you are so brave & strong & true & bright."[32]

Expected to maintain order at home, Breckinridge once more put her own goals on hold: she did not enroll at the University of Michigan, nor did she apply for the settlement fellowship program that her former English professor, Vida Scudder, encouraged her to pursue.[33] Instead, she assumed responsibility both for keeping house and for educating Curry.

While Breckinridge was willing to postpone law school, she was also determined to pursue her dream of practicing law. Within a few months of returning home to Kentucky, she was ready to launch her long-delayed legal career. In the late nineteenth century, lawyers were just beginning to form bar associations and establish standards for legal education and practice; meanwhile, local admission to the bar depended largely on informal apprenticeships and ad hoc oral examinations. In order to qualify to practice at the county level, would-be attorneys in Kentucky were simply required to take an oath that they had never

Issa Breckinridge's sudden death in 1892 struck a devastating blow
to Breckinridge's plans for the future. Instead of studying law at the
University of Michigan, as she had planned, she assumed responsibility for keeping house for her widowed father and—after his sudden
remarriage and the resulting sex scandal—caring for her emotionally
unstable stepmother as well. Although Breckinridge was in mourning
herself, as depicted in this image, she prioritized her father's comfort
over her own welfare, with disastrous results for her physical and
emotional health.

Courtesy Special Collections Research Center, University of Chicago Library

participated in a duel. Breckinridge took the oath and joined her father's law office in the autumn of 1892. At long last, she had reached her goal of practicing law alongside her father.[34]

As luck would have it, however, W.C.P. Breckinridge's legal difficulties would soon overshadow his daughter's legal ambitions. In spring 1893, less than a year after Issa's death, W.C.P. secretly remarried, choosing as his third bride a cousin, Louise Wing. Almost immediately, another woman, Madeline Pollard, filed suit in a Washington, D.C., court for breach of promise, claiming that W.C.P. had reneged on his promise to marry her. She further averred that she and the defendant had engaged in a lengthy extramarital affair that began shortly after their first meeting on April 1, 1884—Nisba's eighteenth birthday—and continued into 1893—during and after Issa's final illness. Testifying that the illicit relationship had resulted in the birth of two children, one in 1885 and another in 1888, she also presented evidence that the affair continued throughout W.C.P.'s term in office; Pollard followed him to Washington, D.C., and he finagled a government job for her. After conceiving a third time, shortly after Issa's death, Pollard secured a promise of marriage, only to miscarry and then to learn that her lover had married another woman.[35]

Unable to deny the affair in the face of overwhelming evidence, W.C.P. instead fought the suit by impugning the plaintiff's character, assembling a team of lawyers and detectives to collect incriminating evidence that at the time of the initial encounter—when he was forty-seven and Pollard was seventeen years old—Pollard was a sexually experienced seductress rather than the innocent schoolgirl she claimed to be. Meanwhile, he hit the lecture circuit, campaigning for reelection on his solid record despite his "secret sin." Notwithstanding W.C.P.'s Herculean efforts to cast aspersions on Pollard's character and veracity, the judge ruled in her favor and ordered W.C.P. to pay her $15,000 in compensation. (Unfortunately for all concerned, W.C.P.'s legal battle had bankrupted him, and Pollard received nothing.) The public also judged him guilty. In mass meetings, prominent community members—including clubwomen and feminist activists—denounced W.C.P. Breckinridge as a menace to society. Some people sent death threats. His political opponents exploited the scandal (and may have funded Pollard's lawsuit), and he was defeated in his bid for reelection to the U.S. Congress in fall 1894. Expulsion from Lexington's Mt. Horeb Presbyterian Church completed his disgrace.[36]

Remarkably, at the same time that W.C.P. angrily denounced what he characterized as "lies fabricated for the purpose of poisening [sic] the minds of my family," he recruited his own children to assist in his defense. Nisba spent her first year as a practicing attorney taking testimonials from boardinghouse keepers, chambermaids, and staff at the foundling hospital and orphanage where Pollard gave birth and left her first child, hoping to establish reasonable doubt that her own father was also the father of Pollard's children.[37]

Almost unbelievably, W.C.P.'s children—including Nisba—supported him unreservedly, even with full knowledge of his betrayal of their mother. In her autobiography, Breckinridge struggled to make sense of her father's infidelity. "As I look back, now, I see how complicated and difficult a burden he carried," she mused. She hastily brushed aside her father's relationship with Pollard (never mentioning her by name), writing, "It is not necessary to give the details of the scandal." Instead, she focused on her father's evident devotion to his wife: "My mother's health was frail and she was entirely unaware of any deviation on his part. He was devoted, he was endlessly kind, and there could not in our minds be any question of his fidelity." At least in her written recollections, Breckinridge accepted her father's version of events, in which the real culprits were his political enemies, who exploited a good man's one weakness "to send in his place to Washington a mediocre representative of certain special interests."[38]

Breckinridge did her best to remain the same loving and dutiful daughter she always had been. From Staunton, Virginia, where she and Curry went to live with their older sister Ella and her husband, Lyman Chalkley, to avoid the worst of the negative publicity during the trial, she wrote often to offer affection and encouragement to her "dearest Papa," assuring him of her continued love and support. "Believe me always, Papa, your loving daughter Sophonisba," she closed one such letter. Although she offered her father unfaltering support and unstinting affection, the revelation of her beloved father's betrayal affected her deeply. Her father and brother worried that her health, still fragile after her bout with influenza, was in jeopardy. Perhaps more to the point, the depression that had plagued her since leaving school also threatened to return. Insisting that she was "perfectly well and strong," she admitted that she felt "dazed" and uncertain.[39]

During this difficult time, Breckinridge continued to prioritize family demands over professional opportunities, relinquishing her renewed plans to study law at the University of Michigan when she learned of her father's objections. Assuring her father that she was "very well and able to work," she vowed, "I would not give you cause for anxiety for the world, and it seems to me now I cannot go."[40]

Instead of going to law school, Breckinridge was "an infinite comfort" to her father. She not only packed his belongings in Lexington in preparation for his return to the capital for the trial but also relocated to Washington for several months during and after the trial to provide around-the-clock care for his new wife, "Cousin Louise," whose pre-existing emotional problems escalated into a nervous breakdown under the pressure of the highly publicized trial, requiring constant monitoring and administration of sedatives. She also assisted her father in his campaign for reelection by copying his speeches, in which he attempted to defend his honor while admitting to the affair. "Of course, you know how faithfully I want you to succeed," she assured him, "& how I will help you in every possible way."[41]

Seeking to reduce her father's financial burdens, in fall 1894 Breckinridge returned to Staunton, where she took a teaching position in a private girls' school. Evidently, she had concluded that teaching was the only remaining option for self-support, for she explained, "While the pay is poor, it is a step towards making a profession of teaching." She whimsically noted, "I already have quite a school-marmish air." Although she did not enjoy teaching in Staunton, she was "glad and grateful to have honest and dignified work" that reduced the "heavy burdens" on her father. Promoting her father's interests, she insisted, was a higher priority than "any false desire for independence."[42]

Determined to be a dutiful daughter, Breckinridge prioritized her father's demands and family responsibilities to the detriment of her own health and happiness. Her physical and mental health declined precipitously, and as she later recalled, by the mid-1890s, "the question of my health and my future became acute." During this dark period, Breckinridge's intellectual interests sustained her. "One year when things were very hard," she reflected many years later, "I think that I saved what little mental power I had working mathematical problems," for "I could keep my mind on an equation as sometimes I could darn!"[43] If intellectual activity helped her survive periods of depression, higher education allowed her to replace melancholy with purpose. In the coming year, she at last would find a way to return to school after a hiatus of seven years. The opportunity to study at the University of Chicago would change her life for good.

"Coming to the University"

In later years, Breckinridge would claim, "My coming to the University was pure accident." In fact, at this critical juncture in her life, her Wellesley College connections served her well. After leaving Wellesley, Alice Freeman Palmer continued her involvement in women's higher education by serving—largely in absentia—as the new dean of women at the fledgling coeducational University of Chicago for the school's first three years, from 1892 to 1895. To enable her to spend time with her husband at Harvard, she arranged for Marion Talbot, a pioneer in the field of domestic science who was then teaching at Wellesley, to live in residence and assist the absentee dean in her new administrative duties. Talbot took over as dean of women in 1895. With Palmer, Talbot had been a co-founder of the Association of Collegiate Alumnae (ACA), an organization dedicated to advancing women's higher education and providing college-educated women with greater opportunities. Breckinridge, a member of the association, had previously corresponded with Talbot to inquire about the ACA's studies of the health of women college graduates, and Talbot had encouraged her to apply for a fellowship with the College Settlements Association. Now, two years after allowing that opportunity to pass her by, Breckinridge was ready to make the most of her college contacts.[44]

By late 1894, W.C.P. and Desha had become so concerned about Nisba's melancholy, sleeplessness, and weight loss that they agreed to send her to visit her college friend May Estelle Cook in Chicago. "I was a miserable person almost down and out when I came up to visit my classmate May Cook," she later recalled. Relieved from domestic responsibilities and reveling in the comfort of Cook's Oak Park home, Breckinridge "came gratefully back into normal relationships." Cook was then taking courses at the University of Chicago, and she encouraged her friend to visit the campus, where they discovered that two other Wellesley graduates had enrolled in graduate programs. Although the "Wellesley presence" at the university was an attraction, it was her meeting with Talbot that helped Breckinridge decide to attend the school. Talbot encouraged her to pursue graduate studies and offered her a job as her personal assistant in order to finance her education. Thinking back on her "inexpressible" obligations to Talbot, Breckinridge later declared, "She rescued me and put me on my feet and clarified my thinking about my future. No words can express the obligation I feel to her."[45]

With Talbot's support, Breckinridge enrolled at the University of Chicago in the fall of 1895, where she spent a "wonderful year taking almost exclusively courses with Professor Freund." Ernst Freund, then a professor in the Political Science Department, was an innovative and influential legal scholar. With such legal luminaries as Roscoe Pound, he promoted "sociological jurisprudence," the use of the legal system to promote social justice. It was doubtless Freund's legal expertise that attracted the would-be law student to a university that, as yet, had no law school. Breckinridge was immediately captivated, taking Freund's courses on international law, administrative law, general and historical jurisprudence, Roman law, and judicial power. In short, she came as close as she possibly could to achieving her longtime goal of studying law.[46]

Studying with Ernst Freund introduced Breckinridge to new theories about social justice and public policy. During the time she studied with Freund, he was writing—and often lecturing from drafts of—his pioneering book *The Police Power* (1904). Freund regarded the law itself as dynamic, capable of—indeed, even necessitating—change in response to social and economic conditions. In handwritten notes, Freund pondered how "public power" could advance "humanitarian work." He argued that "social legislation"—such as laws regulating the labor of women and children—was both a proper use of state power and a sensible response to industrial conditions. Presenting his students with information about such current issues as poor relief, juvenile justice, and labor legislation, Freund contended that laws reflected "changing standards" of social justice, and he chal-

The chance to pursue advanced degrees at the University of Chicago offered Breckinridge an escape from domestic duties and an opportunity to pursue a professional career. She later claimed that once she went to Chicago, she never returned to Kentucky without a return ticket in her possession. In this undated photo, Breckinridge is depicted on the campus she would make her home for more than fifty years.

Courtesy Edith and Grace Abbott Papers, Archives and Special Collections, University of Nebraska-Lincoln Libraries.

lenged his students to envision themselves as "activists of the law." Breckinridge wholeheartedly adopted Freund's views on sociological jurisprudence, which she would later apply to her own work as a social worker, policy consultant, and advocate of "socialized justice" in the Second City's courts.[47]

During her year at the University of Chicago, Breckinridge immersed herself in university life. She spent every day in Cobb Hall, where the Political Science Department offices and classrooms were housed and where Talbot had her office. Once she had a janitor shorten the front legs of one of the big chairs in the lecture hall to accommodate her petite frame, she felt entirely at home there. She dined and lived at Kelly Hall, a women's residence supervised by Talbot. Although she did not know it yet, the year that Breckinridge spent in the social science building and in the women's halls at the University of Chicago would be the first of nearly fifty years on campus.[48]

"A Kentucky Portia"

At the conclusion of the 1895–96 school year, however, Breckinridge returned home to Lexington because, as she later stated, "we did not have the money for me to go back to Chicago." Once more, she became, as her father put it, "the mainstay—the cement of the family." Keeping house for her father, caring for her stepmother, and teaching her younger sister certainly kept Breckinridge busy, but "home matters" failed to satisfy her desire for intellectual stimulation, and she was again plagued by depression, leading her father to advise, "You must not permit yourself to grow morbid, nor get into the habit of looking at the dark side of life."[49]

As she had done before, she sought redemption through education. Determined to complete her master's degree, she maintained a "pro forma" student status at the university and chose a topic that she could research in Lexington, the early judicial system of Kentucky. The subject had an additional appeal because it allowed her to address "the old and new court controversy," the context in which her maternal grandfather had launched his political career in the mid-1820s. Finally, the topic allowed her to build on the work of her mentor, Ernst Freund, by exploring the role of the state in promoting social welfare.[50]

The court controversy, which emerged due to conflicting policies on debtor relief during an economic downturn following the War of 1812, pitted the "Old Court" and a "microscopic minority" of fiscally conservative voters against a "New Court" and a populist "Relief party" that advocated issuing paper money as a relief measure. Breckinridge's sympathetic attitude toward the New Court and the "plain people" who advocated debt relief and her dismissal of the Old Court's cherished ideal of "freedom of contract" were consistent with Freund's advocacy of using state power to promote social welfare and foreshadowed her own later use of the court system to advance social justice. Breckinridge completed the thesis in less than a year, receiving her master's degree in political science in July 1897.[51]

While working on her thesis, she also took steps to establish a legal career. In addition to reading law—especially family law—in her father's office, Breckinridge decided to seek further qualifications as a lawyer. Although she had qualified to practice law in Kentucky's lower courts five years earlier, in order to practice in the appellate courts, candidates had to undergo an examination and be found competent by the judges at the Court of Appeals in Frankfort, Kentucky. In January 1897, while accompanying her brother Desha to Frankfort, she seized the opportunity to ask the chief justice, one of her father's cronies from the Confederate Army, to let her "try an examination." After he and two other justices questioned her for several hours in the judges' chambers, they unanimously agreed that she was "qualified to practice," and they administered the oath on the spot. Newspapers around the country celebrated her as a "Kentucky Portia."[52]

As she had done five years earlier when she initially qualified to practice law, Breckinridge continued to work in her father's office. However, she also began to establish a practice of her own, which benefited from her family connections as well as her family-law specialty. In her autobiography, she remarked that a Confederate veteran, a member of her father's regiment, "brought me my first case," involving a homestead claim, and within a week, she also had "three cases involving special women's interests." One of these cases was that of an abused wife, Elizabeth Swigert, who sought a divorce from her husband, Charles, as well as custody of their younger children. Although Breckinridge declined to discuss the case with reporters and characterized it as "simply a plain divorce case," the Swigerts' domestic situation was a particularly "pathetic and dramatic one." Fearing for her life, the abused wife fled the family home with her five children on a frigid winter night, only to be pursued by the enraged husband, who asserted his authority as the children's sole legal guardian and physically removed them from her custody. Pushing the emerging judicial doctrine of acting in the "best interests" of children as far as she could, Breckinridge won her client custody of the three younger children; the husband retained custody of the two eldest.[53]

Although the highly publicized case brought enough business to prevent Breckinridge from accepting out-of-town speaking invitations, it may also have dampened her enthusiasm for practicing law. Many years later, she told an interviewer that dealing with "the broken-down family" was "hard on the young woman lawyer." While speaking in general terms, Breckinridge may have had the Swigert case in mind. Her father's own trial probably also contributed to her negative assessment of the legal profession. Whether because she was disillusioned by domestic law or for some other reason, evidently even a moderately successful legal practice was not rewarding enough for her to resist the opportunity to return to

Chicago for further education. As she later recalled, "when Miss Talbot snatched for me a fellowship in Political Science which a man student had resigned, I came back to the University and have remained ever since."[54]

Breckinridge's return to Chicago in fall 1897 was a major turning point in her life. In her autobiography, she claimed that after beginning work for her PhD, she never left Chicago without a return ticket. Although almost certainly an overstatement, the comment reflected her shifting loyalties from Lexington to Chicago and from the family claim to her own professional goals.[55]

"Rich and fortunate years"

Breckinridge had good reasons for choosing Chicago as her new home. By the 1890s, the Second City was an epicenter of industry and reform. Railroads transported immigrants from the hinterlands, Europe, and the South to the city to work in the stockyards, factories, and department stores that made fortunes for such companies as Morris, Armour, and Swift; McCormick's American Harvester and Pullman's Palace Cars; and Marshall Field, Sears Roebuck, and Montgomery Ward. Chicago was notable also for its history of labor unrest. The railway strike of 1877, the Haymarket riot of 1886, and the Pullman strike of 1894 punctuated the city's growth, serving as periodic reminders of the vast chasm that separated capital and labor. Women reformers responded enthusiastically to the challenges and opportunities presented in Chicago. Jane Addams and her colleagues made Hull House, established in 1889, a center for social services, social reform, and social science research. Meanwhile, clubwomen organized to promote city services and civic reform. At the 1893 World's Fair, a Board of Lady Managers insisted on showcasing women's abilities and accomplishments in a Woman's Building, prompting one female college graduate to remark that "the clock of time" had "struck the woman's hour."[56]

Certainly "the woman's hour" had arrived at the University of Chicago, which from the beginning admitted women "on equal terms." Coeducation was not the university's only innovation. Seeking solutions to the most pressing problems of urbanizing and industrializing America, faculty and students at the new university combined scholarship with social activism and spearheaded the progressive impulse to use expertise to improve society. In Progressive-era Chicago, research and reform were closely intertwined. The need for urban reform justified the rise of the modern research university, while the professional educators who pursued careers in research-oriented universities promised that rigorous academic research would provide the basis for meaningful social change. The University of Chicago's president and professoriate enthusiastically proclaimed the Second City a laboratory for social engineering monitored by experts in the new social sciences. Faculty in the nascent fields of sociology, economics, and political science all believed that their expertise could and should be harnessed in the interests of the public welfare. The opportunities that the University of Chicago offered to combine serious scholarship and social engagement were ideal for a young woman like Breckinridge, who since childhood had evinced both an intellectual bent and a commitment to social justice.[57]

The University of Chicago's emphasis on social sciences dovetailed with the city's ferment of social reform to produce truly unique opportunities for women to engage in social activism grounded in serious scholarship. Breckinridge was well aware of her good fortune in being able to pursue higher education "in the city that made life a continuous adventure," as she put it in her memoirs. Progressive-era Chicago was the perfect place for intelligent and ambitious women who wished to make their mark on the world, and Breckinridge was determined to take advantage of the opportunity, even though her bankrupt father was unable to assist her with her expenses. Combining her graduate fellowship with paid work provided by Talbot as her administrative assistant and as the assistant head of Green Hall, a new residence hall for women graduate students, she spent the next four years "happily working for my degree at Chicago," completing her PhD magna cum laude in 1901. "Those were indeed rich and fortunate years," she later wrote.[58]

Although she could not have known it at the time, Breckinridge's doctoral-level studies prepared her to become both a social justice activist and a social work professor by strengthening her background in socialized justice and reinforcing her commitment to an activist state. Convinced that careful study of social problems would be the basis for effective social policy, the University of Chicago's political science faculty encouraged intellectual analysis of current issues. Working closely with their faculty mentors, political science graduate students—male and female alike—conducted statistical studies that led directly to social reform. In the years to come, Breckinridge would produce a steady stream of such studies, which helped her establish her own credentials as a social scientist and advance the new profession of social work.[59]

Freund remained Breckinridge's most important intellectual influence. While working toward her PhD, she took Freund's courses in American and European government, constitutional law, and the Illinois constitution, in which she continued to imbibe the principles of sociological jurisprudence and develop support for social legislation. After Breckinridge completed her education, she and Freund would remain lifelong friends and collaborators, frequently meeting to help one another draft social legislation relating to the rights and welfare of women, workers, immigrants, and children.[60]

While her studies with Freund helped lay the intellectual foundations for her commitment to social legislation, Breckinridge's coursework with Harry Pratt

Judson on municipal government introduced her to fieldwork and applied research. Judson required his students to conduct fieldwork in Chicago's urban agencies and municipal departments. For the final paper, students chose their subject from a list of topics that reflected Judson's emphasis on original research on local politics: the city council, the school system, the city's elected officials, the judicial system, and municipal administration, which included budgets, buildings, streets, sewers, gas lines, and public health. In later years, as a social work professor, Breckinridge would supervise similar studies, using them as the basis for policy recommendations.[61]

Although her "principal department" remained political science, she also took a "secondary" field in political economy: the study of the creation and distribution of wealth. Coursework in political economy not only deepened her understanding of the economic underpinnings of society but also exposed her to a wide range of views on economic policy. In addition to including faculty who represented divergent perspectives on economics—from socialism to "sound money"—the Political Economy Department encouraged discussion and debate.[62]

Breckinridge, who had enjoyed her coursework in rhetoric at Wellesley, did not shy away from these debates. Indeed, when it came time to select a dissertation advisor, she chose political economy professor Laurence Laughlin. In some ways, this was an unusual choice for one of Freund's students. Laughlin espoused the principles of classical political economy, especially laissez-faire capitalism. He was also an outspoken critic of the populist movement and a passionate defender of the gold standard. However, he was tolerant of dissenting views—so much so that he recruited radical socialist Thorstein Veblen to the University of Chicago. Moreover, he was extremely supportive of women students. Later in life, Breckinridge would laud Laughlin's complete absence of sexism, remarking that he was "wholly unconscious of the fact of differences of sex."[63]

Probably most important, however, Breckinridge relished the intellectual rigor of working with Laughlin. "He was a genius in suggesting topics and in developing material," she asserted, and "he cared, too, a great deal for correctness in form and elegance in presentation." In later years, she would attribute the prompt publication of her dissertation in book form in 1903 to Laughlin's expert instruction.[64]

At Laughlin's suggestion, Breckinridge chose the history of legal tender (money) in the United States and England as her dissertation topic. *Legal Tender* is a comparative history of monetary policy based largely on an examination of legal records. Although to modern readers it may seem rather dull, to contemporaries it was "the best concise and accurate account of American legal-tender paper money, from the purely legal standpoint" ever written. The overall thrust of *Legal Tender* supports Laughlin's sound money principles. However, the progressive potential of *Legal Tender* was apparent in the argument that early British monetary policy was a well-intentioned, albeit unsuccessful, attempt to monitor the economy for the benefit of the populace, rather than for the profit of the state. As a reviewer for the *Journal of Political Economy* pointed out, this interpretation was "widely at variance with certain general statements that have had much currency among economic writers." Thus, even though apparently supportive of conservative monetary policies, Breckinridge's dissertation also revealed her willingness to engage in independent, even iconoclastic, analysis and her continued interest in using state power to improve social conditions. Her recognition of the potential value of central government regulation to promote the common good—a position that owed more to Freund than to Laughlin—would ultimately make her one of the nation's most outspoken advocates for public programs for social welfare.[65]

When Breckinridge completed her graduate studies, she once again encountered a wide gap between expectations and reality when she found herself unable to secure a faculty position in her fields of expertise. As she put it in her memoirs, "although I was given the PhD degree magna cum laude no position in political science or economics was offered me," while "the men in the two departments . . . went off to positions in College and University faculties." Swallowing her disappointment, Breckinridge enrolled in the University of Chicago's new Law School, where she resumed work with her former advisor, Ernst Freund.[66]

Gaining advanced standing by transferring much of her previous coursework in political science into law, she completed her degree in just two years. She graduated at the top of her class, with honors, in June 1904—the first woman in the United States to earn a juris doctorate. Twenty years after matriculating at Wellesley, Breckinridge had finally achieved her lifelong dream of graduating from law school.[67]

Because of family duties, Breckinridge had passed up multiple opportunities, including the chance to study law at the University of Michigan. Although at the time the series of delays in pursuing further study had been extremely difficult, postponing graduate work ultimately proved to be advantageous for the would-be professional. The University of Chicago afforded her the opportunity for a much broader education than she would have received elsewhere. While she could have earned her law degree sooner at the University of Michigan, such a course of action would have prepared her only for a career in law. The legal profession remained exceedingly hostile to female practitioners, and female lawyers found their opportunities extremely limited. In addition, by the time she attended law school, Breckinridge had become somewhat disillusioned with the practice of the law. The two most significant legal cases in which she was involved—her father's defense and Emily Swigert's divorce—both highlighted the ways in which the law functioned to maintain male privilege. Moreover, her studies in political science and political economy, as well as her legal studies under Freund's tutelage, had awakened her interest in making law rather than practicing the law—in using the law to advance social justice rather than upholding laws that enforced social inequality. As she reflected more than fifteen years after completing her law degree: "The laws are so unjust (age of consent, industrial protection etc) that instead of wanting to help carry them out she [the woman lawyer] wants to get to work to change them. Therefore we find many women lawyers in political and public work." Had Breckinridge prepared exclusively for work as a lawyer, external barriers and internal reservations might have made such a career difficult, dissatisfying, or both. (In 1933 she observed, "Women have a cruelly hard time in law.") As it turned out, she would never practice law again after her short-lived Kentucky career. Instead, she would apply "legal thinking" to solving social problems. Both her training in sociological jurisprudence with Ernst Freund and her broad training in the social sciences at the University of Chicago prepared her for a long career in public service and, ultimately, enabled her to become a leader in the new field of social work. Since the University of Chicago did not open its doors until 1892, then, Breckinridge's oft-postponed plans to pursue graduate study or professional training may well have been a blessing in disguise.[68]

Despite any misgivings she may have had about the legal profession, Breckinridge probably intended to return home to Kentucky and join her father's law practice upon completion of her studies in Chicago.[69] An editorial W.C.P. published in 1902 suggests that he had gained greater understanding of his gifted daughter's difficulties and had come to terms with her ambitions. In "The Problem of the Daughter," W.C.P. reflected on the challenges confronting the New Woman in turn-of-the-century America, particularly the ways in which fulfilling parental expectations prevented young women from pursuing their goals. Eventually, he concluded, "after a season of irresolute and uncomfortable protest" on the part of the daughter, and "reflections and awakenings" on the part of the father, "he begins to comprehend that some of the strange new demands made by women are but the outcome of an unrepressed individuality" and "are but a part of the development of the new social conscience in which women, as well as men . . . have become the heirs."[70]

W.C.P.'s reflections seemed to forecast a new type of relationship between Nisba and her father—one in which she could reconcile female ambition and the family claim. Before such an experiment could be attempted, however, W.C.P. died. In this extremity, Nisba might well have found consolation in a line from the Katharine Lee Bates poem "The Ideal": "All thou dost cherish may perish; still shall thy quest remain."[71] Much as she mourned the death of her beloved father, Nisba also was finally freed from the family claim. In the years to come, she would continue her quest for meaningful work in her adopted city of Chicago.

CHAPTER FOUR

Academic Activism

Social Science and Social Reform in Progressive-Era Chicago

"Labor is different from other commodities"

On January 18, 1915, a "hunger procession" of fifteen hundred unemployed men, women, boys, and girls and their supporters braved below-freezing temperatures and confronted mounted patrols and regular beat officers. As the *Chicago Tribune* breathlessly reported beneath a banner headline that screamed "1,500 Idle Riot around Hull House": "Shots were fired, clothes were torn, eyes blackened and heads cracked." Newspaper coverage compared the scene to the infamous Haymarket riots and hinted at the possibility that the International Workers of the World had been involved. Sophonisba Breckinridge, assistant dean of women at the University of Chicago and dean of the Chicago School of Civics and Philanthropy, gave a statement in support of the protesters. She had been present at Hull House when Lucy Parsons, the widow of Albert Parsons, who had been hanged for his alleged complicity in the Haymarket riot, spoke to the crowd. According to plainclothes detectives, Parsons told the crowd to "go out and break windows and take food if they didn't have money to buy it." Parsons denied uttering these words, and Breckinridge backed her up. "Dean Breckinridge ... said she heard nothing of an incendiary nature," the *Tribune* reported. "'She was explaining,' said Dean Breckenridge [*sic*], 'that labor is different from other commodities, which, if not sold one day, can be kept in stock and sold the next day. I heard nothing in her remarks that might incite a person to riot.'" Nonetheless, the police in attendance telephoned headquarters to report trouble brewing. The police stations broadcast a "riot call" and on-duty officers rushed to meet mounted officers at the scene. After a violent clash between police and protesters in which "clubs, blackjacks, and revolver butts were used with bruising effect on heads, arms, and

After a peaceful protest of unemployed workers turned violent in 1915, Sophonisba Breckinridge and Jane Addams hastened to the police station to arrange for the release of six women who had been arrested for their role in the protest. Breckinridge's role in this protest highlighted the position she established for herself in Progressive-era Chicago, using her privileged position and her advanced education to promote social reform.

Courtesy Chicago Daily News Negatives Collection, Chicago History Museum knuckles," twenty-one protesters, including six women, were arrested; the rest of the crowd quickly dispersed. Breckinridge contacted Hull House leader Jane Addams, and together the two women went to the police station to arrange for the release of the female prisoners.[1] While Breckinridge sat in the police station, a photographer for the *Daily News* snapped a photo of her, dressed formally in a tailored suit, hat, and gloves and gazing steadily and solemnly at the camera.[2]

The incidents of that cold January day encapsulated many of the themes of Breckinridge's activism in Progressive-era Chicago. Breckinridge was a supporter of—and at times a participant in—all forms of activism, including direct protest. But her class status and her dignified demeanor protected her from street violence and police repression. Instead of being arrested, she offered an intellectual justification for the protest; instead of going to jail as a prisoner, she went there to assist less-fortunate protesters. From her privileged position as an educated, white, native-born, middle-class woman, Breckinridge established a niche for herself in Progressive-era reform that relied on her professional status and her scholarly expertise to legitimize political protest and advance social reform.

Breckinridge immersed herself in Chicago's reform milieu in the heyday of Progressivism, from the turn of the century until World War I. A close associate of Jane Addams and others at Hull House, which served as a nexus of reform in turn-of-the-century Chicago, Breckinridge was involved in virtually every reform of the Progressive era. She advocated labor legislation for workers, legal aid for immigrants, civil rights for blacks, and financial support for poor families. She also promoted municipal reforms, including better city planning and measures to protect public health.

While she engaged in political activism in Progressive-era Chicago, Breckinridge also carved out a professional niche for herself in her adopted home as a social work educator and a public policy advocate. Breckinridge epitomized progressives' faith in the central role of intellect in finding solutions to social problems. Building on her expertise in politics, economics, and law, she pursued reform by conducting social science research and recommending what her Hull House colleagues called "social legislation." By engaging in this particular version of social reform—"academic activism"—Breckinridge also laid the groundwork for her promotion of a new profession: social work. By the end of the Progressive era, she had gained recognition as a leading figure in the professionalization of social work.[3]

At the same time that she was creating a place for herself in the new profession of social work, Breckinridge was formulating a principle she would later call a "national minimum," a basic standard of living that the government should guarantee to all citizens. Breckinridge's notion of a minimum standard of living eventually would inform her contributions to the welfare state. It also was a precursor to later human rights activists' notions of social and economic rights: the belief that all people have fundamental rights to housing, healthcare, education, and work.[4]

Between 1905 and 1920, Breckinridge laid the groundwork for a lifelong career as an academic, an activist, and an advocate for human rights.

"I owed my chances to Miss Talbot"

"I owed my chances to Miss Talbot," Breckinridge wrote in her autobiography. Indeed, from the very beginning of her time at the University of Chicago, Breckinridge had the distinct advantage of a close relationship with an extraordinary mentor. Ten years Breckinridge's senior, Talbot was an avid and able advocate for women in academia. Breckinridge became both her protégée and her partner in advancing opportunities for women at the University of Chicago. Breckinridge's relationship with Talbot also facilitated her long career at the University of Chicago.[5]

While Breckinridge pursued advanced degrees in political science and political economy, she also forged strong professional and personal ties with Talbot. At the University of Chicago, the two women shared adjoining offices in the administration building, Lexington Hall, and a "suite" of connecting rooms in the graduate women's residence, Green Hall.[6] They also vacationed together, spending school holidays with Breckinridge's family in Kentucky and summers at Talbot's vacation home in Holderness, New Hampshire. (Talbot's parents later deeded the property to both women as joint tenants.)[7] Students who attended the University of Chicago in the early twentieth century regarded Breckinridge and Talbot as inseparable, often sending regards to one in letters to the other.[8]

Breckinridge's relationship with Talbot made it possible for her to pursue graduate education at the University of Chicago and to remain at the university after she completed her studies. Throughout Breckinridge's graduate career, Talbot exerted constant pressure on the university administration to provide higher pay and more dependable employment for her protégée. "Like an old-time knight who drew his lance to defend a lady," as she described herself, Talbot was Breckinridge's tireless advocate at the University of Chicago.[9]

Despite Talbot's best efforts, the university president was reluctant to provide Breckinridge with rank or salary commensurate with her abilities and qualifications. Throughout her years in the PhD program and the law school, Breckinridge was "very poor" and "shabbily dressed," as she described herself. She earned her room and board by working as Talbot's assistant in the residence halls. She also put her earlier training in shorthand to use as Talbot's clerical assistant, earning, by her recollections, $40 a month. While these positions allowed her to "scrape

"I owed my chances to Miss Talbot," Breckinridge wrote in her memoirs. Indeed, "like an old-time knight who drew his lance to defend a lady," as Marion Talbot described herself, the dean of women was a tireless advocate for Breckinridge at the University of Chicago. Although Edith Abbott would take first place in Breckinridge's life soon after this photo was taken in 1909, Breckinridge and Talbot maintained a close friendship for the rest of their lives.

Courtesy Special Collections Research Center, University of Chicago Library

along," Breckinridge was keenly aware of her lack of official standing. More than forty years later, when writing her autobiography, she pointedly noted: "I was never assistant Dean nor was I assistant Head of Green but always assistant to the Dean or the Head as the case might be."[10]

Talbot's unremitting efforts finally bore fruit during Breckinridge's final year in law school. Ironically, the university's new policy of sex-segregated classes for first- and second-year students, which both Talbot and Breckinridge opposed, gave Talbot the opening she needed to persuade a hesitant university president to offer Breckinridge an official position as assistant dean of women. The fact that other schools were attempting to recruit Breckinridge for similar positions gave Talbot additional leverage. After years of resisting Talbot's efforts, President Harper finally conceded in April 1904, shortly before Breckinridge received her JD. "I am glad to know that Miss Breckinridge feels disposed to remain one of us," he wrote, adding, "There is great possibility ahead."[11]

"Great possibility," indeed. For the next twenty years, Breckinridge and Talbot promoted women's educational equality and protected women's separate space at the University of Chicago, fostering women's intellectual achievements as well as female group solidarity. Their joint administration helped make the University of Chicago far more hospitable to women students than other coeducational universities, where the lack of a separate female community combined with a rowdy male subculture to make women students outcasts rather than equals.[12]

Breckinridge's appointment also made it possible for her to remain at University of Chicago, where she would spend the rest of her long career. She had good reasons to stay in Chicago. Her father's death in 1904 had extinguished the possibility that she would become a partner in his legal practice and severed her strongest tie to her home state of Kentucky. In addition, her adopted home offered unique opportunities for an educated woman seeking professional fulfillment. She was drawn to the idea of meritocracy as well as the ethic of service that characterized the burgeoning professional class in Progressive-era Chicago. In particular, she found the prospects for combining social science research with social justice advocacy virtually irresistible.[13]

Breckinridge discussed her decision to remain in Chicago with these factors in mind. "There were opportunities to go elsewhere," she recorded in her memoirs. Indeed, "for a time it was quite the thing to invite me to take positions as Dean of women," she reflected. But she resisted the blandishments of other schools. "Salary and rank they could provide," she mused, but Breckinridge responded instead to the siren call of scholarly endeavor and social reform in the Second City. "Continued research combined with teaching," she explained, together with "the opportunity to develop new resources" for social services in the Second City, led her to cast her lot in Chicago.[14]

"My great chance"

As Breckinridge's memoirs suggested, one of her chief motivations for remaining in Chicago was the chance for "continued research combined with teaching." Academic administration provided her with a secure position at the University of Chicago, but she had never relinquished her hopes of joining the university's faculty. Supportive as her male professors had been of her when she was a student, they showed little disposition to have her join their ranks, and she was unwilling, as her mentor put it, "to offer instruction except on the full and free wish of the department—either political science or political economy."[15]

Talbot's ingenious solution to this dilemma was to create a position for Breckinridge in a new department under her authority: the Department of Household Administration. Talbot was an enthusiastic participant in a nationwide home economics movement. Although now associated with conventional gender roles and conservative values, in its early years, home economics—also known as domestic science—reflected the Progressive reform impulse and represented a new professional opportunity for women. Many early domestic science and home economics programs prefigured graduate programs in public health and public policy. Moreover, unlike the fields of political science, economics, and sociology, which often were hostile to women, domestic science allowed female faculty to create and define "a department of their own."[16]

Talbot's advocacy of the Department of Household Administration at the University of Chicago reflected these national trends. From the beginning of her tenure at the university, she bombarded the administration with proposals for a new department under different rubrics. The various names proposed for the field in its early days—household technology, domestic science, and home economics—reflected proponents' efforts to establish legitimacy within established fields, such as science, or emerging fields, such as social science, while still claiming a distinctive "domestic" or "home"-based approach that justified women's leadership. After ten years of unremitting effort, Talbot finally convinced the university president to authorize the Department of Household Administration in 1904. Talbot, who had insisted from the beginning that her proposed department would be dedicated to "social progress," may well have chosen this name because she felt it positioned the new department as part of the broader movement for Progressive reform, which emphasized efficient administration in public offices. In addition, the rubric set the new department apart from the university's preexisting Department of Home Economics. Talbot emphasized that the Department of Household Administration would focus on advanced, theoretical courses rather than the basic, technical offerings of the Department of Home Economics. Comparing women's education in the new department to men's training in law, medicine, and business, Talbot insisted that her curriculum would demand the same level of academic rigor as other social science departments.[17]

Talbot envisioned Breckinridge as occupying a key role in the new department. While Talbot would offer courses in her own area, sanitation, which fell under the old "domestic science" rubric, she intended for Breckinridge to offer courses more consistent with the new "household administration" label—courses that applied economic theory to domestic life. This scheme would give the new department a sort of dual legitimacy as based in both science and economics. It also would provide Breckinridge with the faculty position that she had been unable to secure in an established social science department. After some initial hesitation, citing financial constraints, the university president agreed to appoint Breckinridge as assistant professor in the new department in time for the 1905–06 academic year. Breckinridge was overjoyed at the opportunity to teach at her alma mater. "Miss Talbot got me my great chance," she described these developments in her memoirs.[18]

Thrilled to be able to put her extensive education to work in the classroom, Breckinridge took full advantage of the possibilities offered by her new position, designing courses on a wide range of topics, including "The State and the Child"; "The State in Relation to Labor"; and "Modern Aspects of the Household." "The chance to organize those courses in the Department of Household Administration was an incredibly rich opportunity," she explained. "They gave an opportunity to use every kind of material of which I could make use. The legal, the economic, the historical and the social implications were all appropriately considered." Breckinridge was especially proud of her course on "The Legal and Economic Position of Women." In this course, arguably the nation's first women's studies class, Breckinridge analyzed "the position of women in the family group as well as in industry and the professions."[19]

This course also brought her into contact with several women who would later prove to have a major impact on her life. Agnes Nestor of the Women's Trade Union League and other members of Chicago's reform community enrolled in the class. So did Edith Abbott, a Nebraska schoolteacher who came to the University of Chicago to pursue her PhD in political economy with Breckinridge's former academic advisor, Laurence Laughlin. Ten years younger than Breckinridge, Abbott was nonetheless her intellectual equal. Recalling a classroom interaction that would prove to be a turning point in both women's lives, Breckinridge later wrote:

> Among the students who took the course on women was Edith Abbott. I shall never forget the fright she caused me when I said something about the way in which women had carried the work of the world while men were doing the

fighting and hunting. "Do you mean to say?" she asked. "I thought I did," I replied. "I must look into that," she replied. And her "looking into that" resulted in her first publication, *Women in Industry*.[20]

Breckinridge and Abbott quickly formed a close emotional and intellectual bond. Just as Talbot had done for her, Breckinridge sought out professional opportunities for her one-time student. After Abbott completed her PhD in 1905, Breckinridge helped her publish her research and find a job. With Breckinridge's support, Abbott published her dissertation, a groundbreaking study of women's work based on census data, in 1909.[21] In the meantime, the pair collaborated on what would prove to be the first of many co-authored publications, a long article in the January 1906 *Journal of Political Economy* that offered an overview of women's industrial employment based on comparative census data from 1890 and 1900 and made the then-startling assertion: "Women have always worked."[22] Breckinridge also used her contacts to help Abbott find professional opportunities. Abbott conducted research on working women in Boston and Washington, D.C.; completed a fellowship at the London School of Economics and Political Science under the guidance of Sidney and Beatrice Webb; and taught economics at Breckinridge's alma mater, Wellesley College. During Abbott's absence, Breckinridge wrote to her frequently, mixing expressions of profound affection with information about professional opportunities. Always, she was on the lookout for ways to bring Abbott back to Chicago.[23]

"Industry is more perilous than war"

As part of her ongoing effort to find employment for her former student, in 1905 Breckinridge proposed working with Abbott to conduct a statistical study of women's work in the United States. With the enthusiastic support of local settlement-house workers, including Jane Addams, Breckinridge advocated the study at a meeting of the Illinois Federation of Women's Clubs, the state's branch of the nationwide umbrella organization for women's groups, the General Federation of Women's Clubs. Under the headline "University Girl Upholds Toilers," the *Chicago Tribune* credited Breckinridge's "stirring speech" with convincing those in attendance to support both the women's trade union movement and the federally funded investigation of conditions of women's work.[24]

In the meantime, Breckinridge accepted a temporary appointment as inspector of yards, investigating the working conditions of women in Chicago's infamous stockyard district. In the decades following the Civil War, Chicago's location in the nation's heartland, the spread of railways, and the invention of refrigeration all combined to make the city the epicenter of the nation's slaughtering trade. In the late nineteenth century, entrepreneurs such as Philip Armour and Gustavus Swift utilized the division of labor and took advantage of technological innovations to build vast meatpacking plants that, by turning "waste" into "by-products," commodified every ounce of the 400 million cattle, sheep, and hogs that were shipped from the hinterlands to be killed, processed, packaged, and sold between 1865 and 1900, producing revenue of more than $5.5 billion. By the turn of the century, Chicago's scattered slaughterhouses and stockyards had been consolidated into

the vast Union Stock Yards, occupying approximately one square mile on the city's South Side. The nation's greatest concentration of meat-product companies such as Armour's, Swift & Co., and Libby's processed up to forty thousand hogs per day—each. Meatpacking moguls employed approximately thirty thousand workers, more than 10 percent of them women. Breckinridge recruited Abbott to co-author a long study of the women workers of the Second City's stockyards.[25]

This study revealed that the high profits of the meatpacking industry came at a high price for its workers. The "disassembly" procedures of Chicago's meatpacking industry foreshadowed the "assembly" lines that would come to characterize industrial production methods in modern America. By compartmentalizing the skilled trade of butchering and replacing it with repetitive tasks in multiple departments, meatpacking companies were able to pay low wages, demand high productivity, and rely on seasonal labor. The constant influx of desperate immigrants provided a ready supply of unskilled labor, and the stockyard operators successfully resisted workers' attempts to unionize to demand better wages and working conditions. "Ignor[ing] all considerations except those of the account book," and exhibiting "callous disregard" for the workers, Chicago's carcass capitalists earned condemnation from settlement-house workers and so-called muckraking journalists such as Upton Sinclair, whose 1906 novel, *The Jungle*, seared images of downtrodden workers and diseased flesh into the minds of his readers the same year that Breckinridge began her work as inspector of yards.[26]

Breckinridge spent more than four months inspecting the facilities and interviewing the employees of "Packingtown." To complete her assignment, she traversed the unpaved, manure-strewn streets; braved the warren of "dark pas-

Opposite page: Breckinridge first encountered Edith Abbott, an ambitious former schoolteacher from Nebraska, when she came to the University of Chicago in 1903 to study economics under the guidance of Laurence Laughlin, who also had supervised Breckinridge's dissertation. While completing her PhD, Abbott lived in Green Hall, where Breckinridge served as head, and enrolled in Breckinridge's course on "The Legal and Economic Position of Women," arguably the first women's studies course in the United States. Impressed both by Abbott's piercing questions and by her "big brown eyes," Breckinridge soon forged both an intellectual connection and an emotional bond with Abbott. As Talbot had done for her, Breckinridge helped advance Abbott's career after the younger woman completed her studies in 1905. In 1908 Breckinridge engineered Abbott's return to Chicago to assist her in her work at the Chicago School of Civics and Philanthropy. Decades later, asked to reflect on the highlights of her long and successful career, Breckinridge pronounced that bringing Abbott back to Chicago was her "best day's work."

Courtesy Special Collections Research Center, University of Chicago Library

sageways" and damp, decaying wooden buildings; and endured the "indescribably offensive odors" of rotting carcasses and boiling bones to query approximately two thousand girls and women—mostly Slavic immigrants between the ages of sixteen and twenty-two—who worked trimming meat, canning ham, making sausages, packaging "Butterine," producing glue, and processing bones in unspeakably unsanitary conditions. Whether paid by the piece or by the hour, packinghouse workers were subject to periodic layoffs in slack periods and forced to work at a "feverish pace" during the busy season. Laboring in cold, windowless rooms and standing on "dirty, blood-soaked, rotting wooden floors" for ten hours a day, women "toil[ed] without relief in a humid atmosphere heavy with the odors of rotten wood, decayed meats, stinking offal," and human waste from the doorless privies that vented directly into the workrooms. Breckinridge found her task exhausting, both physically and emotionally. To Addams, she confessed, "I was getting where I could not sleep—the vision of the day's work presses in so! Not my own day's work—but that of the crews of girls I see marching past me now."[27]

Characteristically, Breckinridge translated her emotional response to women workers' abysmal working conditions into social scientific scholarship and policy recommendations. In addition to co-authoring with Abbott a long study on women workers in the stockyards, she reported her findings to the U.S. Labor Department to provide ammunition for the request for funding a full-scale investigation. Ultimately, the nineteen-volume report on the working conditions of wage-earning women and children, published between 1910 and 1913, provided the basis for the establishment of two new federal bureaus, the U.S. Children's Bureau and the U.S. Women's Bureau. These government agencies would advocate for a ban on child labor and better working conditions for women for decades to come.[28]

Breckinridge's investigation into the meatpacking industry also convinced her that "industry is more perilous than war," as she put it in a public address in 1908. Convinced that only the power of the state could protect workers from the rigors of industrial capitalism, Breckinridge urged the adoption of labor legislation to provide shorter working hours and safer working conditions.[29] After her encounter with the packinghouses of "Porkopolis," Breckinridge became a passionate advocate of "protective legislation" for women workers.

"A minimum of decency, safety, and healthfulness"

While investigating the working conditions at the Union Stock Yards, Breckinridge launched what would become a lifelong campaign for labor legislation. In February 1906 she wrote a short piece on "Legislative Control of Women's Work" for the *Journal of Political Economy* in which she advocated so-called "protective legislation" for women workers: state laws regulating working women's hours, wages, and working conditions.[30]

Breckinridge's advocacy of gender-specific labor legislation brought her into a powerful alliance of women's organizations—most notably the Women's Trade Union League and the National Consumers' League—that pushed for protective legislation in the Progressive era. While national in scope, the protective legislation movement had strong ties to Hull House and deep roots in Chicago. Hull House alumna Florence Kelley headed the National Consumers' League. In addition, at the time that Breckinridge began her association with Hull House, the Chicago branch of the Women's Trade Union League met there.[31]

Breckinridge entered the fight for labor legislation at a key moment. Originally, Illinois activists had linked labor legislation for women and children. The state's 1893 Factory Act had prohibited child labor and provided for an eight-hour workday for women. However, the Illinois Supreme Court declared the law unconstitutional just two years after it went into effect. Illinois labor activists regrouped. They successfully lobbied for the passage of a new child labor law in 1897. In 1909 they rallied behind a new "Ten-Hour Law" for women workers, modeled on a similar law in Oregon that had withstood a constitutional challenge in the U.S. Supreme Court in the 1908 case *Muller v. Oregon*.[32]

Protective labor legislation advocates had followed the *Muller* case closely because they knew that all labor legislation faced an uphill legal battle. In 1905 the U.S. Supreme Court had ruled, in *Lochner v. New York*, that the ten-hour day provided by an 1895 law was an unconstitutional infringement on (male) workers' "freedom of contract." The outcome of *Lochner* put advocates for labor legislation on notice that in order to provide lasting relief, proposed legislation would have to make a compelling case that public interest justified the use of the "police power" of the state.[33]

Breckinridge wrote her early articles favoring protective legislation for women workers in this context. Like most advocates of protective legislation, she also was a supporter of organized labor. She understood that trade union organization allowed skilled male workers to demand "union" shops, pay raises, shorter workdays, and other benefits.[34] But she also knew that very few women workers joined unions, and so-called "unorganized women" were unable to use collective bargaining to wrench concessions from employers. The limited utility of trade unions for women workers became apparent during two major strikes in Chicago's garment industry, one in 1910 and another in 1915. Despite strong support from Hull House residents, including Breckinridge, neither strike produced significant gains for women workers, and both strikes ended without union recognition.[35]

Thus, Breckinridge regarded labor legislation as the most effective route to improved working conditions for working women. While recognizing that in a few cases such laws might exclude women from certain occupations, she argued that women so rarely competed directly with men for jobs—and were so much more vulnerable to exploitation—that the real benefits outweighed the potential liabilities.[36]

Arguments emphasizing gender distinctions provided the legal loophole supporters of labor laws sought to sidestep the Supreme Court's hostility to labor legislation in the 1908 case of *Muller v. Oregon*. In this landmark case, which relied heavily on sociological evidence compiled by the National Consumers' League, the court upheld Oregon's single-sex ten-hour law, ruling that the state had a compelling interest in protecting the health and safety of women workers.[37]

The decision in *Muller* paved the way for a wave of labor legislation on behalf of women workers. Illinois led the way by adopting a ten-hour workday for women factory workers. Enacted by the state legislature in June 1909, the law was almost immediately challenged, but following the precedent set in *Muller*, the Illinois Supreme Court upheld the law in April 1910.[38]

Breckinridge and her colleagues promptly set their sights on further legal protections for workers. In 1912 Breckinridge spoke at a meeting of the National Conference of Charities and Corrections (later the National Conference of Social Welfare) at which representatives of the Women's Trade Union League and the National Consumers' League demanded a "living wage," unemployment insurance, and workers' compensation for all workers, as well as special protections for women and children in the workforce.[39]

As it turned out, this particular conference had significant implications for national politics. The new Progressive Party adopted the resulting social workers' "Platform of Industrial Minimums" as part of its official platform, known as the "Contract with the People." As a result, Breckinridge and her Hull House colleagues were enthusiastic supporters of the Progressive Party and its presidential candidate, Theodore Roosevelt, in 1912.[40] However, when the third-party candidate failed to draw enough votes to win the election, Breckinridge and her fellow reformers returned their attention to state-level legislative initiatives.

As with laws limiting working hours, legislation designed to guarantee a "living wage" began with women workers. In 1913, drawing inspiration from the adoption of the nation's first minimum wage—for women only—in Massachusetts the previous year, labor advocates around the nation launched a new campaign. Breckinridge collaborated with the Illinois Consumers' League to advocate a minimum wage for women workers. She authored promotional materials for the proposed legislation and personally publicized the campaign; she may have helped also to draft the bill itself. But although Illinois authorized a commission to study living wages for women and children in 1913, the state did not adopt a minimum wage.[41]

Historians differ in their assessment of gender-specific advocacy of workplace protections. Some point out that the Supreme Court's language in the *Muller* decision—"sex is a valid basis for classification"—gave its imprimatur to gender distinctions. While permitting differential treatment in the eyes of the law benefited working women in practical terms, in principle the decision laid the foundation for discriminatory treatment. Other historians, however, argue that protective legislation for women workers was an "entering wedge" for similar legislation for all workers.[42]

Breckinridge's published articles on the subject were consistent with the "entering wedge" strategy. In a 1910 piece for the *Journal of Political Economy*, for instance, she pointed out that in the case of Great Britain, legislation limiting the length of the work day for women led to shorter days for male workers. Perhaps more important, however, Breckinridge's advocacy of labor legislation foreshadowed the policies she would promote throughout her long career. Her 1906 article on protective labor legislation marked one of the first instances in which she began to formulate the notion of a "national minimum," or a basic level of human dignity that a government was obligated to provide for its citizens. Looking to the example of European countries, she was exploring ideas that she would bring to the creation of the American welfare state decades later. At the same time, she advanced the notion that gender distinctions were compatible with women's equality. Identical treatment, such as the Illinois Supreme Court had engaged in when overturning the 1893 Factory Act, resulted in "false equality"; taking difference into account, as in the case of the Ten-Hour Law, allowed the law to promote true equality.[43]

Thus, for Breckinridge, a discussion of labor legislation quickly led to serious consideration of both gender equality and the welfare state. "In many of the advanced industrial communities," she pointed out, "the state not only undertakes to prescribe a minimum of decency, safety, and healthfulness below which its wage-earners may not be asked to go, but takes cognizance in several ways of sex differences and sex relationships." Breckinridge advanced these ideas very early in her career; she would continue to develop them for decades to come.[44]

Breckinridge's early forays into public discussions of the legislative control of women's work also initiated her lifelong commitment to "social legislation." Social legislation had multiple applications. While it encompassed protective legislation for women workers, social legislation was a broader category, embodying the principles of sociological jurisprudence, which held that the state could and should use its power to promote social justice. For Breckinridge, labor legislation was just the beginning.

"A brilliant company of women"

Breckinridge's work on behalf of women workers soon garnered her an invitation to live and work at Hull House. As Russell Ballard, one of the few male residents of Hull House, expressed it, "A brilliant company of women were drawn to the settlement to pioneer in the promotion of social change. The scholarly and talented Sophonisba Breckinridge joined the company in 1907 to become one of Miss Addams' closest friends and most helpful associates." Despite the less-than-pleasant environment of the West Side, with its unpaved streets and "indescribably filthy alleys," Breckinridge quickly felt at home among the circle of women reformers who gathered at Hull House, where she was listed as an official "resident" from 1907 until 1921.[45]

Like other settlements in Chicago and elsewhere, Hull House was "a hive of activity" that functioned as a social center for the neighborhood as well as a home base for social activists. The settlement's "residents"—mostly college-educated women like Breckinridge—organized clubs, concerts, and plays, offered classes in English, art, and drama, and staffed the kindergarten, daycare, and employment bureau. Residents also undertook special projects. For instance, Julia Lathrop served on the Illinois State Board of Charities; Jane Addams supervised garbage collection in the neighborhood; Alice Hamilton researched the health risks of working with toxic chemicals; and Florence Kelley conducted investigations of working conditions in factories and sweatshops. Several residents conducted in-depth investigations into living conditions in the immediate neighborhood, using color-coded maps to indicate nationality and wages in the immigrant, working-class community. The careful compilation of social data included in the 1895 study *Hull-House Maps and Papers* anticipated the later work of social scientists affiliated with the University of Chicago. Small wonder that one neighborhood resident called Hull House "a boarding house for social work students"![46]

Although her graduate education at the University of Chicago had given her the tools to analyze social problems, Breckinridge found that Hull House was her entrée to Chicago's world of social reform. As one resident recalled, "Hull House was the leader . . . in almost every reform movement there was." At Hull House, Jane Addams and her inner circle—including Kelley, Lathrop, and Hamilton—carefully selected residents and groomed them for a career in reform.[47]

Becoming a resident of Hull House encouraged Breckinridge to apply her expertise in social science and her training in sociological jurisprudence to social problems. As one former resident expressed it, because of her knowledge of the law, she "was sometimes asked by her Hull House associates to draft a welfare law or give leadership in sponsoring social legislation." Building on the settlement house's early experiments with statistical data in *Hull-House Maps and Papers* as well as on her own graduate training in social science and administrative law, Breckinridge rapidly developed what would become her hallmark approach to social reform: using social science research as the basis for social welfare legislation.[48]

For Breckinridge, providing social services and conducting social scientific studies went hand in hand. As she gently chided Addams on one occasion, "It is, of course, a very easy thing to give the man who asks for a meal some food and send him on," but "if we are going to feed him, we ought, of course, find out why he is tramping." Acknowledging that such an approach required "a good deal of special knowledge and organized effort," Breckinridge reminded the settlement house leader, "We ought, at Hull-House, to do nothing haphazard, because much is expected of us in the way of setting a standard of efficient work."[49]

Breckinridge clearly enjoyed her time at Hull House. Although her official duties as "head" of the University of Chicago's Green Hall required her to live there during the academic year, she spent all of her vacation quarters—and much of her limited free time—at the settlement house on Halsted Street. Hull House— much like Wellesley College, which Breckinridge had described as her "natural sphere"—provided a unique combination of female community, intellectual stimulation, and social responsibility. She probably would have echoed fellow Hull House resident Alice Hamilton's claim that life at Hull House "satisfied every longing, for companionship, for the excitement of new experiences, for constant intellectual stimulation, and for the sense of being caught up in a big movement which enlisted my enthusiastic loyalty."[50]

"An opportunity to work for human needs"

Breckinridge found life at Hull House stimulating, but the "settlement spirit" also was somewhat unsettling for a no-longer-young woman who had yet to find her true calling. In early 1907 Breckinridge confided to Edith Abbott that she found herself at a crossroads. Writing on letterhead from the Chicago Industrial Exhibit, for which she was organizing a display on "Women in Industry," Breckinridge explained that while Jane Addams urged her to take on a project working with the Juvenile Court, Marion Talbot pleaded with her to stay on at the University of Chicago. Breckinridge, then forty years old, found herself unable to decide whether activism or academia had the strongest claim on her. "Some times I think I must go about and see more," she mused, "and then sometimes I think keeping steadily at the job here is the thing for me to do. Especially if you can go and tell me about the outside world."[51]

The solution to Breckinridge's dilemma came in the form of a job offer from Hull House resident Julia Lathrop, then second-in-command at the Chicago School of Civics and Philanthropy (CSCP). When it was first established in 1903 by Graham Taylor, a professor at the Chicago Theological Seminary and founder of the Chicago Commons settlement, the school—then known as the Chicago Institute of Social Science—focused on providing "practical training" for "efficient helpers" in charitable, correctional, and civic organizations. However, Lathrop was eager to increase the institute's research agenda. In 1907, shortly before the school reorganized as the Chicago School of Civics and Philanthropy, she created a new research department and obtained a five-year grant from the Russell Sage Foundation to support it. The following year, she appointed Breckinridge director of the new Department of Social Investigation.[52]

Breckinridge's work at the Chicago School gave her the opportunity to bring together academic research and activist commitments. Investigating social problems strengthened her commitment to serving society's most vulnerable members. Publishing the results of those investigations helped her develop her trademark approach to social reform: academic activism. By combining social scientific research with social policy recommendations, Breckinridge reconciled her scholarly interests with her commitment to social justice. In short, she found her niche as an activist academic.

Breckinridge's post at the Chicago School also provided her with new professional opportunities. During the years Breckinridge worked there, from 1908 to 1920, she steadily expanded her role at the school. Lathrop left Chicago in 1912 to head up the new U.S. Children's Bureau. Although he continued to serve as both president and director of training at the school, Taylor also decreased his involvement in the day-to-day operations there. Meanwhile, Breckinridge solidified her control of the school. By the time she was appointed dean in 1914, she had expanded the school's curricular offerings, increased its enrollment, and assumed principal responsibility for fundraising for the perennially undercapitalized organization.[53]

Breckinridge's leadership role at the Chicago School positioned her to become a prominent figure in the development of the emerging profession of social work. In the early twentieth century, eager to lay claim to professional status, social workers clamored for recognition of their specialized education in schools of social work and their technical expertise in case work. They formed their own professional organization, produced their own textbooks, and boasted about the high academic standards at their schools. Breckinridge's post at the helm of one of the nation's first social work schools gave her a strong motivation to gain recognition of social work as a profession. Her eagerness to establish her own professional stature also made her an enthusiastic advocate of the profession of social work. For Breckinridge, her own professional advancement and her promotion of the new profession of social work went hand in hand.[54]

Under Breckinridge's leadership, the Chicago School gained recognition as one of the premiere schools for professional social workers. During her tenure there, the Chicago School's publicity ever more insistently touted the importance of advanced specialized coursework for prospective social workers. In particular, Breckinridge emphasized the school's strong focus on scholarly research. In pamphlets such as "The New Profession and Preparation for It" she insisted that "scientific inquiry" was essential to "skilled professional service."[55]

Breckinridge shifted the Chicago School's emphasis from practical training toward serious scholarship. At her insistence, the school raised its standards for both admission and graduation, requiring a college degree or the equivalent of its students and instituting a two-year program. Higher entrance requirements and a longer course of study allowed Breckinridge to dramatically transform the curriculum. A rigorous course on casework methodology replaced Taylor's "survey of the field" as the foundational course. Breckinridge also designed and implemented a new series of advanced courses in social statistics, the history of social welfare, and contemporary public policy.[56]

Breckinridge's work at the Chicago School lent the institution "a distinct status and influence."[57] It also made her a leader in the emerging field of social work. As former CSCP student Louise Marion Bosworth confided to her mother in 1912, it was difficult for Bosworth to resist Breckinridge's advice that she return to Chicago to work for United Charities, even though she herself preferred to remain in New York City. "Miss Breckinridge is too big and influential a woman for me to be able to ignore her advice," she explained, adding, "I am very fortunate in having anyone so nationally prominent as Miss Breckinridge back of me."[58]

Perhaps most important, however, Breckinridge's work at the Chicago School also helped her to figure out where she fit in Progressive-era Chicago: at the nexus of research and reform. Many years later, Edith Abbott said of Breckinridge: "She had been eager to do something that was really useful and was unwilling to be absorbed in the quiet academic life."[59] By juxtaposing "really useful" reform and "quiet academic life," Abbott suggested the distinction that many observers, then and now, draw between academia and activism. Yet, as another of Breckinridge's acquaintances insisted, "these were not separate and distinct lines of activity." Rather, she explained, Breckinridge's research, teaching, and reform "all served one purpose, the improvement of the welfare program so that the disadvantaged in our community might have richer lives."[60]

Perhaps Marion Talbot offered the most accurate assessment of the importance of Breckinridge's affiliation with the Chicago School when she remarked that "Miss B finds in it an opportunity to work for human needs which the Univ[ersity] of C[hicago] has never afforded her." By granting Breckinridge a place to conduct social scientific research on behalf of "the social needs of the community," the Chicago School placed her in the vanguard of an emerging profession that combined scholarly research with social reform.[61]

Breckinridge found her professional niche through her work at the Chicago School of Civics and Philanthropy. Her position there also gave her the chance to invite Edith Abbott to return to Chicago to work with her at the school beginning in spring 1908. Near the end of her life, when asked to reflect on her long career, Breckinridge easily identified her most important accomplishment as bringing Abbott back to Chicago. "That was my best day's work," she pronounced.[62]

Indeed—as discussed in more detail in chapter 10—Abbott quickly became Breckinridge's life partner as well as her collaborator in research and reform. Her presence in Chicago, just as much as Breckinridge's gainful employment there, ensured that Breckinridge would spend the rest of her life in Chicago. Decades later, commenting on the long association between Breckinridge and Abbott that commenced at the Chicago School, a former student mused: "I wonder if they foresaw that they were starting a life partnership that would enrich their personal lives and make their professional careers so intertwined that they would always be thought of together."[63]

"Promoting the welfare of the city"

Breckinridge and Abbott's first research project for the Chicago School's new Department of Social Investigation was a major study of housing in Chicago. Housing—and the related issues of sanitation and waste removal—had long been a concern for Chicago's settlement-house workers, who criticized the practice of dumping garbage in working-class immigrant and black neighborhoods as well as the corrupt and inefficient garbage collection procedures in the city.[64] Hull House residents had conducted a survey of housing in the immediate neighborhood, published in 1895 as *Hull House Maps and Papers*. In 1901 a citizens' committee known as the City Homes Association continued this research. The investigation prompted the adoption of a "new housing" ordinance in 1902, but the new regulations applied only to new construction, not to existing tenements. In addition, city officials routinely overlooked violations of both old and new housing codes, even keeping a "stay book" that listed Health Department suits that were never prosecuted out of "courtesy" to influential officeholders and property owners.[65]

In late 1909, under the auspices of the Chicago School of Civics and Philanthropy, Breckinridge and Abbott launched a new study of housing conditions in the Second City. To facilitate the study, which included not only an investigation of residences but also of the surrounding neighborhoods and their sanitation (or

Breckinridge and Abbott's first study under the auspices of the Chicago School was an examination of housing conditions in the city's working-class, immigrant, and African American neighborhoods. Before launching the study, Breckinridge and Abbott met with investigators from New York's Tenement House Department to discuss the best ways to collect and analyze data. Research fellow Natalie Walker Linderholm recalled that she and her classmates spent several weeks learning "the elements of research," studying statistics, and designing the cards they would use to collect data before dividing into teams and canvassing the city. "I tell you, there were some funny things about it," she reminisced, such as measuring the height of the ceilings while clad in ankle-length skirts. As this undated image from a later decade suggests, social work students at the University of Chicago continued this sort of field research even after women adopted shorter skirts.

Courtesy Special Collections Research Center, University of Chicago Library

lack thereof), Charles Ball, head of the city's Sanitary Bureau, appointed Breckinridge "Tenement Inspector in the Department of Health, without salary."[66]

Before launching the study, Breckinridge and Abbott met with investigators
from New York's Tenement House Department to discuss the best ways to collect and analyze data. They then divided the city into districts and sent teams
of students to investigate conditions in each one and record their observations.
(Although Ball recommended that the study exclude "the negro districts," Breckinridge insisted on including them. She also inquired about the boundaries of the
"so-called red light districts" so that she could take them into account in the study.)
Research fellow Natalie Walker Linderholm recalled that she and her classmates
spent several weeks learning "the elements of research," studying statistics, and
designing the cards they would use to collect data. After "going over it and over it
and over it again to be sure the arrangements, the order of questioning was right,
as were the spacing, and the tiniest detail," the students divided into teams and
canvassed the city. "I tell you, there were some funny things about it," she reminisced, such as measuring the height of the ceilings while clad in ankle-length
skirts. Canvassing the selected neighborhoods residence by residence, students
carefully recorded the conditions they found.[67]

The housing study revealed shockingly unsanitary conditions in Chicago's
working-class neighborhoods. Transcriptions of the students' notes were litanies
of desperate poverty, inadequate sanitation, and irresponsible slumlords:

> 4601 Paulina Street—Rear tenement; sewage water standing in the basement.
> Roof seems to leak; closet walls off bed-room soaked with water. Baby ill, prob-
> ably because of the dampness.

> 4500 Paul[in]a Street—Cellar floor covered with sewage water. Man claims four
> feet in some places. Needs attention at once. Plumbing in whole house bad.[68]

Revelations like these were not new in and of themselves. Throughout American history, reformers had periodically called attention to the dire situation of the
nation's poor. By the end of the nineteenth century, such exposés had become so
common that their authors had a name: "muckraking" journalists. Some of the
best-known works in this genre focused on Chicago, including Upton Sinclair's
The Jungle and William Stead's *If Christ Came to Chicago*. What was innovative
about studies like *The Housing Problem in Chicago* was their systematic approach,
their statistical precision, and their scientific authority.[69]

In the early twentieth century, social scientists increasingly took up the banner
of social reform through social research. By offering incontrovertible evidence of
the scope of social problems, many social scientists believed, they could motivate
authorities to take action rather than dismiss sensational accounts of dire con-

ditions as sentimental drivel. Moreover, these researcher-reformers hoped that their careful studies of underlying problems would pave the way for enlightened and informed policies that would not only redress immediate problems but also prevent future ones.[70]

Breckinridge was at the forefront of this sort of academic activism. Her previous work on the working conditions and wages of women had buttressed arguments for minimum-wage and maximum-hour legislation for women workers. Now, with the housing study, she hoped to change the regulations affecting housing and sanitation. As she explained in a 1910 report on the work of the Department of Social Investigation: "Such a study might bring about needed changes in the tenement house ordinances and in the provisions for their enforcement."[71]

Throughout her career, Breckinridge was committed to promoting social welfare and social justice by adopting sound social policy based in social scientific scholarship. In the case of the housing study, her research produced results, both at a personal level and in terms of public policy.

Whenever Breckinridge's students discovered particularly distressing circumstances, she arranged for social services for the affected families. For instance, in 1910, after her investigators found a baby with diseased eyes, Breckinridge contacted the United Charities of Chicago to have representatives visit the family and arrange for medical care. When she encountered especially distressing domestic situations—like those noted above—she categorized them as "emergency cases" demanding swift attention.[72]

The housing study had an immediate effect in Chicago and exerted considerable influence on urban planning in the Progressive era. As a direct result of the study, the city changed some of its waste-disposal practices, such as coming up with a new plan for treating waste water and a new approach to dumping waste in the stockyards.[73] City planners, civic reformers, and charity workers throughout the nation praised the study and requested offprints of the individual neighborhood reports.[74]

In addition, the housing study prompted Breckinridge to further develop her notion of a "national minimum." In public addresses, she urged clubwomen and city planners alike "to secure and enforce legislation" to create housing standards "below which no [one] living in the community will be allowed to continue."[75]

"Ignorance is the bulwark of prejudice"

The housing study also encouraged Breckinridge to think seriously and systematically about race relations. Her insistence on including the "negro districts" in the housing study increased her awareness of the many challenges African Americans faced in early-twentieth-century Chicago. After completing that study, Breckinridge continued to educate herself about social problems for urban blacks, such as high infant mortality and limited employment opportunities. She also closely monitored the status of African Americans in her native South. In particular, as a member of the National Association for the Advancement of Colored People (NAACP), Breckinridge regularly received reports of horrific crimes against southern blacks.[76]

The dismal situation of African Americans in northern cities and the violent treatment of southern blacks were sufficient to gain the sympathy of well-intentioned whites. Indeed, Breckinridge optimistically predicted that once apprised of the miserable circumstances of Chicago's black population, white citizens and politicians would take immediate and effective action to ameliorate the situation. Invoking her father's values, she asserted: "Most people stand for fair play." Believing that only "a small minority" of whites could be guilty of "race prejudice," she predicted that greater awareness of "the heavy burden of prejudice" would lead to the elimination of "unintentional and accidental" racial discrimination. "It seemed worthwhile to collect and to present the facts relating to housing conditions in the Negro districts of Chicago because one must hope that they would not be tolerated if the great mass of white people knew of their existence," she averred. "Ignorance is the bulwark of prejudice."[77]

Her faith in her fellow citizens' commitment to "fair play" and her confidence that providing information would lead to meaningful change was typical of Progressive reformers. But for Breckinridge, race issues also were deeply personal. Her personal relationships with prominent African American leaders, such as W. E. B. Du Bois, editor of *The Crisis*, antilynching activist Ida B. Wells-Barnett, and educator Booker T. Washington certainly played an important role in her racial consciousness.[78] More important, however, Breckinridge's antipathy to racism was rooted in her own experiences with sexism. For African Americans and women alike, she pointed out, an accident of birth meant that they were "always regarded as members of a group, never as an individual." Moreover, she observed, the "outside restrictions" of discrimination reinforced internal doubts, producing "those inner limitations resting on poverty of the spirit."[79] Well aware of the toll that internalized sexism had taken on her, she committed herself to eliminating all forms of discrimination.

When it came to translating emotions into action, Breckinridge's response was familiar: she advocated social policy to advance social justice. In a 1913 article for a special issue of *The Survey* commemorating the fiftieth anniversary of the Emancipation Proclamation, Breckinridge asserted that African Americans had three fundamental and indisputable rights that the community should uphold: decent housing, equal employment opportunities, and public education.[80]

Breckinridge did what she could to address all these issues. She told the members of the Chicago Woman's Club that "a decent home . . . in a respectable neighborhood and at a reasonable rental" was one of African Americans' fundamental rights and warranted legal protection.[81] She joined the NAACP's correspondence campaign to protest racist treatment of government employees in Washington, D.C.[82] She not only publicly challenged racial segregation in Chicago's public school system but also privately pressured the city's school superintendent to take steps to improve conditions in black schools.[83] Reflecting her commitment to improving race relations, Breckinridge was one of the founders of the Chicago Urban League, an African American civil rights organization created in 1916 at the height of the Great Migration of southern blacks to northern cities.[84]

Breckinridge's local efforts on behalf of Chicago's African American population had limited efficacy. Indeed, by the end of the decade, the situation had become untenable, resulting in the Chicago race riots of 1919. Nonetheless, such activism was not wasted. In the years to come, Breckinridge would include black Americans in federal policy recommendations to ensure minimum standards of living for all Americans.

"Establishing a standard of child nurture"

Breckinridge and Abbott collaborated on several major research projects under the auspices of the Chicago School of Civics and Philanthropy. Arguably their most influential study was an examination of the Chicago Juvenile Court. Established in 1899, the Second City's special court for delinquent youth was the nation's first juvenile court. It also was the first in a series of specialized municipal courts that reflected Chicago's leadership in developing a system of "socialized justice." Chicago's "socialized courts" applied the principles of sociological jurisprudence to the judicial system by using the courts to funnel social services to delinquent youth, wayward women, and troubled families. Located just one block south of Hull House, the juvenile court was an especially promising place for Breckinridge and Abbott to conduct investigations on behalf of the Chicago School of Civics and Philanthropy.[85]

Breckinridge and Abbott conducted research in the records of the Chicago Juvenile Court for its first ten years of operation. In addition, students from the Chicago School interviewed youthful offenders and their families. Based on this data, Breckinridge and Abbott concluded in their 1912 study, *The Delinquent Child and the Home*: "Poverty is in itself often a direct and compelling cause of delinquency." In other words, "delinquent" children were deprived, not depraved.[86]

Like the housing study, the juvenile court study enjoyed a wide readership, partly because Breckinridge mailed complimentary copies to judges all around the country. The study had broad appeal at a time when municipalities everywhere were in the process of developing juvenile justice. The Chicago School's 1912 annual report boasted that *The Delinquent Child and the Home* had been "rated among the 'best sellers' on sale at the annual meeting of the National Conferences of Charities and Corrections."[87]

The study's significance went well beyond the courts, however. Breckinridge's research on youthful offenders provided her with persuasive evidence to advance public policy. In 1910, Breckinridge presented a proposal for public assistance for single mothers at the National Conference of Charities and Corrections. A substantial proportion of juvenile delinquents came from families of single mothers, she noted. Widowed or deserted women struggled to meet their families' financial obligations, manage their poverty-stricken households, and mother their young children. When they failed, their unsupervised children ran afoul of the law. Thus, Breckinridge argued that it was in the public interest to provide single mothers with financial support. The following year, Illinois enacted the Funds-to-Parents Act, which administered the nation's first "mothers' pension" through the municipal court system. The Illinois program became the template for similar programs throughout the nation.[88]

The mothers' pension program was imperfect. Perennially underfunded, it also permitted administrators wide latitude in determining eligibility. In Illinois and throughout the nation, this combination of factors encouraged racial, ethnic, and gender bias. States doled out stingy payments to "deserving" mothers— mostly white, native-born widows—and denied benefits to African American, foreign-born, and divorced or abandoned women.[89] Despite its shortcomings, the mothers' pension program provided many poor families with indispensable financial support. Its adoption also validated Breckinridge's belief that social science research could and should direct social policy.

Breckinridge and Abbott immediately launched a follow-up study, this one on compulsory education and child labor. Just as Illinois was a leader in establishing mothers' pensions, the state was also at the forefront of the national movement to abolish child labor. The Illinois statute was, in Breckinridge's opinion, "a fair model" for other states. The state law prohibited the employment of minors under the age of fourteen and placed restrictions on the employment of youth under sixteen; it also provided that young workers had to demonstrate the ability to read and write simple sentences, either in English or in their native language.[90]

The problem was not the law itself but lack of enforcement. As Breckinridge and Abbott discovered in the course of their research, many poor children left school early in order to find jobs to help their families.[91] Unscrupulous employers and desperate parents often colluded to evade laws governing child labor and compulsory education. As a result, many teenagers left school and entered the workforce without even the rudimentary education required by law. In a letter to Breckinridge, one clubwoman highlighted the hazards resulting from this situation:

> Florence Kelley tells of a Polish Boy unable to read a word of English and therefore unable to read the signs of direction and warning on the machine at which he was placed who was killed caught in the machinery, the third killed at this machine. If America is to mean the door of opportunity to the Foreigners the children must be educated and start in the industrial life without such serious handicaps as a lack of English and education entail.[92]

Breckinridge was horrified at the "haphazard" enforcement of compulsory education and child labor laws that allowed such disasters to occur.[93] She was determined to prevent such unnecessary tragedies. Moreover, she was resolute in her conviction that it was the responsibility of the state to curb "the wastage of young life, [and] the destruction of youth and vigor which goes with low wages and long hours of work."[94]

Just as she had during the housing study, Breckinridge devoted personal attention to problems encountered in the course of the research for the truancy study. For instance, a note recorded by a student about 817 Galt Street tersely recorded: "Mother sick in bed. Send visiting nurse. Girl of 8 and one of 6 stay at home to attend to the baby. Also when mother is well and goes to pants shop to work." Breckinridge promptly contacted the city superintendent of education to alert him to the children's absence from school, and he referred the matter to a truancy officer for "immediate attention."[95]

As usual, Breckinridge hoped that providing reliable information would prompt official action. Even before completing the research, she wrote to the Illinois Commissioner of Education to ask for advice about making the study widely available to educators throughout the country.[96] Once *Truancy and Non-Attendance in the Chicago Schools* was published in 1917, it circulated widely, garnering praise from schoolteachers and settlement workers alike.[97]

In *Truancy and Non-Attendance*, as in *The Delinquent Child and the Home*, Breckinridge and Abbott identified poverty as the source of the problem. They asserted that in the case of truancy, "the only solution in accord with the standards of a democracy is such a permanent lifting of the wage levels as will make possible the higher standard of living that is, in practice, demanded by the state." In other words, if state law required children to attend school, then the state was obligated to enforce wage standards that would enable children to remain out of the workforce.[98]

Both the juvenile court study and the truancy study provided Breckinridge with another opportunity to apply the principle of a minimum standard of living. Children, like working women and African Americans, were entitled to a basic threshold of human comfort and dignity. As Breckinridge expressed this idea in 1911:

> Among the difficult and delicate tasks to which the community is now setting its hand, none is more compelling in interest than that of establishing a standard of child nurture, which shall be recognized by social agencies and public officials as one below which no family or group in which there are children shall be allowed to go.[99]

"New Homes for Old"

In 1907, Breckinridge was a member of a special committee of the Chicago Women's Trade Union League investigating the conditions confronting young, single, immigrant women who arrived in the city, lost and alone and vulnerable to sexual and economic exploitation. A typical case was that of Bozena, "a nice young Bohemian immigrant girl" who was "so eager for work . . . that she had taken the first job she could find—in a saloon. The saloonkeeper had abused her shamefully and then turned her out when he found that she was to become the mother of his illegitimate child."[100]

Breckinridge and other Hull House residents helped this particular immigrant woman in a variety of ways. Breckinridge accompanied Bozena to court in an unsuccessful effort to prosecute the saloonkeeper. Settlement workers helped the young mother find employment and bring her own mother over from Czechoslovakia to America to assist with childcare. Bozena also took evening classes in English at Hull House, enabling her to become a naturalized citizen. Later, Bozena became a social worker specializing in the needs of foreign-born women. Breckinridge and Bozena stayed in touch for over a decade, and Bozena credited "*dear* Miss Breckinridge" for introducing her to the field of social work.[101]

While such personal relationships could make a difference for individuals, it soon became clear that the problem of "lost immigrant girls" was too widespread for existing service agencies to address. Breckinridge proposed the creation of a new organization, and the Immigrants' Protective League (IPL) was established in 1908. As Edith Abbott explained: "This problem of the unaccompanied girls proved to be challenging; but nothing that ought to be done seemed impossible to Miss Breckinridge!"[102]

Unwilling to leave the university to take on full-time work as the director of the new organization, Breckinridge instead suggested appointing Grace Abbott, then working toward her PhD at the University of Chicago. Grace's sister Edith loved to tell the story about how Jane Addams, attempting to convince Breckinridge to take the post, asked her to seek "a competent man" to assist her in the work. Breckinridge retorted: "We don't need to waste any time looking for a man at the university or anywhere else. We have a young woman, Grace Abbott, in the Political Science Department at the university who will be much better than any so-called 'competent man' that I know or can possibly find." Breckinridge remained closely involved in the work, however, as the organization's secretary and as a member of the board of trustees.[103]

One of the league's first major accomplishments was establishing "a kind of immigration station" to welcome new arrivals. Immigrants who arrived in Chicago by train met with IPL agents—chosen to represent the nationalities and speak the languages of their clients—who helped orient newcomers to the city. Agents provided new arrivals with information about employment opportunities, social services, and evening classes. One of the principal goals of the league was to protect immigrants from exploitation. At the welcome station, agents helped new arrivals steer clear of unscrupulous cab drivers, fraudulent employment agents, and the ever-present "cadets" who recruited young women into prostitution. Breckinridge also persuaded local women's clubs to issue funds for the league to provide temporary lodging for young immigrant women. In only four years, the league served close to eighty thousand immigrants at its welcome station.[104]

Hoping to provide similar services on a larger scale, Breckinridge and the IPL lobbied for federal and state assistance. However, increasing anti-immigrant sentiment quickly doomed public funding for social services aimed at the foreign-born.[105] In the absence of either state or federal support, the league continued to provide essential assistance to Chicago's immigrants. In its first decade, the league investigated approximately twenty-five thousand complaints about economic exploitation, including being cheated by banks, steamship companies, employment agencies, and "shyster lawyers" and "quack doctors." Breckinridge's membership on the board of directors for Chicago's Legal Aid Society provided useful contacts, as the IPL frequently referred immigrants to the society for assistance in obtaining unpaid wages and fee refunds. The league also supplied interpreters for non–English-speaking immigrants in the criminal court system and sent representatives to municipal courtrooms to protect immigrants against legal discrimination.[106]

Reflecting Breckinridge's special interests in working women and socialized justice, the IPL also served as a liaison between immigrants and the authorities charged with upholding labor legislation and compulsory education. The league helped enforce the Ten-Hour Law by reporting violations to the factory inspector and providing interpreters when the affected workers were unable to testify in English. Similarly, the league helped enforce compulsory education laws by keeping track of all school-age immigrant children affected by the compulsory education laws. League agents communicated with truancy officers and school superintendents throughout the state to ensure that children between ages six and sixteen were enrolled in and attending school.[107]

In addition to providing social services to immigrants, the league also conducted "special investigations" into immigrant life, including studies on employment, housing, healthcare, education, Americanization, and naturalization and citizenship.[108] From the beginning, the Immigrants' Protective League and the Chicago School worked closely together. The agencies occupied adjoining offices downtown, where "a connecting door" facilitated frequent contact and allowed the two organizations to collaborate on research projects.[109] Chicago School student Natalie Walker Linderholm completed her fieldwork at the immigrant aid organization; she also assisted Grace Abbott in an investigation into the 1915 textile workers' strike.[110]

Breckinridge built on this foundation when she launched her own study of immigration with the help of a grant from the Carnegie Corporation, published in 1921 as *New Homes for Old*. Based on detailed "schedules" on recent arrivals' lives, the study exhibited some of the ethnocentrism characteristic of other Progressive experts, as for instance when Breckinridge critiqued immigrants' family situations as failing to meet "certain standards and requirements for wholesome family life" established by U.S. home economists. However, the bulk of the book was a sympathetic exploration of "the difficulties encountered by foreign-born families" and an effort to outline social services that might alleviate those difficulties.[111]

Breckinridge's resistance to the strain of Americanization that required immigrants to abandon their own culture was reflected in her special interest in providing social services in immigrants' own language. Breckinridge had a strong preference for so-called "foreign visitors," much like Bozena, the Bohemian-immigrant-turned-social-worker she had befriended at the beginning of her work with the Immigrants' Protective League. This priority suggested that Breckinridge was indeed, as she expressed it in a 1919 article for the *Journal of Home Economics*, committed to "reciprocal understanding and respect" between old-stock Americans and new arrivals.[112]

In this article as well as in *New Homes for Old*, Breckinridge argued that there were certain "minima of sound family life," including decent housing and adequate income, that the United States owed immigrants. By insisting that the host country should offer immigrants adequate economic, social, and civic opportunities, Breckinridge expanded her notion of a "national minimum" to include foreign-born immigrants as well as native-born citizens.[113]

"She was relentless with herself"

Between 1905 and 1920, Breckinridge maintained a grueling pace. She continued to work as assistant dean of women at the University of Chicago, located south of the city center in Hyde Park, while also serving as director of research and then dean of the Chicago School of Civics and Philanthropy, located downtown. In addition, she spent a great deal of time at Hull House, located west of downtown. Simply traversing the city between these three regular destinations was a major undertaking.

The logistics alone, when the chief means of travel were by streetcar or via the new elevated rail system, were daunting. Breckinridge, however, refused to concede weakness. Former University of Chicago student Gertrude Wilson recalled meeting Breckinridge for the first time on the "El" platform as she and a group of students were on their way to visit a juvenile group home west of Chicago. Breckinridge allowed the students to board first; by the time she entered the train, no seats remained. Wilson, who "had been taught how to treat elders," recounted her first conversation with the older woman: "I jumped up, and I said, 'Oh, Miss Breckinridge, please take my seat.' She straightens herself up straight as a ramrod, and she says, 'Young lady, I'm just as capable of standing as you are.'"[114] Wilson's recollections revealed the daily challenges Breckinridge confronted in fulfilling her many commitments in and around Chicago.

Moreover, Breckinridge's responsibilities in each place were heavy. Administrative matters took up a tremendous amount of her time. Breckinridge corresponded constantly regarding matters at the Chicago School of Civics and Philanthropy, replying to queries about education for social work, assisting students in finding housing, offering advice to job seekers, making suggestions for open positions in social agencies, and writing letters of recommendation for graduates of the program.[115] She devoted special attention to the needs of the school's African American students. In particular, she collaborated with philanthropist Julius Rosenwald to subsidize and staff an African American settlement house, the Wendell Phillips Settlement, which provided employment for the Chicago School's black graduates.[116]

At the University of Chicago, Breckinridge dealt with administrative matters in Harper Hall during the day and then presided over the evening meal at Green Hall each night. She often returned to her administrative office in the evening to finish up her day's work, leading her to write to the superintendent of buildings and grounds to ask if it were possible to leave the doors open after 8 P.M.[117] Her stubborn determination, her strong work ethic, and her "simply incredible energy" were legendary on campus. Decades later, former Green Hall resident Mary Jane Tilley reflected: "I shall always vividly remember her valiant figure, hurrying past our house to her office each morning—whatever Chicago's weather might be doing."[118]

Breckinridge's teaching responsibilities, on and off campus, also were substantial. Between the Department of Household Administration and the Chicago School of Civics and Philanthropy, she taught up to five courses each term; she also held weekly individual meetings with fellowship students to discuss their research projects. Preparing for new courses and grading papers also were time-consuming endeavors. Decades later, one former student recalled the familiar sight of "Miss Breckinridge sitting at the long table in Cobb 112 spending countless hours on student papers and apologizing for going to sleep over them at 2:00 A.M."[119]

Breckinridge also continued to play an active role at Hull House, where she had become one of Addams's closest colleagues. She helped to raise funds for the settlement, served as a substitute speaker when Addams was unavailable, and assisted Addams with her correspondence. Breckinridge's papers are filled with hastily scrawled notes from Addams, invariably beginning with the exclamatory greeting "Dear Lady!" and closing, "Hastily yours, Jane Addams." In response to such letters, Breckinridge assisted Addams in innumerable ways, large and small, leading Addams to close one typical letter asking Breckinridge to perform a task, "I do hope that I am not putting too many things 'off' on you." Breckinridge always came through for Addams, signing one letter, "Yours to command always."[120]

Interspersed between all these commitments, Breckinridge attended frequent meetings of the many clubs and organizations to which she belonged, fielded repeated requests to lecture to various groups on a wide array of topics, and served on numerous committees and boards. She also found the time not only to research and write numerous academic publications but also to respond to the press's demands that she edit and return page proofs. She was always ready to take on extra work that she deemed important. For instance, in 1917 she initiated an investigation into the services provided by Legal Aid for an abused wife seeking a divorce from her violent husband.[121]

Breckinridge's ever-increasing workload did not result in increased compensation, however. Although by mid-decade she was—at least on paper—earning $5,000 annually, her income was uncertain, and her amenities were nonexistent.[122] An illustrative month was July 1914, when the Chicago School was too strapped financially to pay either Abbott or Breckinridge. That same month, Breckinridge had to plead with the superintendent of buildings and grounds at the University of Chicago to supply her office in Harper Hall with a desk lamp and a telephone. When her sister-in-law, Kentucky suffragist Madeline McDowell Breckinridge, wrote to ask her to participate in a "sacrifice day" for suffrage, Breckinridge wryly responded, "It doesn't seem to me that I have anything left to sacrifice."[123]

Given the heavy workload and unremitting pace, it is small wonder that Breckinridge sometimes felt overwhelmed by her many responsibilities. In 1917 she confided to Edith Abbott: "I feel all the time as if I should wake up and find the essential things ignored, as is truly the case, now."[124] Despite private complaints, however, she always maintained a public posture of professional competence. As a later tribute expressed Breckinridge's tireless determination: "She was relentless with herself, never admitting in word [or] gesture that there is such a thing as weariness."[125]

Although Breckinridge shouldered all of these responsibilities with remarkably few complaints about the hard work, long hours, and poor pay, it was a constant irritant that her work did not result in a full-time appointment. When in 1913 Talbot issued one of her periodic requests for a salary increase for Breckinridge, the university president denied her plea on the basis that Breckinridge gave only half of her time to the university. Given that the university had steadfastly refused to grant Breckinridge full-time faculty status, this must have seemed like a gratuitous insult to both Talbot and her protégée.[126]

Similarly, Breckinridge's position at the Chicago School was officially half-time, despite the seemingly endless work it entailed. As Abbott and Breckinridge rather acerbically noted in a memo about the school:

> Since 1913–14 the details of the educational program have been under the direction of a Dean [Breckinridge] and the Director of Social Investigation [Abbott], who have been supposedly devoting half their time. It goes without saying that the work hitherto done by them on a part-time arrangement could occupy the entire time of educational experts in both fields.[127]

"A genuine triumph"

Breckinridge had good reasons, therefore, for wishing to relocate the work of the Chicago School to the University of Chicago campus, a move she began to advocate in the mid-1910s. Such a move would dramatically simplify Breckinridge's daily schedule; it also would further her own professional status and advance the professionalization of social work.

There were practical considerations, as well as personal and professional ones, that propelled Breckinridge in the direction of seeking university affiliation for the Chicago School. The school's funding had never been secure. Unlike other private social work schools, such as the New York School of Philanthropy (later the New York School of Social Work), the Chicago School had no endowment. Income generated from tuition covered only a small fraction of the school's operating expenses; from the beginning, the school relied heavily on private donations from a small but dedicated group of supporters. Thus, financial considerations had long made the prospect of affiliation with a university an attractive prospect for the school's founder and trustees. Indeed, Graham Taylor had investigated this option as early as 1906. Over the next decade, as the school's expenses increased, the trustees—who doubled as the school's benefactors—ever more insistently recommended that the school's leaders explore the possibility of university affiliation.[128]

Finally, philosophical differences between Breckinridge and Taylor inclined Breckinridge toward a reorganization of the Chicago School of Civics and Philanthropy. Social work struggled to find a professional identity in early-twentieth-century America. By the time Breckinridge assumed the deanship of the Chicago School of Civics and Philanthropy, two distinct schools of thought about the future direction of the field had emerged. The first, known as "scientific philanthropy," grew out of religious organizations and charitable agencies and emphasized efficient administration and individual casework. The second, "social justice," emerged from settlement houses and research universities and advocated public policy to address structural inequality. These divergent approaches soon came into conflict at the Chicago School.[129]

Although Taylor was critical of scientific philanthropy, in many ways the Chicago School of Civics and Philanthropy, like other private social work training schools, seemed poised to adopt the principles of scientific philanthropy and the techniques of individual casework. Taylor's course notes, including those for his "Survey of the Field," the original foundational course at the Chicago School, evinced the strong religious orientation of many early charity workers. Moreover, even though Taylor's social gospel beliefs prevented him from blaming the poor for their plight, his emphasis on personal relationships aligned him with case work methods. Finally, the Chicago School employed at least two faculty members, Mary Richmond and Amelia Sears, who were major figures in scientific philanthropy and strong advocates of individual casework.[130]

Breckinridge brought very different ideas about social work to the Chicago School. Unlike the members of the Charity Organization Society who advocated scientific philanthropy, she regarded poverty as a symptom of "social malaise" rather than as the result of immoral behavior. Thus, she favored social welfare programs over individual casework. Breckinridge and Abbott's joint leadership of the Department of Social Investigation and their publications for the Chicago School reflected these convictions. Their emphasis on social scientific research offered an alternative approach to professional social work, one that prized research rather than efficiency, policy rather than casework. Clare Tousley, a social worker trained at the New York School of Philanthropy, described a "parting of the ways" between her school, led by Mary Richmond, and the Chicago School under Breckinridge and Abbott's influence: "They thought it was a waste of time . . . to do case work one by one. . . . They'd get at the larger questions."[131]

To "get at the larger questions"—and to buttress their credibility as social scientists—Breckinridge and Abbott enthusiastically promoted social work as a profession grounded in social scientific research. Meanwhile, impatient with any sort of "scientific" approach to social work—whether of the Charity Organization Society (COS) brand of "scientific philanthropy" or the Breckinridge-Abbott brand of social science research—Taylor became increasingly critical of the professionalizing impulse, which he saw as compromising the personal relationships that he viewed as essential to social work.[132]

By the time Natalie Walker Linderholm, who completed her training in 1915, came to the Chicago School, these divisions had created a rift between Breckinridge and Taylor. Linderholm rarely saw the school's official leader, although she recalled that Taylor "talked of the meaning of helping people . . . off and on throughout the year." By contrast, as a research fellow, she worked closely with Breckinridge and Abbott. Linderholm fully embraced the social-justice orientation of her mentors. She developed a "violent aversion" to scientific philanthropy, to which she was exposed in a class taught by Amelia Sears. She was profoundly impressed, instead, by Breckinridge and Abbott's shared view "that research . . . was basic to the development of a profession that was going to try to find the causes of social malaise as well as help the people that were caught in its toils." More than six decades later, Linderholm still espoused her former teachers' belief that "only when you look for facts can you begin to think about remedies."[133]

Differences of opinion between Taylor and Breckinridge probably accounted for his growing resistance to her efforts to incorporate the Chicago School into a local university. Initially, Breckinridge and Taylor enjoyed a cordial relationship. Eager to increase the school's influence, Taylor supported Breckinridge's efforts to increase the school's claims to professional status. He enthusiastically promoted the work of the Department of Social Investigation, and he supported Breckinridge's proposal to increase the school's graduation requirements.[134] But as it became clear that Breckinridge was consolidating her control of the school and his own leadership was in jeopardy, Taylor became increasingly critical of the social scientific bent that Breckinridge had brought to the school. At the same time, Breckinridge became more determined to shape the future direction of the school—and more convinced that she would have to do so in spite of, rather than with, Taylor.[135]

As soon as she was promoted to dean of the school in 1914, Breckinridge—initially with both the trustees' backing and Taylor's support—began conversations with the University of Chicago's president about absorbing the curriculum of the

Chicago School into the university curriculum. Although the university president was favorably disposed to this plan, the United States' entry into World War I complicated the negotiations as the University of Chicago, like other universities, directed resources toward war service rather than new academic programs. Breckinridge and other members of the special committee formed to address the issue continued to court the University of Chicago throughout the war, while the trustees agreed to continue their support until the situation stabilized.[136]

Despite his earlier support for university affiliation, Taylor continued to hold out hope for a solution that would allow the school to maintain its independent status. In 1919 he launched a capital campaign to raise money from alumni. Taylor hoped to create an endowment that would allow the school to continue as an independent entity along the same lines as the New York School. Although fundraising efforts continued into the spring of 1920, Taylor had to admit that the school was approaching "a very serious crisis."[137]

His health suffering under the strain, Taylor went on unpaid leave in April. Breckinridge, who had been named acting president in Taylor's absence, wrestled with the school's accounts, which once again were in arrears. Indeed, by early July the Chicago School was insolvent. Breckinridge informed Taylor, "We have in the bank substantially no balance," and advised him to seriously consider the prospect of having the school "go out of business."[138]

Breckinridge took decisive action to deal with what she deemed a "desperate situation." In Taylor's absence and with the end of the fiscal year looming, she resumed negotiations with the University of Chicago. Acting quickly, she arranged a meeting with the university president and with Chicago School trustee Julius Rosenwald on July 3, the same day that she had warned Taylor about the school's imminent collapse. Less than a week later, on July 9, she submitted a draft proposal for university affiliation to the Chicago School's board of trustees.[139]

Although Breckinridge maintained that the plan "met at first with Dr. Taylor's cordial approval," Taylor later claimed to be "surprised" by this "sudden turn of affairs." Whatever the truth of the matter, by the time Taylor returned to Chicago to attend the meeting of the board of trustees to consider the proposal, it was a fait accompli. Taylor was unable to halt the approval process, despite what Breckinridge described as a last-minute change of heart that led him to detail "not the reasons *for* the plan, but the reasons *against* it" to the trustees. However, Breckinridge already had secured the support of the majority of the trustees, who had long favored university affiliation as a solution to the school's financial woes. Overwhelmed and outvoted, Taylor reluctantly conceded that university affiliation was preferable to "total extinction" and joined Breckinridge in signing preliminary agreements with the university in August 1920.[140]

From Washington, D.C., Julia Lathrop, who had hired Breckinridge and Abbott to direct research at the Chicago School of Civics and Philanthropy more than a decade earlier, wrote to congratulate both women on the creation of the University of Chicago's Graduate School of Social Service Administration. Recognizing that university affiliation lent greater legitimacy to the nascent field of social work education, she reflected, "There is much to be said for the success you have achieved in gaining recognition as a graduate school. That is a genuine triumph which will descend in the history of education."[141]

For Breckinridge, the establishment of the new School of Social Service Administration was a signal achievement. For fifteen years, Breckinridge had balanced the demands of three separate but related arenas of activity: academic administration at the University of Chicago, progressive politics in the Second City, and social work at the Chicago School of Civics and Philanthropy. Moving the Chicago School to the University of Chicago allowed her to braid these three strands together, making a whole that was stronger than its parts. At the University of Chicago's School of Social Service Administration, Breckinridge could combine her commitment to higher education, her advocacy for the underprivileged, and her interest in advancing the social work profession. Over the next twenty years, she would use the school as her power base for continued professional development, political activism, and policy work.

CHAPTER FIVE

The *Other* Chicago School

The School of Social Service Administration

"The school is yours"

Mention "the Chicago School" in academic circles today, and most people will likely assume you refer to the University of Chicago's Sociology Department, which gained national renown in the early twentieth century. At the same time that the Sociology Department gained prestige and name recognition, however, so did the University of Chicago's new Graduate School of Social Service Administration (SSA), the nation's first graduate school of social work affiliated with a major research university.[1] Indeed, among social workers, public welfare administrators, and social welfare policymakers, it was the *other* Chicago School—the SSA—that enjoyed the distinction of being "the" Chicago School. After wresting control of the Chicago School of Civics and Philanthropy away from Graham Taylor and establishing the Graduate School of Social Service Administration at the University of Chicago, Breckinridge worked closely with Edith Abbott to make the SSA the premier school of social work in the United States. Working in tandem, Breckinridge and Abbott shaped the SSA's distinctive approach to social work, basing social welfare policy on social science research and emphasizing public programs rather than individual responsibility.[2] Breckinridge and Abbott's work at the University of Chicago's School of Social Service Administration in the 1920s positioned both women to become major players in the development of the welfare state in the 1930s.

"About one thing I am certain," Julia Lathrop wrote to Edith Abbott in August 1920. "The School is yours and S.P.B.'s in a peculiar sense and your judgment as to the best practicable turn is backed by such generous devotion that I accept it and only feel grateful to you for what you have done and will do to uphold the standards of applied social science." Although she was sorry to see Taylor leave the school, and she preferred for the school to remain independent, Lathrop conceded: "I am sure that the only path is ahead on the university plan. Of course I am sorry, but there is much to be said for the success you have achieved in gaining recognition as a graduate school. That is a genuine triumph which will descend in the history of education."[3]

Lathrop's comments would prove to be prescient in several ways. First, Lathrop was undoubtedly correct in her reluctant admission that the Chicago School of Civics and Philanthropy's shaky finances made it highly unlikely that the school could have continued on the old basis. By July 1920, the CSCP was insolvent. The trustees unanimously agreed to offer Breckinridge "without charge two desks and a Noiseless typewriter" from the old CSCP offices. Breckinridge personally paid the costs of moving the school equipment from downtown to campus. "The university plan" was indeed the only way forward.[4]

Second, Breckinridge and Abbott shared both the responsibility for the survival of the new Graduate School of Social Service Administration and the credit for its eventual success. The pair worked ceaselessly to establish social work education at the University of Chicago. As a result, the SSA became firmly identified with their joint leadership. Students and colleagues invariably linked the two women in their recollections. As one correspondent put it in a letter to Abbott, "You and she together have made a contribution to the University that will stand as a proud beacon for other women."[5]

Third, the new school allowed Breckinridge and Abbott, who accepted appointments as associate professors in the Graduate School of Social Service Administration, to attain new stature in academia. Chicago School of Civics and Philanthropy founder Graham Taylor, however, was not offered any position in the new school. Stung at his exclusion, Taylor opined that preparation for social work was being "academicized to death at the university to gratify the pride of *S.P.B.!*"[6]

Fourth, the Graduate School of Social Service Administration would indeed make history as the first school of social work affiliated with a major research university. Widely known for its rigorous academic standards for preparing students for the new profession of social work, the SSA also developed a distinctive approach to social work education that emphasized social policy based on social science. Many decades later, loyal alumni continued to measure social work education against the standards Breckinridge and Abbott established at the University of Chicago.[7]

Finally, Breckinridge and Abbott positioned the University of Chicago's social work program to shape public policy. Because of their unswerving commitment to public welfare programs—what some referred to as "the Abbott-Breckinridge point of view"—the School of Social Service Administration ultimately would play a major role in the development of the American welfare state.[8]

"Making the school go"

The move to the University of Chicago was, as Lathrop put it, "a genuine triumph" for Breckinridge and Abbott. However, for its first four years on campus, the new school eked out a precarious existence. Initially, the program was placed under the aegis of the School of Commerce and Administration, whose dean, Leon Carroll Marshall, showed little interest in helping to raise the matching funds required by the agreement with the university. Thus, while "on the academic side the situation on the whole seems reasonably satisfactory," Breckinridge observed, "what we have done has been done on a very slender budget, even smaller than the old School of Civics budget." Breckinridge and Abbott's position also was tenuous. Despite their faculty status, neither woman had any administrative authority—or even any office space—in the School of Commerce and Administration. Indeed, Breckinridge described the two women as "homeless," pointing out that "no where is there a spot, not a sign indicating our right to be and to work." Breckinridge and Abbott's lack of funds and space reflected the lackadaisical leadership of Dean Marshall, who devoted little attention to the school and contemplated "abandoning" it entirely at the end of the five-year trial period.[9]

As the five-year deadline approached, Breckinridge became increasingly anxious about the school's future. She appealed to her old mentor, Ernst Freund, as well as to former CSCP trustee Julius Rosenwald, who had proved to be a strong ally. Fortunately for the future of the school, Rosenwald not only greatly admired Breckinridge and Abbott and their work but also was a trustee and benefactor of the University of Chicago. Relying on arguments Freund provided, Rosenwald appealed directly to the university president. Arguing that "practically all the work accomplished has been done by Miss Breckenridge [*sic*] and Miss Abbott," he made a strong case that the two "gifted women" should take over the school's administration:

> The school's work should not be jeopardized by a failure to put forward every effort to make it a success. Will you permit me to suggest, in the interest of making the school go, that Miss Breckenridge [*sic*] and Miss Abbott, who are recognized authorities in their fields and who have the confidence of social workers and students, be given charge of the present situation and responsibility for planning ahead.[10]

Rosenwald's intervention was critical. Within months after his meeting with the university president, the school had been removed from the oversight of the business school and Edith Abbott—at Breckinridge's insistence—had been ap-pointed as its new dean. "The new captain is wonderful!" Breckinridge exclaimed in a letter to Grace Abbott. "It is too good to be true."[11]

The following year, another one of Breckinridge's steadfast supporters, Marion Talbot, further guaranteed the success of the school and its new leaders. After Talbot's retirement in 1925, the Department of Household Administration ceased to operate as an independent department, and Breckinridge's half-time position there was combined with her half-time position in the School of Social Service Administration. At long last, Breckinridge had achieved a full-time position on the faculty of the University of Chicago.[12]

Thanks to Talbot, Breckinridge also advanced in the faculty ranks. Before her retirement, as part of her broader commitment to promoting women faculty at the university, Talbot was determined to see Breckinridge promoted to full professor. To encourage the upper administration to comply with her demands, Talbot established a generous trust fund "for the advancement of the education of women" at the university. Talbot's combination of coercion and philanthropy proved to be a blessing for both Breckinridge and Abbott. After nearly two de-cades of part-time and often unpaid work, Breckinridge was finally promoted to a prestigious position as professor of social economy. Abbott also was promoted to full professor. Both women received significant pay increases as well.[13]

"The challenge of pioneering"

Although their new positions provided them with greater autonomy, higher sta-tus, and better pay, Breckinridge and Abbott still had much work to do. What one mutual acquaintance called "the challenge of pioneering" could be daunting indeed.[14] However, the women's personal relationship (explored in more detail in chapter 10) facilitated their professional work. As one friend observed, "pioneer-ing is hard work," but "the fact that your and her ideas and ideals were the same" helped both women to confront and overcome obstacles.[15] The combination of "personal and professional," as one former student observed, made Abbott and Breckinridge effective advocates for the School of Social Service Administration and for the profession of social work.[16]

Breckinridge and Abbott faced the difficulties of establishing a new school to-gether. Although Abbott was the school's dean—and Breckinridge always insisted on acknowledging Abbott's leadership—the two women were widely recognized as partners at the University of Chicago's Graduate School of Social Service Ad-ministration.[17]

The unremitting labors of both women were essential to the school's success. Their work ethic was legendary among their students.[18] Tales of the women's long hours and rigorous standards also circulated widely among social workers throughout the nation. Commenting that "stories about these two unusual women were legion," Mildred Mudgett recounted one of them in the form of a conversation between Edith Abbott and a graduate student:

> MISS A.: 'How are you getting along?'
> STUDENT: 'Pretty well, except I haven't been able to do anything about my thesis.'
> MISS A.: 'Why not?'
> STUDENT: 'Well, I study every night until 11.'
> MISS A.: 'What do you do between 11 and 1?' [19]

Similarly, former student Helen Wright recounted an oft-told tale about a conversation Breckinridge had with a student at the university who complained that he found it difficult to study past 11 o'clock because he found it difficult to stay awake. "You must remember," responded Breckinridge, "that the work of the world is not done by going to bed when you get sleepy."[20]

The School of Social Service Administration thrived under Breckinridge and Abbott's guidance. First and most obviously, the curriculum expanded tremendously. In just three years, from 1924 to 1927, the SSA's course offerings more than doubled. Initially, other departments—including political economy and political science—had provided instructors for elementary and intermediate courses. Breckinridge and Abbott assumed primary responsibility for the advanced courses. Teaching individually and also in tandem, they continued to offer the core courses in social statistics and social research methods they had developed at the "old" Chicago School; at the "new" school, they also developed new courses on public welfare history and public welfare administration, which became a staple of the curriculum. In addition, they each offered courses reflecting their particular interests; while Abbott emphasized historical themes in courses on the history of social welfare and the history of social policy, Breckinridge emphasized law and government in courses on social work and the law and the family and the state. After Abbott became dean in 1924 the faculty grew and the curriculum expanded still further. By 1930 the SSA had three full professors, five associate professors, two assistant professors, and four instructors, as well as several assistants and fellows. Abbott and Breckinridge maintained their core curriculum—emphasizing research and policy—while the new faculty members offered more practice-oriented courses on topics such as case work, child welfare, and community organization. SSA students also continued to complete coursework in other departments and schools. In official reports, Breckinridge and Abbott celebrated their "cordial relationships with the Law and Medical Schools" as well as the SSA's cooperation with the "Social Sciences."[21]

The student body at the School of Social Service Administration also increased in numbers and diversity. The school more than tripled its enrollment in the first decade from fewer than one hundred students in 1920 to more than three hundred students in 1930. Abbott was especially proud that the School attracted a growing number of male students, although female students continued to predominate. She also praised the "mixture of races" at the SSA, boasting: "Few of the schools of social work have made so definite an effort to meet the need for negro social workers." Indeed, building on their work at the CSCP, Breckinridge and Abbott gave special attention to African American graduate students, supervising their research on topics related to African American social welfare and helping them find field placements that provided financial support for their studies. The SSA consequently produced several black graduates who would go on to prominent careers in education and social work.[22]

The school's proportion of graduate students also showed a marked increase. Reflecting Breckinridge and Abbott's desire to ensure that the "new" school was a graduate program intended for future professionals, the SSA, unlike many other social work schools, offered master's and doctoral degrees rather than certificates. After taking over the school from the School of Commerce and Administration, Breckinridge and Abbott gradually phased out the undergraduate program inherited from that school, shifting remaining undergraduate students into a "pre-professional" track in social science while actively recruiting graduate students, including experienced social workers. Between 1920 and 1929 the total number of graduate students increased from 31 to 191; this represented an increased proportion of graduate students from 40 percent to 72 percent. By the end of its first decade, the school had awarded ninety-six MA degrees and eleven PhD degrees. Abbott attributed the school's success, in part, to demand for graduate degrees rather than certificates. "That this is appreciated is shown by the number of students coming here for degrees after they have had work in the independent Schools of Social Work," she noted in a report to the supporters of the CSCP and its successor institution.[23]

Teaching more courses and hiring new faculty required money. Fortunately, the SSA's finances stabilized under Breckinridge and Abbott's leadership. In particular, the school's success at attracting outside funding improved markedly after Abbott and Breckinridge took charge. In 1923–24, the Local Community Research Council (discussed in more detail below) began to provide funding for research projects and student fellowships. In 1926 the school won a five-year matching grant from the Laura Spellman Rockefeller Memorial, later extended for an additional three years; in 1927–28 the Leila Houghteling Fellowship, established by alumni, began to offer additional support for promising graduate students; in 1928–29 the Samuel Deutsch Memorial Fund began to subsidize research, publication, and a new Samuel Deutsch Professorship for Breckinridge; and in 1929 the Common-wealth Fund established a fellowship for students of psychiatric social work. The school also continued to receive substantial financial backing from loyal support-ers of the "old" CSCP, particularly Julius Rosenwald, throughout the 1920s.[24]

Rosenwald's support was critical, as well, in helping Breckinridge and Abbott to launch a new series of books on social service, published with the University of Chicago Press. When Rosenwald decided to press for Abbott and Breckin-ridge's promotion to leadership positions, he also provided funds to permit the prompt publication of the first two books in the Social Service Series, Abbott's *Immigration* and Breckinridge's *Family Welfare Work.* For the next twenty years, Breckinridge and Abbott produced a steady stream of publications for the Social Service Series. Works in the series provided a broad historical overview of national social welfare policy as well as in-depth examinations of state policies on issues ranging from poverty to prisons. Breckinridge and Abbott's contributions, com-posed of carefully selected case records and government documents, offered an alternative approach to "casework" by using case records to inform social policy, thereby emphasizing public welfare rather than individual treatment. In the in-troduction to her *Family Welfare Work,* for instance, Breckinridge explained that she organized the book to "convey an idea of the extent to which our older social machinery fails," thus using the collection of cases to persuade would-be social workers of the necessity of advocating on behalf of public welfare programs, not just on behalf of individual clients. In Breckinridge's hands, then, case records became a crucible for "community action" on behalf of "community resources." The Social Service Series solidified Breckinridge and Abbott's reputation as the nation's preeminent social work scholars, raised the profile of the School of Social Service Administration, and disseminated Breckinridge and Abbott's ideas about social work as a tool for shaping public policy.[25]

In addition to working together at the School of Social Service Administra-tion and co-editing the Social Service Series for the University of Chicago Press, Breckinridge and Abbott collaborated in founding and editing the *Social Service Review,* the first professional social work journal, beginning in 1927. For the first several years, Abbott and Breckinridge produced most of the content them-selves. They also worked closely with their own students to include publications based on graduate research. Even after submissions began to filter in from other sources, the two women continued to perform almost all of the editorial work on a "Lilliputian budget." Although this required great "personal sacrifice," it also allowed Abbott and Breckinridge to control the content and tone of the journal. Insisting that "the duties of social workers require a broad intellectual grasp of basic social issues," the *Review* addressed a "remarkable range of topics—legal, economic, social, political, international." The *Review* thus solidified the con-

The original power couple, Abbott and Breckinridge shared responsibility for guiding the University of Chicago's social work program. At the School of Social Service Administration, "A and B," as their students called them, occupied adjoining offices, passed each other correspondence and memos with hastily scrawled notes and queries, and consulted with one another frequently throughout their long workdays. Indeed, Breckinridge and Abbott worked so closely together that many of their correspondents treated them as interchangeable; one even addressed a letter to "Dr. Edith Breckinridge."

Courtesy Special Collections Research Center, University of Chicago Library

nection between Breckinridge and Abbott, social work's claim to professional status, and the SSA's reputation as the premiere school of social work. "I just got started yesterday on your review of the work of the school in the Social Service Review," Abbott's sister Arthur wrote to her in 1943, adding, "it is a wonderful work you and Miss B. have done."[26]

"A wonderful work," indeed. Abbott and Breckinridge's partnership sustained what one admirer called "the warm pioneer spirit," ensured the success of the

School of Social Service Administration, and made both women key players in the professionalization of social work.[27]

"A and B"

The original power couple, Abbott and Breckinridge shared responsibility for guiding the University of Chicago's social work program. At the School of Social Service Administration, "A and B," as their students called them, occupied adjoining offices, passed each other correspondence and memos with hastily scrawled notes and queries, and consulted with one another frequently throughout their long workdays. Indeed, Breckinridge and Abbott worked so closely together that many of their correspondents treated them as interchangeable; one even addressed a letter to "Dr. Edith Breckinridge"![28]

Breckinridge and Abbott's correspondence during their infrequent separations reveals their reliance on one another in everything related to the smooth operation of the School of Social Service Administration and the editorship of the *Social Service Review*. In 1928, when Breckinridge was in Paris for a series of social welfare conferences, Abbott wrote to inform her about registration figures for the fall term and to give her a progress report on the school's pilot program for foster care for African American children. Meanwhile, Breckinridge took careful notes on conference proceedings and pondered publishing them in the *Review*. The pair continued to share responsibility for school business throughout their lives. In 1933, when Breckinridge went to South America, Abbott assured her that "everything [is] all right here" at the school and reported that Breckinridge's temporary replacement "got your class going along nicely." Abbott used Breckinridge's file copy of the previous year's exam to test their progress. In 1938, while on the train, Breckinridge read a student's thesis and wrote to Abbott to give her impressions of it. "It has such a lot of material," she reflected, "but so little appreciation—but it can go—with a little more editing." In 1942, when Abbott was temporarily away from Chicago, Breckinridge forwarded her mail and assured her that she and the rest of the staff and faculty were getting along in her absence. In 1944, when both women were away from the university, Breckinridge had her office mail forwarded to her onboard a ship in the Great Lakes. When she wanted Abbott's insights, she sent the mail on to her in Nebraska. Given the difficulties in conferring long distance about school business, it's not surprising that Breckinridge confessed, "I'll be glad when the vacation time is over and we are back in the regular program."[29]

In addition to sharing responsibility for administration and editing, Abbott and Breckinridge worked closely together on research and teaching. Student reminiscences indicated the intimate way in which Abbott and Breckinridge interacted, either by easily moving back and forth between each other's separate residences or by sharing a home. (Until 1940, Breckinridge resided at Green Hall, while Abbott lived in rented quarters near campus; as discussed in chapter 10, they combined households after Breckinridge relinquished her role as head of Green Hall). Abbott's one-time student assistant, Eleanor Taylor, recalled that when Abbott wanted a particular document, she "sent me scurrying back to the library stacks or in search of Miss Breckinridge, whom she regarded as a good substitute for an original source." Former student Arthur Miles gently poked fun at both women in an anecdote about how Breckinridge had mislaid his thesis, only to find it months later at Abbott's residence in one of the untidy stacks of books and papers that littered her home. Breckinridge explained, he reminisced, "with great affection and without a trace of criticism in her gentle voice—'you know, Mr. Miles, this just goes to show that Miss Abbott really isn't a housekeeper!'" Another SSA graduate recalled that her first night at Green Hall, after arriving in the graduate residence as an incoming sociology student, she went to Breckinridge for advice after she realized that she was more interested in social work than in sociology. Breckinridge assured her that Abbott would arrive momentarily, and soon thereafter the two women "helped me work out a plan which fitted in with the preparation for the kind of professional career that I was hoping to prepare for." And Ben Meeker and his wife never forgot spending time in front of Abbott and Breckinridge's "cheery fireplace" while their young daughter sat in a child-size chair "treasured, as I recall, from either yours or Miss Breckinridge's childhood."[30]

Breckinridge and Abbott complemented one another in their approach to teaching as well. Both women conducted formal classes based on rapid-fire lectures, interspersed with occasional pointed queries to students to test their reading and comprehension of the thick packets of primary source documents both women used as texts. Their shared interest in the historical development of the welfare state, their mutual preference for public welfare over private charity, and above all their strong sense of social justice infused both women's courses. However, while students often felt intimidated by both women's demanding expectations, encyclopedic knowledge, and growing reputation as the leaders of social work education, some found the soft-spoken Breckinridge, who never lost her southern accent, more approachable than Abbott, who struck many students as overbearing and autocratic. Students universally agreed, however, that the two women had earned their positions of authority, were inspiring role models, and were endlessly helpful in advancing the careers of their former students. In addition, students commented on both women's quick wit as well as their keen intelligence. Clearly, despite their somewhat different personalities, the two women were one another's intellectual equal, and their shared values made them an effective team in transmitting what one former student called "the Abbott-Breckinridge point of view."[31]

"The Abbott-Breckinridge point of view"

The "Abbott-Breckinridge point of view" combined social justice with social science. Although many accounts of the professionalization of social work indicate that academic social work was entirely distinct from the settlement-house movement, Breckinridge and Abbott consistently incorporated their Hull House experience and ethos into their courses. Breckinridge related the conditions she encountered en route from the University of Chicago to Hull House; Abbott devoted a lecture to settlements and their innovative programs, such as summer camps, mothers' pensions, and juvenile courts. In addition, Breckinridge and Abbott used the research compiled by Hull House residents, *Hull House Maps and Papers*, in their SSA classes. Always, they maintained the settlement-house perspective—as distinct from the "scientific philanthropy" view—that the underlying "causes of destitution" were not individual failures but rather the result of a nation-state's failure to make "provision for old age, for the sick, for children, for the insane and mentally handicapped, for invalidity."[32]

While Breckinridge and Abbott never abandoned the commitment to social justice they had adopted during their years at the settlement house, they also were determined to give their social work program the scholarly credibility they associated with the social sciences. Their insistence on rigorous scholarship was not simply a matter of raising the status of social work as a profession. Rather, they firmly believed that only by engaging in serious scholarship could social workers fulfill their most important mission: creating social change through social policy based on social science. While this ethos was evident in the school's many reports and publications, it comes through most clearly in records of Breckinridge and Abbott's classroom instruction.[33]

The two women shared responsibility for developing and teaching the essential curriculum of the SSA. Their approach was strongly historical; after all, as Abbott headed one lecture, *"Poor Law [was] our Oldest Form of Social Security."* This insight, gleaned from Abbott's time at the London School of Economics, informed several of the SSA's course offerings. To learn from experience, Breckinridge and Abbott favored courses with names such as "History of American Philanthropy," "History of Social Politics," "History of Social Welfare in America," and "History of American Public Welfare." In these courses, Breckinridge and Abbott assigned essays on pioneering social workers. Building on Breckinridge's original course on women's status, their social welfare history courses paid special attention to women social reformers and settlement-house leaders such as Jane Addams, Clara Barton, Dorothea Dix, Florence Kelley, Julia Lathrop, and Lillian Wald. Such assignments demonstrated by example that women had the capacity to be leaders in both social welfare and social reform. They also provided students at the SSA with inspiring role models. Thirteen years after studying with Breckinridge, one former student assured her, "I haven't forgotten the women we studied and the difficulties they endured."[34]

In keeping with Breckinridge's legal background, and especially the emphasis on sociological jurisprudence that she imbibed from her studies with Ernst Freund, the SSA curriculum also emphasized the key role of the law, especially labor legislation, juvenile justice, and prison reform. Breckinridge offered an entire course on "Social Work and the Law," in which she introduced the key documents she later included in her book by that title—which Abbott later assigned in her own classes. Abbott also taught an entire course on "American Prisons," in which she explored the relationship between "prisons and public welfare."[35]

Both women also emphasized the importance of public welfare. Abbott's 1944 lecture notes for "Public Assistance" opened with the bold statement: "PUBLIC RESPONSIBILITY FOR THOSE IN NEED AN ESTABLISHED AMERICAN POLICY." Students in the SSA's courses completed term papers on "State Welfare Institutions in New York," "State Institutions in Wisconsin," "State Welfare Institutions in Minnesota," "Public Welfare Institutions in Massachusetts," "State Welfare Institutions in New Jersey," and so forth. In the opening decades of the twentieth century, when localities were just beginning to develop publicly funded welfare programs, studying public welfare was a revelation to many students. Decades later, Ruth Colby confided to Abbott that "the closing session of our class in Public Welfare" with Breckinridge was "one of the high points in my life."[36]

This focus on public welfare programs, rather than on private charitable organizations, was one of the defining features of the Chicago social work program and reflected Breckinridge and Abbott's shared belief that public policy, not private charity, was the solution to economic inequality. Indeed, Breckinridge and Abbott's common commitment to public welfare infused all their courses. Both women argued that the government had a responsibility to ensure basic education, healthcare, safe working conditions, programs for people with disabilities, and old age pensions. Abbott's course notes for "Housing and Public Health" contrasted the "old idea" of "relief of destitution" with the "new idea" of "maintenance of standard of life," while Breckinridge lectured her students on the necessity of using a "broad basis of resources (broad as need)" in order to provide "comprehensive" support for all.[37] Abbott also incorporated into her courses

Breckinridge's cherished concept of a "national minimum"—which Breckinridge attributed to Sidney and Beatrice Webb, with whom Abbott had studied at the London School of Economics.[38]

By reinforcing common themes, Breckinridge and Abbott's teaching immersed students in a well-integrated curriculum. The overlap between the two women's teaching is suggested by the commonalities between Abbott's typed lecture notes and a student's handwritten notes from Breckinridge's course. For a class on "Federal Government Reorganization," Abbott included a section on grants-in-aid in which she briefly rehearsed her main points about the superiority of public programs over private charity: Public funding ensures "uniformity," "efficiency," and "economy"; while public administration provides "a superiority of knowledge and breadth of view" and results in "more equitable" programs. With less detail but no less emphasis, Breckinridge's student hastily recorded her edict: "No excuse for public money in pvt [private] hands."[39]

Breckinridge and Abbott always maintained an emphasis on public policy, but that does not mean they lost sight of the personal dimensions of social work. Rather, both women evinced strong sympathy for "those in greatest need of social welfare." Abbott assigned an English poem titled "The Little Street-Sweeper" in her course on "Social Welfare in America." The poem follows the day of a "weary" and "sad" orphaned girl who traversed "a squalid street,/With bare and bruised feet," swept the intersections, and begged passersby for pennies. Nor did Abbott limit her sympathy to innocent children. In a lecture on solitary confinement for a course on "American Prisons," she included the story of a prisoner whose feet froze in his unheated cell.[40] Similarly, one of Breckinridge's former students averred, "No one could possibly have associated with Miss Breckinridge without learning to care more deeply for people."[41]

Abbott and Breckinridge's "rigorous standards for scholarship," as well as their concern for others and their commitment to advancing social welfare through public policy, had a profound effect on their students.[42] Both women took pains to read their students' work with an eagle eye, insisting on in-depth research, rigorous analysis, and clear writing. Breckinridge's careful reading of her students' work is evident in her handwritten comments on a student's 1935 paper on the care of mentally ill persons in Indiana. Breckinridge's suggestions included incorporating more evidence from primary source materials, correcting and expanding footnotes, examining evidence more critically, clarifying explanations about public welfare administration procedures, integrating statistical evidence into a paper based primarily on legal statutes, elaborating on the relationships between and among public and private institutions, eliminating extraneous material, and correcting typographical errors—all on a nine-page paper that she pronounced "very good"![43]

This dedication left an indelible mark on students. Edith Finlay explained that part of what made Breckinridge "a wonderful teacher" was that she impressed her students with her own high standards and inspired them to live up to her expectations, even many years after concluding their formal educations: "Sometimes when I'm in a hurry & am tempted to take short-cuts, a silent voice says 'That would never pass Miss B!' and then I go back and do a better job."[44]

Approximately fifty years after graduating from the SSA, Arlien Johnson reflected the opinions of many of her peers when she described Abbott and Breckinridge as "great pioneers and great characters" who left an indelible mark on their students. She did not resent their insistence on formal teaching or their pressure to live up to their high expectations, she explained, because "they had such backgrounds of knowledge that you respected them. . . . And they had such conviction about the injustices in certain things and how they should be changed. . . . So I have, you know, I had a very grateful feeling about these two women and what they had meant, not only to me but to generations of students—actually to generations of students."[45]

"Do gooders" and "old maids"

Breckinridge and Abbott were not universally beloved, however. As the SSA's reputation grew, Abbott and Breckinridge drew criticism from other departments at the University of Chicago as well as from rival social work educators. Specialization and professionalization fostered such antagonisms by encouraging competition within and among emerging fields of expertise, particularly those in the social sciences: political science, economics, sociology, and social work. While academic departments struggled to define the parameters of their disciplines and thus to justify their own existence, educators and practitioners laid claim to professional status by asserting that their work required mastery of a specialized body of knowledge and that highly educated practitioners used that knowledge for the public good, as did the traditional professions of medicine, religion, and law. By founding an academic journal, producing a series of scholarly books, and promoting specialized coursework, Abbott and Breckinridge played a central role in shaping social work education and the social work profession in this increasingly "credentialed society." Their leadership roles in the American Association of Social Workers—Abbott was president of the national organization, Breckinridge the chair of its Chicago chapter—further reinforced their prominence as leaders in the movement to professionalize social work.[46]

Professionalization could be problematic for women, since codes of professional conduct and standards of academic scholarship often were constructed in ways that marginalized women and made them "unequal colleagues." In particular, while professionalization often was linked to disassociation from advocacy, for Breckinridge and Abbott, professionalization and activism were closely intertwined. The two women fought an uphill battle to define social work as a profession while maintaining their commitment to social reform. In different ways, this tension informed their conflicts both with the University of Chicago's Department of Sociology and with the New York School of Social Work.[47]

The pair's visibility as female leaders in a still-nascent profession attracted some criticism. At a local level, this came primarily from the University of Chicago's Department of Sociology. Early social scientists at the University of Chicago, much like the residents of Hull House and the research division of the Chicago School, had emphasized empirical research based on careful fieldwork in the Second City—and combined sociological research with social reform. However, in keeping with national trends that increasingly associated professionalism with "objectivity" rather than with "advocacy," in the 1920s the Sociology Department, as part of its efforts to boost its stature as a discipline, distanced itself from applied research and methodically erased its early ties to social reform.[48]

In Chicago, as elsewhere in the nation, previously harmonious relationships between early sociologists and early social workers were undermined by acrimonious debates over the compatibility of academic scholarship and activist commitments. This was especially evident in the case of Sociology Chairman Robert Park, who had languished for years as an adjunct before finally achieving status as a tenured professor. Park subsequently shored up his own position by disparaging Breckinridge and Abbott's scholarship at the same time that he spearheaded the Sociology Department's rise to national prominence. Hostile to women in general and to Breckinridge and Abbott in particular, he classified them as "do-gooders" instead of serious scholars.[49]

The divide between the two departments had just as much to do with gender as it did with content. While Breckinridge and Abbott held the reins of the SSA and trained female students to become leaders in their field, the Sociology Department marginalized women students and refused to hire women faculty. In addition, at least among students, the Sociology Department had a reputation as being anti-woman and the SSA had a reputation for being anti-man. According to one female graduate student in sociology, it was common knowledge that "Park didn't like women at all." A male sociology student recounted an anecdote about Abbott: "There were two kinds of people that she didn't like. One was sociologists and the other, people who wore long pants."[50]

Because of these gender dynamics, both faculty and students tended to exaggerate the differences between the two departments. In terms of teaching and research, the similarities outweighed the differences. The members of the Sociology Department, much like Breckinridge and Abbott, regarded themselves as social scientists, recognized that they were in the process of establishing a new field of academic endeavor, cooperated on research projects, encouraged their students to engage in collaborative research, upheld high academic standards, relied on both statistical and qualitative evidence, emphasized fieldwork in the "social laboratory" of the Second City, and used their studies of urban communities as the basis for policy recommendations. Precisely because there was so much overlap between sociology and social work, however, members of both groups were anxious to differentiate between them to shore up their own status. As one sociology student recalled, in the 1920s and 1930s, "a Sociologist . . . didn't have the highest status," which made it all the more imperative to clarify that although sociologists worked directly with the same populations that interested social workers, such as juvenile delinquents, for "objective" sociologists, any intervention was "incidental." The chief goal was "to get first hand data"; reform was "a dirty word." Thus, the sociologists ridiculed Abbott and Breckinridge as "old maids . . . wet-nursing social reformers." For their part, Abbott and Breckinridge were, according to sociology students, "Anti-Sociologist."[51]

There was some truth to this claim. Breckinridge consistently downplayed the similarities between sociology and social work and always disassociated herself from the discipline of sociology. When Kathryn McHale, a fellow member of the American Association of University Women, referred to Breckinridge as a sociologist in the context of making arrangements for a public speaking engagement, Breckinridge firmly disavowed the label. "Please don't think of me as a sociologist," Breckinridge wrote. "My work has been in economics, government and law, and I certainly make no claim whatever to be classed with the sociological group."[52]

As Breckinridge's reference to her graduate training in economics, political science, and law suggests, disciplinary boundary setting also played a role in the growing differentiation of the fields of sociology and social work. In the early twentieth century, both sociologists and social workers were in the process of defining their fields and establishing their credentials as professionals, which required specialized expertise. While disciplinary boundary setting was part of a broader trend in early twentieth-century academia, it was especially important for the field of social work and its female leaders. From the beginning, Breckinridge and Abbott understood that gender discrimination in the social sciences made it essential for social work to maintain a distinct identity. During the negotiations to bring social work education under university auspices, Breckinridge and Abbott had insisted that their program should be independent from the control of other departments. As they expressed it in a draft memo: "It was clear to us that professional education for our field would make necessary the use of courses given in several different university departments and we were not willing to be submerged in any one of them." The pair's inability to obtain permanent, full-time positions in the university's established departments had made it clear that the costs of being "submerged" were high. Only by establishing their own discipline—as Talbot had done with the Department of Household Administration—could Breckinridge and Abbott claim authority within academia. While at many universities social work was subsumed under the rubric of sociology, Breckinridge and Abbott insisted on developing a completely new discipline in which women could assume positions of leadership. As Abbott explained to her graduate advisor, economics professor Laurence Laughlin, "I think we have succeeded in putting our Social Service work very closely in relation to the Departments of Political Economy and Political Science, instead of letting it drift along as a sort of appendage to the Sociology department. This, I think, is our real contribution to the educational field."[53]

While keeping sociology and social work separate protected Breckinridge and Abbott from being relegated to second-class status, this division also may have contributed to other problems. In addition to the conflicts associated with gender dynamics and disciplinary squabbles, competition for graduate students, agency placements, and employment opportunities also created tension between the SSA and the Sociology Department. Park discouraged his students from taking courses in the SSA, while Breckinridge attempted to lure away the few female sociology students. One sociology student recalled that Breckinridge and Abbott even sabotaged her attempt to establish a divorce clinic. "They killed the idea," she explained; "they didn't want a Sociologist involved in it you see."[54]

Competition for funding also may have heightened tensions between the SSA and the Sociology Department. In the late 1920s the SSA had a larger instructional budget than the Sociology Department, even though sociology enrolled far more graduate students. Part of the reason for this discrepancy was that the SSA was more successful in attaining outside funds for assistants, lecturers, and fellows. While both academic units benefited from cooperation with the Local Community Research Council (discussed below), only the SSA could draw the support of organizations like the Wieboldt Foundation, created to fund "charities designed to put an end to the need for charity." In other words, the sociologists' adamant refusal to consider the policy implications of their research disadvantaged them in the competition for grant funding, which probably only increased their disdain for "applied" social science.[55]

Personal animosity clearly also played a role in the division between sociology and social work at the University of Chicago. Where Park ridiculed social workers as "do-gooders," Abbott characterized his research as "sloppy." The "hostility" between the two programs was sometimes baffling to students, but they generally agreed that it went both ways. "I never did understand the whole setting for that opposition, but Park did not get along with the two [Abbott and Breckinridge] and vice versa," one former sociology student explained.[56]

The conflicts between the Sociology Department and the School of Social Service Administration both reflected and reinforced disciplinary boundaries and gender stereotypes. While students who attended the University of Chicago in the first two decades of the twentieth century moved easily across departments and between the university, the CSCP, and Hull House, later generations of sociology students were remarkably ignorant about both the SSA and Hull House. Harriet Bartlett, who attended the London School of Economics before she received her degree from the Sociology Department and devoted her professional career to social work, never took courses with Abbott and Breckinridge, because she was under the impression that "they were pretty well involved with social welfare programs and things like that, and not themselves working out the concepts and principles as much as I wanted. It was more directly service and operational, you see." Bartlett clearly was misinformed about the SSA's emphasis on "concepts and principles"; she evidently also was unaware of either Abbott's tenure at the London School or of *Hull House Maps and Papers*, since she also believed that "settlement people" were not interested in "a disciplined scientific approach."[57]

The result of all this tension and ignorance was that the male-dominated Sociology Department came to be identified with "pure" research, while the female-led School of Social Service Administration became known as the home of "applied" studies. These characterizations were so oversimplified and exaggerated as to be caricatures, but they persisted because they reflected stereotypes about gender, reified an emerging belief in a dichotomy between research and reform, and reinforced professional and disciplinary boundaries.

"Bitter struggles"

When it came to fellow social workers, the gender dynamics were different, although still related to the process of professionalization. Because of the difficulties women encountered entering traditional male-dominated professions, many, like Breckinridge and Abbott, carved out new areas of expertise. In many cases, however, these new professions—sometimes referred to as "helping" professions, "semi-professions," or "feminized" professions—were auxiliary positions that kept women under male leadership. For instance, male doctors held more authority than female nurses. In other cases, such as teaching and librarianship, women predominated numerically, but they did not hold positions of authority or leadership, and they earned less than men.[58]

Social work was an anomaly insofar as it was initially led as well as staffed by women. As former SSA student Katherine Kendall put it, social work was "a woman's world" when she had entered the field in the 1930s; "women ran the show." Even in a field dominated by women, however, there were significant rifts. For many social workers, as for sociologists, professionalization meant rejecting social action. Instead of rejecting social reform to focus on social science scholarship, however, many social workers turned from social action to direct service to individual clients. Often, the emphasis on case work went hand in hand with the adoption of the "scientific philanthropy" approach associated with the Charity Organization Society (COS). Emerging from social work's origins in private charitable organizations (rather than from the settlement-house tradition), scientific philanthropy aimed to make the administration of aid more efficient, in part by determining eligibility based on whether or not clients were "deserving." In the nation's private social work training schools, such as the New York School of Social Work, this became the dominant approach to social work by the 1920s.[59]

As both settlement-house residents and leaders in the professionalization of social work, Breckinridge and Abbott fused reform and professionalism into a distinctive version of social work. Just as they shared the daily work of the SSA, they also collaborated in producing the annual reports that announced their intention to make the School of Social Service Administration the premier social work program in the country and asserted their belief that the SSA's emphasis on academic research and public policy was the way to do so. Frequently reiterating their pride that "the University of Chicago has maintained the only professional school in the field of social welfare that has made the social research program an integrated part of the curriculum," they rejected the "narrow . . . so-called 'techniques' of family casework" and insisted on "a sound disciplinary education in fundamental principles" of "social legislation and social politics."[60]

Abbott and Breckinridge's academic and activist approach to social work, using social science research as the basis for social change, set them apart from other social work educators, particularly those associated with the New York School of Social Work. Under Mary Richmond's guidance, the New York school, a private institution that resisted incorporation into academia, became the foremost exponent of the casework approach, with strong overtones of COS ideology. The New York and Chicago schools thus offered alternative visions of the central mission of social work. While the New York school "stood for practice" and "service to the individual," the Chicago school insisted on addressing "the larger questions" and engaging in "social activity to improve and increase the responsibility of the state for all people in need." In short, the University of Chicago's SSA came to stand for the "macro" approach to social work, emphasizing structural causes of poverty and public policy solutions to change the social order, while the private New York school represented the "micro" approach, focusing on casework with clients to help individuals adjust to the larger society.[61]

Breckinridge and Abbott's outspoken—even arrogant—insistence on the superiority of the SSA's approach to social work education, focused on social science scholarship and public welfare policy, sometimes brought them into conflict with other social work educators. Arlien Johnson, who attended the New York school before earning her doctorate at the SSA, recalled that "the New York School and Chicago School of Social Service Administration fought all the time" over these issues at annual meetings of the American Association of Schools of Social Work. While casework proponents regarded the SSA's emphasis on policy as cold and impersonal, Breckinridge and Abbott disparaged casework as narrow and limited. These conflicting views—expressed by strong personalities—resulted in "really bitter struggles, bitter struggles."[62]

"The Chicago plan"

Undaunted—perhaps even invigorated—by these "bitter struggles," Breckinridge and Abbott persevered. Beset on one side by sociologists' accusations of a lack of academic rigor and on the other by social workers' suspicion that they were overly academic, they sustained one another and stood together, withstanding all criticism and promoting what one loyal alumna called "the science of social welfare": social policy based on social science.[63]

Breckinridge and Abbott insisted on maintaining what they called "University of Chicago standards of instruction" by demanding "scientific research" and shaping public policy even as other schools increasingly focused on technical training and individualized treatment. Their approach to field work was just as distinctive as their classroom teaching. As they detailed in seemingly endless reports and memoranda, the SSA strove for a "principle of unity in social work" by combining "intimate and cordial relations . . . with social organizations" with "a broad conception of the field of social work."[64]

At the SSA, Breckinridge and Abbott implemented "the Chicago plan" of combining scholarship with social services by supervising graduate students in agency job placements and associated research. Rejecting the idea of "learning on the job," they hewed to a strict policy of "direct supervision" of fieldwork by faculty members, regular "conferences" between faculty advisors and their students, and weekly seminars "for presentation and discussion of plans and results." With this sort of careful guidance, Breckinridge and Abbott expected their students to use agency placements to conduct research and collect data, rather than simply to gain work experience.[65]

Under "the Chicago plan," graduate students at the SSA simultaneously fulfilled the fieldwork requirement, conducted social scientific research, and reformed social services. For instance, when the Chicago Orphan Asylum (COA) sought a qualified person to study the institution and make recommendations, Breckinridge promptly volunteered a doctoral student, Ethel Verry. Fellow SSA alumna Helen Wright explained: "Miss Verry says that before anyone—least of all herself—quite knew what was happening, she was installed on the staff of COA and given the responsibility of transforming its program."[66]

Beginning in 1924–25, the Local Community Research Committee (later the Social Science Research Committee) facilitated the connection between scholarly research and social reform for the SSA leaders and their students. Based at the University of Chicago, the Committee drew its support from a variety of sources, including philanthropists, private charities, and public agencies. Taking its cue from its funders, the committee sponsored empirical research in the social sciences and promoted interdisciplinary cooperation and applied research, countering the postwar trend toward more rigid disciplinary boundaries and a more "objective" attitude of detached scholarship.[67]

Funding from the Local Community Research Committee facilitated the Abbott-Breckinridge team's penchant for combining research with reform. Typically, a private or public agency would commission Breckinridge or Abbott—frequently, both—to conduct a study of a particular aspect of social service. Funding provided by the requesting agency was matched by the University of Chicago and outside funders. Breckinridge and Abbott shared responsibility for supervising the fieldwork of social work graduate students who collected the requested data; Breckinridge and Abbott then wrote a final report for the agency's use and/or publication. In many cases, students published portions of their research in the *Social Service Review* prior to using it to complete their MA or PhD in the School of Social Service Administration. Studies undertaken through the Local Community Research Committee and directed by Breckinridge and/or Abbott included a review of state institutions for the mentally ill, an investigation of the employment of disabled youth, and a study of African American domestic servants, as well as evaluations of courts, charities, and county welfare programs.[68]

In all these cases, reform and research were closely linked. Empirical research on social conditions was undertaken for the express purpose of reforming social services. One project that eventually fell under the purview of the Local Community Research Committee—the study of social services for dependent black children—casts this relationship between research and reform into sharper relief. Beginning in 1913, when they served on a committee convened by the Cook County Board of Visitors to investigate the county's orphanages, Abbott and Breckinridge advocated extending services to black children, who were usually excluded from private orphanages. Seven years later, in 1920, they helped establish a foster-care placing agency for African American youth. Drawing its funding from both private and public sources, the program not only placed children in foster homes but also provided a boarding home for unwed mothers and their children, support services for poor families as an alternative to the separation of parents and children, and services for children with physical disabilities and behavioral problems. Beginning in 1928, the program began receiving funding from the Local Community Research Committee, and the School of Social Service Administration took charge of its administration. The program was directed by a social work instructor and staffed by social work students, including the University of Chicago's first black social work students; Breckinridge and Abbott served on the Local Community Research Committee, which oversaw the project. Breckinridge also served on the weekly case-review committee.[69]

Breckinridge worked tirelessly to acquire funds from the Local Community Research Committee and from private donors to fund the project. She explained the logic of providing services for children with funds earmarked for research: "So little was known about the needs of the negro child and the problem presented by their care that it was felt necessary to do the work for them after the method of a research project." Despite constant fundraising efforts, the program was perennially short of cash. Breckinridge repeatedly justified the expense of the program to the executive secretary of the Local Community Research Committee, basing her arguments on practical considerations (such as using committee funds for dispensary fees because black children were not served by public hospitals) and scholarly ones (including the "interesting facts" that the program revealed, which "will be an extremely valuable addition to our body of social-case-record material," as well as students' use of the project as a basis for their degree requirements).[70]

In 1932, after more than a year of repeated requests from both Abbott and Breckinridge, who each served on the Advisory Board of the Cook County Bureau of Public Welfare, the county assumed responsibility for the program, financing it through state and federal emergency relief funds and renaming it the Children's and Minors' Service, which served children regardless of race. In a typical combination of social science and social policy, this project facilitated the education (and employment) of the University of Chicago's first black students of social work as well as the creation of Chicago's first public child-welfare agency.[71]

Research projects like those undertaken by Ethel Verry and the African American students who worked in the black foster-care program prepared SSA graduates to become policymakers and educators in their own right. "The Chicago plan" of carefully supervised field work and related social science research was an essential part of Abbott and Breckinridge's shared vision of producing not simply social work practitioners but public policy experts. Repudiating what they characterized as "narrow, technical 'training courses,'" Breckinridge and Abbott insisted that the goal of social work education was "not merely the training of routine case workers but the larger and more constructive policy of working with the social agencies to develop the science of public welfare."[72]

Breckinridge and Abbott groomed their students for leadership. By placing them with social agencies in need of reform and linking their thesis research with onsite internships, they simultaneously helped students complete their degrees and created career opportunities for them. As one SSA report boasted, former students "frequently occupy 'key positions' in social work largely because of the broader educational preparation they have had." Indeed, throughout the 1920s more than half of SSA graduates held positions in higher education or public welfare administration. This accomplishment was all the more notable since many newer public welfare agencies, eager to distinguish themselves from charitable organizations associated with benevolent female volunteers, favored hiring men in leadership positions. Breckinridge and Abbott's insistence on preparing their students—most of whom were women—to "develop the science of public welfare" helped to counter this trend.[73]

A sampling of SSA graduates' careers, highlighted in annual reports to funders and alumni, indicates that the SSA was strikingly successful in producing leaders in social work and public policy. Whether as professors of social work or sociology; directors of public agencies or private charities; researchers at policy think tanks both in the United States and abroad; or superintendents of detention homes, guidance offices, and hospital social work departments, SSA graduates amply fulfilled their mentors' faith in "the Chicago plan."[74]

At the same time, of course, SSA graduates disseminated the "Abbott-Breckinridge point of view" around the country. As SSA alumna Arlien Johnson explained, a group of "second-generation" social workers spread the "science of social welfare" well beyond the University of Chicago. Speaking particularly of Breckinridge, she reflected:

> She has left an indelible stamp upon the development of the professional schools of social work. The rich knowledge and the discipline of mind gained from her study of economics, political science, and law, which she brought to bear upon the emerging formulations of social work education from its inception, were not limited to one school but have permeated the whole fabric of professional education.[75]

"Unique and priceless"

Breckinridge and Abbott's collaboration at the School of Social Service Administration allowed them to achieve more together than they could have done individually. As Children's Bureau chief Katharine Lenroot reflected in a letter to Abbott, "You and she together . . . have made a contribution that is completely unique and priceless."[76]

By sharing responsibility for the often arduous task of developing the University of Chicago's social work program, Breckinridge and Abbott achieved professional success against sometimes seemingly insurmountable odds. As one acquaintance admiringly wrote: "Both of you have exemplified the finest in the professional woman."[77]

At the same time that they advanced their own professions, Breckinridge and Abbott also promoted the profession of social work. The curriculum they developed at the School of Social Service Administration "influenced all professional education for social welfare" for decades to come. Moreover, their shared vision of "the science of social welfare"—social policy based on social research—provided an important counterpoint to the one-on-one casework with individual clients advocated at other schools of social work.[78]

Ultimately, Breckinridge and Abbott's shared vision of social work as a tool for promoting social policy based on social science made the School of Social Service Administration an effective engine for political activism. As explored in more detail in chapter 9, during the New Deal they used the school as a platform for promoting public policy, allowing them to play a key role in the development of the American welfare state.

CHAPTER SIX

Defining Equality

Fairness and Feminism

"Public life"

In 1930, Breckinridge's name appeared on a commemorative plaque dedicated to those "whose labors have won for the women of this country entrance into its public life" alongside such feminist luminaries as Elizabeth Cady Stanton, Susan B. Anthony, Lucretia Coffin Mott, Charlotte Perkins Gilman, Jane Addams, Anna Howard Shaw, Carrie Chapman Catt, and other prominent women activists. Highlighting the importance of successive generations taking up the struggle for women's rights, the bronze tablet not only included both nineteenth- and twentieth-century leaders but also depicted allegorical women "bearing torches" and "pass[ing] them from hand to hand."[1] At least in the eyes of the League of Women Voters, which designed the panel, feminism was alive and well in the interwar period, and Breckinridge was one of its foremost proponents. Yet later generations of feminists have allowed both Breckinridge's memory and the history of women's activism in the interwar era to fade into obscurity, almost into nonexistence. As far as her own role was concerned, Breckinridge may have preferred it this way. To Belle Sherwin, president of the League of Women Voters, she confessed: "Frankly I don't like to be 'in bronze.' I like what I do to slip in, and through, and out again; but I am very grateful."[2] Breckinridge's self-effacing attitude notwithstanding, recognizing her important role in women's rights activism, as well as reexamining the significant debates in which she took part, offers important insights into feminism in modern America.

Debates over the best way to improve women's status—indeed, disagreements about the very nature of "equality"—both animated and antagonized women activists in the early twentieth century. The central issue that concerned Breck-

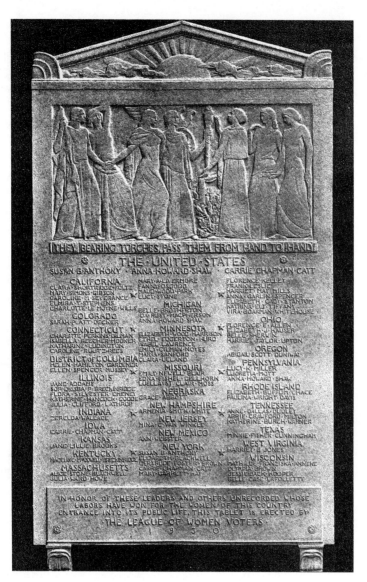

In 1930, Breckinridge's name appeared in a list of suffrage leaders, including Elizabeth Cady Stanton, Susan B. Anthony, Anna Howard Shaw, and Carrie Chapman Catt, on a commemorative plaque designed by the League of Women Voters that both celebrated veteran feminists and called young women to activism with the motto, "They bearing torches pass them from hand to hand." Both during and after the suffrage movement, Breckinridge was an important feminist activist, not only for her leadership roles in both the National American Woman Suffrage Association and the League of Women Voters, but also for her role in defining the essence of equality for American women. Debates over how best to achieve what Breckinridge called "effective equality"—an equality that both acknowledges gender differences and demands fair treatment—persist to this day.

Courtesy Woman's Journal

inridge and her contemporaries—how to acknowledge gender difference while also demanding women's equality—continues to be a divisive issue in contemporary America. Yet our understanding of the historical origins of this feminist fissure is overly simplistic. Most histories of U.S. feminism either conclude that feminism waned in the interwar period or devote their attention to the National Woman's Party's unsuccessful attempts to adopt the Equal Rights Amendment. Thus, Breckinridge and her fellow activists' continued attempts to reconcile equality and difference either have received scant attention or have been dismissively characterized as a lesser type of feminism, "social feminism," whose proponents supposedly privileged "protection" over "equality" and based their arguments on "difference" rather than on "equality." Such formulas suggest that "difference" and "equality" are mutually exclusive categories—an assumption that has hobbled women's continued advancement. Yet for Breckinridge and many of her political allies—sometimes referred to as "social justice feminists"—the central question was not whether to prioritize equality *or* difference but rather how to reconcile equality *with* difference. Both earlier feminists' earnest efforts to address these knotty questions and the unfortunate results of their failure to resolve their political differences offer useful insights for contemporary activists.[3]

From the first, Breckinridge was determined to reconcile feminist assertions of women's equality with her cherished sense of "fair play." Thus, at the same time that she worked to ensure women's equal opportunities, Breckinridge also promoted measures that would allow all women an equal ability to pursue those opportunities—including gender-specific legislation designed to benefit working women and poor mothers—as a necessary aspect of what she called "true equality." Breckinridge's simultaneous support for women's rights and women's welfare infused all her work in feminist organizations, both before and after the achievement of the federal suffrage amendment.[4]

While Breckinridge had been interested in women's rights since her teens, she first became active in the woman suffrage movement in her early thirties, when, after attending a national suffrage convention, she co-founded the Equal Suffrage Association at the University of Chicago and the Committee for the Extension of Municipal Suffrage for Chicago Women in 1907.[5] Breckinridge's entry into suffrage work coincided with her introduction to the Women's Trade Union League and her residence in Hull House, and her approach to organized feminism would remain strongly influenced by her concerns for working women and social welfare. When Breckinridge became a leader in U.S. feminism, she brought her dual commitment to women's rights and women's welfare to the national stage.

Even before she became second vice president of the National American Woman Suffrage Association (NAWSA) in 1911, Breckinridge had become a highly visible feminist figure. Her status as the University of Chicago Law School's first female graduate and one of the country's leading "learned women" made her a popular subject for the women's pages of local newspapers, which often sandwiched her discussions of women's legal and economic status between fashion features and advice columns.[6] In 1910, for the summer session at the University of California at Berkeley, Breckinridge gave a series of lectures in home economics on "the economic position of women and its relation to matrimony" in which she forthrightly demanded full equality and predicted that "the time was coming ... when man and woman would stand on the same industrial plane and their wages would be equalized by an equal social condition."[7]

Breckinridge not only believed that women deserved to be "on the same industrial plane" as men, earn the same wages as men, and share "an equal social condition" with men, but also that equal voting rights would help women achieve these ends. At the same time, she insisted that gender-specific labor legislation was entirely compatible with—and, indeed, necessary to—true female equality. This logic is apparent in a pamphlet she co-authored with Edith Abbott, *The Wage-Earning Woman and the State: A Reply to Miss Minnie Bronson*. In 1910 Bronson had published an antisuffrage pamphlet under the auspices of the Massachusetts Association Opposed to the Further Extension of Suffrage to Women. Bronson's chief argument was that there was no connection between woman suffrage and labor legislation in the various states and thus that there was no tangible benefit to political equality. Writing on behalf of the Boston Equal Suffrage Association for Good Government, Breckinridge and Abbott vigorously disputed Bronson's arguments, asserting that woman suffrage was indeed a vital tool in promoting women's social, economic, and legal status. In particular, they argued that woman suffrage was "the swiftest and surest way to bring about the reforms which are asked by and for the women workers of this country," such as protective legislation for women workers.[8] In a special volume on *Women in Public Life*, published under the auspices of the American Academy of Political and Social Science, Breckinridge reiterated this argument, explaining that "political equality" was not simply a goal in and of itself but, more important, an "efficient instrument" with which to advance women's "economic status."[9]

Breckinridge's emphasis on woman suffrage as political leverage made her an ideal candidate for leadership in the national suffrage movement, which was gaining popularity in the early twentieth century precisely because activists of many different stripes could agree that suffrage was a practical tool with which to improve women's status, even if they disagreed on the particulars of how to better women's lives. Yet the same chameleon-like quality that made Breckinridge's message—and the suffrage movement more generally—so successful in the years leading up to 1920 would prove problematic for continued activism in the decades following the Susan B. Anthony amendment.

Of course, disagreements among feminists did not emerge from a void in the postsuffrage years. Breckinridge's tenure as an officer of NAWSA, while brief, offers insight into the complicated dynamics of the organization and the tensions plaguing feminism in the final decade of the suffrage movement. Indeed, both Breckinridge's selection as second vice president in 1911 and her decision to leave office after only one year resulted from the difficulties plaguing the organization as a result of political infighting within U.S. feminism. Reflecting personality conflicts and philosophical differences alike, the fissures apparent in the suffrage movement would only widen in the decades to follow. Breckinridge's determination to advance both women's rights and social welfare remained constant, however, making her an important—if sometimes controversial—figure in twentieth-century feminism.

"You can be of splendid service to the cause"

Breckinridge's vice presidency coincided with a difficult period of adjustment for the nation's leading suffrage organization. Membership in NAWSA doubled between 1910 and 1912 and again between 1912 and 1915.[10] A larger membership necessitated a more formal organizational structure and a more central official headquarters, while the organization's appeal around the nation also led to regional tensions between the old leadership, based in the Northeast, and the new membership, coming out of the South, Midwest, and far West. Successful western and midwestern state campaigns shifted the focus of the movement—although not the headquarters—westward, while southern suffragists, seeking to protect states' rights and white supremacy, offered only lukewarm support for the federal suffrage amendment. Finally, the organization confronted increasing expenses in reaching its growing membership and carrying on multiple state and federal campaigns simultaneously. The decision to sponsor Alice Stone Blackwell's weekly newspaper, the *Woman's Journal*, as its official weekly publication further complicated the organization's finances.[11]

The growing movement also developed ideological differences, as some suffragists adopted an argument based on women's difference from men rather than women's equality with men. While the original Declaration of Sentiments, penned by New York suffrage pioneer Elizabeth Cady Stanton in 1848, proudly insisted that "all men and women are created equal," many of the movement's new adherents instead capitalized on the notion that women's superior morality meant that with suffrage, women could "clean up" corrupt politics. Of course, this shift "from justice to expediency" did not happen either overnight or all at once, and many suffragists—including Breckinridge—routinely mixed "social housekeeping" arguments with "natural rights" claims.[12]

A newspaper account of a suffrage speech Breckinridge delivered in Chicago early in her vice presidency illustrates the way in which she combined elements of domesticity and equality. The speech's title, "Domesticity and the Ballot," contrasted with the speech's contents, wherein Breckinridge argued that women needed the ballot to combat "poverty, disease, unequal distribution of wealth, special privilege, and unequal justice." While her references to using the ballot to combat poverty and disease might be cast in terms of social housekeeping, her challenges to unequal distribution of wealth, special privilege, and unequal justice smacked more of justice than expedience. Similarly, her stated goals for the ballot ranged widely, from public health to social justice.[13]

So long as feminists agreed on the goal of suffrage, their rationale for seeking the vote—whether based on natural rights or social housekeeping—was not problematic. Likewise, women activists with a variety of aims, ranging from prohibition and moral reform to labor legislation and social welfare programs, to full equality and the elimination of all forms of gender discrimination, could agree on suffrage as the best way to achieve their different goals.[14] Nonetheless, the different views that lurked beneath the surface of the suffrage consensus ultimately posed a serious threat to a unified feminist movement.

Suffragists who based their claims on difference also sometimes emphasized differences of race, class, and ethnicity. Lingering resentment over the fact that the Reconstruction amendments enfranchised African American men but not women—few people noticed, or cared, that African American women were entirely missing in this equation—led former abolitionists like Elizabeth Cady Stanton to decry the enfranchisement of uneducated former slaves ahead of educated white women. By the turn of the century, as immigration expanded and newcomers increasingly came from southern and eastern Europe and adhered to Judaism or Catholicism, some suffragists began to call for "educated suffrage," code for suffrage requirements that would restrict the voting rights of immigrants, the working class, and blacks, while granting the right to vote to educated, white, middle-class women.[15]

Breckinridge, however, steered clear of racist, classist, and nativist rhetoric. In addition to being a charter member of both the Immigrants' Protective League and the Chicago branch of the National Association for the Advancement of Colored People, she actively combated efforts to restrict immigration and joined the growing antilynching movement. Moreover, as a social worker and educator, she advocated public schools for all, rather than privileging an elite literate class. In the months leading up to her election to office in NAWSA, she joined forces with Jane Addams and Grace Abbott to protest a proposed literacy test for immigrants, responded to NAACP leader Oswald Garrison Villard's request to investigate a lynching in Kentucky, and co-authored a report with Edith Abbott advocating education (rather than employment) for working-class youth.[16] Breckinridge sometimes used arguments emphasizing gender distinctions to advance suffrage, but she refused to sanction racial, ethnic, or class discrimination.

While employing multiple arguments in support of woman suffrage helped the movement grow, suffragists' varied strategies also could result in conflict. In the early twentieth century, new tactics such as open-air speaking, suffrage parades, lobbying representatives, and even engaging in civil disobedience alarmed some of the old guard while also attracting increased media attention. Although NAWSA's leadership increasingly condoned most of these new strategies, the organization remained wary of so-called "militant" action as practiced by England's "suffragettes," followers of Emmeline and Christabel Pankhurst, who stormed Parliament, went to jail, and staged hunger strikes. When Alice Paul returned to the United States fresh from the battles in Great Britain in 1912, the stage was set for a showdown between "moderate" suffragists and "militant" suffragettes.[17]

Personal conflicts also played a role in the suffrage movement's difficulties. Indeed, NAWSA, founded in 1890, had a long history of such conflicts, which magnified political differences. In the aftermath of the Civil War, during the debate over citizenship and voting rights in the reunited nation, suffragists split into two rival organizations, the National Woman Suffrage Association (NWSA), which opposed extending citizenship and voting rights to African-Americans but not to women, and the American Woman Suffrage Association (AWSA), which held that "half a loaf is better than none." Because so many first-generation advocates of woman suffrage were also veterans of the abolitionist movement, the "Negro's hour" led to bitter recriminations between the leaders of the two organizations, with the NWSA's Elizabeth Cady Stanton and Susan B. Anthony insisting on the primacy of women's rights, and the AWSA's Lucy Stone accusing her former colleagues of apostasy, even racism. It took two full decades for the personal antagonisms to subside enough for the two suffrage groups to combine as the National American Woman Suffrage Association. However, it did not take long for the new organization to develop similar tensions.

Anna Howard Shaw, president from 1904 to 1915, was an excellent public speaker but a poor administrator. Touchy and tactless, she antagonized her colleagues and exacerbated tensions. Suspicious of her fellow officers and jealous of her authority, Shaw only compounded the numerous challenges facing the growing organization. Her acceptance of the financial support of Alva Belmont, a wealthy New York socialite, created friction since Belmont attached several conditions to her support, including moving the national headquarters from Ohio to New York. Dissatisfaction with Belmont's financial influence and Shaw's administration created dissension among officers and led to several resignations. The election of new officers based in the Midwest and the South only increased problems as the officers not based in New York felt increasingly alienated from the central New York office. These self-styled "insurgents" objected to both Belmont's influence and the New York leadership and lobbied to relocate headquarters to Washington, D.C., or Chicago. Shaw not only resisted these calls but also proposed amendments to NAWSA's constitution that would have made meaningful participation of midwestern and southern officers nearly impossible. The Louisville convention in 1911 became a focal point for these disputes.[18]

In Louisville, eastern suffragists ousted Kentucky insurgent Laura Clay from office while filling three open positions with midwesterners—Sophonisba Breckinridge, Jane Addams, and Belle Case La Follette—who not only were not in attendance at the meeting but also were unaware that their names had been proposed for office. When Breckinridge learned of her election, she fired off a frantic telegram to former NAWSA vice president and fellow Chicagoan Catharine McCulloch: "I don't see how it happened. I can't take Miss Clay's place—help me do the right and loyal thing."[19]

In her response, McCulloch explained that a peculiarity in the organization's constitution that allowed delegates present from any state to cast the entire vote of the state had allowed a small group of "Eastern women" to "control the entire situation." "I was on the platform with Miss Clay at the time," McCulloch explained, "and I said to her, 'this is the cleverest sort of work I ever saw; to use the names of these famous Western women as candidates is much better than putting in some unknown Easterners, for of course we of Chicago cannot complain and Kentucky which loves Miss Breckenridge [sic] will not complain." As a result of Clay's defeat, "the Board now has no Southern woman on it and no woman from Kentucky, which was our hostess state." McCulloch remarked, "It reminded me of the days of barbarism when we would eat our host's salt and then stick a knife in his back."[20]

The eastern faction's decision to champion three midwestern women was, as McCulloch recognized, a strategic one. All three women were prominent reformers, Addams because of her leadership of Hull House; Breckinridge because of her deanship of the Chicago School of Civics and Philanthropy; and La Follette because of her association with her husband, progressive Wisconsin senator Robert La Follette. They thus had contacts that might be exploited to raise funds for the financially struggling organization, and they were geographically ideally situated to spearhead the ongoing suffrage campaigns in several midwestern states, especially Illinois and Wisconsin. In addition, all three women's residence in the Midwest—and especially Breckinridge's southern roots—would appeal to the growing western and southern membership and hopefully placate the insurgents. At the same time, however, even though all three women supported suffrage in their home states, all were newcomers to the national organization; indeed, there was some question, after the election, whether or not La Follette was even a member of NAWSA. Rather than a drawback, eastern leaders probably regarded this as an advantage, believing that the new officers might be more amenable to eastern leadership than those they replaced. Finally, both Breckinridge and Addams were known for their diplomacy and charisma, and NAWSA leaders probably hoped they could help resolve the organization's internal conflicts. When M. Carey Thomas, the president of Bryn Mawr College and a prominent NAWSA supporter, visited Hull House and "talked National" with Addams and Breckinridge later that year, she was pleasantly surprised to find that both new officers were "awfully nice," making her optimistic that the Chicago officers might help resolve the problems that plagued the national board.[21]

The insurgents also saw benefits in the selection of new officers. Despite the underhanded tactics of the eastern delegates, McCulloch urged Breckinridge and Addams to accept the office and use it as an opportunity to counterbalance the overweening power of the eastern officers. "I have felt this year that the three headquarters' officers"—meaning President Anna Howard Shaw of Pennsylvania, Treasurer Jessie Ashley of New York, and Secretary Mary Ware Dennett of Massachusetts—"had little idea of real national work," McCulloch opined. "They do not appreciate what is going on in the West and the South and you two Chicago women do know the whole country well and you can be of splendid service to the cause."[22] Similarly, southern insurgent Laura Clay encouraged Breckinridge to accept the office and use her "political sagacity" to help bring the South into the suffrage fold. "The South is yet in a great measure unawakened and backward," Clay reflected on the region's resistance to suffrage organization. "I believe your name and family influence, combined with your abundant personal abilities to wield them advantageously, are worth more to the cause in the South than those of any other woman of whom I know."[23]

The initial months of Breckinridge's term seem to bear out the hopes of both the old guard and the insurgents. Breckinridge spent much of her time unraveling the organization's tangled finances and attempting to "placate" discontented members. She traveled widely to deliver speeches on behalf of suffrage, and she successfully used her fundraising prowess on behalf of the organization. However, the insurgents had underestimated the seriousness of the organization's internal problems, while the easterners had underestimated the new officers' independent thinking. Despite Breckinridge's hope that she and the other officers could "keep away from politics and personalities and concentrate on work," politics and personalities continued to disrupt the organization.[24]

While initially the eastern leadership was enthusiastic about the midwestern women's ability to raise funds within their circle, the national board had a positive genius for miscommunication and misunderstanding, leading even the gentle Addams to exchange bitter recriminations with her eastern colleagues over the organization's financial difficulties. Possibly in response to these problems, although using the excuse of assisting her husband with his work, Belle La Follette, the other midwestern suffragist elected at Louisville, resigned after only two months. Although tempted to follow suit, Breckinridge and Addams continued on as vice presidents of the organization, sharing speaking duties throughout the country in 1911 and 1912, carrying on official correspondence, and attending meetings of the national board, which Addams compared to being immersed in "boiling oil."[25]

With both of the national suffrage organization's vice presidents hailing from Chicago, the Second City quickly became a "stronghold for the cause."[26] Despite—or perhaps because of—Breckinridge and Addams's successful organizing in Chicago, relationships within the national organization remained strained. In spring 1912, Breckinridge and Addams turned their attention to an annual midwestern suffrage conference. Misunderstandings soon emerged about the national organization's role at the midwestern convention. Most Chicago suffragists regarded the convention as a purely local or regional gathering and therefore resisted the presence of the national leadership; however, the eastern leadership insisted that the national organization's presence was necessary and resented their possible exclusion. Frustrated with the continuing antagonisms, Addams confided to Breckinridge: "I am inclined to think Miss Shaw's suspicions exaggerate everything."[27]

Bad as the situation was, it became still worse, in part due to continuing financial difficulties, and in part because Shaw and other eastern leaders used accusations of financial malfeasance to discredit anyone they regarded as a threat to their leadership.[28] To Breckinridge's dismay, despite all her efforts to keep the organization's financial records in "the best order," complaints soon arose about the intermingling of state and national suffrage funds in Illinois. She exclaimed: "I think Miss Adams will be surprised and I was shocked to learn that our little understanding had been such a drain on the State resources."[29]

Further exacerbating the already tense situation, by the fall of 1912, both Breckinridge and Addams had become outspoken supporters of Progressive Party presidential candidate Theodore Roosevelt, disregarding the national suffrage organization's traditional commitment to nonpartisanship. As discussed in chapter 4, Breckinridge and other activists had helped shape the third party's "Platform of Industrial Minimums," which included several measures to promote workers' welfare, including protective legislation for women workers. Breckinridge's insistence on publicly supporting the Progressive Party despite the nonpartisan stance of the suffrage organization thus demonstrated the potential conflict between women's rights and labor legislation and highlighted Breckinridge's insistence on combining these goals. She failed to convince national leaders that the suffrage movement should use party politics to promote social welfare, however; indeed, Shaw publicly denounced "party ties." This uncomfortable situation led Breckinridge to resign her post after just one year in office, and Addams soon followed suit.[30]

The tensions that plagued NAWSA throughout Breckinridge's tenure as second vice president only escalated after she stepped down from office. In December 1912, Alice Paul, recently returned to the United States after engaging in militant civil disobedience in Great Britain, revitalized the national organization's Congressional Committee, which focused on adoption of a federal woman suffrage amendment. Paul soon ran afoul of Shaw, who disapproved of a lavish parade she organized in Washington, D.C., the same day in early 1913 as the inauguration of the new president, Woodrow Wilson. Shaw also disapproved of Paul's strategy, modeled on the tactics of British suffragettes, of holding the party in power responsible for women's disfranchisement. With fellow militant Lucy Burns, Paul founded a separate but related organization, the Congressional Union, which urged women voters in the western states that had adopted woman suffrage to oppose Democratic candidates in the fall 1913 elections. Because many suffragists regarded Democrats as allies, this tactic angered the old leadership. Once again invoking financial mismanagement, Shaw and other eastern leaders forced Paul and Burns off the Congressional Committee in December 1913 when they refused to relinquish partisan politics as a tool to win woman suffrage. Two months later, under the pretext of requiring all NAWSA affiliates to reapply for auxiliary status, NAWSA officially severed all ties with the Congressional Union, which became a rival suffrage organization, the National Woman's Party (NWP).[31]

Although they remained active in the suffrage movement, after leaving office Breckinridge and Addams shifted their focus away from NAWSA and toward the Woman's Peace Party, which they co-founded in 1915. In their opposition to the war in Europe and in their support for a federal suffrage amendment, Breckinridge and Addams philosophically aligned more with the National Woman's Party than with the National American Woman Suffrage Association. However, despite their support for Alice Paul's Congressional Union and British suffragette Emmeline Pankhurst, both women remained members of the mainstream organization. In fall 1916, when women voters were torn between suffrage and peace, the NWP attempted to counter the Woodrow Wilson slogan "He kept us out of war" with the slogan, "He kept us out of suffrage." NAWSA, by contrast, under the leadership of a new president, Carrie Chapman Catt, adopted a resolution announcing the organization's "unswerving loyalty to the Government in this crisis."[32]

Catt's so-called "winning plan," which called for NAWSA to connect continuing work at the state level with advocating the federal amendment, and the NWP's wartime protests, which earned Paul and her followers the moniker "Iron-Jawed Angels" for their participation in a hunger strike after being jailed for picketing the White House, both played a role in the successful adoption and ratification of the Susan B. Anthony amendment in 1920.[33] Breckinridge's pacifist commitments, as discussed in chapter 7, prevented her from participating in the final stage of the suffrage struggle. However, her commitment to women's equality extended well beyond the achievement of suffrage.

"The greatest good for the greatest number"

Speaking in her home state of Kentucky shortly before the ratification of the Susan B. Anthony amendment, Breckinridge hailed "the full enfranchisement of the American woman" as the beginning of a new era for the nation's welfare as well as women's rights. With full voting rights, she predicted, women would be able to "develop every faculty they inherit in common with men without hindrance from him. There is henceforth to be a fair field and no favor." Not only would woman suffrage advance women's equality, she explained, but it would also advance public welfare, "the greatest good for the greatest number." The newly enfranchised female electorate, Breckinridge proclaimed, would help the entire nation deal with "the leading issues of the day."[34]

Breckinridge's optimism seemed warranted in 1920, when organized feminism in the United States appeared not only victorious but also more unified than ever before. Beneath the surface, however, lay unresolved tensions that threatened the unity of women activists and the political effectiveness of organized feminism. While Breckinridge forecast a future in which equal rights and social welfare not only coexisted easily but also reinforced one another, strains soon developed between advocates of social welfare legislation and proponents of an equal rights amendment. Continuing the earlier rivalry between the National American Woman Suffrage Association and the National Woman's Party, these divisions would prevent women activists from working together toward a shared goal in the 1920s and 1930s.

In the early 1920s, however, the future seemed bright. An encouraging series of victories in the immediate aftermath of suffrage seemed to augur an era of unprecedented feminist cooperation and legislative success as a series of bills passed with the enthusiastic support of a variety of women's groups united under the auspices of the Women's Joint Congressional Committee (WJCC).[35] In 1920 women gained new visibility in politics with the creation of a federal agency, the Women's Bureau, within the U.S. Department of Labor.[36] In 1921, Congress passed the Sheppard-Towner Act, better known by its supporters as the Maternity and Infancy Act, which provided matching funding for states for pre- and postnatal care for poor mothers and their children.[37] In 1922 the Cable Act offered "independent citizenship" to married women, partially redressing discriminations introduced in previous legislation that deprived women of their citizenship based on marriage to aliens or residence abroad (marital expatriation) and that linked married women's access to naturalization to the citizenship status of their husbands (derivative citizenship).[38] In 1923, Congress considered an Equal Rights Amendment that declared: "Men and women shall have equal rights throughout the United States and every place subject to its jurisdiction."[39] And in 1924, Congress passed a child labor amendment and sent it to the states for ratification.[40]

Unlike the suffrage movement that immediately preceded it, this flurry of political activity did not represent concerted action by multiple groups on behalf of a single goal. Rather, different organizations offered both different legislative agendas and divergent strategies for further improving women's status in the United States.

Initially, with victory finally reached, it appeared that the rival suffrage groups might achieve greater cooperation. When the National Woman's Party held its National Convention in Washington, D.C., in 1921, its leaders reached out to former members of the National American Woman Suffrage Association as well as other women's groups.[41] The 1921 gathering thus raised hopes among many other groups that the National Woman's Party, from its home base in Washington, D.C., might represent a variety of issues in the nation's capital. However, to the disappointment of other women's organizations, it soon became apparent that the NWP intended to continue as a single-issue organization, replacing the demand for the federal suffrage amendment with the demand for an equal rights amendment.[42]

When the National Woman's Party committed itself exclusively to the promotion of the Equal Rights Amendment, it foreclosed the possibility of cooperation with many other women's organizations, which feared that the proposed amendment would invalidate so-called protective legislation for women workers, which had circumvented challenges to regulating working hours and conditions by appealing to women's potential motherhood and particular vulnerability in the industrial workplace. Indeed, at the same time that the NWP was formulating the ERA, labor advocates were holding a Women's Industrial Conference under the aegis of the Women's Bureau of the Department of Labor in Washington, D.C., where Breckinridge gave a speech emphasizing the importance of maintaining and extending special protections for women in the workforce.[43]

Although NWP members sometimes argued that such laws would be extended to all workers in the near future, labor legislation advocates regarded this argument as specious. Breckinridge's former law professor and fellow protective legislation advocate Ernst Freund was one of several legal experts who weighed in on this matter at the request of the National Women's Trade Union League and the National Consumers' League. Freund opined that the courts would not uphold an eight-hour workday for men, and therefore the amendment would "destroy labor laws for women"; indeed, he asserted, "I believe [this] is its purpose." In fact, while early versions of the ERA, first drafted in 1921, specified that the amendment "does not undertake to deal with the field of industrial legislation," by 1923 the NWP was openly hostile to protective legislation. Therefore, despite the apparent inoffensiveness of the official language eventually adopted—"Men and women shall have equal rights throughout the United States and in every place subject to its jurisdiction"—trade union activists and their allies were convinced "that the purpose of the National Woman's Party, . . . is to destroy any labor laws that apply to women only, as well as to prevent the enactment of any such legislation in the future."[44]

Breckinridge, like her mentor, feared that the proposed amendment jeopardized not only gender-specific labor legislation, or "protective legislation," but also other forms of "social legislation" designed for women and children that she championed, such as the mothers' pensions provisions she had helped to initiate and the maternity and infancy healthcare program created by the Sheppard-Towner Act.

The federal government's actions in the 1920s gave social legislation advocates like Breckinridge good reason to fear for the future of programs designed to benefit working women and poor mothers and children. Because of stingy allotments, the mothers' pension programs had never really fulfilled their intended function as compensation for the work of childrearing. Rather, many recipients had to combine paid work with pension checks, or send their children into the workforce, in order to make ends meet. The situation only worsened in the 1920s and 1930s as the deepening economic depression placed a strain on local and state budgets. The failure to ratify the Child Labor Amendment exacerbated these difficulties by leaving the burden of enforcing child labor laws on state and local authorities. Meanwhile, the Sheppard-Towner Act encountered strong opposition from the American Medical Association. After a last-ditch effort to save the program in 1927, when it was extended for an additional two years, the federal grants-in-aid to states for subsidized healthcare for mothers and infants were discontinued in 1929. And the U.S. Supreme Court's decision in the 1923 case *Adkins v. Children's Hospital*, which ruled minimum-wage legislation for women an unconstitutional abridgement of the due process clause of the Fourteenth Amendment, emphasized the vulnerability of state-level protective legislation laws. For all these reasons, Breckinridge and other supporters of social legislation regarded the Equal Rights Amendment as a profound threat to their hard-won victories.

"Nothing can be more unequal
than calling unequals equal"

Disagreement over the Equal Rights Amendment and its potential effect on protective legislation sharply divided women activists in the 1920s. Organizations such as the National Consumers' League and the Women's Trade Union League, both of which had been represented at the National Woman's Party's National Convention, protested the amendment.[45] So too did NAWSA's successor organization, the League of Women Voters. Breckinridge, a longtime member of the National Consumers' League and the Women's Trade Union League and a former officer of NAWSA, as well as one of the chief framers of gender-specific legislation such as mothers' pensions, not surprisingly cast her lot with the League of Women Voters, joining both the state and the national leagues.[46]

Originally a committee of NAWSA, the League of Women Voters (LWV) was committed to three objectives: educating newly enfranchised women; promoting responsible citizenship; and supporting legislation to remove discriminations against women. By 1920 the LWV was an independent national organization with branches in all but two states. Priding itself on nonpartisanship, the league established standing committees on issues ranging from voter education to efficiency in government to the legal status of women. By adopting a regularly updated "Program of Work," the national organization encouraged state branches first to study political issues and then make recommendations for legislation. Although the LWV was committed from the outset to eliminating discriminatory laws, its membership also was convinced of the necessity of gender-specific social legislation, such as limiting the hours of work for women workers, subsidizing low-cost healthcare to mothers and infants, and providing mothers' pensions to assist poor mothers to care for children in their own homes. Thus, league literature carefully distinguished between the single-issue "feminism" of the National Woman's Party defined by the Equal Rights Amendment and the league's standing as "an every woman's organization" committed to developing "well-rounded citizen[s]."[47]

The league's goals aligned well with Breckinridge's beliefs. "The greatest question before the women . . . is not to which political party they are going to belong," Breckinridge asserted, "but rather to which class of citizens are they to belong." In order for the majority of informed citizens to "vote intelligently and so make possible the greatest good for the greatest number," it was imperative that "women should at once familiarize themselves" with both the principles of self-government and "the leading issues of the day."[48] Moreover, Breckinridge, like most long-time women activists, remained committed both to removing laws that discriminated against women and to promoting social legislation that supported them.

Although the LWV and the NWP originally coexisted peacefully, by 1923 it had become clear that the Woman's Party's priority would be the Equal Rights Amendment. Thus, the short-lived unity of the former suffragists dissipated quickly as longtime feminists divided into opposing camps, with the NWP carrying the standard for the Equal Rights Amendment and the LWV staunchly defending social legislation. Because of this opposition, historians sometimes label the ERA supporters as "radical feminists" or "equal rights feminists" and the ERA opponents as "social feminists," who were supposedly more concerned with social welfare than with women's rights. But it is overly simplistic to divide these women activists into "social feminists" and "radical feminists" or into those who represented "difference" and those who represented "equality." A close examination of Breckinridge's published writings and public statements shows that this is a false dichotomy.

Like other members of the LWV, Breckinridge rejected both the Equal Rights Amendment and the equal rights arguments of the NWP, which she regarded as theoretical rather than practical, based on abstract notions of equality rather than being grounded in women's real-life experience. It was counterproductive, she argued, to assert women's equality with men as an ideal when in fact women were at a distinct disadvantage as both workers and citizens because of their inferior educations, their limited occupations, their exclusion from office, their childbearing potential, and their greater responsibility for domestic life. "Nothing can be more unequal than calling unequals equal," she pronounced.[49]

Breckinridge carefully parsed the meaning of equality. For instance, in a 1923 article in the *Journal of Political Economy* pointedly titled "The Home Responsibilities of Women Workers and the 'Equal Wage,'" Breckinridge questioned the notion of "equal work" and "equal pay." Because women rarely had the opportunity to perform work that was "equal" to that of their male counterparts, she pointed out, the demand for equal pay for equal work was "somewhat meaningless." Instead of equal pay for equal work, she argued, what women workers truly needed was protective legislation guaranteeing "just treatment."[50] For Breckinridge, as for the vast majority of women activists in the 1920s and 1930s, justice, not sameness, was the goal.

Breckinridge's analysis of "equality" and the law reflected a broader division between proponents of legal formalism, who believed in interpreting the law narrowly and conservatively, and advocates of sociological jurisprudence, who argued that the law should respond to socioeconomic conditions to promote social justice. Having studied with Ernst Freund, who was, with Roscoe Pound and Felix Frankfurter, one of the nation's foremost spokespeople for sociological jurisprudence, Breckinridge was, not surprisingly, committed to the notion that the "police power" of the state should be used to mitigate real inequities, not to legislate formal equality.[51]

Women's equal citizenship, Breckinridge argued, necessitated both equal rights and special treatment. While women's natural rights as human beings entitled them to civil rights, their gender roles as family caretakers demanded social accommodation. Rather than privileging "equality," Breckinridge advocated "justice." Like her father, she was for "fair play." In practical terms, this meant that she favored using the law to ensure equal opportunity for all—while also using the law to compensate for the particular disadvantages women confronted. In political terms, it meant that she allied herself with the League of Women Voters' commitment to "specific bills for specific ills" and opposed the National Woman's Party's advocacy of the Equal Rights Amendment, which its opponents called a "Blanket Amendment."

Opposition to the Equal Rights Amendment did not correspond to hostility to women's rights, however. Far from it. Opposed to what it called "blanket legislation" such as the Equal Rights Amendment, the league instead addressed women's rights by way of specific state legislation. In this way, the LWV's state-by-state approach mirrored that of its predecessor organization, NAWSA, while the NWP's advocacy of the Equal Rights Amendment paralleled its support of the Susan B. Anthony amendment.

Just as it is overly simplistic to divide former suffragists into those who advocated "equality" and those who represented "difference," it is also inaccurate to read the division between the LWV and the NWP as a product of the postsuffrage ERA battle. Rather, the differences between mainstream activists, represented first by NAWSA and then the LWV, and militant feminists, represented by the NWP, predated both the achievement of suffrage and the ERA. The ERA battle simply continued the two groups' rivalry and reflected their different strategies for improving women's position in the United States. Nonetheless, disagreement over the ERA deepened the divide between the NWP and virtually every other women's organization in the interwar period, pitting feminist activists against one another instead of uniting them in the face of the challenges posed by the Red Scare and the Great Depression.

Ironically, while the NWP and the LWV traded barbs and vied with one another to sway public opinion about the ERA, the organizational records of the two groups in the 1920s and 1930s demonstrate that they shared many aims. At the state level, both groups worked to make women eligible for jury duty. At the federal level, both groups opposed Section 213(a) of the National Recovery Act, which sanctioned discrimination against married women in federal employment. At the international level, both groups worked to ensure women's independent citizenship.[52] But the Equal Rights Amendment was the wedge that kept the two organizations apart and its leaders at odds.

Because of mutual animosity between the NWP and the LWV, the two national organizations carried on a nearly continuous battle over the fate of the federal equal rights amendment at the same time that state branches of both organizations busily worked to ensure equal employment rights, party representation, and jury duty, among other issues. Rather than joining forces, however, party leaders competed for credit for each victory.[53]

In the interwar years, there was no equivalent to Carrie Chapman Catt's "winning plan," which had tied together NAWSA's state-by-state strategy with the NWP's federal amendment focus and thus brought both groups together for the triumphant adoption of the suffrage amendment. Back in 1911, Breckinridge had been brought into NAWSA with the goal of smoothing over differences within the organization. In 1928, when she became chair of the Committee on the Legal Status of Women, her trademark diplomacy, characteristic courtesy, and southern charm might have made her a logical choice to repair relations between the NWP and the LWV.[54]

However, Breckinridge did not take advantage of opportunities to heal the breach between the NWP and the LWV. Rather, she played a prominent role in the LWV's public-relations campaign against the Equal Rights Amendment. Breckinridge joined the League of Women Voters' anti-ERA campaign because she, like many other longtime women activists, opposed a proposed amendment that asserted women's absolute equality in order to preserve existing social legislation that improved women's daily lives.

When the National Woman's Party proposed the Equal Rights Amendment, Breckinridge was concerned about not only "protective legislation" in particular but also what she preferred to call "social legislation" more broadly. In addition to her worry that the amendment would invalidate labor laws that regulated women's working hours and work conditions, she also feared that the amendment would endanger mothers' pension laws, which compensated women for their work as caregivers, and healthcare programs such as those set forth in the Sheppard-Towner Act.

Behind Breckinridge's championship of protective legislation, mothers' pensions, and maternal and infant welfare programs lurked her vivid memories of exhausted factory workers, sickly infants, and despairing widows. Earlier in her career, her exposure to these circumstances had inspired her to promote legislation to address the pressing needs of poor women and their families. Now they led her to oppose new legislation—the Equal Rights Amendment—that might well undo all the work she and her colleagues had accomplished in the preceding decades.

From firsthand investigations into the conditions in Chicago's infamous Stock-yards and in the city's notorious sweatshops, Breckinridge knew the dire conse-quences "of being mastered by the machine," as she put it in the *Handbook of the Chicago Industrial Exhibit*. She related the cost in human lives:

> Girl lives, killed by the speed it sets or demands; woman lives, crushed by the conditions of noise, vibration, unwholesome fumes, long hours, and work at night which kindly nature meant for human rest; and infant life given up be-fore it comes to light, not because the mother works, but because she is and has been worked in so cruel a fashion that there is no surplus life upon which the child can draw.[55]

Remembering the harsh conditions in factories and sweatshops prior to protective legislation, Breckinridge was determined to protect labor legislation.

Having lost two siblings to childhood ailments and observed her own mother's delicate health and premature death, it is no surprise that Breckinridge decried the "hideous waste" of infant deaths and the "immeasurable" consequences of maternal morbidity,[56] leading her to become a passionate supporter of the Shep-pard-Towner Act. When the program eventually was discontinued in 1929, she blasted the federal government for what she called "its indifference with regard to the chances of life provided for mothers and babies."[57] Here, too, Breckinridge had good reason to fight fiercely to maintain social legislation.

Finally, as one of the original proponents of mothers' pensions, Breckinridge was convinced of the need to provide public assistance to poor women with young children. Her careful research in the records of Chicago's Juvenile Court had convinced her that it simply was not possible for unmarried, abandoned, or widowed women to earn enough to support their families and also provide suf-ficient supervision for their children. In the course of investigating the homes of youthful offenders, Breckinridge had discovered troubling scenarios in which "the mother took in washing and had a hard struggle for years; . . . was not able to look after the children properly," or "went out to work and left the children with a neighbor who did not treat them properly," or "the children were left alone all day" while the mother went to work.[58] During the Red Scare of the 1920s, pub-lic welfare programs such as mothers' pensions were in jeopardy; Breckinridge, therefore, felt it necessary to be vigilant in defense of all forms of gender-specific legislation.

Because of her strong commitment to social legislation, Breckinridge played an important role in the anti-ERA campaign of the 1920s. In 1924, as part of a set of hearings on the proposed Equal Rights Amendment, the *Congressional Record* published her debate with NWP representative Anna Kelton Wiley over whether mothers' pensions could operate under the Equal Rights Amendment.[59]

The National Woman's Party insisted that the amendment would not invalidate either mothers' pensions or "maternity legislation"; moreover, the party argued that it would pave the way for higher workplace standards for both men and women. "The demand for a shorter work-day is based upon the need of leisure, health, recreation, and the fulfilling of one's duties to society," a party pamphlet asserted. "These needs bear no relation to sex and the laws which provide for a shorter work-day should therefore be regardless of sex."[60] Most women activists, including Breckinridge, were not convinced.

Breckinridge conceded that so-called "mothers' pensions" were in fact support for indigent children as an alternative to institutional care and that the "great social experiment" of providing financial assistance to poor families should not be affected by the amendment. However, she cautioned that the courts could not be "counted on" to see the matter in this way. Breckinridge warned that there were "enemies in every jurisdiction" who would use the "ambiguity" of the "Blanket Amendment" to undermine the mothers' pension program, which by 1924 existed in some form in forty-two states, plus the territories of Hawaii and Alaska.[61]

Breckinridge also was well aware that the "enemies" of the maternal and child health program created by the Sheppard-Towner Act would also use any opening to torpedo that program, which already had fallen prey to red-baiting in the *Woman Patriot*, a periodical originally published by the National Association Opposed to Woman Suffrage that reinvented itself after the Susan B. Anthony amendment as a publication "Dedicated to the Defense of the Family and the State AGAINST Feminism and Socialism."[62] Practical considerations, therefore, played a role in Breckinridge's opposition to the Equal Rights Amendment.

But Breckinridge also had ideological reasons for opposing the ERA. She regarded "equality" as a slippery concept. In her foreword to the LWV's 1929 anti-ERA booklet, *Toward Equal Rights for Men and Women*, Breckinridge questioned simplistic definitions of "equal rights," separating "the principle of equality" from the "qualitative considerations" that negated true equality. "With independence should come equality," she pronounced, "but the independence comes first, and often the problem of independence will give rise to grave doubts, not as to whether equality is desirable, but wherein equality exists." Breckinridge challenged a "doctrinaire" definition of equality as absolute sameness in the law with respect to men and women. "Equality is one principle to be applied in working out the change from what has been and what is to what should be," she conceded, but she insisted that "no quantitative or mechanical or mathematical conception"—such as the ERA—"can comprehend the entire undertaking. There are qualitative considerations—matters of emphasis, of stress, of social importance that should also affect these decisions." Ignoring "qualitative considerations," such as women's poor bargaining position in the workforce, and insisting on the "arbitrary uniformity" of gender-neutral laws, Breckinridge charged, indicated that the amendment's proponents were "tragically remote from the realities of life."[63]

Because virtually every national women's organization except the National Woman's Party vigorously opposed the Equal Rights Amendment, it is impossible to either credit or blame Breckinridge for its failure. However, examining her steadfast opposition to the amendment further illuminates the divisive nature of the amendment and suggests how concerns about social legislation and differences of opinion over the true nature of equality led to increasingly doctrinaire opposition to the Equal Rights Amendment. For instance, in addition to her other anti-ERA activities, as chair of the LWV Committee on the Legal Status of Women from 1928 to 1930, Breckinridge insisted that each update of the committee's proposed program include a clause indicating its opposition to "blanket" legislation such as the ERA. Moreover, she even attempted to have all the other committees adopt similar language.[64]

"Practical equality"

Breckinridge's work with the Committee on the Legal Status of Women reveals that in her stubborn opposition to the Equal Rights Amendment, she ran the risk of becoming just as inflexible as the steadfast supporters of the amendment. Her position as the chair of this committee also exposes the complexity of the LWV's position on women's rights in the 1920s. Despite its adamant opposition to the ERA—which almost certainly detracted from its effectiveness in other areas— the LWV was committed to women's rights. The LWV coordinated its women's rights advocacy through the Committee on the Legal Status of Women, which recommended programs of study and supported legislation to remove discriminations in a variety of areas, including jury duty, citizenship, office holding, property ownership, employment rights, guardianship, and divorce.[65]

Far from regarding women's rights as a dead issue, the members of the Committee on the Legal Status of Women regarded their group as *the* national women's rights organization. Breckinridge, who chaired the committee from 1928 to 1930, regarded it as the rightful heir to the suffrage movement. At the 1930 LWV annual convention, she declared, "It seems to me that my Committee on the Legal Status of Women, which has been devoted to the removal of discrimination, is very much the channel of the efforts of the old suffragists."[66]

As chair of the Committee on the Legal Status of Women, Breckinridge attempted to maintain a balance between opposition to the Equal Rights Amendment and support for women's rights. At the 1928 annual convention of the League of Women Voters, she argued that it was the federal government's responsibility to acknowledge and counterbalance real differences, rather than simply to deny them and legislate formal equality. "It is important to examine closely every measure proposed," she explained, to determine "whether, in view of the actual biological, social, and occupational differences between men and women, it tends to secure for women a true equality and a greater freedom." The LWV should support legislation that achieved "effective equality" or "practical equality," she argued, as opposed to the Equal Rights Amendment, which offered only the illusion of theoretical equality.[67]

This stance committed Breckinridge's committee to a course of state-by-state action. Breckinridge kept a busy schedule as chair of the Committee on the Legal Status of Women (CLSW). She produced biennial updates of the CLSW program in consultation with the chairs of state-level committees, conducted a study of the legal status of women in Illinois, distributed questionnaires to state chairs about the laws and pending legislation in their states, and updated the survey of laws pertaining to women's rights in the forty-eight states. In addition to corresponding with state chairs about their activities, Breckinridge also produced an internal mimeographed newsletter, *Legal Status News*, to keep the LWV membership informed about strategies, setbacks, and successes in state campaigns.[68]

In her own community, Breckinridge was an effective advocate for women's legal rights, both by promoting the adoption of a women's jury bill and by spearheading a campaign to protect the rights of accused prostitutes. At the end of her two-year campaign, she and her fellow activists had succeeded in obtaining jury trials for female defendants in a new "Woman's Court" and in passing a law allowing women to serve on juries. By 1932 a Cook County woman accused of a crime, for the first time in the history of Chicago, was assured a trial before a jury of her peers.[69]

As Breckinridge's two-year struggle to reform one court in one city suggests, addressing individual discriminations in every state was a complex, arduous, and seemingly never-ending task. When Breckinridge stepped down from her post, she handed over to her successor a three-page bibliography of books addressing women's rights of citizenship, suffrage, jury duty, office holding, public employment, party management, marriage, domicile, property rights, custody rights, and divorce.[70] Her compendium of state laws affecting women, *Survey of the Legal Status of Women in the Forty-Eight States*, ran to more than two hundred pages.[71]

As yet, no historian has attempted a systematic analysis of the Committee on the Legal Status of Women's work in all the states. One of Breckinridge's successors as chair of the committee, Edith Valet Cook, credited the League of Women Voters with enacting a total of 159 statutes in forty-six states between 1921 and 1940, including twenty-one office-holding statutes, sixteen jury-service statutes, twenty-three equal-guardianship statutes, and twenty-seven property-rights statutes. She also gave the organization credit for defeating seventy-two bills, including forty-seven bills authorizing discrimination against women in business and five state equal rights amendments, in the first two decades following the achievement of woman suffrage. Yet it is difficult to escape the conclusion that the LWV's greatest accomplishment was a negative one: blocking the Equal Rights Amendment.[72]

"Family unity" and "full independence"

Breckinridge's most visible *positive* accomplishment as chair of the Committee on the Legal Status of Women was the successful promotion of a revised Cable Act, adopted in 1930. Prior to the adoption of the original Cable Act in 1922, women's citizenship depended on the nationality of their husbands; American women who married immigrant men lost their citizenship status and therefore also lost voting rights and eligibility for mothers' pensions. One of the former suffragists' first steps, therefore, was to work for "independent citizenship" for married women, a goal partially advanced by the adoption of the Cable Act in 1922. However, strict immigration quotas put into place by the "national origins" formula in 1924 and troubling questions about women who resided separately from their husbands persisted, separating family members and raising "questions of individual discrimination." Breckinridge expressed particular concern that women, but not men, were deported for "immoral conduct," a catch-all category for exclusion that applied to suspected homosexuals and alleged prostitutes. In addition, with the memories of World War I still fresh, immigrant women who had difficulty obtaining citizenship through the naturalization process expressed concern over the possibility of forced deportation in the event of another international conflict.[73]

As the secretary of the Immigrants' Protective League (IPL) and as chair of the Committee on the Legal Status of Women for the League of Women Voters, Breckinridge frequently received queries about these and other issues, including cases of domestic violence and divorce proceedings. *Marriage and the Civic Rights of Women* (1931), a study on marriage and women's rights, brought together her concerns about immigrant welfare and women's rights. While working on the book, in addition to holding office in both the IPL and the LWV, Breckinridge also served on an ad hoc committee that sought to modify immigration restrictions (cumbersomely named "The Illinois Joint Committee to Secure Legislation to Unite Families Separated by the Restrictive Immigration Act") and was active in an effort to amend the state mothers' pension law to eliminate the citizenship requirement. As part of her research, Breckinridge engaged in extensive correspondence with local charity organizations, asking each to fill out questionnaires about women's citizenship status, the naturalization process, and eligibility for aid.[74]

Breckinridge's surveys revealed both the importance of citizenship and the difficulty of obtaining it. Many of the case histories revolved around women's unsuccessful efforts to obtain mothers' pensions—an issue of special importance to Breckinridge, since she had played a role in enacting the original Funds-to-Parents Act. An Italian widow, despite her poor health, did night work to support herself and her four children and attended English classes to qualify for citizenship. Even though she was "very faithful and diligent in her attendance," her multiple responsibilities made it difficult for her to keep up in her classes, so she failed the language examination necessary for citizenship and therefore was ineligible for state assistance. A native-born American woman who married an Englishman in 1916 did not realize the consequences until her husband became "totally incapacitated with tuberculosis," and she found herself solely responsible for the support of herself, her husband, and their seven young children. Because she had lost her citizenship by marrying a foreign national, she was not eligible for a mother's pension. An African American woman whose husband, a Native American, had abandoned her, encountered difficulties when she applied for a pension because of questions pertaining to her absent husband's birthplace. Her pension was delayed for a year while she sought to prove that her husband had not been born on a reservation, meaning that he was eligible for citizenship and she was eligible for a pension.[75]

Marriage and the Civic Rights of Women combines these and other case studies with a review of the laws pertaining to domicile and citizenship. It is clear that Breckinridge's sympathies are for women who sought increased independence both in the form of separate domicile and in the form of independent citizenship, as well as that she objected to sex discrimination in the new immigration laws, which shortened the period of required residency for wives of naturalized citizens but did not do the same for husbands. Once the book was complete, she sent it to lawyers, legislators, and government officials, including the director of naturalization, who thanked her for the book and promised to recommend that his staff read it closely "for their guidance in future examinations."[76]

Breckinridge used her expertise on citizenship laws to help the League of Women Voters promote a revised Cable Act and shape the league's recommendations on women's citizenship. Ironically, by insisting on equal treatment for women and men, the league's position on the Cable Act contradicted its position on the Equal Rights Amendment. By holding that "temporizing reservations and special rulings made by apply [sic] to one sex only prolong confusion in the law and injustice to many persons," the league undermined its own longstanding tradition of supporting "special rulings" such as protective legislation.[77]

Nonetheless, league leaders insisted on distinguishing between LWV and NWP work on behalf of independent citizenship. Commenting that in previous sessions of congress representatives of both organizations had appeared to support amendments that would "do away with the discriminations" contained in the third, fourth, and fifth sections of the 1922 Cable Act, league executive secretary Julia Margaret Hicks cautioned Breckinridge: "We are especially anxious that our point of view should be re-registered at an early date because the Woman's Party is already widely advertising the fact that it will be very active in this matter."[78] The need to highlight differences between LWV and NWP positions pressured Breckinridge to avoid overt criticism of sex discrimination and to comply with league practice of piecemeal legislation.

As Breckinridge saw it, the Cable Act had been poorly drafted because it attempted two different purposes: first, granting independent citizenship by removing discriminations against women who either were themselves immigrants or were married to immigrants; and second, promoting family unity by simplifying naturalization procedures for individuals married to native-born or naturalized citizens. By combining these two goals in a single act, the Cable Act eased some discriminations against women while imposing new ones, in the process actually interfering with family unity in some instances by creating barriers to citizenship for women who married noncitizens. Breckinridge therefore initially favored a complete overhaul or substitute act rather than piecemeal amendments to the existing act, and she turned to her longtime friend and legal counselor Ernst Freund for advice.[79]

Although she ultimately agreed to support specific amendments rather than a wholesale overhaul of the act, Breckinridge nonetheless had a significant influence on the League of Women Voters' final set of recommendations. Collaborating closely with Adena Miller Rich, her colleague in the Immigrants' Protective League as well as chair of the LWV Immigration Committee, Breckinridge made subtle but important changes to the league's recommendations.[80]

In recommending changes to the original Cable Act, as in other areas, the league preferred a point-by-point approach to individual issues rather than a "blanket" commitment to equal treatment. However, many of the league's critiques of the Cable Act revolved around differential treatment of women and men. League leaders criticized Section 3, which provided that a female citizen marrying an alien ineligible to citizenship would lose her citizenship, while "the reverse of this, that a man marrying a woman of a race ineligible for citizenship" would lose his citizenship, was not provided. Section 3 also provided that a woman married to a foreign national who resided either in her husband's home country for two years or outside the United States for five years would be presumed to have renounced her citizenship. Again, these provisions did not apply to men marrying foreign nationals. The League of Women Voters regarded this clause as "needless discrimination" and thus supported amendments to repeal the provisions of Section 3, or changes "to make it applicable to men and women equally."[81] The league also criticized the "arbitrary and unreasonable discrimination" contained in Section 5, which provided that any woman married to a man not eligible for citizenship was disqualified from becoming a naturalized citizen. Here too, the league proposed either eliminating this clause or making it equally applicable to both men and women.[82]

However, in early drafts of its position, the league did not oppose all provisions that treated men and women differently. Section 2, on first glance, treated women more favorably than men, permitting an immigrant woman married to either a U.S.-born citizen or a naturalized citizen to apply for naturalization after just one year of residence in the United States, rather than five. "This is a clear distinction," the league admitted, but "the League, however, does not at present favor any modification." Conceding the possibility of making the provisions of Section 2 apply to men as well as to women, the League of Women Voters nonetheless hesitated to take a definite position on this issue. Further study was necessary, a draft proposal indicated, into what measures "would best promote the principle of equality of status without injury to the family unity and welfare." Here, as in the case of other rights legislation, the league insisted that it was necessary to pay attention to "social considerations" as well as equal rights.[83]

In general, Breckinridge's recommendations aligned with those proposed by other league leaders. However, in the case of Section 2, she favored amendment to give the husband of a naturalized citizen the same streamlined process of naturalization as a wife of a naturalized citizen. This would not only equalize men's and women's naturalization procedure, she explained, but would also positively increase women's rights: "In that case the wife who came first would have the same rights the husband has to enjoy after a brief period the sense of a common loyalty in the family group," she explained. Therefore, "social considerations" and equal-rights considerations would both be taken into account, and the new Cable Act would support both "family unity" and "full independence."[84]

Ultimately, Breckinridge prevailed on the issue of easing naturalization requirements for all spouses of citizens (rather than only for wives of male citizens). The league's official recommendations echoed her language in supporting "giving to the alien wife *or husband* of a native born or naturalized citizen the same privileges in respect to the acquisition of citizenship," as well as substantiating her conviction that immigration and naturalization procedures could and should support both the principle of independent citizenship for women and the principle of family unity.[85]

When it came to the Cable Act, as with other issues, although both the National Woman's Party and the League of Women Voters supported amendments to the act, they worked at cross-purposes. The NWP and the LWV actually engaged in similar activities in spring 1930, when both groups testified on behalf of the revised Cable Act and opposed various proposed amendments they believed would interfere with the act's passage. Once again, however, rather than joining forces, both groups claimed credit for the act's passage. In addition, when the

NWP offered suggestions for additional changes to the act, the LWV sharply criticized their proposals, which Gladys Harrison characterized as "ill adapted to accomplish any purpose whatsoever, except to create confusion."[86]

Although the offending amendments were removed from the final version of the 1930 Cable Act, much to league members' disappointment, the original proviso in Section 5 of the 1922 Cable Act that a woman marrying an alien ineligible for citizenship became herself ineligible for citizenship remained intact. In combination with the immigrant restrictions of the National Origins Act of 1924 and other legislation, this meant that women who married men from groups deemed neither "white" nor "black"—Japanese, Chinese, Indian, and other "yellow races"—effectively assumed the racial category of their husbands and lost their own eligibility for citizenship. The obvious racism encoded in this provision was further complicated by vague and variable definitions of race. For instance, both Assyrians and Armenians were sometimes categorized as white, at other times as nonwhite. Additional confusion arose from the questionable status of mixed-race groups coming from places such as Mexico and Malaysia, and by the unclear status of people from U.S. possessions and protectorates, such as Puerto Rico, Hawaii, and the Philippines. But Section 5 sanctioned sex discrimination as well as race discrimination by applying only to women who married ineligible men, and not to men who married ineligible women.[87]

These unresolved issues in U.S. nationality law left the door open for further activism related to women's "equal nationality" on the international stage. As discussed in chapter 8, Breckinridge would continue to play an important role in these debates, in which antagonisms between the National Woman's Party and the League of Women Voters again would come to the forefront.

Breckinridge's involvement in organized feminism in the first three decades of the twentieth century confirms as well as complicates established narratives of the history of U.S. feminism. While her involvement in the National American Woman Suffrage Association and her participation in the Equal Rights Amendment conflict reaffirms historians' characterization of American feminists as a fractious bunch, her insistence on enacting gender-specific social legislation as well as advancing women's equal rights challenges scholars' understanding of the "difference versus equality" debate. Moreover, Breckinridge's ongoing commitment to organized feminism and her consistent support for meaningful equality offer a counterpoint to extant histories of U.S. feminism, which suggest a sharp break between the feminist ferment of the suffrage struggle and the disagreements and divisions of the equal rights debate. Rather, Breckinridge's continuous efforts to advance women's equality and uphold social legislation highlight the vitality and the diversity of modern American feminism throughout the early twentieth century. Future generations would continue the struggle to define women's equality and unite feminists behind a common cause.

CHAPTER SEVEN

Women against War

An International Movement for Peace and Justice

"The best and worthiest women in our country"

In April 1915, Breckinridge and fellow Hull House residents Jane Addams and Grace Abbott traveled to The Hague as U.S. delegates to the International Congress of Women. An official letter of introduction from the governor of Kentucky described the trio as "three of the best and worthiest women in our country." Originating as a replacement for the annual meeting of the International Woman Suffrage Alliance, the congress became the first international meeting of women to discuss the ongoing war in Europe. It was an eventful journey. On board the *Noordam*, Breckinridge and her fellow delegates met "morning, afternoon, and evening" to "study and deliberate" programs for peace. Although they had, according to Breckinridge, "a wonderful passage, smooth all the way," the delegation soon ran into difficulties. British authorities delayed the ship for three days. Cut off from all sources of information and "waiting powerlessly to know what next," as Breckinridge put it, they were "strangely removed from all sources of information. . . . We know no news—and dread what we learn." Nonetheless, the American delegation and the other women aboard were fortunate by comparison to some other would-be attendees; many British women were denied passports, and Russian and French women also were unable to attend. Despite a brief encounter with "a little machine gun trained full upon us by a boat alongside while two German stowaways were taken off and searched and carried away" and other delays en route, the *Noordam* passengers "got through the formalities of passports and customs" just in time for the first session of the congress.[1]

Despite the delays and obstacles, ultimately more than one thousand delegates from twelve countries gathered at The Hague, representing neutral and belligerent nations alike. Indeed, the assembly was so large that it had to be moved to a larger

Along with other feminist pacifists, Breckinridge traveled to The Hague in 1915 in an effort to find a peaceful resolution to the ongoing conflict in Europe. Her position in this photo, taken on board the *Noordam*—in front, but off to the side—in some sense reflected her role in the peace movement. Although fully committed to femi-nist pacifism, Breckinridge was never as prominent a leader as Jane Addams, whose opposition to World War I gained her the moniker "the most dangerous woman in America." Breckinridge's decision to avoid the most public leadership positions may have helped to protect her from the worst of the "Red Scare."

Courtesy Swarthmore College Peace Collection

venue. According to the minutes, "A series of brilliant evening meetings were held during the Congress." Addams chaired the congress; Breckinridge spent her time "looking out for her." Addams worried that Breckinridge spent all her time "sav-ing her from the un-interesting persons while she had the interesting ones," but Breckinridge formed important relationships with other delegates, including Dr. Aletta Jacobs, a prominent European feminist who was responsible for inviting the American women to participate in the congress. In addition, Breckinridge and Addams—who were frequently linked in materials from the congress—were both invited to dine with several British delegates. According to Alice Hamilton, another delegate from Hull House, "Miss Breckinridge has been a great help," and she, Grace Abbott, and Emily Greene Balch all had been "acknowledged by the leaders" of the congress.[2]

The congress adopted a series of resolutions protesting "the madness and the horror of war;" calling attention to the particular dangers war posed to women, including sexual assault; proposing an International Court of Justice and a Council of Conciliation and Investigation to mediate international disputes and "establish a just and lasting peace"; and demanding national self-determination, continuous mediation, universal disarmament, free commerce, and woman suffrage. After considerable debate, delegates agreed to accept "two fundamental planks" as a condition of membership in a new international organization, the International Committee of Women for Permanent Peace: a commitment to peaceful resolution of international disputes and a commitment to support woman suffrage.[3]

The International Congress of Women was Breckinridge's introduction to an international women's movement dedicated to both world peace and women's rights. While Breckinridge, like many of her counterparts in the United States and Europe, initially was drawn to this movement because of her opposition to World War I, her participation in the congress initiated a decades-long commitment to world peace through international cooperation. Breckinridge and her feminist-pacifist counterparts continued to seek peaceful alternatives to war long after the conclusion of World War I. While their efforts did not prevent another world war, feminist-pacifists eventually would help design the United Nations in the aftermath of World War II.[4]

The international women's peace movement also introduced Breckinridge to a transatlantic network of women dedicated to universal human welfare. By the time Breckinridge and her colleagues traveled to The Hague, a social justice consensus had begun to emerge among women peace activists on both sides of the Atlantic. Many of these activists, like Breckinridge, were engaged in social work and social reform in their home countries. As social justice activists as well as feminist pacifists, they regarded world peace and social welfare as inextricably intertwined. In keeping with this logic, Breckinridge praised Jane Addams for her insights in *Newer Ideals of Peace*: "first that the social worker to do her work must have peace, and second, that where the ideas of the social worker prevailed peaceful relations are possible."[5] Breckinridge's participation in international social work in the interwar period suggests the importance of social justice work in sustaining the international women's movement well after woman suffrage had been achieved. Ultimately, as discussed in chapter 8, women's engagement in international politics would help to ensure that women's rights were central to post–World War II discussions of human rights.

This chapter examines Breckinridge's participation in international feminist, pacifist, and social justice circles from 1915 through the 1930s, with a focus on the interactions between the United States and Europe. Chapter 8 addresses her related work in Pan-American context. Whereas chapter 6 highlighted the continuity of U.S. feminism before and after the Susan B. Anthony Amendment, chapters 7 and 8 call attention to the continued vigor of women's internationalism in the interwar period. By participating in an international network of women committed to peace and justice during and after World War I, Breckinridge expanded her influence to the world stage.

"Peace baby"

As discussed in chapter 1, Breckinridge attributed her pacifism to her childhood experiences in the Reconstruction-era South. Although her father dubbed his favorite daughter, born just a year after the cessation of hostilities, his "peace baby," he could not protect her from the war's aftermath. Breckinridge's exposure at a young age to the deep-seated antagonisms that had ruptured the Union, decimated the Confederacy, and divided families had a profound effect on her. Instead of defending "states' rights," as so many southern whites did, Breckinridge instead, as an adult, came to advocate "an indestructible union of indestructible states" dedicated to ensuring all countries, groups, and individuals "full enjoyment of community rights" in a peaceful world.[6]

Breckinridge's opposition to militarism led her to oppose the first major international conflict of her adult life, the Spanish-American War. In April 1898, when her brother Desha enlisted, she wrote from Chicago to express her concern. "I hate the war, and feel that it is a humiliating position the country is in," she remarked. Commenting, "I know men look at things differently from women," she promised not to "nag" her brother. Nonetheless, Breckinridge was greatly relieved when Desha's training at Newport News, Virginia, delayed his service at the front. "Ella says she would much rather have you impatient than dead," she relayed their eldest sister's views in July 1898, "and we all feel that way." The "splendid little war," as President Teddy Roosevelt dubbed it, lasted for only ten weeks, and despite his eagerness to participate in the conflict, Desha returned home to Lexington without ever seeing active duty.[7]

The gender dynamics of the Breckinridge family's response to the Spanish-American War—with Ella and Nisba opposing their brother's military service—revealed not only the sisters' concern for their brother's safety but also Americans' gendered understanding of war itself. Just as many young men had regarded the Civil War as an opportunity to prove their manhood, so too did a later generation of men, like Desha Breckinridge, see in the Spanish-American War a way to mark their coming of age as adult men. More broadly, public discourse about the conflict over the fate of Cuba, the Philippines, Puerto Rico, and Guam cast the United States itself as a powerful masculine nation coming to the rescue of a feminized subject people. The gendered discussion of the conflict melded with racialized depictions of residents of the Pacific Islands and the Caribbean. By opposing the war, Breckinridge also was rejecting militaristic, imperialistic values strongly associated with masculinity and whiteness. She also began to regard her own preference for a peaceful resolution of the conflict as a distinctly female perspective on international relations. Well before the outbreak of the conflict that would become known as World War I, Breckinridge was primed to join the nation's first feminist-pacifist organization, the Woman's Peace Party.[8]

"Women's protest against war"

While Breckinridge's conviction that war was "a festering sore on the body politic" dated to her childhood and informed her response to the Spanish-American War, she became an outspoken advocate for peace in the context of feminist pacifism and World War I.[9]

By the time Breckinridge became a charter member of the Woman's Peace Party, pacifism already had established a firm foothold in the United States. However, the outbreak of war in Europe, coinciding with a burgeoning movement for woman suffrage, spurred the creation of the Woman's Peace Party, which quickly distinguished itself from other U.S. peace groups in its commitment to women's rights. The group's founding members, including Breckinridge and Addams, were veterans of the suffrage movement. When Breckinridge and Addams co-founded the Woman's Peace Party in 1915, their actions revealed the vital connection between feminism and pacifism in early twentieth-century America as well as the fault lines within the suffrage movement that required the creation of a new organization to respond to the looming conflict in Europe.[10]

In summer 1914, as the diplomatic crisis created by the assassination of Archduke Franz Ferdinand of Austria moved a complex web of European alliances in the direction of world war, Breckinridge, Addams, and other members of the Woman's City Club of Chicago were celebrating the achievement of limited suffrage for Illinois women. Both Addams and Breckinridge, who had been campaigning for municipal suffrage since 1907, were founding members of the club, established in 1910. As club president (1912–1913) and a member of the board of directors (1914–1916), Breckinridge enthusiastically supported the club's successful suffrage campaign. After Illinois women gained the right to vote in federal and municipal (but not state) elections in late 1913, Breckinridge not only edited a guidebook for women voters but also ran for a seat as a city alderman. While she was unsuccessful in her bid for office, she continued to urge Illinois women to register to vote, inform themselves about the issues, and go to the polls.[11]

Although engrossed in local suffrage politics, Breckinridge and her fellow clubwomen were keenly aware of alarming developments overseas. After Austria-Hungary declared war on Serbia on July 28, 1914, the situation in Europe escalated rapidly as preexisting alliances drew additional nations into the conflict. "Everything is swamped by the war news," Breckinridge reflected in a letter to her sister-in-law on August 1, 1914—the same day that Germany declared war on Russia, initiating a series of events that led to global conflict between the Central Powers (Austria-Hungary and Germany) and the Allies (Russia, France, and the United Kingdom).[12]

The onset of hostilities, including the invasion of Serbia, Belgium, and France by the Central Powers in August and September 1914, did not deter Breckinridge and other Chicago clubwomen from advocating for women's civic engagement, however. To the contrary, in October 1914, as trench warfare raged on the western front, the club's bulletin urged its members to the polls to promote peace: "Remember that by using the ballot we are adopting the quickest method of securing peace, the surest method of assuaging suffering, and the *only* method of attaining compulsory arbitration and international courts of justice."[13]

Chicago clubwomen continued to advocate civic engagement as a solution to international conflict. In December 1914 the Woman's City Club hosted British suffragist Emmeline Pethick-Lawrence, who was then engaged in a national speaking tour to promote peaceful solutions to the war in Europe. In her address to club members on "Woman's Movement for Constructive Peace," Pethick-Lawrence articulated many of the principles that would later become staples of feminist pacifism, including the assertion that "articulate citizenship" by "the mother-half of the human race" would promote democracy, the call for democratic participation in foreign policymaking, and the demand that nations form an international body to mediate differences.[14]

Woman suffrage and world peace were closely linked at the national and international levels as well as at the local level. Both Addams and Breckinridge were well-known American suffragists. As discussed in chapter 6, in 1911 they had been elected to serve in tandem as vice presidents of the National American Woman Suffrage Association. NAWSA's president, Carrie Chapman Catt, was also closely affiliated with the International Woman Suffrage Alliance. In 1914 Catt invited Hungarian suffragist Rosika Schwimmer to speak in the United States on feminism and pacifism during the same time that a rival suffrage organization, the Women's Political Union, sponsored British feminist Pethick-Lawrence's speaking tour, which had brought her to the Chicago Woman's City Club. Afterward, Catt urged Addams to issue a call for a women's peace meeting. Addams agreed, inviting all women's organizations that had standing peace committees to convene at the New Willard Hotel in Washington, D.C., in January 1915. This meeting became the organizational conference of the national Woman's Peace Party (WPP), which elected Addams as chairperson and Breckinridge as treasurer.[15]

The Woman's Peace Party was the first U.S. pacifist group to treat "peace as a women's issue." Many members believed that women had a special responsibility to protect life and thus to prevent war. The party preamble and platform called on women, as "the mother half of humanity," to oppose the "reckless destruction" of human life that resulted from armed warfare. At the same time that they emphasized women's particular responsibility for peace work, feminist pacifists also demanded equal political rights for women. Believing that women's full participation in the political process was essential to ending global conflict, members of the Woman's Peace Party worked for both women's rights and world peace.[16]

Like many of her contemporaries in the feminist-pacifist movement, Breckinridge believed that women had a special affinity with pacifism. In part, this was because women had the most to lose in wartime. "Where force prevails," she opined, "the interests of women being dependent upon cooperation, sympathy, and good will must suffer." Unlike some members of the Woman's Peace Party, however, Breckinridge eschewed "maternalist" arguments for pacifism. Instead, she argued that it was her professional identity as a social worker, rather than her biological identity as a potential mother, that fueled her commitment to peaceful resolution of conflict. She averred: "Both as a woman and as a social worker, the barbarities, cruelties, and fatalities of war are, of course, especially obvious to me."[17]

While Breckinridge's emphasis on social work reflected her commitment to the emerging profession, many other feminist pacifists shared her interest in social welfare and social justice. Indeed, many members of the Woman's Peace Party were drawn to pacifism, in part, by their conviction that women had a special responsibility to ensure the highest possible quality of life to all people. Moreover, they believed that inequality itself—whether within or among nations—was one of the "fundamental causes of war." To avoid war and promote peace, they regarded a democracy with "no limitations of race, color, class or sex" as "essential." Thus, an important ingredient in their "distinctive and most earnest appeal as women" was to "protest against war and all that makes for war," including "race prejudice," "territorial aggression," "imperialistic policies," "economic exploitation," "secret diplomacy," "vast armies," and "a narrow patriotism unchastened by the spirit of world fraternity."[18]

Soon after participating in the creation of the Woman's Peace Party, Breckinridge and Addams represented the new organization at the International Congress of Women at The Hague. The congress enthusiastically adopted many of the measures proposed by the U.S. representatives, including the "Principles for a Permanent Peace," modeled on the Woman's Peace Party's "Program for Constructive Peace," that called for the creation of an international peacekeeping body as well

At the International Congress of Woman at The Hague, Breckinridge and her fellow delegates from the Woman's Peace Party proposed "Principles for a Permanent Peace." Breckinridge herself introduced the resolution demanding that national governments should submit international disagreements for peaceful arbitration. Subsequently, Breckinridge and fellow members of the Woman's Peace Party attempted to persuade President Woodrow Wilson to serve as a neutral mediator in the European conflict. Instead, in the aftermath of escalating German aggression, Wilson encouraged the U.S. Congress to declare war.

Courtesy Women's International League for Peace and Freedom Collection, Special Collections and University Archives, University of Illinois at Chicago Library

as for national self-determination for all countries and equal political participation for women. Breckinridge personally introduced the resolution demanding that, in the future, national governments should submit international disputes for peaceful arbitration. After returning home to Chicago, Breckinridge carefully typed out all the resolutions from the International Congress of Women.[19]

Following the congress, two delegations made a total of thirty-five visits to political and religious leaders of neutral and belligerent nations alike. When Addams, who participated in the visits, returned home, she did so as the first president of the new International Committee of Women for Permanent Peace (later the Women's International League for Peace and Freedom, or WILPF).[20]

Meanwhile, back in Chicago, Breckinridge used her position at the Chicago School of Civics and Philanthropy to advance pacifism. In summer 1915 the school offered a public lecture series on pacifism. Breckinridge delivered the commencement address for the "peace course" based on her experiences at The Hague. She also continued to serve as treasurer of the Woman's Peace Party.[21]

While founded as a U.S. organization, the Woman's Peace Party always had internationalist tendencies. After all, American women's participation in the pacifist movement owed much to the outreach efforts of European feminist pacifists. Moreover, feminist pacifists regarded internationalism as essential to promoting peaceful resolutions to international conflict and thereby preventing warfare. The International Congress of Women strengthened the internationalist tendencies of the Woman's Peace Party by bringing U.S. feminist pacifists into personal contact with their European counterparts. While some of these women were already acquainted through their participation in the suffrage movement or in social work circles, the congress strengthened preexisting ties and created new ones. The creation of WILPF formalized this growing international feminist pacifist movement.[22]

Affiliation with WILPF strengthened the U.S. group's internationalism. It also firmly committed members to both pacifism and feminism. Although local affiliates had considerable latitude to set their own priorities, the national organization (WILPF-U.S.) insisted on "substantial" agreement with the international group's two chief priorities: political power for women and peaceful resolution of conflicts. The dual demands for woman suffrage and world peace had stirred controversy at the International Congress of Women. The Woman's Peace Party also struggled with this issue as members debated the relative importance of pacifism and feminism.[23]

The movements for woman suffrage and world peace converged—and sometimes conflicted—in the Woman's Peace Party. At the organizational meeting in January 1915 delegates had easily and unanimously agreed upon the goals of arms limitation, international law, and neutral mediation. But the demand for woman suffrage had aroused controversy from the outset. Even though the woman suffrage plank was officially adopted, some members of the group continued to object to the emphasis on women's rights.[24]

At the first annual meeting of the Woman's Peace Party after it had affiliated with the International Committee of Women for a Permanent Peace, held in Washington, D.C., in January 1916, attendees vigorously debated the international group's requirement that affiliated organizations support woman suffrage as well as world peace. In the ensuing discussion, Breckinridge and Addams sought to persuade participants to support affiliation with the international group. Ultimately, the U.S. group not only supported affiliation but also voted overwhelmingly to maintain the language about membership being contingent upon being "substantially" in agreement with the international priorities.[25]

Although WPP/WILPF-U.S.'s refusal to compromise on woman suffrage may have alienated some potential members, its inclusive definition of pacifism appealed to many others. While demanding substantial support for the central aims of the international organization, the WPP did not insist that U.S. members support "in full" the official platform, which included arms limitation, international law, economic diplomacy, and opposition to militarism as well as "the further humanizing of governments by the extension of the franchise to women." As the platform pamphlet stated, "We have sunk all differences of opinion on minor matters and given freedom of expression to a wide divergence of opinion in the details of our platform . . . in a common desire to make our woman's protest against war and all that makes for war, vocal, commanding, and effective."[26]

Despite the emphasis on diversity and compromise, the group's commitment to both pacifism and feminism continued to excite controversy. In June 1916 the WPP executive board held a meeting in conjunction with delegates for the International Committee of Women for Permanent Peace. Acting in a dual capacity as an executive board member of the WPP as well as a delegate for the international committee, Breckinridge read reports from similar delegations in Great Britain, Denmark, Norway, and Hungary. A lively discussion followed as those in attendance debated whether or not the U.S. chapter of the international group should combine with other reform organizations and groups concerned with related issues, including "the Socialists, the Jews, Labor, Suffragists, etc." Differentiating themselves from both male pacifist groups and nonpacifist women's groups, the WPP determined that their organization "should keep itself distinct" from other types of reform groups. "Our special relationships would be with peace and suffrage organizations," they declared.[27]

Despite internal differences, the Woman's Peace Party quickly became the largest pacifist organization in the United States. Within a year of its founding, the party had attracted a national membership of forty thousand women organized in more than two hundred local branches and affiliated groups spanning the entire nation.[28]

"Constructive internationalism"

The Woman's Peace Party took the lead in attempts to find a peaceful solution to the ongoing war, which quickly involved Asia and Africa as well as Europe. After

Addams's return to the United States, Breckinridge and Addams worked with members of the Chicago and New York branches of both the Woman's Peace Party and the American Peace Society (a mixed-gender group) to pressure President Woodrow Wilson to intervene in the European conflict as a neutral intermediary. At a meeting held "in the headquarters of the peace forces"—the WPP's Chicago office—Addams selected Breckinridge and Grace Abbott as the other female members of the gender-balanced committee assigned to consult with other pacifists within and beyond the U.S. on strategies to "make propositions to the belligerenets [sic] in the spirit of constructive internationalism." As the memoranda detailing the decision explained, those selected needed to be "American citizens of recognized international spirit and qualified because of their genuine experience in great human activities inherently international in character."[29]

The idea of a "negotiated peace" may seem quixotic in hindsight. Yet for the first two-and-a-half years of the bloody conflict—prior to the U.S. entry into the war in spring 1917—a variety of pacifist groups and individuals in the United States and Europe advanced proposals for a mechanism by which mediation could end the bloodshed. Advocates of a negotiated peace hoped that one or more national leaders, working in conjunction with some sort of governmental, quasi-official, or private commission, could intervene and bring the war to a swift end, preventing additional loss of life and paving the way for a "new diplomacy," based on international law and voluntary arbitration, that would ensure lasting peace.[30]

The Woman's Peace Party, which had endorsed the mediation movement in its official platform, led these efforts in the United States. Throughout the war, WPP representatives maintained steady pressure on President Wilson, as the leader of the largest and most powerful of the neutral nations, to intervene in the war either in conjunction with other neutral nations or independently. Wilson had made initial overtures in this direction at the war's outset, but his offer was rebuffed. Thereafter, Wilson adopted a pose of watchful waiting. Although he steadfastly maintained his intention to offer mediation when the time seemed propitious, that time never arrived. However, Wilson's willingness to meet with pacifist delegations, his cordial relationship with Addams, and his assurances that he considered the women's proposals at The Hague "by far the best formulation" for world peace, encouraged the pacifist women to continue their efforts.[31]

Although she evidently never had a personal audience with the president, Breckinridge eagerly engaged in the "citizen diplomacy" practiced by feminist pacifists throughout World War I. The first documented instance of her efforts to directly affect foreign policy, in 1915, demonstrated her commitment to the antipreparedness movement as well as her interest in international mediation.

The antipreparedness movement was separate from, but related to, the mediation movement. Regarding the European arms race of the previous decades as a contributing factor to the outbreak of war—as well as a major reason for the tremendous casualties in the trenches—antipreparedness advocates sought to prevent a military buildup in the United States. Their mission took on new urgency after a German submarine torpedoed and sank a British ship, the *Lusitania*, in May 1915. As American public opinion shifted away from neutrality and toward preparedness, antipreparedness forces established the American Union Against Militarism. Breckinridge was one of the original members and an executive officer of the new organization.[32]

For many pacifists, antipreparedness and mediation went hand in hand. After all, the U.S. president's credibility as a peacemaker would suffer if he seemed to be compromising his commitment to neutrality. Thus, in the aftermath of the *Lusitania* episode, Breckinridge and other members of the Woman's Peace Party urged Wilson to steer clear of what they called "a preposterous 'preparedness' against hypothetical dangers" and instead to provide "the epochal service which this world crisis offers for the establishment of permanent peace"—that is, to offer his services to mediate the ongoing conflict.[33]

Breckinridge's initial forays into "foreign policy feminism" may not have brought her into the Oval Office in person, but they did familiarize her with the U.S. House of Representatives' Committee of Foreign Affairs. In 1916 Breckinridge, Addams, and other representatives of the Woman's Peace Party testified before the committee on behalf of two bills they believed would prevent future armed conflicts. Breckinridge's testimony on these occasions indicated her determination to translate feminist-pacifist principles into feminist foreign policy.[34]

Breckinridge's first appearance before the Committee of Foreign Affairs occurred in January 2016. On this occasion, which coincided with a meeting of the Woman's Peace Party in Washington, D.C., Breckinridge and her fellow feminist pacifists offered support for a House joint resolution proposal to establish a "Commission for Enduring Peace." Breckinridge's address included a review of "the fundamentals of government organization" that amounted to a primer of political theory, including explanations of Montesquieu's notion of "a government of laws and not of men," the English government's "King's Peace," and the U.S. "separation of powers." Informing the committee that "all the women in the country" were familiar with these principles, she suggested that planning for peace was simple common sense. "Therefore, if you would start upon a program of world organization you will find that these women can not quite see why you could not apply the very same line of reasoning and justice" to contemporary conflicts, she concluded.[35]

In December 1916 Breckinridge and other delegates from the Woman's Peace Party again appeared before the Committee on Foreign Affairs, this time in support of a bill to provide for a commission on relations between the United States and "the Orient" (China and Japan). Breckinridge and her colleagues urged the committee to establish a commission to consult with "authorities, high in the service of their respective countries," rather than relying on rumor and innuendo, to guide foreign policy in the Far East. Moreover, they suggested that if such a commission had been established to regulate relations among European countries, the current war might have been averted.[36]

Breckinridge's testimony on these occasions displayed her familiarity with political theory, supporting her contention that American women were informed, intelligent citizens who deserved a voice in the government, even if they did not yet have the right to vote. She also indicated her commitment to internationalism and the rule of law by highlighting her interest in creating a "world organization" to prevent future wars. Finally, Breckinridge's comments demonstrated that progressives' faith in expert knowledge as the basis for social reform easily translated into pacifists' belief in fact-finding commissions as the basis for foreign policy. While the Woman's Peace Party did not succeed in convincing the Committee on Foreign Affairs to adopt their proposals, the principles that Breckinridge and her fellow WPP members outlined for the committee would continue to inform women's distinctive approach to international relations.

"Patriotic women"

Despite their best efforts, American pacifists were unable either to halt the ongoing war or to prevent the United States' entry into it. Proponents of mediation seemed on the brink of success in late 1916 and early 1917, when Wilson sent a "peace note" to Germany and delivered an address touting the idea of "peace without victory" in the U.S. Senate. Ironically, just a week later, the German government, which had seemed to be on the verge of welcoming mediation, announced a new policy of unrestricted naval warfare. Once German U-boats began to sink U.S. ships, Wilson abandoned his earlier commitment to neutrality. In April 1917, he asked Congress to declare war on Germany.[37]

Breckinridge and other pacifist women found themselves helpless to avert U.S. entry into the war. As Breckinridge later recalled, "We knew . . . what it meant to us as women and as social workers to have war anywhere and especially for the United States to participate. The sad thing was that not even Miss Addams could speak so that what we said would be heard. And it is no comfort, only a crushing source of humiliation, to be able to now [in 1936] to say that 'we told you so in 1915, '16, and '17!' It was a war that no one now wants to claim and those who foresaw are perhaps in some ways unhappier than those who did not understand."[38]

In the weeks leading up to the United States' entry into the war in April 1917, disagreements between pacifists and militarists were intense. Some, like Wisconsin senator Robert La Follette, regarded intervention in the European war as an ill-disguised attempt to protect U.S. capitalist interests overseas. He therefore opposed the Armed Shipping Bill, a measure intended to promote military preparedness that was debated in Congress in March 1917. Breckinridge, who had expressed similar concerns before the Committee on Foreign Affairs the previous year, was "inexpressibly grateful" to Senator La Follette for his steadfast opposition to U.S. involvement in the war, even in the form of "armed neutrality." Breckinridge praised the senator's "valiant courage" in the face of overwhelming pressure to support President Wilson's increasingly hawkish foreign policy and urged him to "carry on the struggle in whatever new shape it may assume."[39]

Disagreements over "preparedness" not only led to debates in Congress but also weakened and split many peace organizations in the months leading up to U.S. entry into the war. These struggles highlighted divisions within women's rights organizations about the relative importance of pacifism and feminism. Such conflicts, which had been present since the founding of the Woman's Peace Party, shattered the fragile accord that feminist pacifists had achieved during the period of neutrality, requiring women activists to take sides on U.S. entry into World War I.[40]

The U.S. declaration of war thus was a critical moment for women activists. Feminists and pacifists alike disagreed among themselves about what position to take on war service. Without consulting the membership, Carrie Chapman Catt committed the mainstream woman suffrage organization to the war effort. Writing "as an individual suffragist and not as a member of the Woman's Peace Party," Breckinridge chided Catt, "protesting against her action in offering the services of the National [American Woman Suffrage Association] for war and relief work." Catt angrily defended herself and asked to have her name removed from WPP letterhead. After Catt's departure from the WPP, she organized a Woman's Committee (or Division) of the Council of National Defense, which she chaired.[41]

At the other end of the spectrum, the New York branch of the Woman's Peace Party adopted a "nonresister" stance, asserting, "We should enter into no sort of war work direct or indirect," including relief work. So-called nonresister organizations insisted that members should not aid any war in any way for any reason; this meant that members should not only abstain from defense work such as in the munitions industry but also should not participate in war relief work such as that provided by the Red Cross. Nonresisters also objected to international peacekeeping bodies since these used coercion to regulate international relations.[42]

In response to these challenges, Addams appointed a select committee, including Breckinridge, to offer suggestions for wartime activities for Woman's Peace Party members. The committee's "Suggestions for Work in War Time" emphasized the importance of continuing to support such peacetime progressive reforms as promoting child welfare, maintaining labor standards, and protecting immigrant rights. The group also suggested countering war fever by opposing military training in schools and defending the civil liberties of war protesters and draft resistors. Although intended for the Chicago group, because of the overlap between the Chicago branch and the national board, these recommendations were widely circulated throughout the nation.[43]

Breckinridge and Addams also collaborated closely with each other and with other WPP members about phrasing and issuing an official (and vague) "statement of principles" for the national organization. Writing from her colleague Marion Talbot's New Hampshire vacation home in September 1917, Breckinridge responded to one of Addams's frequent queries: "I accept the suggestion of Mrs. [Lucia Ames] Mead about substituting milder terms for demands and I am always glad to put in Mrs. [Alice Thacher] Post's commas and semi-colons[.]" After a meeting of the WPP's executive board in October the group issued an official statement defining the group's purpose in the broadest possible terms: "Our business is to help mitigate all horrors of war."[44]

Breckinridge thus played a key role in helping the Woman's Peace Party to stake out a middle ground between NAWSA's unqualified support for the war effort and the nonresisters' absolute opposition to any war-related activity. The moderate pacifism espoused by the WPP was reflected in a brochure titled "A Program During Wartime," in which the organization reaffirmed its commitment to peaceful solutions to war, international cooperation, civil liberties, and human welfare while also proclaiming the WPP's patriotism. By coming out in support of Wilson's Fourteen Points in January 1918, the organization reiterated its commitment to peaceful resolution of international conflict while also acknowledging the United States' entry into the war. For the most part, however, the WPP was conspicuously quiet during the war years. Ostensibly, the national board focused on international issues, leaving local branches to work out their own responses to the situation. This left individuals like Breckinridge in a tenuous position as they sought new ways to reconcile patriotism and pacifism.[45]

Pacifism of any stripe was not a popular stance in wartime America. After the United States formally declared war on Germany in April 1917, pressure to support the war intensified with the adoption of the Alien and Sedition Acts, which made opposition to the war and criticism of the wartime president federal offenses punishable by up to ten years in federal prison. The WPP and its leaders came under government surveillance, and membership declined. At the Chicago headquarters, Addams recalled, "the door was often befouled in hideous ways." Both government repression and popular opinion forced what remained of the WPP to retrench. Many branches simply disbanded; others vigorously debated whether war relief work was appropriate for WPP members. Addams, as the head of the organization, found herself branded "the most dangerous woman in America."[46]

Breckinridge, like Addams, continued her commitment to pacifism despite widespread suspicion of Americans who refused to support the war effort. The fact that both the University of Chicago and the Chicago School of Civics and Philanthropy offered special courses to prepare for defense work highlighted Breckinridge's difficult situation. The University of Chicago relaxed guidelines about student course load in order to encourage every student to take at least one course to prepare for "patriotic service." Meanwhile, the CSCP began a special series of courses on public nursing and war service that drew more than five hundred students in a single year, 1918.[47] As assistant dean of women at the University of Chicago, Breckinridge was charged with advising students to enroll in war-related courses. As dean of the School of Civics and Philanthropy, she was responsible for balancing the budget, and she understood that the CSCP's always-shaky funding would fail completely without these special courses. This was a precarious situation indeed for a committed pacifist.

Nationwide, public intellectuals and university faculty enthusiastically supported military intervention and joined new government agencies that geared the nation's research institutions toward the war effort. At the University of Chicago, as well, the pressure to respond to the exigencies of war was intense. University of Chicago president Harry Pratt Judson published a prowar pamphlet, *Threat of German World Politics*; supported the creation of a Department of Military Science and a Reserve Officers Training Corps (ROTC) on campus; committed the university's scientific laboratories to war-related research; and encouraged faculty to sign up for the 4-Minute Man program, a series of brief but compelling prowar speeches. With the exception of a few notable dissenters such as John Dewey and Thorstein Veblen, most University of Chicago faculty vigorously supported the war effort. Professor H. B. Clark gave a speech that was approvingly quoted in a newspaper article titled: "You Are Either All American or All Traitor, There Is No Middle of the Road." Female faculty and students at the University of Chicago also joined the campaign. Faculty member Elizabeth Wallace appealed to "all patriotic women of the University of Chicago" to take a pledge of loyalty to the president and the flag and to engage in war-related work. Wallace also recruited students to join the Woman Students' Training Corps, an organization similar to the ROTC, which sponsored military drill activities.[48]

In this atmosphere, Breckinridge's association with Addams, arguably the nation's most well-known pacifist, aroused concerns on campus. In August 1917 Wallace objected to a campus reception in honor of Addams that Breckinridge and Talbot had arranged. As soon as she saw the announcement in the university calendar, Wallace fired off a memo to the university president: "It seems to me ill-advised, to say the least, to give her any special distinction at the present moment," she pronounced. The reception was held as planned, however; Talbot proudly reported that a crowd of five hundred people "seemed highly appreciative of the opportunity of meeting Miss Addams." To reassure President Judson, she added, "There was no demonstration of any kind and every thing went off in a way that I am sure would have been pleasing to you. There was a peculiar lack, I should say, of special interest in her peace activities"; rather, at least according to Talbot, the assembled crowd wanted to meet Addams as "the devoted worker in behalf of social justice." Referring to Wallace's rumor-mongering, she assured the president that columns in the Chicago *Tribune* critical of Addams were "malicious and deliberate untruths" that did not warrant the university's attention or concern.[49]

Talbot also acted to reassure the president and other critics by co-founding a new organization, Woman's War Aid of the University of Chicago. This group offered a more nuanced approach than Wallace's ultra-patriotism. Rather than establishing an auxiliary ROTC and holding military drills, participants established a branch of the Red Cross and studied proposals for what would become the League of Nations. Instead of taking a loyalty oath, female students and faculty wives who joined the group pledged, "[I will] do all in my power to build a new social order based, not on mutual distrust and selfish competition, but on confidence and good-will, upon the spirit of service and co-operation." Moreover, the organization specifically opposed nativism, including in the pledge a promise "to establish friendly relations with persons whose families came to this country more recently . . . and in this and every possible way to help promote a feeling of international sympathy." Although Breckinridge's name does not appear in the memo detailing the group's founding, her influence is clear in these passages. Portions of the pledge referring to child welfare, school nursing, and infant health also reflected Breckinridge's close relationship with the Children's Bureau.[50]

Hull House alumna Julia Lathrop, Breckinridge's former employer and now head of the U.S. Children's Bureau, praised the pledge. Concerned that the defense effort might undermine legislation regulating working hours and conditions for women and children, she made a pointed suggestion for the pledge: "I hope it will be construed to include a definite effort to keep up in every way standards of industrial protection. . . . [which] should not be lightly thrown aside at the outset of the war."[51]

"Industrial protection" provided a way for Breckinridge to engage in war service without supporting the war effort. Building on her earlier efforts on behalf of protective legislation, Breckinridge joined the Woman's Division of the Council of National Defense (the group founded by Carrie Chapman Catt after she left the WPP), serving on that organization's Committee on Women in Industry. The

committee conducted in-depth investigations of conditions in defense industries, such as the factories that produced navy uniforms, where women made up
a majority of the workforce. Their final report called attention to poor working
conditions and racial discrimination in war industries and argued that wartime
conditions did not justify relaxing workplace regulations.[52]

Public health and public welfare also offered a form of wartime patriotism
that was palatable to moderate pacifists like Breckinridge. In the Department of
Household Administration at the University of Chicago, Breckinridge taught a
special course on "social service in war time"; a similar course titled "Modern Care
of Families in Distress" prepared students to engage in social welfare investigation
and treatment in a variety of venues, including the American Red Cross.[53]

Even though they brought her into contact and even cooperation with supporters of U.S. involvement in the war, Breckinridge's war-time activities were entirely
consistent with the moderate pacifism espoused by the Woman's Peace Party.
(Given Breckinridge's role in designing official materials for both the national
organization and the Chicago branch, this was perhaps to be expected.) The Chicago group had issued a "Declaration of Principles" reaffirming the goal of "permanent peace" while also making "suggestions for work in war time." Although
the WPP remained adamantly antimilitaristic—as manifested, for instance, in
its opposition to military training in public schools—Breckinridge's branch also
carefully pointed out that pacifism was entirely compatible with "civilian relief,"
such as work through the Red Cross, and public welfare work, such as "industrial
protection." This position defined a positive role for pacifist patriots as engaged
citizens and public servants, rather than only a negative definition of pacifism as
opposition to U.S. military involvement.[54]

While Breckinridge engaged in her own forms of patriotic pacifism and helped
shape the Chicago WPP's wartime stance, her younger sister, Curry, served as a
Red Cross nurse in France. Curry had followed in her older sister's footsteps by
seeking advanced education in Chicago and dedicating her life to public service.
After acquiring her nursing degree from the Presbyterian Hospital Training School
in 1908, she worked first in a state hospital for the mentally ill in Illinois and then
in a tuberculosis sanitarium in Michigan. During World War I she spent twenty-six
months in France working in Red Cross hospitals before returning to the United
States to seek treatment for heart problems. Despite the best medical care and her
sister's personal attention, she died at Chicago Presbyterian Hospital, the same
hospital where she had completed her nurses' training, in June 1918.[55] Emphasizing
the nurturing rather than militaristic nature of this service, one admirer decorated
a page in her souvenir album with a watercolor showing uniformed Red Cross
nurses assisting an injured child while men and boys rushed away bearing swords

The United States' entry into World War I ushered in a vigorous debate about the nature of pacifism and women's responsibility in wartime. Many pacifist groups split over the question of whether humanitarian aid, such as serving in the Red Cross, was appropriate for pacifists. As an officer of the Woman's Peace Party, Breckinridge helped craft statements for the group that defined a moderate pacifism that condoned nonmilitary war-related service; as the dean of the Chicago School of Civics and Philanthropy, she offered special courses on humanitarian aid in wartime. Meanwhile, her younger sister, Curry Breckinridge, served as a Red Cross nurse in France. Her premature death as a result of her wartime service strengthened Breckinridge's commitment to pacifism.

Courtesy of the Library of Congress

and flags. The artist dedicated the painting to Curry with thanks for "her goodness and the devoted care that she gave to the unfortunate wounded."[56]

The loss of her beloved sister only reinforced Breckinridge's adamant opposition to militarism. During the debates over military preparedness, a mixed-gender coalition of pacifists and progressives, including Breckinridge and Addams, had formed a new peace group, the American Union Against Militarism (AUAM). Breckinridge and other members of this organization protested civil-liberties violations such as legal harassment of conscientious objectors and deportation of suspected subversives. In accordance with these aims, the Union established a Bureau of Conscientious Objectors, which evolved into the Civil Liberties Bureau and eventually, in 1920, into the American Civil Liberties Union (ACLU).[57]

Although federal authorities initially took a tolerant view of the union's civil liberties activities, in 1918 government officials raided the organization's New York headquarters and confiscated records of its defense of pacifist, socialist, and anarchist groups and individuals. Legal harassment did not deter Breckinridge from engaging in civil liberties work, however. In addition to being a member of the Executive Committee of the American Union Against Militarism, she was executive director of the Chicago branch of the Civil Liberties Bureau and a member of the Chicago Amnesty Committee, which advocated for amnesty for political prisoners arrested under the Alien and Sedition Acts and worked on behalf of conscientious objectors.[58]

In addition, through her work with the Immigrants' Protective League, Breckinridge provided legal assistance to immigrants whose civil rights were in jeopardy in wartime. Although not officially a civil-liberties organization, the league was committed to seeking asylum for political refugees, assisting immigrants to gain entry to the United States, and preventing the deportation of immigrants under the restrictive Immigrant Act of 1917, which allowed for denial of entry to or deportation of a wide range of "undesirables," including those suspected of opposing the war. In addition, the league provided interpreters for non-English speakers at Selective Service Bureaus and helped foreign nationals gain exemptions from military service. Breckinridge's work with the league allowed her to engage in the same sorts of civil-liberties activism undertaken by groups such as the beleaguered AUAM/ACLU and a separate but similar organization, the New York Bureau of Legal Advice—which provided legal assistance to war protesters, conscientious objectors, and hyphenate Americans who were deprived of the rights of free speech, subjected to legal harassment, and threatened with deportation—without committing to the latter group's absolute opposition to Wilson and his wartime policies.[59]

Nonetheless, in a 1919 Senate Judiciary Committee hearing, Breckinridge was named, along with Addams, as one of one hundred Americans who "had not helped to win the war" and should be investigated.[60] This federal investigation marked the beginning of the postwar "Red Scare" that, as discussed below, regarded a wide range of activist women as dangers to national security. However, despite this heightened scrutiny, Breckinridge maintained her commitment to pacifist and internationalist work throughout the 1920s and 1930s.

"A peace of justice"

In late 1918, in a handwritten draft of an editorial in response to the query "What kind of peace do women want?" Breckinridge emphasized the importance of social justice. As a feminist, Breckinridge demanded fairness. "Women want a peace of justice," she insisted, defining justice as "a fair chance for all, great and small, mighty and humble, to do their part, to live their life[,] to make their contribution in a world fellowship." As a social worker, Breckinridge insisted that "ministering to the weak and needy" was essential to maintaining world peace. She extended her notion of a "national minimum" to the world stage, asserting: "Women want a peace that will make possible an international minimum standard of comfort and opportunity."[61]

Breckinridge's vision of a "peace of justice" required a "permanent peace." War, she argued, was a wrong-headed approach to resolving grievances. "War is itself a symptom, of deep seated pathology, the result of a sense of wrong, lack of facilities for adjusting conditions to need, what the social worker would describe as unsound practice, retarded diagnosis and inadequate treatment," she declared. When "a sense of an unrighted wrong" was combined with "the willingness to use force," war was the unhappy result. Therefore, the "path to peace" required a refusal to resort to force and a commitment to "international cooperation" in "investigation, diagnosis, and treatment" of social inequalities, including the exploitation of weaker nations by stronger ones. No "abstraction" such as national sovereignty or democratic government, she argued, excused "the barbarities, cruelties, and fatalities of war."[62]

While "abstractions" did not excuse militarism, Breckinridge did not shy away from abstract notions. Rather, she was an early advocate of both national self-determination and international law. Later in her life, Breckinridge stated: "I am one of those who even before 1915 hoped and who still hopes for the organization of a world state, governed by the principles of constitutional justice, sound administration and democratic recognition of the rights of all peoples."[63]

Breckinridge's profession as a social worker and her passion for social justice informed her commitment to peaceful resolution of international conflicts. It was never enough to supply basic human needs; rather, the aim of social work was to eliminate the sources of inequality and poverty. She insisted that the "enemies" of "the highest good" were "poverty and ignorance, and injustice." Social inequality, she argued, created both individual difficulties and international conflict.[64]

Breckinridge's vision of a postwar world thus included new opportunities for social work on a global scale. She hoped that a bevy of "international agencies" would "succeed the agencies developed by the Allies and the U.S. during the war" so as to "conserve those experiences, gained during the war" and "make possible an international standard of comfort and opportunity determined by the world supply of commodities and the state of the arts." She dreamed of "an international distribution of food and international sanitary police and international probation staff, and international labor department and international control of the world's highways by land and water, and international guardianship of the weaker people, [and] an international commission on resources for the benefit of the coming generations."[65]

Breckinridge's long wish list typified feminist pacifists' ambitious program for international cooperation and social justice in the postwar era. Women who had engaged in wartime pacifism were eager to prevent war by promoting social justice. They believed that equitable distribution of resources and democratic principles of national self-determination would help to eliminate sources of conflict, while mechanisms for international governance would facilitate peaceful resolutions of future conflicts.[66]

From its inception, the Woman's Peace Party had emphasized the importance of postwar planning, what it called a "program for constructive peace." This program included establishing an alliance of nations committed to "the peaceful settlement of all international disputes by means of a world court"—ideas adopted in President Wilson's Fourteen Points and eventually translated into the League of Nations. But beyond creating an international organization and equipping it with peacekeeping mechanisms, feminist pacifists also believed that it was important to foster the conditions for lasting peace. Thus, they abjured a "narrow patriotism" characterized by militarism, imperialism, and "economic exploitation" and instead promoted international cooperation, universal welfare, and "a truer and broader democracy" that "will know no limitations of race, color, class or sex." Above all, it was up to women to "lessen the bitterness and misunderstanding engendered by this war" and "save the next generation from renewing conditions that breed war."[67]

At the conclusion of the war, as "miles and miles of barbed wire [were] being rolled up in Europe," according to Grace Abbott's letters from overseas, the leaders of the "Big Four"—the United States, France, the United Kingdom, and Italy—gathered at the Paris Peace Conference in Versailles to sign peace treaties, establish new national boundaries, impose reparations on Germany, and discuss proposals for a League of Nations. Breckinridge, along with other internationalists and pacifists both in the United States and Europe, anticipated that the proposed League of Nations would prove to be an effective mechanism "for adjudication of disputes" in accordance with "international law."[68]

However, Breckinridge and her fellow feminist pacifists had higher hopes for the peace talks. Immediately after the armistice was signed on November 11, 1918, board members of the Woman's Peace Party, including Breckinridge, began to hold meetings to recommend proposals for a second International Congress of Women, to be held in Zurich at the same time that the all-male representatives of the Big Four met in Versailles. At this gathering, delegates officially established the Women's International League for Peace and Freedom. They also proposed several measures that went well beyond ending the war and establishing a League of Nations. Taking a firm antimilitarist stance, they recommended total disarmament and an end to the draft. To prevent new international conflicts, they suggested an end to purely regional diplomacy, such as the Monroe Doctrine, as well as ending the practice of protecting capitalist interests through foreign policy. To promote social justice, they demanded the abolition of child labor and the adoption of a "world economy" that would equitably distribute "the necessities of life" to all people. Finally, the assembled delegates adopted a "Women's Charter" that demanded not only "full equal suffrage" for women but also "the full equality of women with men politically, socially and economically."[69]

Women's high hopes for creating conditions for a lasting peace met with disappointment, however. The delegates to the second International Congress of Women, held in Zurich in May 1919, protested the terms of the Versailles Treaty, especially its prejudicial treatment of Germany. Feminist pacifists protested both the denial of League of Nations membership to Germany and the demand that Germany pay reparations. They also expressed disappointment that the treaty disregarded the principle of national self-determination and the peace talks' failure to address issues such as child labor, arms reduction, and women's rights. American feminist pacifists confronted further disappointment later that year when the U.S. Congress voted against joining the League of Nations.[70]

Despite these disappointments, feminist pacifists were determined to continue their work in the aftermath of World War I. By the end of the war, Breckinridge's name was well known in pacifist and feminist circles, including among the outspoken antiwar women of New York. When the WPP officially changed its name to the Women's International League for Peace and Freedom, Section for the United States (WILPF-U.S.) and moved from Chicago to Washington, D.C., New York member and U.S. chair Anna Garlin Spencer proposed that Breckinridge become the new chair of the organization. "My first choice of all American women I am frank to say would be Miss Breckinridge," Spencer wrote to Addams "in the strictest confidence." Acknowledging Breckinridge's residence and responsibilities in

Chicago, Spencer hoped that with skilled support staff "the office of Chairman would not be so exacting and it would not be necessary to have the Chairman live in the same city as the Headquarters," and "then the Chairman could be chosen just because she was wise, well-known and beloved, wherever she resided."[71]

However, contrary to Spencer's suggestions, Breckinridge could not "find time and strength to undertake that office." At the time, as detailed in chapter 5, she was deeply invested in the transformation of the Chicago School of Civics and Philanthropy into the University of Chicago's School of Social Service Administration, a move that significantly advanced both her own professional status and the professionalization of social work. Although Breckinridge always insisted that social workers should concern themselves with welfare policy and international affairs rather than concentrate exclusively on case work and direct services, she found her niche as an academic rather than as an activist.

Breckinridge was an activist academic, however. Just as she fused her dedication to social work and social reform in the domestic arena, she also combined her career in social work with her commitment to social justice in international context. In the postwar years, she sought to realize the feminist-pacifist movement ideal of constructing a durable peace by promoting social justice on an international scale.

"We are all marching together"

Building on ideas they had begun to develop in the heady days of the organization's founding, Breckinridge and other members of the Woman's Peace Party were eager to enact their full program for permanent peace. The "constructive pacifism" they envisioned carved out a place for women in international affairs. Still excluded from the highest levels of foreign policy even after the achievement of woman suffrage, women like Breckinridge hoped to advance international cooperation by engaging in "constructive social reform" abroad as well as at home.[72]

Breckinridge and other feminist pacifists continued to promote their vision of a peaceful postwar world in the 1920s. In 1923 Breckinridge and Addams discussed submitting "our" set of principles for the American Peace Award, a prize offered by former *Ladies' Home Journal* editor Edward W. Bok for a "practicable plan" for peace. The plan that Breckinridge and Addams proposed called for the United States to join the World Court and the League of Nations. The ultimate winner of the prize, male pacifist Charles Herbert Levermore, made similar suggestions. However, Breckinridge and Addams also demanded that the U.S. military refrain from defending the interests of private businesses abroad, that the U.S. end the production and the sale of armaments, and that the U.S. cooperate with other nations in a process of universal disarmament. Significantly—and reflecting both feminist pacifists' concerns at the time of the Paris Peace Conference and the worsening economic distress in postwar Germany—they also recommended "cancelling or reducing debts due to the United States" from the other Allied countries in return for an agreement to "divide the costs of commissions hitherto charged against Germany alone equally between Germany and the former allies" and offering "a long moratorium to Germany" to allow that nation "eventually to pay the balance on her reparations debt as estimated by an impartial commission of experts to be constituted for the purpose." Their plan thus called for the United States to promote peace not only by agreeing to abide by arbitration in future disputes but also by removing the reasons for rising resentment in Germany that would soon allow Adolf Hitler to rise to power.[73]

Whether "practicable" or not, feminist pacifists' plans were not put into place. Thus, Breckinridge and her fellow internationalists sought other avenues for promoting peace in the postwar era. Many feminist pacifists were concerned with the urgent need for humanitarian aid in war-torn Europe. International WILPF leaders determined that the organization should not engage in direct relief but instead address the underlying causes of suffering, such as war. However, national chapters—including WILPF-U.S.—and individual members of the organization—including Addams—were at the forefront of efforts to address food shortages in postwar Europe.[74]

Many pacifist feminists, like Addams, saw the problem of hunger as a major obstacle to a peaceful future. They critiqued the Allied forces' blockade of Central Europe and urged the victorious and the vanquished countries alike to "develop the inter-allied organisations formed for the purposes of war into an international organization for purposes of peace, so that the resources of the world—food, raw materials, finance, transport—shall be made available for the relief of the people of all countries from famine and pestilence."[75]

In keeping with her social work background and her social justice principles, Breckinridge fully supported such initiatives. She was convinced that the inequitable division of resources, whether within or among nations, not only created individual difficulties but also contributed to international disputes. By engaging in international social work, which fused humanitarian aid with international pacifism, she took feminist pacifism to its logical conclusion in the postwar era.

In the 1920s Breckinridge was an integral part of a growing international network of social justice feminists who promoted both social welfare policies and the social work profession. In the late nineteenth and early twentieth centuries, social welfare programs and social work education developed in tandem on both sides of the Atlantic. In the United States, Great Britain, France, and Germany, social workers, clubwomen, and feminist activists collaborated in establishing nascent welfare states. Healthcare services for pregnant and nursing women, infants and small children, and schoolchildren were especially widespread, reflecting pronatalist ideology and concerns about depopulation as well as responding to shockingly high infant death rates. Several countries also adopted mothers' pensions and protective legislation for women and children. France even provided paid maternity leave and public childcare for working mothers. Although specifics varied from country to country, in all of these nations social work developed as a women's profession closely associated with women's voluntary associations and organized feminism. To lay claim to authority within national welfare policy or to establish "shadow welfare states" in nations lacking such policies, voluntary women's associations and professional social work organizations used both the language of maternalism, which valorized women's role as mothers and applied it to society more broadly as "social mothers," and the discourse of social science, which allowed educated women to claim a role in public policy as social workers. Breckinridge, as an advocate of social science research as the basis for social service programs, fell in the latter camp.[76]

Social work educators and social justice advocates held numerous international gatherings of social welfare professionals to exchange information about each nation's social welfare programs and social work education. These interwar gatherings formalized the preexisting ties among pacifist feminists around the world and emphasized international cooperation as the key to both social welfare and world peace. As one fellow reformer in England wrote to Breckinridge and Abbott about a joint trip to Europe in 1923: "I am so glad you are making this trip to the continent at this critical moment for you will do so much on your return to make America appreciate the situation and recall her to a sense of her obligations in relation to it."[77]

Throughout the 1920s, Breckinridge attended numerous European conferences on issues such as prison reform, immigration policy, and child welfare. Revealing the continuity between women's participation in international social work circles and their involvement in the international peace movement, at the First General Congress on Child Welfare, held in Geneva, Switzerland, in 1925, Breckinridge urged national governments to accept responsibility for "permanent adequate support" for mothers' and children's healthcare and economic security—a position that was consistent with the "Woman's Charter" proposed at the 1919 Congress of Women in Zurich, which had included a call for "adequate economic provision for the service of motherhood."[78]

The culmination of these international gatherings was the First International Conference of Social Work (ICSW), held in Paris in July 1928 in conjunction with several other international congresses addressing a range of topics, including public assistance, affordable housing, and child welfare. Approximately half of the more than five thousand delegates attending the "Social Welfare Fortnight" attended the inaugural ICSW. Together with Alice Salomon of Germany and Alice Masaryk of Czechoslovakia, Breckinridge was one of the leaders of the First International Congress of Social Work. She was also vice chairperson of the section on social work education, out of which came the International Committee (later Association) of Schools of Social Work (IASSW). The new organization facilitated the exchange of students, faculty, and ideas across national boundaries, primarily in Europe and the United States.[79]

In keeping with her priorities at the School of Social Service Administration, Breckinridge urged her European colleagues to give equal attention to direct services, social science, and public policy. "The Social Research Field is an essential portion of the Social Work field and sound education for it is available and necessary," she declared. In addition to promoting international social work education, Breckinridge was an eloquent spokesperson for international cooperation. "It has been suggested that the Americans have come here with an idea that they are in the forefront of this great effort," she addressed the assembled delegates, representing forty-two countries. "We do not feel that we are in the forefront," Breckinridge pronounced. "We are all marching together."[80]

"Setting our own house in order"

Breckinridge's participation in international social work circles added a new dimension to her work as a social work professional by highlighting the ways in which social welfare agencies and social work education could facilitate international cooperation. It also indicated the international implications of Breckinridge's longstanding interest in immigrants. While this connection was highlighted by a trip that Breckinridge and Abbott made to Geneva in 1927 to attend the International Conference of Private Organizations for the Protection of Migrants, Breckinridge did not have to travel abroad to promote immigrant welfare.[81]

At home in Chicago, she continued to protect immigrants' rights and to promote their welfare. Her work with immigrants had important internationalist dimensions. She had long drawn connections between U.S. immigration policy and international relations. When she testified before the Committee on Foreign Affairs in 1916, she had urged reconsideration of a proposal, originally introduced by former President Taft in 1914, to give the federal government responsibility to "protect" foreign nationals residing in the United States. Only by "setting our own house in order," she quoted Taft, could the U.S. government play an effective leadership role in international affairs.[82]

In the aftermath of World War I, Breckinridge worked with the Immigrants' Protective League in efforts to reunite family members separated as a consequence of the conflict. Many Assyrians and Armenians who had been driven from their home countries during the war found themselves unable to join family members who had come to the United States before the war because of the restrictive immigration quota, which resulted in a thirteen-year waiting list even for the "preferred class" of would-be immigrants who were parents or children of naturalized U.S. citizens. These problems were compounded by the wartime destruction of Armenian records, making it impossible for Armenian Americans to provide official documentation of the age and identity of family members.[83]

Throughout the 1920s, as immigration policy became increasingly restrictive, Breckinridge was an outspoken advocate for immigrants. As discussed in chapter 6, she sought to modify laws relating to immigration and citizenship through her work with both the League of Women Voters and the Illinois Joint Committee to Secure Legislation to Unite Families Separated by the Restrictive Immigration Act.[84] She also continued her work with the Immigrants' Protective League, which documented and deplored a series of "deportation drives" fueled by fears of subversives in the 1920s and 1930s.[85] And she worked with the Immigrants' Protective League, the Illinois League of Women Voters, and local women's clubs to promote an adult education bill to provide public schooling to immigrants.[86] Breckinridge also used her professional prowess to influence public opinion. In her 1921 study of immigrants, *New Homes for Old*, she reminded her readers: "We are all 'pilgrims and strangers.'"[87]

"A new international order"

Breckinridge also used her status as an educator to promote "international understanding and friendship." In 1926, for instance, she traveled to Holland to represent the American Association of University Women at a gathering of the International Federation of Women, whose members promoted world peace and attempted to forge a "transnational identity." As a charter member of the Illinois League of Women Voters, she also may have helped organize a "week-end school of foreign affairs" held in Chicago in 1929 as part of the national organization's postwar efforts to promote "international friendliness between women, and through women, between their governments."[88]

Perhaps the most significant of Breckinridge's educational efforts was the International Summer School on the theme of "A New International Order" that she directed in 1924 on behalf of the U.S. chapter of the Women's International League for Peace and Freedom. Created for foreign delegates to WILPF's Fourth International Congress, which was held in Washington, D.C., the summer school was open to "men and women of every nationality, race, or creed." In addition to reports from the delegates to the congress, who traveled from the congress to Chicago aboard a charter railway car, the *Pax Special*, the summer school included lectures and workshops on a wide range of subjects, including "the historic, legal, and political bases of internationalism." Among featured speakers were distinguished professors at well-regarded universities and activists from the labor, civil rights, and women's movements, as well as representatives of a variety of peace groups.[89]

Breckinridge continued to support WILPF and its foreign-policy feminism throughout the interwar years. In 1929 the U.S. section of WILPF issued a foreign policy statement expressing support for national sovereignty, disarmament treaties, free trade, and a "well-equipped Department of State supported by ample appropriations" to foster good diplomatic relations with other nations. The 1930–31 WILPF-U.S. program pushed for the withdrawal of American troops from foreign countries; a cessation of arms dealing with other countries; and demilitarization of the Mexico–U.S. border.[90] As discussed in chapter 8, Breckinridge would use her position as an official delegate of the U.S. State Department to advance these aims during and after the Seventh Pan-American Conference of 1933.

In the interwar period, new feminist foreign policy groups also appealed to Breckinridge. After the conclusion of World War I, new feminist-pacifist organizations such as the Women's Peace Union sought legal solutions to international conflict, including collective armed intervention by the League of Nations, international mediation in the World Court, and the "outlawry of war" by enacting laws making war an international crime. Breckinridge, who would later contend that World War II was the result of a tragic "failure to establish a world state," was entirely in sympathy with these aims, although there is no evidence that she joined the Women's Peace Union.[91]

She did, however, join a new organization created by Carrie Chapman Catt. As the president of NAWSA's successor organization, the League of Women Voters, Catt had committed that organization to internationalism by sending representatives to the Pan-American Conference of Women in 1922. Two years later she formed an umbrella organization for pacifists, the National Committee on the Cause and Cure of War. Catt's actions evidently healed the wartime rupture between Catt and Breckinridge; in the 1920s and 1930s, Breckinridge was not only a leader in the League of Women Voters (as discussed in chapter 6), but she also participated in the annual Conference on the Cause and Cure of War, sponsored by Catt's new pacifist group.[92]

"Red Peril"

Despite the postwar "Red Scare," throughout the 1920s and 1930s, Breckinridge was active in numerous feminist, pacifist, and internationalist organizations. Indeed, she was a member of many of the groups featured in the infamous "Spider's

Web" chart, which literally drew connections between women's groups, international committees, pacifist organizations, and socialist governments. The chart, designed in 1924 by a librarian in the War Department and featured prominently in such fear-mongering government publications as the Lusk Report, was headed: "The Socialist-Pacifist Movement in America is an Absolutely Fundamental and Integral Part of International Socialism."[93]

Groups implicated in the chart included WILPF, the National Child Labor Committee, the ACLU, the National Consumers' League, the General Federation of Women's Clubs, the Women's Trade Union League, the American Association of University Women, and the League of Women Voters—all organizations in which Breckinridge was an active member. Although she held local leadership positions, served on executive boards, and headed committees for these organizations, evidently Breckinridge's work was low-profile enough for her name to be omitted from the chart. Many of Breckinridge's colleagues, however, including Jane Addams, Lucia Ames Meade, Florence Kelley, Julia Lathrop, Emily Greene Balch, Vida Scudder, and Mary McDowell, appeared in versions of the chart.[94]

Hull House and its associates also came in for special scrutiny. In 1926, during one of several debates over the Children's Bureau and its programs, a conservative senator read into the *Congressional Record* an article originally published in the *Woman Patriot* that collectively indicted all the women activists affiliated with Hull House and the Children's Bureau as supporters of both social welfare legislation and international "'bread and peace' propaganda":

> It is of the utmost significance that practically all the radicalism started among women in the United States centers about Hull-House, Chicago, and the Children's Bureau at Washington, with a dynasty of Hull-House graduates in charge of it since its creation.

Because Breckinridge, a Hull House alumna, was a frequent consultant for the Children's Bureau, because her friends and colleagues Julia Lathrop and Grace Abbott were the first two directors of the bureau, and because graduates of the School of Social Service Administration effectively staffed the federal agency throughout the 1920s, statements like these certainly pointed toward her as a dangerous subversive, even though they did not name her outright.[95]

One organization that did name Breckinridge as a "doubtful" character was the Daughters of the American Revolution (DAR). Although Breckinridge had helped to establish the organization—"If they had had five instead of only four 'Founders,' I might have been the fifth," she later reflected—she eventually had resigned from the organization, probably well before the DAR listed her along with many of her friends and fellow reformers as a pacifist and socialist on a blacklist circulated in the mid-1920s. However, the DAR's blacklist, which listed

131 men, 87 women, and 306 organizations as communist, socialist, pacifist, feminist, internationalist, radical, pro-Soviet, pro-German, or simply "defeatist," was simply too all-encompassing to be persuasive. Carrie Chapman Catt and others angrily defended the "doubtful" individuals, and major newspapers ridiculed the DAR, which later repudiated the list. By that time, Catt and her own organization, the National Committee on the Cause and Cure of War, had come under attack. Breckinridge, who had attended the organization's 1925 meeting, remarked to Addams: "You will have seen the accounts of the attacks . . . on Mrs. Catt" and her fellow NCCCW members. "I think they have learned a great deal about the kinds of attack that have been made on you. Of course, no one wants them to learn by sad experience but I think they are wiser if not sadder."[96]

Whether this was her intention or not, Breckinridge's decision not to pursue the top levels of leadership in the many pacifist, feminist, and internationalist organizations to which she belonged may have protected her from the worst of the Red Scare. Although University of Chicago faculty and students frequently faced accusations of communist sympathizing, these were never substantiated. Even the campus's very own Red Scare, a 1935 probe into an alleged "Red Peril" on campus, did not cast suspicion on Breckinridge, despite the fact that she supported the aims of the targeted groups and individuals, including unionized labor, aid to Russia, opposition to the ROTC, and racial integration.[97]

Breckinridge was featured prominently in *The Red Network: A "Who's Who" and Handbook of Radicalism for Patriots* in 1934, compiled by Chicago conservative Elizabeth Dilling, who also played a key role in promoting anti-Communist hysteria on campus in the mid-1930s. Among other affiliations, the book noted Breckinridge's membership in such groups as the ACLU, the Committee on Militarism in Education, the Chicago Committee for the Struggle Against War, and, of course, WILPF.[98]

Although Breckinridge dismissed the listing, averring that Dilling "is treated as something in the nature of a joke," she was keenly aware that her involvement in internationalist and pacifist circles exposed her to public scrutiny, even though she somehow managed to avoid both official investigation and governmental repression.[99] Breckinridge later recalled that during the war, some of her colleagues dismissed her as a "half-baked pacifist." Even though she "had done what those arrested had done," she reflected, she never went to jail for her antiwar activism. She mused: "It may be that they [the police] recognized me as essentially harmless and so took others and left me."[100]

By surviving the war and postwar years with her professional reputation and personal freedom intact, Breckinridge was able to continue her commitment to internationalist pacifism. In the interwar years, Breckinridge belonged to a dizzying array of organizations dedicated to women's rights, national self-determination, democratic government, free speech, and world peace. In addition to WILPF, she also was active in the National Committee on the Cause and Cure of War, the People's Mandate to End War, and the American League Against War and Fascism. Concerned about the civil rights of immigrants and political dissidents, she supported the American Committee for Protection of the Foreign Born and the American Civil Liberties Union. As fascist and authoritarian governments came to power and war swept through Europe, she donated to Aid to Great Britain, the Fighting French Committee in America, the International Relief Association for Victims of Nazism, the Medical Bureau to Aid Spanish Democracy, and the National Council of Soviet-American Friendship. She also assisted the work of German Scholars in Exile, which helped Jewish and dissident intellectuals flee Nazi Germany, and actively participated in several organizations to aid refugee children, including the U.S. Committee for the Care of European Children.[101]

Just as she had done at the outset of World War I, when global conflict again appeared imminent, Breckinridge opposed entry into the war in no uncertain terms. In 1940, on the brink of U.S. involvement in the conflict, she used a book review of a history of the Woman's Peace Party as an opportunity to defend opponents of U.S. entry into the war against "the charge of lack of patriotism" and to celebrate pacifism as "true patriotism."[102]

When the United States entered World War II, Breckinridge, now in her seventies, responded in much the same way that she had during World War I. She deplored the violence of warfare at the same time that she maintained a cordial correspondence with members of the U.S. military. She criticized the U.S. internment of Japanese Americans and discrimination against African American soldiers. She supported aid organizations in war-torn countries and corresponded with her friends in Europe, especially with the British women she had met at the International Congress of Women. She helped German Jews, dissident intellectuals, and British children enter the United States and obtain homes, jobs, and citizenship.[103]

As she did in so many other arenas, Breckinridge persisted in the face of repeated setbacks because she recognized the necessity of pursuing the goal of peace with what she called "passionate patience." After all, as she pointed out in a radio address in 1936, "If it has taken centuries to replace vengeance by public law, we need not despair if it takes decades to substitute law for war in the settlement of disputes between nations."[104]

The Potential and Pitfalls
of Pan-American Feminism

"One of the great and decisive battles of feminism"

In late 1933, Breckinridge attended the Seventh Pan-American Conference in Montevideo, Uruguay, as the United States' first official female delegate to an international diplomatic conference. Breckinridge's selection as one of the "U.S. 'Big Four'" to attend the "Pan-American Parley," at which the United States formally announced its "Good Neighbor" policy, aroused considerable interest in the news media. Breckinridge carefully preserved a clipping of a story that listed her alongside Secretary of State Cordell Hull, businessman Spruille Braden, and former Mexican ambassador J. Reuben Clark as the "quartet of experts from the state department."[1] Both local and national newspapers reveled in the novelty of a woman delegate, publishing numerous profiles of the "feminine brain trustee."[2] Journalists especially delighted in pairing details of Breckinridge's impressive credentials with commentary on her appearance and personality, noting that "the small sapient and scintillating Sophonisba" was sure to win admirers because of her "charming southern manners." "She is said to be able socially as well as scholastically, to be witty as well as wise," one article commented.[3] According to a laudatory article in a Kentucky newspaper, "Miss Breckinridge is capable of holding her own with any of the experts. Exchange, tariffs, trade are subjects in which she is as deeply versed as women in industry and child labor."[4] But most accounts suggested that it was generally understood that Breckinridge was selected for her expertise on feminist foreign policy—or, as one piece expressed it, "the several subjects, significant to women, on the agenda for the conference, including child welfare and the civil and legal status of women in the Americas."[5]

Breckinridge's participation in the gathering—officially known as the Seventh International Conference of American States—highlighted both her expertise in international affairs and her interest in women's issues. Speaking before the assembled delegates, Breckinridge criticized U.S. interventions into Latin American affairs—including the military occupations of Veracruz, the Dominican Republic, and Haiti—in no uncertain terms. Like other members of the Women's International League for Peace and Freedom, Breckinridge opposed military intervention and economic imperialism in Latin America. "The United States has not been the good neighbor," she charged. "Issues have been determined by force," she lamented. "Power and not reason has been the basis of adjudications." Breckinridge found economic imperialism perhaps even more troubling than military intervention, however, describing "the predatory character of business" as producing "economic conflict" that then led to armed conflict. Breckinridge even hinted that the United States was implicated in the ongoing Chaco war, suggesting that "our armament firms are probably supplying munitions" to both belligerent nations, Paraguay and Bolivia.[6] However, Breckinridge also had a grand vision of women's role in repairing international relations, predicting: "The field of Inter-American relations will offer the women of the United States rich opportunities ... for responsible participation in the development of a new order on this hemisphere."[7]

Breckinridge's comments suggested the potential for Pan-American feminists to play an important role in international affairs by fostering cooperation rather than conflict. As discussed in chapter 7, following World War I, feminist pacifists encouraged international cooperation and transcended national boundaries in an effort to find solutions to global problems. Drawing on a long tradition of women's cooperation in social movements, feminist internationalists (who addressed state-to-state relations) and transnational feminists (who worked across national borders) hoped that women's shared gender identity would enable them to overcome national differences and become effective ambassadors for international understanding and world peace. With the Pan-American Union revitalized, the International Conferences of American States reinstated, and the U.S. president committed to a Good Neighbor policy, Pan-American feminism seemed to be a particularly promising strand of feminist internationalism and transnational feminism in the 1920s and 1930s.[8]

Yet Breckinridge's participation in the Seventh Pan-American Conference soon brought her into conflict with another feminist internationalist, Doris Stevens.[9] Although not an official delegate, Stevens also attracted considerable attention from the press. A veteran of the National Woman's Party, Stevens attended the conference in an unofficial capacity as the leader of a relatively new international women's group, the Inter-American Commission on Women, which had been established at the Sixth Pan-American Conference in Havana, Cuba, in 1928. Prior to the 1933 gathering, the commission had conducted an extensive study of women's status in the Americas. Armed with incontrovertible evidence of women's inferior legal status, Stevens planned to force the issue of women's rights by proposing two instruments dealing with women's rights—the Equal Nationality Treaty and the Equal Rights Treaty—with the hope that international action would break the deadlock in the United States over the stalled Equal Rights Amendment.[10]

As contemporary political observers understood, these proposals set Breckinridge and Stevens on a collision course.[11] As an official U.S. delegate, Breckinridge had received orders from Secretary of State Cordell Hull to avoid any discussion of nationality, because the Roosevelt administration considered the proposal a threat to national sovereignty.[12] Consequently, even though the Equal Nationality Treaty upheld the principle of independent citizenship (which, as discussed in chapter 6, Breckinridge had promoted in the United States in the form of the Cable Act), Breckinridge was obligated to vote against it. More important, she was personally opposed to the Equal Rights Treaty, modeled on the National Woman's Party's Equal Rights Amendment, which threatened to reopen the debate over the amendment and thus endanger protective legislation for working women and poor mothers both in the United States and abroad. Breckinridge's views on these subjects were well known; indeed, many reporters correctly surmised that it was because her attitudes mirrored those of the Roosevelt administration and the State Department that she was selected as a delegate.[13]

Thus, the stage was set for a showdown between Breckinridge and Stevens. At the Pan-American Conference, the two women engaged in a vicious campaign complete with personal attacks and underhanded tactics. Breckinridge characterized Stevens as a "highly nervous, over-wrought and fanatical type," while Stevens said of Breckinridge, "She's a witch and a bitch and she makes my ass tired." Each woman accused the other of tampering with official conference documents. U.S. delegate Spruille Braden described the "women's rights fight" as a "perfectly ridiculous tempest in a teapot."[14]

Braden's dismissive comments notwithstanding, the Breckinridge-Stevens battle at Montevideo put women's rights on the international agenda in a highly visible way. Calling attention to the importance of the issues at stake, National Woman's Party leader Alice Paul predicted that that the fate of the controversial proposals relating to women's rights at the Pan-American Conference would represent "one of the great and decisive battles of feminism."[15]

The "feminine fracas" at Montevideo also revealed ideological differences among women activists that threatened to undermine their efforts to develop a Pan-American women's rights movement.[16] In the 1930s, what contemporary newspapers referred to as "two opposing schools of feminine thought"[17] fractured the transnational feminist movement. Although the immediate issue was the debate over the proposed women's rights treaties, the larger question concerned competing definitions of women's equality.

Feminists like Breckinridge supported so-called protective legislation for working women—laws regulating working hours and mandating minimum wages for women workers—as the only avenue to what she termed "true equality." As discussed in chapter 6, Breckinridge built upon the work of her former mentor, legal scholar Ernst Freund, and the principles of sociological jurisprudence by insisting that government had a responsibility to level the playing field for its citizens. Because women were disadvantaged in the workforce by limited opportunities, weak unionization, and domestic responsibilities, it was, therefore, the government's job to enact legislation to create "a basis of effective equality of opportunity and protection."[18] When she traveled to Uruguay, Breckinridge represented not only the U.S. government but also a wide swath of women's groups, including the League of Women Voters, who shared these ideas. For Breckinridge and others like her, equality fundamentally meant fairness.

Feminists like Stevens, by contrast, insisted that the only way to eliminate discrimination was to treat men and women identically before the law. Any legislation that differentiated between women and men, they argued, ultimately disadvantaged women by casting them as dependents in need of protection, rather than as free citizens entitled to equal rights. A veteran of the National Woman's Party as well as the leader of the Inter-American Commission on Women (IACW), Stevens came to Montevideo resolved to ask the assembled nations "to outlaw the anti-social system which now stigmatizes one half the adult membership of their communities as irresponsible wards of man and of the State."[19] For Stevens and those like her, equality essentially meant sameness.

Pan-American feminists were unable to bridge the divide between "equal rights" and "special protections" until they could frame political and civil rights as well as social and economic welfare as basic human rights. Although both U.S. and Latin American activists sometimes pointed in this direction, in the 1930s they had not yet developed a coherent human-rights framework. Without that shared understanding of human rights, women internationalists proved unable to realize their vision of a global community—what Breckinridge called "a world fellowship." Instead, by the 1940s, U.S.-based transnational feminists, like their counterparts around the globe, found themselves swept up in a second world war.[20]

Nonetheless, by bringing feminist concerns into international politics and by keeping women's political and civil rights as well as their social and economic needs at the forefront of the discussion, Pan-American feminists—for all their differences—ensured that women would help shape the world order that emerged from global conflict. Women's participation in international relations ultimately helped to create an expansive definition of human rights and to promote the notion that "women's rights are human rights."

"The disagreement persists"

By the time Breckinridge set sail for Montevideo in November 1933, U.S.-based feminists had firmly established the battle lines over women's rights. As discussed in chapter 6, disagreements over the best route to women's equality had played out a decade earlier in the United States in the form of debates over the Equal Rights Amendment, originally proposed in 1923 by the leader of the National Woman's Party (NWP), Alice Paul. The League of Women Voters (LWV), together with most other U.S. women's groups, had blocked the proposed amendment, which they feared would jeopardize the gender-specific legislation they had worked so hard to implement. Acrimonious debates over the amendment divided U.S. feminists into opposing camps, deepened the divide between the NWP and the LWV, and fostered personal animosity among women activists. When they shifted their focus from the United States to abroad, U.S. feminists brought their ideological differences, their political rivalries, and their personal antagonisms with them. As one reporter explained, U.S. feminists' debate over equal rights versus protective legislation was "purely a local issue, but the feeling on the part of the league leaders runs deep, and they oppose on principle almost everything the Woman's party ever stands for."[21]

Thus, the League of Women Voters led the opposition to the National Woman's Party's proposals internationally as well as domestically. The groups' differences had been exacerbated at the Conference for the Codification of International Law at The Hague in spring 1930, where the Nationality Convention became a flash point of contention for U.S. women's rights advocates. Most U.S. feminists, in both the LWV and the NWP, denounced derivative citizenship. The question was what should replace it: equal citizenship or independent citizenship? The National Woman's Party supported equal citizenship—that is, all laws governing citizenship should be absolutely identical for both men and women. The League of Women Voters, however, advocated independent citizenship: married women should be able to elect their own citizenship, either adopting that of their husbands or retaining their original citizenship. Because both organizations were in favor of changes in the international law of citizenship, for a brief period, it seemed that the LWV and the NWP might come to agreement on the issue of married women's nationality. This potential coalition fell apart, however, in the course of preparation for, debates during, and the aftermath of the conference at The Hague. Desperate to differentiate the LWV from the NWP, league leadership began to question the effectiveness of international law to promote women's rights. While the NWP moved ever more decisively into international activism, the LWV increasingly retreated from the international arena.[22]

Similar tensions plagued feminist activists at the League of Nations. European, Latin American, and U.S. feminists all converged on Geneva in the 1920s and 1930s, hoping to persuade the League of Nations to adopt a convention on women's equality. But while there was broad agreement on the principle of equality, women's rights activists at Geneva, as elsewhere, found themselves unable to resolve conflicting impulses toward absolute equality between women and men with recognition of women's particular needs as workers and mothers. Policies already adopted by the International Labor Organization, such as the Maternity Convention of 1919, became a point of contention for international feminists, just as so-called protective legislation was a contested issue in the United States. Disagreements about how to define equality as well as how to achieve it fragmented the internationalist feminist coalition.[23]

The Seventh Pan-American Conference became yet another platform for the pro- and anti-ERA forces in the United States to air their disagreements. "Always the line-up is the same," New York Times correspondent Mildred Adams observed, whether the debate took place in Washington, D.C., Geneva, The Hague, Cuba, or Uruguay. Adams concluded: "The disagreement persists, until one wonders if it really is the anachronism it seems, or if its very strength may perhaps indicate that it is necessary to the health of a lively movement, and that without it all feminist endeavor might sink into a complacent rut."[24]

"A lively movement"

Debates over women's rights were anything but anachronistic at the Seventh Pan-American Conference, however. Rather, when U.S. feminists arrived in Latin America, they discovered "a lively movement" already deeply engaged in many of the same questions that interested members of the LWV and the NWP. For Latin American activists as well as for their U.S. counterparts, the burgeoning interest in Pan-Americanism opened up new opportunities to discuss women's rights on a world stage. Adding new voices to the debate, however, only highlighted the extent to which competing definitions of women's equality characterized not only U.S. feminism but also international feminism in the twentieth century.

Many scholars of Latin American women's history suggest that the "difference-versus-equality" debate had no currency among Latin American feminists; rather, for Latin American activists, equality-based feminism and difference-based maternalism coexisted peacefully under the aegis of "compensatory feminism"—at least until U.S. feminists brought the issue to the forefront.[25]

However, a close examination of Breckinridge's work at the Seventh Pan-American Conference reveals that tensions between women's equal rights as citizens and their particular demands as women were endemic to feminism throughout the Americas. Pan-American feminism, therefore, was fraught with conflict not only because of differences between U.S. and Latin American feminists but also because of divisions among women activists throughout the Americas. At Montevideo, as at The Hague and in Geneva, competing definitions of "equality" posed a significant challenge for the development of transnational feminism in the interwar period.[26]

Latin American feminists approached the conference with a mixture of hope and concern. As Grace Abbott noted, "Suffrage is still a burning issue in South America," and many Latin American feminists, still without the franchise, saw advantages in gaining the Pan-American Union's support for women's rights. Indeed, Latin American women were leaders in international organizing in large part because of their exclusion from politics in their own countries, and Cuban feminists had taken the lead in orchestrating the creation of the IACW in Havana in 1928 precisely because they hoped that international action might prompt national progress.[27]

At the same time, however, keenly aware of condescending attitudes among North American feminists in both the NWP and the LWV, Latin American feminists were wary of U.S. activists who might use the international gathering to advance North American women's rights at the expense of Latin American women's interests. Because many Latin American countries did not have functioning representative democracies, Latin American feminists initially showed less concern about political rights than social welfare, prompting some U.S. feminists to label them "backward" and ignorant. These tensions increased in the 1920s when U.S. women, despite winning the franchise, failed to put an end to U.S. military and economic imperialism in Latin America, disappointing Latin American feminists who had hoped that their U.S. counterparts would support their campaigns for national independence.[28]

The location for the Seventh Pan-American Conference in some ways exemplified these cross-currents in Latin American feminism. Uruguay enfranchised women in 1932, one of the earliest Latin Americans nations to do so. However, as in other Latin American countries, women in Uruguay gained political leverage by positioning themselves as members of groups—as mothers or as workers—rather than by demanding rights as individuals. The Uruguayan welfare state, like other modernizing Latin American nation-states, thus envisioned woman suffrage as a "shield of the weak" rather than as a right of citizenship.[29] When feminists from throughout the Americas converged on Montevideo in 1933, then, they were well positioned to consider competing notions of female citizenship and women's equality.

Breckinridge was in many ways an ideal person to address these issues at the Pan-American Conference. Her participation in the Pan-American Child Con-

Breckinridge's work at the Sixth Pan-American Child Congress in Lima, Peru, in 1930 laid the groundwork for her selection as an official State Department delegate to the Seventh Pan-American Conference in Montevideo, Uruguay, in 1933. It also reinforced her support for gender-specific policies such as protective legislation and maternity programs, a position that was consistent with the Roosevelt administration's stance but that brought her into conflict with Doris Stevens and the Inter-American Commission of Women.

Courtesy of the Columbia University Rare Book and Manuscript Library (Katharine Lenroot Papers)

gresses—begun by Latin American feminists in 1916—had familiarized her with the outlines of Latin American feminism and revealed the points of convergence between her own social justice feminism and Latin American maternalist feminism, which focused on "child welfare as a strategy for female empowerment" and used women's roles as mothers to justify their political participation and to make claims upon the nation-state.[30]

As discussed in chapter 7, in the 1920s Breckinridge had been an active participant in the international social work movement, which intersected in important ways with an international movement for child welfare, particularly in the United States, England, France, and Germany.[31]

By the 1930s the focus of international child welfare work had shifted to Latin America. Breckinridge was an official delegate to the Sixth Pan-American Child Congress, held in Lima, Peru, in 1930. At this gathering, several streams of child welfare advocacy converged to produce a demand for a strong welfare state that provided healthcare, education, financial assistance, and legal protection for children. The congress thus represented the culmination of several decades of child welfare reform in the United States, Europe, and Latin America and the coming of age of a truly international child-welfare movement.[32]

The 1930 congress also helped to promote a particular strand of Pan-American feminism. U.S. and Latin American activists demonstrated remarkable unanimity in supporting gender-specific legislation as a means to advance child welfare, including state-supported prenatal care and well-baby clinics; direct financial support for needy mothers and their children; and protective legislation and "maternity insurance" for working women. Interestingly, the congress also unanimously adopted language upholding "the rights of motherhood," thus linking maternalism with citizenship and moving in the direction of defining welfare programs as a necessary guarantee of social and economic rights.[33]

Breckinridge fully supported the measures proposed at the 1930 Pan-American Child Conference, which echoed many of her policy initiatives in Progressive-era Chicago and foreshadowed her work in designing the New Deal welfare state. Following the conference, she promptly helped found the U.S. Committee on Cooperation in Pan-American Child Welfare Work. This organization facilitated her continued work with Latin American feminist activists and social workers, extending her international social work connections to include Latin American as well as European social-welfare advocates.[34]

Breckinridge's participation in Latin American child-welfare circles also reinforced her preference for social legislation benefitting women in their roles as workers and mothers and, therefore, her suspicion of sweeping equal rights legislation. These thoughts were at the forefront of her mind as she prepared to undertake her responsibilities at the Seventh Pan-American Conference.

"Go to it"

The Pan-American Conference of 1933 was not intended to be a forum on women's rights. Rather, the conference aimed to reduce international tensions and promote hemispheric cooperation. At this historic gathering, the United States formally announced its "Good Neighbor" policy (which opposed U.S. armed intervention in Latin America), and assembled delegates from nineteen countries adopted the Convention on the Rights and Duties of States, which established the declarative theory of statehood as international law. Delegates also discussed reducing trade tariffs and signing an antiwar treaty.[35] Although the "extensive agenda" included "the political and civil rights of women" along with "such important subjects as the organization of peace, international law, . . . social problems, [and] intellectual cooperation," Secretary of State Cordell Hull did not initially anticipate that "any undue importance should be given to the discussions of the political and civil rights of women during this particular Conference."[36]

Nonetheless, women's concerns quickly came to the forefront. According to an in-depth article by journalist Jonathan Mitchell, while the principle issue of the conference was President Roosevelt's new "Good Neighbor" policy and the extent to which the U.S. delegation could convince suspicious Latin American representatives that the United States was sincere in its commitment to international cooperation, women's rights threatened to eclipse questions of international relations. Mitchell concluded: "The only question of comparable importance, in its long-range significance, will be the proposal of the official Inter-American Commission of Women, of which an American, Miss Doris Stevens, is chairman, to establish by treaty complete political and civil equality for women throughout the hemisphere. The changed position of women in recent years is a phenomenon with more far-reaching ultimate consequences than any political or economic issue whatever." For Breckinridge, as for Stevens, women's status was indeed the most pressing issue at the Pan-American Conference. Although Mitchell was clearly sympathetic to Stevens—the two would marry in 1935—Breckinridge evidently found his insights compelling, for she chose to keep a copy of this article in her personal papers.[37]

Although the Secretary of State attempted to downplay the importance of women's issues at the conference, government officials tacitly acknowledged the issue by sending Breckinridge to Montevideo. For many reasons, Breckinridge was the logical choice as the United States' first woman delegate to the Seventh Pan-American Conference. For maternity-program and protective-legislation advocates in the U.S. Children's Bureau and the U.S. Women's Bureau (both located within the U.S. Labor Department), her long-standing support for mothers' pensions and labor legislation made her an ideal representative. For the League of Women Voters, eager to squelch the National Woman's Party and maintain its own preeminence among U.S. women's organizations, Breckinridge's work as the chair of the Committee on the Legal Status of Women made her a strong selection. And for pacifists and internationalists, her standing as a founding member of both the U.S. chapter of the Women's International League for Peace and Freedom and the U.S. Committee on Cooperation in Pan-American Child Welfare Work made her an exceptionally qualified candidate.

Perhaps most important for the Roosevelt administration and the State Department, however, Breckinridge's expertise on women's citizenship and nationality lent her credibility and made her an effective representative of the government's

official position that women's rights were a matter of national policy, not international law. Determined to maintain national sovereignty and hoping to counter the influence of the IACW, government officials saw distinct advantages in
Breckinridge's selection. As Stevens later asserted in her memoirs: "Miss B. was
put on the U.S. Delegation for a special purpose the main ingredient of which
was some form of wrecking [the IACW] or, failing that, reprisal."[38]

Stevens was not far off the mark. With considerable understatement, Breckinridge explained that, since she was the chair of the LWV Committee on the Legal
Status of Women, which had spearheaded the anti-ERA campaign, and because
the Roosevelt administration considered the Equal Nationality Treaty a threat
to national sovereignty, "it could be inferred that I was appointed partly at least
because of that experience and of that agreement on my part with the views of
the present administration." Official records—including an exchange between
Secretary of Labor Frances Perkins and Secretary of State Cordell Hull—confirm
that Breckinridge's appointment reflected government officials' desire to have a
qualified woman present both to support the Roosevelt administration's priorities and to rein in the IACW and its chair.[39]

For Breckinridge and her circle of supporters in the federal government, the
central issue was the pending women's rights debate at the conference—in particular, concerns that the IACW proposals threatened labor legislation. Breckinridge's allies at the Children's Bureau, Grace Abbott and Katharine Lenroot,
actively promoted her selection as delegate. Frances Perkins, U.S. Secretary of
Labor, also campaigned on Breckinridge's behalf, sending word to her friends
to "go to it on Nisba's appointment to the Pan American delegation and she will
back it up from the inside."[40] The "women's network" in Washington, D.C., was at
the peak of its influence in the early 1930s, and Breckinridge's appointment flew
through the approval process in under two weeks.[41]

Armed with background material about the Pan-American Commission from
the Children's Bureau,[42] instructions from both the State Department and the
Labor Department, and suggestions from the League of Women Voters,[43] Breckinridge was prepared for a confrontation over the proposed treaties. "I shall, of
course, undertake so far as lies in my power to express the views of the administration," she promised Lenroot.[44]

While her goals aligned with those of the Roosevelt administration, Breckinridge agreed to represent the federal government's position because of her long-
standing commitment to special legislation on behalf of women and children,
and she accepted the post only at the urging of her colleagues in the Children's
Bureau.[45] Moreover, while she was undeniably antagonistic to the Inter-American
Commission, her views were consistent with those of many—perhaps most—
Latin American feminists.

Breckinridge, like many Latin American feminists, rejected a narrow definition of "feminism" as exclusively dedicated to equal political and civil rights
and instead favored a broad definition of feminism that included social welfare,
international cooperation, and feminist pacifism. In particular, her commitment
to labor feminism—although generally expressed in terms of her support for
social legislation—aligned her with Latin American activists' interest in advancing social and economic rights and, ultimately, Pan-American feminists' comprehensive vision of women's human rights. In addition, her commitment to
national self-determination and international law resonated with Latin American
feminists' efforts to advance Latin American nations' independence as well as
women's equality. Finally, her vision of women's central role in peacekeeping fit
well with Latin American feminists' goal of advancing women's representation
in international affairs.

Thus, while Breckinridge clashed with the IACW and with its U.S. leader,
Doris Stevens, she had much in common with other women involved in the Pan-
American feminist movement, which sought to bring together women's rights and
workers' rights in the context of international anti-imperialism and presaged the
notion of "women's rights as human rights." These shared attitudes would pave the
way for Breckinridge to cooperate with Brazilian feminist Bertha Lutz. Whereas
during the conference Breckinridge and Lutz focused their efforts on thwarting
Stevens and obstructing the IACW, afterward they would work together to promote peaceful solutions to international conflict as well as an expansive vision
of women's equality.

"A definite cleavage"

Breckinridge's duties as a delegate to the Pan-American Conference began well before she arrived in Montevideo. In addition to corresponding with her colleagues
in the Children's Bureau and the Labor Department, she visited the White House
in person on November 6, 1933, three days prior to the delegation's departure, to
receive final instructions. But her work began in earnest once she embarked on
the sea journey to Uruguay.[46]

On board the USMS *American Legion*, Secretary of State Hull, who chaired
the delegation, divided up assignments among the other five delegates. (In addition to the "Big Four" highlighted in the press, the delegates included Alexander Weddell, U.S. ambassador to Argentina, and J. Butler Wright, the Minister
to Uruguay). Breckinridge and Weddell were both assigned to Committee III:
Political and Civil Rights of Women, which had been charged with reviewing
the recommendations of the Inter-American Commission. Once they reached
Montevideo, Breckinridge and Weddell would work closely together to thwart

Stevens and the IACW proposals she championed. Weddell brought his authority as a diplomat to bear on the situation; Breckinridge brought her expertise on
the women's movement.[47]

During the eighteen-day voyage, both Breckinridge and Stevens courted support for their positions. U.S. delegate Spruille Braden, who confessed total ignorance about the "very marked schism" in the U.S. women's movement prior to
boarding the ship for Montevideo, later recalled, "I've never seen such lobbying
in my life."[48]

Breckinridge used the journey to inform her fellow delegates about divisions
within U.S. feminism and to justify her mission to stall the IACW. In a memorandum about her experiences, Breckinridge recalled: "I was given the opportunity
on the boat of informing the members of the delegation of the general development of the movement for women's rights in the United States." In fact, Breckinridge's overview of feminism in the United States was an extended screed against
the National Woman's Party and a concerted effort to undermine the IACW's
proposed Equal Nationality Treaty and Equal Rights Treaty.[49]

In a nineteen-page document, Breckinridge reviewed the history of the movement for woman suffrage in the United States from 1848 to 1920 and highlighted
the "definite cleavage" in the 1920s between the advocates and opponents of the
Equal Rights Amendment. Noting that in the United States opponents of the ERA
far outnumbered its supporters, she praised the gradual removal of discriminations with respect to nationality in the United States by means of the Cable Acts
and questioned the efficacy of broad-brush legislation, promoting instead the
"general doctrine of special remedies for definite evils." Turning her attention to
the international arena, she again noted "a definite cleavage" among international
women's organizations with respect to the issue of codifying women's nationality
rights both at the conference on international law held at The Hague in 1930 and
before the League of Nations in 1931. Given that there was no "widespread agreement" on this issue, she explained, the Roosevelt administration had determined
to review the nationality laws of the United States and recommend reform but to
treat nationality as a domestic issue rather than debating it "in an international
platform." Arguing that the IACW did not represent the majority of women in
the Americas, Breckinridge urged her fellow delegates not to approve any treaties
pertaining to equal rights at the Seventh Pan-American Conference.[50]

Stevens also used the voyage to prepare for the upcoming meeting, largely by
lobbying the U.S., Haitian, Venezuelan, Cuban, and Honduran delegates who also
were on board the ship. Stevens also attempted to gain Breckinridge's support, or
at least to ascertain her attitude toward the IACW proposals, but she complained
that Breckinridge was vague and dismissive and responded with "total indifference" to her explanation of the IACW's report and recommendations. Although

initially "baffled" by Breckinridge's noncommittal response, Stevens eventually concluded, "Either she was not versed in international procedure or she was not her own man and had to wait upon someone elses [sic] 'word.'"[51]

In fact, operating along the lines suggested by the State Department but consistent with her own priorities, Breckinridge was scheming about how to subtly sabotage Stevens. With advice from Secretary of State Cordell Hull, Secretary of Labor Frances Perkins, and Children's Bureau Chief Grace Abbott, Breckinridge met with Alexander Weddell to determine how best to limit the IACW's impact, oust Doris Stevens from leadership, or even eliminate the IACW entirely. Stevens's interactions with State Department representatives at The Hague codification conference in 1930 had not endeared her to the Roosevelt administration, which in any event was determined not to relinquish authority over nationality and citizenship to any international organization. Indeed, to forestall such developments, at the suggestion of the secretary of state, Roosevelt had assembled an interdepartmental committee and charged it with overhauling nationality laws, with particular attention to eliminating remaining discriminations against women. Since the U.S. government was conducting its own inquiry, then, he directed the delegation at the Seventh Pan-American Conference to keep mum on any proposals on nationality that might come up there. At the conference itself, Breckinridge and Weddell hoped to convince another delegate to express appreciation for the IACW's work, call attention to the complex issues involved, and assign further study to individual nation-states or a panel of experts—thus bypassing the IACW without coming into overt conflict with it.[52]

Although both Breckinridge and Stevens laid the groundwork for their campaigns while still aboard ship, their efforts kicked into high gear once they reached Montevideo and the official headquarters of the conference at the Hotel Parque. "Montevideo!" Stevens exclaimed upon arrival. "The long journey was at an end. The battle was about to begin." After unloading seventeen pieces of luggage—including four boxes of documents, two typewriters, and borrowed summer clothing—Stevens and the other members of the IACW established a battle station in "an excellent corner suite on the mezzanine, just below the headquarters of the U.S. delegation."[53]

From this base Stevens orchestrated a sophisticated lobbying campaign. She assembled information about and solicited support from numerous Latin American feminist organizations, keeping a tally of visitors' political positions and influence. She also maintained detailed records of committee members assigned to interview the delegates and notes on the delegates' attitude toward the IACW proposals. Finally, Stevens and other members of the IACW met with a never-ending stream of representatives of Latin American women's groups, fellow conference attendees, and journalists to promote the organization's proposed treaties.[54]

Meanwhile, Breckinridge focused on soliciting support from the five other women who attended the Seventh Pan-American Conference in an official capacity: delegates from Paraguay and Uruguay and technical advisors from Brazil, Mexico, and the United States. "My relations with all five of these women were pleasant," averred Breckinridge, even though "two of them were evident adherents of the Inter American Commission, one as ardent an opponent."[55] One of the adherents was Dr. Sofía Álvarez Vignoli de Demicheli, a lawyer and a delegate from Uruguay; Bertha Lutz, a technical advisor from Brazil, proved to be an opponent, although initially, Breckinridge remarked, "Both Miss Lutz and Madame Demichelli [sic] are distinctly political and I am, therefore, as yet rather uncertain as to exactly what are the items in the program of either."[56] The second supporter of the IACW was the technical advisor from Mexico, Margarita Robles de Mendoza, who also was the Mexican representative to the IACW. Mendoza, who owed her official appointment to Stevens, arrived convinced of the need to "fight for our rights."[57] The other women were María F. González, a delegate from Paraguay, and, from the United States, technical advisor and State Department official Anna A. O'Neill.[58]

Breckinridge wasted no time in developing friendly relationships with the Latin American women while carefully avoiding Stevens. She quickly formed an especially close friendship, however, with Bertha Lutz. Stevens complained bitterly about the "close alliance" between Breckinridge and Lutz. After having tea with Lutz, who had assisted with the IACW study of laws affecting women's status, Stevens had counted the Brazilian among her supporters. Now, however, she angrily observed as Breckinridge and Lutz teamed up to conduct an "intensive lobby" to stall the IACW's proposals, undermine its leader, and even dissolve the organization entirely.[59]

According to Stevens, the Latin American feminists at the conference were confused by Breckinridge's overtures because "they were wont to think of all our women being as one in the advance of women's rights."[60] This was certainly not the case for Lutz, however. The daughter of an English mother and a Swiss-Brazilian father, Lutz studied at the Sorbonne before completing her law degree at Rio de Janeiro with a thesis in support of equal citizenship rights. Lutz subsequently attended the Pan-American Conference of Women in the United States in 1922 organized by Carrie Chapman Catt. Lutz maintained a lifelong friendship with Catt. Despite her intimacy with the head of the League of Women Voters, Lutz also formed a close relationship with National Woman's Party member Mary Wilhelmine Williams, who attempted—unsuccessfully—to persuade her Brazilian friend to abandon protective legislation. Fluent in English, French, Portuguese, and Spanish, Lutz also was familiar with a variety of feminist tactics and ideologies. She would soon prove to be Breckinridge's strongest ally at the Pan-American Conference.[61]

The Mexican woman at the conference, Margarita Robles de Mendoza, also was conversant with feminist debates over maternity and equality. Mendoza, who had studied in New York, was the founder and director of the *Unión de Mujeres Americanas*, a Latin American feminist organization that focused on political rights, especially the vote. Mendoza's commitment to equal rights and distaste for protective legislation were consistent with the philosophy and the position of the National Woman's Party; her extensive writings also make it clear that she was intimately familiar with debates about protectionism and equality. Both as a veteran of the equal nationality campaign at The Hague and as an official commissioner for the IACW, Mendoza arrived at the conference ready to promote the IACW's proposals.[62]

Sofía Álvarez Vignoli de Demicheli, the Uruguayan delegate, likewise was quite familiar with the tensions between protectionism and equality. A veteran of the suffrage movement, Demicheli left the short-lived Uruguayan women's party (Partido Independiente Democratico Femenino) in early 1933 as a result of a disagreement over women's right to divorce that highlighted differences between protection and equality. As an advocate of equal divorce laws, Demicheli had gone on record as opposed to gender-specific legislation well before the Pan American Conference commenced.[63]

Less information is available about the final Latin American woman representative to the conference, Paraguayan delegate María Felicidad González. A pioneering educator who held a post as professor of pedagogy at the Normal School of Paraguay, González had, like Lutz, attended the Pan-American Conference of Women in the United States in 1922; she later served as the vice president of the Asociación Feminista Paraguaya (Paraguayan Feminist Association), founded in 1929. While she was obviously well informed about both U.S. and Latin American feminism, González's position on the IACW was unclear.[64]

Breckinridge thus found herself with powerful allies, formidable opponents, and unknown quantities at the Pan-American Conference. Of the six women delegates, four—Breckinridge, Demicheli, Mendoza, and González—served on Committee III, charged with studying the IACW proposals and making recommendations to the conference. Lutz served as technical advisor to the Brazilian delegation, while Anna O'Neil served as technical advisor to the U.S. delegation.[65]

Breckinridge soon found herself outnumbered and outmaneuvered by IACW supporters on Committee III. She was "quite unhappy" following the first substantive meeting of the committee on women's rights. Breckinridge and Weddell had hoped to postpone any action on the IACW's proposals, but instead, after delivering a "brilliant speech in defense of the rights of women," Sofía de Demicheli proposed the formation of a subcommittee to consider the proposals. "After an exchange of ideas in which the majority of the Delegates intervened," the assembled delegates approved this plan. Demicheli was the only woman on the subcommittee. This meant that the only female voice on the subcommittee to address the IACW's proposals was that of an IACW supporter. However, Bertha Lutz evidently had some influence on the Brazilian member of the subcommittee, Francisco Luis da Silva Campos. This was fortunate from Breckinridge's standpoint, because Lutz shared Breckinridge's antipathy for Stevens and her desire to displace Stevens as the head of the IACW.[66]

The IACW leader's emphasis on equal rights, even at the expense of protective legislation, ran counter to Lutz's goals. In 1919, soon after organizing the League for the Intellectual Emancipation of Women, Lutz represented Brazil at the International Labor Organization (ILO) conference on the conditions of working women, where the ILO endorsed legal regulation of women's work and provisions for paid maternity leave. As the founder of the Brazilian Federation for Feminine Progress (FBPF), founded in 1922 and active until 1932, Lutz advocated women's rights to education, employment, voting, and office-holding, but she also consistently supported legislation to protect working women and provide support for mothers. Shortly before the Seventh Pan-American Conference, Lutz collaborated with women lawyers to create her *Thirteen Principles*, which the FBPF hoped to incorporate into Brazil's new constitution. The aims included paid maternity leave and tax-supported programs for mothers and children as well as equality before the law and equal pay for equal work.[67]

Lutz thus was an enthusiastic ally in Breckinridge's efforts to undermine the IACW and its leader, and she did not hesitate to use her influence with the Brazilian member of the subcommittee to shape the group's report to the Third Committee. The subcommittee, "in harmony with the indication of the delegate from Brazil"—and incorporating aspects of Breckinridge and Weddell's original scheme—made three recommendations:

1. That the Inter-American Commission of Women should be warmly thanked and should be continued.
2. That a treaty providing for equality in nationality should be approved and adopted.
3. A recommendation that the principle of equality should be called to the attention of the various states, and that in the organization of the Inter-American Commission of Women, the principle of rotation in office should be applied to the chairmanship.[68]

While these recommendations applauded the IACW's work and conceded the point of equal nationality, the support for only a "recommendation" on "the principle of equality" and the proposal for a "principle of rotation in office" in the IACW represented both a political challenge to the IACW's proposals and a personal attack on its leader. Indeed, as Breckinridge remarked, the rejection of the Equal Rights Treaty was "a definite defeat" for Stevens, and the proposed rotation of leadership was clearly intended to remove her from power.[69]

At subsequent meetings of Committee III, however, the other Latin American women present expressed strong support for women's rights and for the work of the IACW. (In a later account, Stevens claimed that she enjoyed "virtually unanimous support" among the Latin American delegates.)[70] In addition, arguing that the IACW was an independent entity not subject to the Pan-American Union's oversight, they objected to the proposed change in the leadership of the nongovernmental organization.[71] Instead of bowing to the logic offered by IACW supporters, Lutz responded by offering a resolution proposing a mechanism for the rotation of the chair of the IACW. The resolution, possibly written with Breckinridge's input, specified that Brazil would provide the next chair. The resolution also pointedly insisted that commissioners to the IACW had to be ratified by the government pursuant to approval "by the associations of women leading the national feminine movement . . . most representative of organized feminine opinion." Breckinridge and Lutz, of course, considered their organizations—the League of Women Voters and the Brazilian Federation for Feminine Progress—to be the most influential and representative women's organizations in the United States and Brazil, respectively.[72]

However, Mendoza vigorously opposed Lutz's proposal, and "after a very considerable amount of discussion" and "a lengthy exchange of ideas" involving delegates from Brazil, Mexico, Paraguay, and Ecuador, the assembled delegates determined that they lacked a quorum.[73] Stevens and the IACW mobilized to have the Latin American delegates boycott the final sessions of the Third Committee, and without a quorum the committee was only able to forward the original, weaker resolution to the plenary conference for approval. The language ultimately adopted merely "present[ed] as an aspiration . . . the suggestion that the Presidency of the Inter-American Commission of Women . . . may rotate."[74]

Breckinridge and Lutz had not succeeded in their plan to oust Stevens from office, but they were able to claim a qualified victory with respect to the Equal Rights Treaty. While the Third Committee had recommended adopting the Equal Nationality Treaty, it had withheld judgment on the Equal Rights Treaty, recommending instead only continued consideration of the "principle of equality." In all likelihood, Lutz's informal influence on the Third Committee had helped to defeat the Equal Rights Treaty.

The fate of the Equal Nationality Treaty still hung in the balance, however. Pro- and anti-treaty forces rallied support up to the last minute, and when the delegates assembled to consider the recommendations of the Third Committee, "there was an atmosphere of great excitement." Both Breckinridge and Weddell spoke out against the Equal Nationality Treaty. Further, Weddell announced that the United States "desires to dissociate itself in the future from the work of the Inter-American Commission of Women," stating that the U.S. government preferred to work through official, national channels rather than with unofficial, international organizations. Stevens rebutted by reading a long list of organizations in the United States that supported the Nationality Treaty, demonstrating that "a considerable number of women in powerful organizations in the United States do want to act internationally with other women." Inter-American Commission delegate Minerva Bernardino also spoke on behalf of both the treaty and the IACW, assuring those in attendance that she spoke for "my sisters of the entire continent" in demanding equal rights and urging the "Gentlemen of the Conference" to "give way to Woman!"[75]

Ultimately, the Seventh Pan-American Conference endorsed all the recommendations of Committee III, as presented by the subcommittee. The U.S. delegation continued its obstructionist tactics, however, by abstaining from the vote in favor of the continuation of the IACW.[76] Breckinridge and Weddell also refused to support the Equal Nationality Treaty until—as a result of a public relations campaign conducted by the IACW and the NWP—President Roosevelt cabled them at the last moment to direct them to vote in favor of the treaty. Flushed with victory, Stevens and her allies sent telegrams to political leaders and women's groups in all nineteen nations represented at Montevideo to urge them to ratify the treaty.[77]

Once Roosevelt changed his position on the treaty, Breckinridge lent it her support. Perhaps she was even somewhat relieved at the outcome. After all, she had been an outspoken advocate of both women's nationality rights and international law prior to the developments at The Hague that had prompted members of the League of Women Voters to retreat from international women's rights activism. Moreover, prior to receiving orders from the State Department to oppose the nationality treaty, Breckinridge had read favorable reports on that instrument from Secretary of Labor Frances Perkins.[78] On her return to the States, when the LWV was disposed to lobby to prevent ratification, Breckinridge pointed out that "we [in the LWV] are committed to the doctrine of independent and equal rights in nationality for the husband and wife" and argued that unlike the Equal Rights Treaty, the Equal Nationality Treaty, "like all policies pursued by the League of Women Voters," was "an admirable illustration of applying the principle of specific treatment for special evils." Breckinridge thus urged the league to support the Equal Nationality Treaty, which was ratified by the U.S. Senate in May 1934.[79]

"The witch is after you again"

Although Breckinridge gracefully—if belatedly—conceded defeat with respect to the Equal Nationality Treaty, she did not soften her attitude toward Stevens. Instead, she chose to interpret the Third Committee's recommendations as evidence of "the prompt and unanimous and convinced rejection by the South American groups" of the Equal Rights Treaty. Further, she regarded the conference's support for a rotating chair for the Inter-American Commission—rather than keeping Stevens on in perpetuity—as "a definite device to eject and evict her."[80]

Breckinridge thus continued her efforts to oust Stevens. She used her membership on the Eighth Committee, which was responsible for planning future conferences, to continue her offensive against Stevens and the IACW. In later memoranda and reports about her experience at the Pan-American Conference, Breckinridge explained that the U.S. delegation wished to "disassociate" itself from the IACW to enable the United States to work in the future only with "agencies responsible to the Government." In essence, the State Department argued that its delegates should not be answerable to a nongovernmental body such as the IACW, in which the commissioners did not have the implicit or explicit endorsement of their national governments. Breckinridge presented a resolution to this effect to the Eighth Committee, but, according to her, "difficulties in language" prevented the Spanish-speaking delegates from comprehending "the different principles applicable to the two sets of agencies"—that is, government-sanctioned delegations and nongovernmental organizations—and they unanimously rejected the resolution.[81]

Official minutes from the meeting, however, suggest that the Latin American delegates understood the proposal perfectly and that they rejected it because they realized the threat it posed to political freedom: in unstable political situations, corrupt governments might use it to disfranchise citizens.[82] Stevens and her allies also understood the proposal to be another attempt to oust her; Manuel Sierra, a Mexican representative on the Eighth Committee, warned Stevens about the resolution, saying, "The witch is after you again."[83]

Breckinridge was bitterly disappointed. "Everything has been distorted and disturbed by Doris Stevens," she complained to Edith Abbott.[84] Before leaving the conference, Breckinridge made a last-ditch attempt to outmaneuver Stevens, introducing what the IACW chair referred to as a "ripper bill" at the final plenary session of the conference, held on Christmas Eve.[85]

Breckinridge's resolution—which she funneled through Cuban delegate Angel Giraudy—provided that the Seventh Pan-American Conference would create a standing committee composed of women who had attended the conference as part of an official national delegation. She further charged this group with "framing the future program of all the matters referring to cooperation and interests of woman in the Peace of America, and regarding the feminine aspects of social, juridical and international questions." In effect, Breckinridge's proposed women's committee would supplant the IACW, which, at best, might be consulted if the new committee's members—including Breckinridge and Lutz, but not Stevens— "deemed [it] advisable." Clearly this resolution was intended to displace Stevens. However, since the proposal would have made Mendoza and Demicheli, both IACW supporters, permanent members of the new committee, it also would have provided a balance between advocates of protective legislation and proponents of equal rights legislation.[86]

Breckinridge's proposal created "pandemonium" at the closing plenary session of the conference. Braden later detailed the furor:

When we went into this final plenary session, Miss Breckinridge, who was seated next to me, was exulting. She had pulled one of the fanciest bits of diplomacy that she thought had ever happened. She told me in confidence that she had gotten this resolution through . . . to the effect that any woman of any American republic who served as a delegate at any one of our principal conferences automatically became a member for life of the Inter-American Woman's Bureau—or whatever the name is—that's supposed to look after women's rights in inter-American affairs. They just stayed put. They never had to bother about elections or anything else.

Of course, this was really pulling a fast one because she was the only American woman that we'd ever had as a delegate up to that time and Doris Stevens was not a delegate—she was merely a lobbyist working on the outside. . . . I couldn't help smiling. The whole thing to me seemed to be a perfectly ridiculous tempest in a teapot.

Sure enough, the Mexican [sic] got up, he delivered himself of an oration, and proposed the resolution. It was unanimously approved instantaneously— there was no discussion at all. There was blanket approval. Miss Breckinridge had taken the pains to make sure, talking to several of the Latin delegates, that they were all going along.

Everything went along fine until apparently the portent of this resolution got out to Doris and her girl friends and a bevy of them came right in and interrupted the meeting.[87]

At that point, Stevens alerted the "somnolent" delegates to Breckinridge's intent to oust the IACW leader and convinced them to postpone a vote on the proposal. The delegate who had originally made the resolution withdrew it, "so poor Miss Breckinridge lost out entirely on this thing," Braden concluded.[88] Undeterred, Lutz declared: "We will carry the fight into the eighth Pan-American Conference."[89]

"The special problems of women workers"

Breckinridge's conflicts with Stevens highlighted the fissures in transnational feminism; her collaboration with Lutz, however, revealed the potential of women's international activism. Although initially drawn to one another by their joint mission to curtail the influence of the IACW, Breckinridge and Lutz soon discovered other commonalities. The two women shared a vision of social justice that included equal rights, special protections, and world peace through women's collective efforts. Thus, although Stevens complained that Breckinridge offered no constructive proposals of her own to counter the IACW treaties, the two women did offer an alternative program at the Seventh Pan-American Conference—and afterward.

At the same time that Breckinridge and Lutz worked together to undermine Stevens, they also were concocting a plan to promote working women's interests. Initially, Lutz had attempted to address this issue in the Third Committee, where she offered a multipart proposal intended to ensure "complete equality of rights between both sexes." Pointing out that given "centuries of [male] tyranny ... it is necessary that women be defended by special laws which will help her to gain the same position which man reached before her," Lutz's proposal demanded both equal opportunities in the workplace and gender-specific labor legislation, including maternity insurance.[90]

Lutz's ambitious proposal went nowhere, however. Although the IACW plan to boycott the final meetings of Committee III allowed Stevens to keep her post, it also meant that Lutz's proposal never got a full hearing. Instead, it was referred to the Committee on Initiatives before returning to Committee III, which by then could not achieve a quorum.[91]

Unable to advance her proposal in the Third Committee, Lutz recruited Breckinridge to help her promote a similar initiative in Committee V, Subcommittee 1—a committee that both women attended only in an unofficial capacity. This subcommittee was formed to discuss the possible creation of an Inter-American Bureau of Labor, which would coordinate its work with the International Labor Office at Geneva. Prior to the conference, Breckinridge obtained copies of—and may have helped to write—Secretary of Labor Frances Perkins's memorandum on the potential Pan-American labor bureau. Some of the aims of such an organization were to provide "fair and reasonable wages, hours, and conditions of labor for both men and women," to eradicate child labor, and to provide unemployment and accident insurance.[92]

When they appeared before the labor subcommittee, Breckinridge and Lutz both made proposals for protective legislation for women workers, including the creation of "a special division" within the Labor Bureau to address the "special interests of women wage-earners." Breckinridge also supported the establishment of mothers' pensions and a minimum wage.[93] As she subsequently remarked, her proposals at the Pan-American Conference were intended to ensure "the protection of women as mothers, of women as home-makers, and of women as industrial workers."[94]

Breckinridge and Lutz's proposals regarding working women and mothers' pensions assumed that while a small group of privileged women (like themselves) might pursue higher education and professional careers, most were destined for motherhood, wage labor, or both. By demanding both equal access to power and protection from abuse, they sought to meet the needs of both groups. While Lutz and Breckinridge passionately defended married women's right to work and working women's right to marry, they also recognized that women's different life paths required different kinds of rights. Moreover, by supporting women's rights as citizens, mothers, and workers, they found common ground between equality and difference.

However, their proposals were unsuccessful. Both because of possible conflicts with the International Labor Office and because the United States could not authorize additional expenditures, the creation of a Pan-American labor organization was postponed. Notwithstanding the United States' interest in "the special problems of women workers," Breckinridge regretfully remarked, her government was not prepared to spearhead a program dedicated to them.[95]

Although Breckinridge and Lutz had yet again failed to achieve their immediate objective, they continued their association. After Breckinridge's return to the United States, she and Lutz carried on a cordial correspondence in which they rehashed the events of the conference and devised various schemes to unseat Stevens. In particular, Lutz still hoped it would prove possible to "reorganize women[']s collaboration" by establishing a new—or rival—inter-American women's organization, preferably with Latin American leadership.[96]

Both Lutz and Breckinridge remained particularly interested in promoting labor legislation for women workers—precisely the agenda they feared would be "poisoned" by Stevens and the Equal Rights Treaty. In the aftermath of a revolution in her country in 1930 and under a provisional government that granted women suffrage, Lutz was "fighting valiantly" to ensure that the new Brazilian constitution contained the reforms she favored, including equal pay for equal work and paid maternity leave. Hoping for support from prominent U.S. women such as Frances Perkins, Katharine Lenroot, and Eleanor Roosevelt, Lutz suggested that perhaps a future meeting of the Pan-American Union might be dedicated to "women workers." Breckinridge, who sent copies of Lutz's letters to both Belle Sherwin at the LWV and Ruth Shipley at the Department of State, also wished to organize some sort of conference on women's labor issues in Pan-American context—what she called "some definite piece of research in the Pan-American labor field"—possibly in conjunction with the U.S. Women's Bureau. Unfortunately, she explained, the LWV had no money to spare for such an effort.[97]

"Another aspect of the women's movement"

Breckinridge and Lutz also hoped to use Pan-American feminism to advance peace. After the 1933–34 election cycle, in which Lutz ran for federal office but gained enough votes only to be an alternate, the Brazilian women's movement experienced "a great slump" that coincided with dangerous militaristic and authoritarian trends. "There is a very male-spirit rampant in the world now," Lutz worried. "Every day military training and Fascist doctrines grow stronger here and elsewhere. . . . Can we do nothing to prevent this spirit from undermining all our work?"[98]

Lutz wrote to her U.S. allies seeking counsel and encouragement, hoping to "work up the panamerican again" and collaborate with U.S. feminists to counter the growing threat of fascism. In particular, she hoped that the Committee on the Cause and Cure of War might extend its reach to South America. She offered to put the organization's leader, Carrie Chapman Catt, in touch with all the women's organizations in Buenos Aires. Lutz also promised to solicit support from a Latin American organization, the Women's Confederation for American Peace, for a women's conference to be held in conjunction with a Special Conference for the Maintenance of Peace, called by the United States but slated to held in Buenos Aires, Argentina, in 1936.[99]

During preparations for the 1936 peace conference, Lutz again wrote to Catt to find ways both to counter the IACW's influence and to raise the profile of women's peace work in the Americas. To thwart Stevens as well as to promote the peace movement, Lutz proposed, the "cloven hoof of Doris Stevens in the item: civil & political rights of women" on the agenda of the conference should be replaced by "collaboration of women for Peace." In addition, she suggested, all unofficial attendees (in other words, IACW commissioners) should be excluded from the conference entirely, and the official delegates should include "women plenipotentiary delegates, with a right to vote."[100]

Breckinridge also hoped to reenergize women's international pacifism. In a lecture she delivered at the 1936 Conference on the Cause and Cure of War, she argued that the Seventh Pan-American Conference had offered an instructive example of international peacemaking:

> The Conference dealt with every device for adjusting difficulties,—through securing ratification of earlier treaties and the drafting of new ones; establish-

ing procedures for carrying on the work of codifying international law; recognizing the economic sources of conflict; urging many forms of cooperation; and asking some new exercise of self-restraint. A temporary truce between the warring countries, and now at last what is to be hoped to be a permanent peace and possibly a peace of reason and justice, not simply a peace of victory, has been achieved.[101]

Breckinridge therefore had high hopes of what might be achieved at a Pan-American Peace Conference.

While unable to attend the Buenos Aires conference herself, Breckinridge was eager for the United States to send at least one woman delegate to the peace conference. She corresponded extensively with her government contacts about potential candidates, preferably "someone who speaks Spanish and someone well grounded in the Peace Movement"—as well as someone who would counter proposals that might endanger protective legislation.[102]

The individual eventually selected, Ellen Musser, was fluent in Spanish but less conversant with competing ideas about women's equality. However, Breckinridge and other influential women in the Roosevelt administration—including Secretary of Labor Frances Perkins; Mary W. Dewson, head of the Women's Division of the Democratic National Committee; Women's Bureau chief Mary Anderson; and Breckinridge's former student, minimum-wage advocate and New York Industrial Commissioner Frieda Miller—quickly brought the newcomer up to speed. Members of the League of Women Voters and other women's groups also urged Musser—who described herself as "a feminist, but not militant," thereby distinguishing herself from the NWP—to avoid the subject of women's rights. Spruille Braden, who attended the conference in an unofficial capacity, described Musser as "of the same Mrs. Roosevelt—Sophonisba Breckinridge school of thought in respect to women's rights."[103]

Breckinridge hoped not only to keep Stevens in check at the conference but also to advance labor legislation there. To this end, she urged Frieda Miller, who had represented the United States at the 1936 meeting of the International Labor Organization in Santiago, Chile, to send her report about those experiences to the State Department, explaining that by taking advantage of U.S. women's previous experience in Latin America, she "wanted to salvage whatever could be salvaged in the way of [an inter-American] organization of women."[104]

Miller's visit to Santiago had brought her into contact with Marta Vergara, a Chilean advocate of "Popular-Front Pan-American Feminism." While Popular-Front feminists eschewed protective legislation, they championed maternity legislation. Moreover, they did so by casting state support for mothers as a right rather than as a protection. Popular-Front feminists thus pointed the way toward a new feminist synthesis that supported both equal rights for women and social programs especially tailored to women's needs.[105]

For Vergara, provisions for state support of working mothers seemed entirely compatible with demands for women's equal rights. Soon after Chile ratified the International Labor Organization's Maternity Convention (stipulating benefits for working women during maternity leave) in 1934, Vergara represented the IACW at the 1936 ILO Conference by reframing maternity legislation as a social and economic right rather than as a gender-specific protective policy. Miller remarked on this innovative approach in a confidential report to the Labor Department, calling it "striking evidence of difference of viewpoint and interest" between the United States and Latin America and commenting on the greater emphasis on "the position of women in the social and economic scheme of things" in Latin America.[106] Presumably these were precisely the observations that Breckinridge hoped that Miller would share with the State Department, since they meshed with her long-standing dual goal of advancing women's social and economic status as well as their civil and political rights.

Even as some Pan-American feminists groped toward a resolution of the difference-versus-equality conundrum, the international feminist community remained deeply divided. After Montevideo, both the Equal Nationality Treaty and the Equal Rights Treaty came under consideration at the League of Nations. Latin American feminists urged the league to address women's rights, including their right to participate in the workforce, in light of discriminatory labor legislation enacted in authoritarian regimes. International agitation prompted the league to solicit information from member countries about political and civil rights in their countries. The league also requested the ILO to study the issue of equal rights and protective legislation. However, disagreements about the wording of the nationality treaty and concerns about the effect of the equal rights treaty on working women created rifts on both the Liaison Committee of Women's International Organizations and the Women's Consultative Committee on Nationality. Unable to arrive at a compromise, international feminists in Geneva instead demanded that the league undertake a comprehensive study of the legal status of women around the world, while the ILO conducted a parallel study on women's economic status.[107]

Against this backdrop, in 1936 Stevens and Vergara agreed to meet at the Popular Peace Conference in Buenos Aires, which preceded the official Pan-American Peace Conference. To maintain Vergara's support for an endorsement of the Equal Rights Treaty at the conference, Stevens, for the first time, made a public statement that equal rights were compatible with maternity legislation. The strategic alliance between Stevens and Vergara overpowered U.S. reformers' objections to the Equal Rights Treaty, and the Popular Peace Conference passed a resolution recommending Pan-American enforcement of the Equal Rights Treaty. Vergara subsequently facilitated an alliance between Stevens and the IACW and an Argentinian organization, the *Unión Argentina de Mujeres*, at the official peace conference in Buenos Aires. Again, by proclaiming herself in support of maternity legislation and by at least rhetorically supporting Latin American feminists' support for "a broader social justice agenda," Stevens succeeded in putting women's rights on the agenda of the conference and in persuading the attendees to endorse the women's rights resolution.[108]

The successful collaboration between Vergara and Stevens in Buenos Aires marked a significant shift in Pan-American feminism. Following the conference, Vergara praised the IACW for its support of "the full recognition of women's political, civil, and economic rights." Stevens continued to express public support for maternity legislation, issuing a memo to Latin American affiliates, titled "Maternity Legislation Not Incompatible with Equal Rights." At the Eighth Pan-American Conference in Lima, Peru, in 1938, she announced that the IACW was undertaking a hemispheric study of maternity legislation.[109]

Stevens's new tactics were not enough to maintain her leadership of the IACW, however. Instead, at the Eighth Pan-American Conference, the U.S. State Department joined forces with Latin American feminists to pressure Stevens to resign. The IACW itself reorganized, becoming an official branch of the Pan-American Union rather than an independent organization. Its headquarters moved to Buenos Aires, and Argentinian Ana Rosa de Martínez Guerrero became the new chair. In 1939, when Stevens resigned her post as commissioner, U.S. Women's Bureau member Mary Winslow, a member of the League of Women Voters and an advocate of protective legislation, became the new U.S. representative. Although Stevens was convinced that Breckinridge had conspired with government officials to force her out of office, Breckinridge's role—if any—in the reorganization of the IACW is not detailed in extant documents. However, she enthusiastically supported Winslow's appointment "as a person representing a different type in manner and bearing from the characteristic of the present Chairman," adding, "I should be happy if we might have another aspect of the women's movement representing [*sic*] on that body."[110]

The same year that Stevens stepped down as the leader of the IACW, the League of Nations appointed an expert committee to conduct an official inquiry into the status of women. However, before the study was complete, World War II resulted in the demise of the League of Nations.[111] Any resolution of the longstanding disputes among transnational feminists would have to wait until international peace was restored.

Breckinridge's participation in Pan-American feminism in the 1930s suggested the potential of international cooperation to advance both women's rights and world peace. However, she was soon embroiled in a bitter conflict among international feminists. This "ill-timed woman's quarrel," as the *New York Times* described it, fragmented the international feminist movement just as the rise of fascism posed ever greater threats to both women's rights and world peace.[112] Yet, although Pan-American feminists had failed to find common ground in their quest to advance women's status and women's rights, their often bitter disagreements nonetheless had the effect of ensuring that women's issues took center stage in international relations. Ultimately, women activists who forged their ideas about female equality in the fierce battles of the Pan-American Conference—including Bertha Lutz—would bring their hard-won insights to bear on the creation of the United Nations and the contents of the Universal Declaration of Human Rights.[113]

CHAPTER NINE

Toward a National Minimum

Women Building the Welfare State

"Minimum Standards"

In summer 1919, a group of influential child-welfare advocates, medical profession-als, and government officials all converged on Washington, D.C., for the Second White House Conference on Children. Breckinridge was among those who at-tended. Her work there was important not just for setting the standards for child welfare for more than a decade—the next such conference did not take place until 1930—but also because it laid out the principles that subsequently led her to become a major player in public welfare policy in the United States, culminat-ing in the Social Security Act of 1935.[1]

Ten years earlier, delegates to the First White House Conference on the Care of Dependent Children had affirmed the importance of "home life," thereby en-dorsing the principle that led to the mothers' pension program that Breckinridge had advocated in Illinois in 1910.[2] This time, the conference had a more ambi-tious purview, seeking to establish "Minimum Standards of Child Welfare" in three broad areas: child labor; maternal and infant health; and "the protection of children in need of special care," which included poor, illegitimate, "mentally defective," rural, and delinquent children.[3]

Breckinridge made key contributions in each of these areas. Perhaps more important than any of her contributions to the three areas of interest, however, was the opportunity to bring to a national audience her ideas about "minimum standards" of living, which she had been developing at the local and state levels for more than a decade. As a member of the committee on "the Economic and Social Basis for Child Welfare Standards," Breckinridge prepared a report on "Family Budgets" in which she enunciated her conviction that the federal govern-ment owed all its citizens a basic level of economic security. "A level can be fixed below which no one should be allowed to fall," she pronounced. "Having seen the possibility, we can 'do no other' than seek it as a matter of national honor."[4] Breckinridge's participation in the 1919 White House Conference on Children thus foreshadowed her role in the development of the welfare state committed to establishing a basic minimum standard of living for all Americans.

"Miss Breckinridge and the Bureau"

The 1919 White House Conference on Children was the culmination of the U.S. Children's Bureau's "Year of the Child" campaign, launched during World War I by Breckinridge's old friend from Hull House and former employer at the Chicago School of Civics and Philanthropy, Julia Lathrop. Lathrop had moved from Chicago to Washington to become the nation's first female head of a federal agency in 1912. She was succeeded in office in 1921 by another Hull House alumna, Grace Abbott, who had cut short her graduate training at the University of Chicago to direct the Immigrants' Protective League (discussed in chapter 4) before moving to the nation's capital in 1917 to assist in enforcing the nation's first (and short-lived) federal child labor law. Abbott remained in office until 1934, when she returned to Chicago to join the faculty of the School of Social Service Administration. Before she departed, Abbott hand-picked her successor, Katharine Lenroot, who, as Abbott's assistant, had been integral to the Bureau's Pan-American activities, discussed in more detail in chapter 8, which were of great interest to Breckinridge. From the beginning, then, Breckinridge had a special relationship with the U.S. Children's Bureau and its female leadership. As Lenroot put it: "The path between Miss Breckinridge and the Bureau was well traveled in both directions."[5]

Shared principles as well as personal relationships made Breckinridge an avid supporter of the Children's Bureau. Breckinridge appreciated the bureau's long-standing emphasis on both "civil service standards" and sound social science. As she explained: "What I want is what the Children's Bureau wants, because I think they know more what is needed and what can be done than anyone else in the country."[6]

Institutional ties further strengthened Breckinridge's association with the Children's Bureau. Under Breckinridge and Abbott's joint leadership, first the Chicago School of Civics and Philanthropy and then the School of Social Security Administration enjoyed a long and productive relationship with the Children's Bureau. The bureau's modus operandi—investigate, educate, legislate—meshed well with Breckinridge and Abbott's strong emphasis on social science scholarship as the basis for social welfare legislation. Breckinridge, Abbott, and their students conducted numerous studies on behalf of the Children's Bureau. Breckinridge and Abbott were also largely responsible for staffing the agency. Modeling the

Breckinridge met Julia Lathrop when both women were residents of
Hull House; in 1908, Lathrop invited Breckinridge to head up a new
research department at the Chicago School of Civics and Philanthropy.
After Lathrop left Chicago to direct the new U.S. Children's Bureau
in 1912, Breckinridge worked closely with the Children's Bureau to
promote child labor legislation, aid to single mothers, and maternal
and child health. Her advocacy on behalf of the often-beleaguered
agency paved the way for her participation in the New Deal "women's
network" and her promotion of a welfare state to ensure a "national
minimum" for all Americans. In this image, Breckinridge and Lathrop
are depicted early in their association outside of Green Hall on the
University of Chicago campus.

Courtesy Special Collections Research Center, University of Chicago Library

School of Social Service Administration curriculum on the bureau's civil service exams, Abbott and Breckinridge gave their students a significant advantage in competing for both state and federal positions with the Children's Bureau, which functioned practically as an employment service for SSA graduates.[7]

Breckinridge's close ties to the Children's Bureau prompted her to engage in political lobbying on behalf of public policy on the national stage beginning in the 1920s, when the bureau assumed responsibility for administering the United States' first federally subsidized public welfare program. First proposed in 1918 and finally enacted in 1921, the Sheppard-Towner Act provided federal funding to states to provide health services to pregnant women, new mothers, and young children.[8] Breckinridge, who had been profoundly affected by the childhood deaths of two siblings as well as by her own mother's premature death—resulting, she suggested in her memoirs, from poor health as a consequence of repeated pregnancies— became a fervent supporter of the proposed public health program.[9]

Breckinridge, the Abbott sisters, and their allies in such women's organizations as the National Consumers' League, the Women's Trade Union League, the League of Women Voters, and the Women's Joint Congressional Committee all worked feverishly to rally support for the bill, known colloquially as "the M & I," for "Maternity and Infancy." Although the bill's sponsors were forced to accept some amendments during the legislative process, Grace Abbott was optimistic that these were face-saving measures for congressmen who had originally opposed the bill but who had been overwhelmed with supportive messages from their constituents. "It is too ridiculous the way these grown men have behaved," she confided to Breckinridge. As it turned out, the amendments—which included a five-year "test period" for the bill and required congressional approval for reauthorization—would prove to be far more significant than Abbott originally estimated. Nonetheless, Breckinridge and other supporters of the bill were thrilled at its adoption.[10]

The Sheppard-Towner Act provided funding through an innovative grants-in-aid system, in which the federal government offered matching grants for states that agreed to establish maternal and infancy services. Although the Children's Bureau generally oversaw these services, individual states had considerable latitude in the design and implementation of their programs. Breckinridge described the program as a "magnificent and successful experiment of federal-state cooperation" that combined "a unified administration from Washington" with a "recognition of the different needs of the different states." While the responsiveness to "local capacity and local need" no doubt encouraged states to "opt in" to the program, this decentralized approach also opened the way for localities to engage in discriminatory practices that reflected prejudices against African American midwives and Native American healers and resulted in inferior services on reservations and in black communities.[11] Despite its shortcomings, the "M & I" provided essential services to many women and children, especially to poor white women in rural areas who had limited access to quality healthcare.[12]

Notwithstanding its success rate and its popular appeal, the "M & I" struggled throughout its tenure, from 1921 to 1929, to maintain political support and essential funding due to opposition from red-baiting antifeminist women's groups as well as the male-dominated medical establishment, which wished to maintain control over healthcare. The proviso that the program would have to be resubmitted to Congress for continued funding, which Abbott had hoped was mere window dressing, proved to be an Achilles' heel. Although legislators grudgingly extended funding for a two-year period in 1927, they included a clause specifying that the program would be terminated for good in 1929—just as the nation entered a prolonged period of economic crisis that would come to be known as the Great Depression. "A magnificent piece of skilled administrative organization was allowed to go out like the flame of a candle, as though it were of no national importance whatsoever," Breckinridge lamented.[13]

After the program lost funding, there were several efforts to revive it. Breckinridge supported these efforts in a variety of ways. She planted editorials in the *Lexington Herald*, the newspaper her brother Desha had inherited from their father, under the byline of the editor, Thomas Underwood. She also flattered and cajoled congressmen, including Morton Hull (R-IL) and Virgil Chapman (D-KY), attempting to persuade elected officials from both major parties and from her home state as well as her adopted state to support continuing health services for mothers and infants. However, all of these efforts were unsuccessful. "It was so mean of these men to hit the children," Breckinridge complained.[14]

Although unsuccessful, Breckinridge's lobbying efforts on behalf of the "M & I" represented the beginning of an ever-increasing commitment to using all the forces at her disposal to promote public welfare at the federal level. Initially focused on supporting the Children's Bureau, ultimately Breckinridge would use the lobbying skills she honed in support of the bureau to advocate for the creation of the American welfare state.

The Children's Bureau fought from its inception to maintain both its autonomy and its funding. These tensions led to a major battle between women child-welfare reformers and male public-health officials at the White House Conference on Child Health and Protection in 1930, where women activists, including Breckinridge, strongly opposed efforts to transfer child health services from the Children's Bureau to the Public Health Service. Ultimately, the "overwhelming opposition" presented by approximately five hundred angry bureau supporters prevailed, and the conference not only preserved child welfare under the purview of the female-dominated Children's Bureau but also produced a nineteen-point Children's Charter recognizing "the rights of the child as the first rights of citizenship."[15]

Referring to the charter as the "Magna Charta [*sic*] of American childhood," Breckinridge praised it as "the most comprehensive statement of what should be the heritage of every child that could be conceived by America's ablest educators and wisest social workers." In keeping with Breckinridge's commitment to a national minimum, the charter included a demand that all children—"regardless of race, or color, or situation"—should be entitled to "an adequate standard of living and the security of stable income." As the Depression deepened, the Children's Bureau's commitment to child welfare would require the agency to become increasingly active in efforts to promote first a federal relief program and then a broader set of policies that would ultimately become enshrined as "social security."[16]

By the time the United States entered the Great Depression, the Children's Bureau had an established record as a trusted source for social statistics. Throughout the 1930s the bureau was the principal source for statistical data on the impact of the economic crisis on the citizenry. As Breckinridge put it, "It is the channel through which information was brought to the American people of the extent and character of this misery now prevailing."[17]

In part because of the bureau's importance in providing reliable information to politicians, policymakers, and the public, Breckinridge was one of the beleaguered agency's most passionate supporters, organizing many letter-writing and public-relations campaigns on behalf of the bureau. One illustrative instance came in 1932, when the bureau faced a proposed $100,000 budget cut. After receiving an urgent appeal from Katharine Lenroot, Breckinridge mobilized her fellow social workers to contact their legislators to express their support of the bureau and its work. She also prevailed upon her brother, Desha, to lend his support. Breckinridge herself wrote to her representatives to express her support for the bureau and to explain that the proposed budget cut would inhibit the agency's fact-finding mission and thus undermine efforts to promote an informed approach to the economic crisis. Unfailingly polite, Breckinridge also was persistent. She exchanged several letters with a fiscally conservative senator in an effort to preserve funding for the Children's Bureau, for instance, in which she assured him that the organization was "a model both of efficiency and of economy." Grace Abbott believed that "all the letters about the Bureau" helped to preserve the bureau's funding, specifically for the statistical research that would be used in support of New Deal welfare legislation.[18]

"The need was so dire and so widespread"

While the Children's Bureau collected national data on Americans who sought financial assistance during the Great Depression, the School of Social Security Administration conducted its own study on the effects of unemployment on Chicago residents. Breckinridge, who supervised the study, needed to look no further than her own adopted hometown to find evidence that drastic action was called for to address the dire situation confronting the nation in the 1930s.

During the Depression, Breckinridge agonized over the plight of the unemployed and the homeless. One of her students at the School of Social Service Administration during the 1930s vividly recalled a remark Breckinridge made about "being so troubled sleeping in her good warm bed. She seriously thought that she really ought to give it to someone who needed it, when the need was so dire and so widespread."[19]

Breckinridge was well aware of the extent of the crisis, because she had responded in characteristic fashion to this national emergency by directing a study of the Chicago Renters' Court, the specialized court responsible for hearing cases in which tenants were subject to eviction within twenty-four hours for nonpayment of rent. Student researchers' case notes from the Renters' Court revealed the difficult, even desperate, circumstances confronting working-class Chicagoans in the depths of the Depression. Breckinridge, who received daily reports from the court, described the situation as "unendurable." She noted that in spring 1932, between forty and seventy cases were heard in the court each day. In addition to pointing out the ways in which the housing crisis led to "separation of families," on the one hand, and "fearful crowding," on the other hand, Breckinridge observed that each day, new applicants were from "a constantly higher occupational level"—that is, the Depression was affecting more and more people, including people who had previously been financially secure.[20]

Except in the cases involving individuals unable to work because of disease or disability, case files from the Renters' Court recorded the renters' previous employment and income. In nearly every instance, the file included a notation that the householder(s) had been unemployed for a lengthy period, often two or three years. While some had found temporary or part-time work, the family income had dropped precipitously. For instance, the Whitney family, who appeared at the Renters' Court in 1932, had previously had three earners: Floyd Whitney had worked for a publishing company, but he had been out of work for two years in 1932. His wife, Carrie Whitney, had worked as a maid but had been out of work for five months. And her brother, Rufus Rice, who worked in a pickle factory, had been out of work for seven weeks. The family's total monthly income had dropped from $261 to zero.[21]

Some families and individuals who appeared in the Renters' Court were "re-peaters," who had been evicted repeatedly since the onset of the Depression. Their case files recorded that prior to 1930, they had been long-term tenants, owing nothing; by the time they appeared in the Renters' Court, however, they had endured a succession of short-term rentals and a rapid series of evictions. Anton Czipowski had worked as a pile driver for twenty years but had lost his job in 1930. By 1932, he, his wife Elizabeth, and their five children had been evicted three times. "Very quiet" throughout the interview, at its conclusion Elizabeth burst into tears and began to "repeat over and over a refrain that went something like this:—I can't stand this moving, moving, moving; I can't stand it! Why can't they let me stay in one place? I can't stand this all the time moving! . . . I can't stand this moving, moving, moving!"[22]

Other clients were appearing before the court for the first time. Such families and individuals reported having steady incomes, acquiring savings, and in some cases even purchasing property prior to the Depression. By 1932 or 1933, however, they had lost everything. Tom and Margaret Riley were in this position. Prior to the Depression, Tom had worked as a barber, earning $108 a month; Margaret earned $143 a month at International Harvester. Both Rileys lost their jobs in 1929–30, however. Although they had been getting by, using Tom Riley's veterans' pension to cover rent and "depending on relatives for food," they had run out of resources entirely by 1932. "Had savings, gone now," the case file tersely recorded.[23]

To survive, families sold their furniture, clothing, and other belongings, moved repeatedly to cheaper and cheaper quarters, borrowed and begged from relatives and friends, and finally turned to charitable and relief agencies for support. By spring 1932, however, most private charities had exhausted their funds. Charitable agencies passed needy families on to other sources when they could, but eventually applicants had nowhere else to go. The McNerney family, for instance, had been receiving assistance since 1929, when Thomas McNerney, a World War I veteran who had been gassed in the war but nonetheless held a job as a machinist prior to the Depression, lost his job. The McNerneys first received aid from the Salvation Army, then the Red Cross, then the Catholic Charity Bureau, and finally the Cook County Veterans' Service, but the latter agency could not provide rent assistance when the family was threatened with eviction in 1932.[24]

Many unemployed Chicagoans lost all hope. The Labedz family received assistance from their local parish for eighteen months before funding ran out. With nowhere else to turn, "Mrs. L. is about frantic," the worker noted, alternating "hysterical weeping" and "almost shrieking" with threats to "smother the baby" or to "turn on the gas and kill the whole family."[25]

"National Funds for a National Crisis"

The dire circumstances recorded in the Renters' Court study played a decisive role in inspiring the first serious attempts at legislation for federal relief. Edith Abbott later maintained that Senator Edward Costigan's inspiration for drafting his relief bill was a conversation he had with the Abbott sisters about conditions in Chicago while they were on vacation in his home state of Colorado in fall 1931. Abbott informed the senator that local resources were entirely incapable of dealing with the current crisis: "Our schools are full of hungry children, our streets are full of tired and resentful men," she told him. Homelessness had become a terrible problem. "The Renter's Court, I told him, was a nightmare—women crying, children crying, everyone in despair." Edith Abbott backed up her emotional appeal with "a lengthy recitation of statistics and facts" taken from the Renters' Court study, but it was Grace Abbott who drove the point home: "Now Senator Costigan," she demanded, "if this is what happens in Chicago—'the Queen of the West'—do we need federal relief or do we not?" Breckinridge subsequently corresponded with Senator Costigan about the Renters' Court study, providing him with ammunition for his efforts to enact federal relief legislation.[26]

Along with the Abbott sisters, Breckinridge was one of the earliest and most outspoken advocates of federal programs to address the Great Depression. She had undertaken a study of "the present crisis of unemployment" for the National Conference of Social Work in May 1930. By the following summer—sometime before the Abbott sisters had their fateful conversation with Senator Costigan—Breckinridge had become convinced that "national sources should be drawn upon to meet this national distress" and had begun to advocate for a federal relief bill.[27]

Breckinridge had promoted public welfare programs for decades. In Progressive-era Chicago, her academic activism had helped establish the nation's first mothers' pension program. In the interwar period, her activity in international social welfare circles strengthened her commitment to state-supported social welfare policies. During the Great Depression, her research in the Renters' Court convinced her that the time had come to advocate for a national welfare program. Drawing on her experience with social-welfare programs in Progressive-era America, her expertise on emerging welfare states in post–World War I Europe, and her statistical research on the effects of the Great Depression, she asserted that an emergency situation justified federal action. By casting the current economic downturn as a national disaster, she advanced her longstanding goal of adopting social policy to ensure a "national minimum" for all Americans.[28]

Breckinridge and Abbott dedicated the entire December 1931 issue of the *Social Service Review* to articles highlighting insufficient local efforts to address the current crisis and suggesting the potential for national solutions to widespread poverty and unemployment. To reinforce this message, Breckinridge included an editorial under the headline "National Funds for a National Crisis" that called attention to "the inadequacy of private relief" and asserted that "federal aid" was "clearly necessary in this emergency."[29]

Breckinridge was not alone in her desire to see the federal government take decisive action, of course. The "female dominion" of child welfare workers based in the Children's Bureau had long advocated federal welfare programs. Women soon expanded their influence under the presidency of Franklin Delano Roosevelt, developing a powerful "women's network" with close ties to both women's organizations and the Children's Bureau.[30] This network used their newfound power to translate the reforms they had long backed at the local and state levels into a comprehensive welfare state at the federal level.

When Roosevelt took office in spring 1933, his administration offered women reformers like Breckinridge new opportunities to shape federal policy. The most visible signal of Roosevelt's willingness to take women's concerns seriously was the possibility that he would choose Frances Perkins as the secretary of labor—and the first woman member of the cabinet. Eager to see more women in influential positions in the federal government and enthusiastic at the possibility of placing Perkins, a long-standing supporter of labor legislation, in a position of political power, Breckinridge enthusiastically endorsed Perkins. "To recognize the capacity of women is to raise the marginal level of service and so benefit the community," she asserted.[31]

Perkins's appointment gave Breckinridge and her fellow advocates of social-welfare legislation a powerful ally within the Roosevelt Administration. "It is wonderful to have Miss Perkins in the department, isn't it?" Breckinridge wrote to her Children's Bureau colleague Katharine Lenroot. "To think that the head of the department really understands what one is talking about and wants the same things that one wants is certainly the source of great happiness."[32] Breckinridge immediately made the most of the opportunity. She wasted no time in contacting the new secretary of labor to urge her to advocate for a national minimum wage and a renewed maternity and infancy program.[33] When the National Industrial Recovery Act passed in early 1933, authorizing maximum-hour and minimum-wage legislation for male and female workers alike, Breckinridge assumed that Perkins would turn to social workers like herself to help "formulate satisfactory principles" to guide minimum-wage legislation and promptly offered suggestions on how to create a minimum-wage policy that would ensure "a minimum standard of living" for all and suggested some of the measures that should be used to establish that minimum, including physical health, adequate diet, child welfare, and recreational opportunities.[34]

Perkins's appointment was not a one-hit wonder. Rather, she was the first of numerous appointments of women reformers to public office. These appointments owed a great deal to the work of Democratic Party insider Mary W. Dewson, known as "More Women Dewson" for her success in placing women in high-ranking positions in the Roosevelt administration. The resulting women's network, which drew from the ranks of female reformers and maintained close ties to women's groups, amplified the influence of Breckinridge and her fellow women activists in the New Deal era.[35] It also seemed to pave the way for a brighter future for the Children's Bureau and its longtime supporters. Thus, Breckinridge was "extremely happy" when longtime labor legislation and healthcare advocate Josephine Roche was appointed assistant secretary of the treasury, commenting that this development "seems to indicate that a way may be found for constructive relationships between the Children's Bureau and the Public Health Service."[36]

Throughout the 1930s Breckinridge carried on a cordial correspondence with "More Women Dewson"—to whom she once referred as "My dear and Honorable Colonel"—and other members of the women's network. Her close relationship with these influential women gave her a voice in the White House, allowing her to take advantage of the women's network to promote social policy.[37] But Breckinridge's standing as a prominent social worker also gave her a powerful—and nonpartisan—platform from which to advocate, first for federal relief and ultimately for a comprehensive social security program underwritten by the U.S. government.

At the same time that she collaborated with the Washington, D.C., women's network to promote federal welfare programs, Breckinridge made it her mission to persuade her fellow social workers to mobilize in support of national action on behalf of the nation's needy. In 1931 Breckinridge criticized the apathetic response of social workers to the economic crisis, commenting that it was "humiliating that the group of social workers is so little heard from in connection with all of this." She added, "I hope that the time will come when the American Association of Social Workers will have some professional influence at times like this." Not content merely to "hope" for change, Breckinridge used her influence with the American Association of Social Workers (AASW) and other professional social-work organizations to prompt them to investigate social and economic difficulties, publicize their findings, and promote federal welfare programs.[38]

Breckinridge must have been pleased when her efforts began to bear fruit. By late 1931 a growing number of her fellow social workers were becoming convinced of "the necessity of federal aid in this emergency." Her friend Frank Bane, who had founded the American Public Welfare Association in 1930 and would later become executive director of the Social Security Board, must have given her spirits a lift when in late 1931 he opined that the nation was entering "a public welfare era." If the difficulties of the era succeeded in demonstrating "the absolute necessity" of addressing the "age-old" problems of poverty through governmental action, he optimistically predicted, "I think we may say the depression has taught us something."[39]

Breckinridge also used her recognized expertise to shape the form of the first federal relief bill. In 1931 two senators—Republican Robert La Follette Jr. of Wisconsin and Democrat Edward Costigan of Colorado—proposed federal relief measures. Ultimately, these would be combined as the Costigan-La Follette Bill. During the drafting of and debate on the bill, Breckinridge corresponded with Senator Costigan, who appealed to her—as well as to other "experts in the field of social service and public welfare"—for advice and assistance.[40]

The Costigan-La Follette Bill, like the now-defunct Sheppard-Towner Act, provided for federal grants-in-aid to states to support programs offering financial assistance to victims of the Great Depression. Because its backers included Grace Abbott, chief of the Children's Bureau, and because its funding system echoed that of the bureau's most well-known and ambitious program, opponents quickly labeled the bill "a Children's Bureau bill."[41]

For Breckinridge, of course, the bill's reputation as "a Children's Bureau bill" was a plus rather than a minus. Once convinced that the Children's Bureau favored the proposed legislation, Breckinridge declared herself "an ardent supporter of the bill" and enthusiastically joined the effort to promote its adoption. Breckinridge's colleague from the League of Women Voters, Marguerite Owen, an experienced lobbyist who had helped to orchestrate the original campaign to adopt the Sheppard-Towner Act, solicited Breckinridge's assistance in lobbying on behalf of the relief bill. "The problem now is to get those in the country who are really concerned to express their interest," Owen remarked. "Any assistance that you can offer in that way will be greatly appreciated."[42]

In response, Breckinridge escalated her lobbying efforts. As she had done in support of the Children's Bureau, she wrote to her own elected representatives and urged others to send "helpful letters" in support of the bill. On this occasion, however, she also used her professional position to promote policy, serving on the AASW Committee on Federal Action on Unemployment, which Grace Abbott referred to as "your Committee of the A.A.S.W." The committee endorsed the bill and assembled prominent social workers—including Edith Abbott—to appear on its behalf at the hearings.[43]

Although the bill ultimately failed, Breckinridge was encouraged by her foray into the political fray. During the debates she confided to a colleague, "I am very happy because they treat the bill with such seriousness for after all I never did anything just like this before." After the bill was defeated, Breckinridge continued to "consider the fight successful from an educational viewpoint," commenting, "It does serve as the basis of discussion and as something from which to depart."[44]

"To mobilize a public opinion"

Breckinridge's work on behalf of the Costigan-La Follette Bill was just the beginning. As detailed above, Breckinridge was no newcomer to lobbying federal officials on behalf of the Children's Bureau and its programs. Prior to 1932, however, she engaged in such political activities primarily as a private citizen—albeit an outspoken private citizen with an impressive professional pedigree. When it came to advocating for federal welfare programs, however, Breckinridge developed a new strategy. She used her position as a pioneering social work educator and as a prominent figure in the professionalization of social work to push professional social work organizations both to lobby for public welfare programs and to shape the form those programs took. Other historians have pointed out that women's "official" work in federal agencies was greatly amplified by women's "unofficial" work in voluntary organizations. Breckinridge's advocacy from within mixed-gender professional organizations reveals another layer of women's (and men's) civic engagement and highlights the important role that public intellectuals played in promoting public welfare and shaping the welfare state.[45]

After the failure of the first relief bill in early 1932, Breckinridge was more determined than ever to ensure that professional social workers would be at the forefront of the fight for social security. She prompted the executive secretary of the national organization, Walter West, to escalate the AASW's efforts on behalf of federal relief. "It seems to me that the American Association [of Social Workers] is the body to move," she wrote, explaining: "These social workers have known of the need, have helped work out the good plans, and they are aware that the need must be met."[46] West responded to Breckinridge's overtures by asking her to join a new AASW committee on the subject of federal relief. The successor to the Committee on Federal Action on Unemployment, which Grace Abbott previously had called "your committee," this committee eventually become the AASW's Committee on Federal Action on Social Welfare. Its charge was to collect information from social workers and "supply information where it can be of use in connection with proposals for legislation." As a member of this group, Breckinridge helped devise "a set of administrative principles for a federal relief program" and prepared testimony in support of federal relief in 1932 and again in 1933.[47]

Breckinridge also used her position as the chair of the Chicago Chapter of the American Association of Social Workers to urge social workers to offer public support for a "legislative program" for public welfare.[48] Breckinridge's leadership transformed the Chicago Chapter into a major player in the promotion of

During the New Deal, Breckinridge used her position as a pioneering social work educator and prominent figure in the professionalization of social work to push professional social work organizations both to lobby for public welfare programs and to shape the form those programs took. Her work highlights the important role public intellectuals played in promoting public welfare and shaping the welfare state.

Courtesy Special Collections Research Center, University of Chicago Library

federal welfare programs. Gertrude Wilson, who had been pursuing her MA at the School of Social Service Administration in the 1930s, later averred that there were no "quiescent social workers" in Depression-era Chicago; rather, they were "just as active as can be."[49]

Throughout the 1930s Breckinridge tirelessly promoted public welfare. In July 1932 she conceived the notion of putting out "The Social Worker's Creed" to express the profession's agreement on the necessity of "adequate knowledge, adequate service and adequate relief."[50] Although "The Social Worker's Creed" never became an official platform for professional social workers, Breckinridge continually pushed her vision of public welfare. In both her public speeches and her private correspondence, Breckinridge consistently advanced a set of principles to guide public welfare policy.

According to Breckinridge, social programs should be both "comprehensive" and "continuous." By "comprehensive" Breckinridge meant that services should be available to everyone, and that they should be sufficient to ensure not only a basic minimum of food, shelter, and clothing but also medical care, educational opportunities, and leisure and recreation. An article in *The Nation*, published under Edith Abbott's byline, but no doubt influenced by Breckinridge, summed up these ideas by insisting that a "comprehensive plan" for social welfare should provide "adequate dignified relief for all in need."[51]

Breckinridge also insisted that welfare programs must be publicly funded and publicly administered, and she frequently reiterated these principles, both of which followed logically from the need for "comprehensive and continuous" coverage. As she explained in the introduction to her 1927 book, *Public Welfare Administration*, public assistance was preferable to private charity, "for the social worker can be satisfied with nothing less than a universal provision for a continuous service," and "only the state can be both universal and continuous."[52] Just as important as the public provision of ample funding was the principle of "public money in public hands." Breckinridge never tired of advancing this principle, which she saw as necessary to ensuring adequate support for those in need.[53] As she explained: "It is the only principle any hope can be based on securing standards not too low and a comprehensive service."[54]

Finally, Breckinridge insisted that the "public hands" in charge of dispensing "public money" should be those of qualified professionals. While this principle obviously reflected Breckinridge's own self-interest, in her many statements on this issue she insisted that the need for professionally trained social workers was twofold. First, only professional social workers had the necessary expertise to render a "social case work diagnosis"—that is, to determine needs accurately and respond appropriately. Second, social work professionals were guided by "professional standards of social work" rather than by "sinister" party politics.

Throughout her career Breckinridge was an outspoken critic of "partisan politics" in public appointments. Instead, she advocated hiring qualified experts, preferably through a civil-service process, for positions of public responsibility. Nowhere was this more important than in the area of administering public-welfare programs. Breckinridge insisted that only professionally trained social workers were qualified for the important task of determining needs and providing assistance.[55]

In addition to enunciating guiding principles for public-welfare policy, Breckinridge elaborated on the specific programs she saw as necessary for social security—what she called a "national minimum." Breckinridge believed that the federal government should provide financial assistance, medical care, and legal services for everybody in need, as well as special programs for mothers and children and the elderly or disabled. She also insisted that the nation-state was responsible for enacting and enforcing labor legislation, including the abolition of child labor and the adoption of minimum-wage and maximum-hour legislation for all adult workers. Breckinridge had advocated these measures for decades; by the 1930s she also had become a supporter of old-age pensions and unemployment insurance. In short, her vision of a comprehensive federal welfare program anticipated— and exceeded—the provisions that ultimately would be included in the Social Security Act of 1935 and the Fair Labor Standards Act of 1938.[56]

Breckinridge's efforts to "mobilize a public opinion" on behalf of a public-welfare program were not always obvious. More interested in results than in recognition, she believed that "a body of informed public opinion on the professional aspects of social legislation" should come from professional organizations rather than from their individual members.[57] The important thing, she once remarked, was "real service to the people who need it. . . . That is, after all, what we spend our lives trying to get."[58]

Thus, much of Breckinridge's work building the welfare state took place behind the scenes. For instance, Breckinridge provided "talking points" to official (male) representatives of national professional organizations, suggested policy proposals to be discussed at national conferences, and drafted official statements that appeared in the national news media. While her ideas thus informed many public-policy discussions, her authorship went unremarked. Only combing through her personal papers reveals that her role in promoting public welfare went well beyond her official contributions.[59]

"A national program in our field"

Breckinridge's most visible role in the New Deal was her collaboration with the Federal Emergency Relief Administration. She had played an important, if nearly invisible, role in establishing this federal agency. As a consultant to the AASW

Committee on Federal Action on Unemployment, Breckinridge had helped to devise "a set of administrative principles for a federal relief program" and to prepare congressional testimony in support of such a program. These efforts finally came to fruition with the adoption of the Federal Emergency Relief Act of 1933.[60]

The act established a new relief agency— the Federal Emergency Relief Administration, or FERA—to administer a temporary relief program begun in summer 1933. Set to last for just two years, the new agency was placed under the leadership of Harry Hopkins, who promptly announced that as of July 1, only public agencies could administer FERA funds. The new administrator's commitment to Breckinridge's cherished principle of "public money in public hands" encouraged her to see the new relief agency as providing "the opportunity for which we have been waiting . . . to establish a national program in our field."[61] As it turned out, she was correct.

Breckinridge insisted there was "no reason to think [Hopkins] values my opinion especially!"[62] Indeed, there is no evidence that Breckinridge ever followed up on Democratic Party insider Mary Dewson's suggestion, in February 1934, that she should "help him perfect his plans" by sending a carbon copy of any correspondence with Hopkins to the First Lady, who "will see that it gets into Mr. Hopkins' hands."[63] Breckinridge used other channels to reach out to the new FERA official, however. In addition to corresponding with him personally, she persuaded the American Association of Social Workers to suggest that Hopkins establish an advisory committee of social work professionals.[64] She also helped set the agenda for a "Conference on Governmental Objectives for Social Work" in Washington, D.C., in February 1934, featuring special guests Harry Hopkins and Frances Perkins, at which the Chicago Chapter of the AASW recommended taking up the questions "Could Social Workers Frame Standards and Requirements for Personnel for Federal, State and Local Positions in Social Work Programs? What Help Could Be Offered in Training Workers Selected on an Emergency Basis?"[65] However, none of these overtures seems to have had any measurable outcome, despite Dewson's (apparently unanswered) demand for an update.[66]

Instead, Breckinridge's entrée into FERA came from Josephine Brown, who was appointed as administrative assistant at FERA in April 1934. Within a month of Brown's appointment she and Breckinridge were collaborating on an innovative training program for emergency relief workers that allowed Breckinridge to bring to bear on the most pressing needs of the nation her decades of experience in professionalizing social work.

In some ways, Brown seemed an unlikely ally for Breckinridge. Although she was a fellow graduate of a Seven Sisters school (Bryn Mawr), Brown's social work education was limited to a short stint at the New York School of Social Work, which emphasized casework rather than Breckinridge's preferred focus on social policy. Moreover, much of her social work experience was in private rather than public agencies, which Breckinridge favored. However, Brown recently had spent a year at the Social Science Research Council in New York City, where she did innovative research on social work in rural areas and worked with two graduates of the Chicago School of Civics and Philanthropy, Gertrude Vaile and Emma O. Lundberg. These experiences may have heightened Brown's interest in serious research and in public relief. Contact with Breckinridge's former students—especially Lundberg, who worked at the Children's Bureau and became Lenroot's life partner—probably also brought Breckinridge to Brown's attention. Alternatively, given Breckinridge's recent election as the new president of the American Association of Schools of Social Work (AASSW), it may simply have seemed like a logical step to contact the leader of the national social work education association when faced with the problem of educating the army of unprepared relief workers who had been hastily hired to staff the new emergency-relief offices around the country. Whatever the reason, within a month of beginning her new job Brown contacted Breckinridge in May 1934 to invite her to attend a three-day conference in Washington, D.C., to discuss possible collaboration between the AASSW and FERA to design a special training program for the nation's relief workers.[67]

Breckinridge took office just as the desperate need for workers in both public and private relief agencies during the Great Depression brought long-standing tensions over professional standards of social work training—and different schools' visions of social work education—to a head. Within the American Association of Social Work, left-leaning social workers attempted (but failed) to take control of the organization. An independent organization of "untrained relief workers" also posed a dilemma for the AASW, which was dedicated to advancing the status of the social work profession by establishing prerequisites for membership. Although the organization still had rather minimal expectations in the 1930s—a high school diploma and social work experience sufficed—its chapters had been actively investigating the possibility of establishing definite certification standards for social workers. Breckinridge, who had an abiding interest in this issue, undertook this initiative with enthusiasm. Establishing professional standards was also a major preoccupation of a relative newcomer to the professional social work scene, the American Public Welfare Association, established in 1930. True to form, Breckinridge took part in this organization's professionalizing drive as well.[68]

Meanwhile, the American Association of Schools of Social Work took a different tack by adopting a new "minimum curriculum" for its thirty member schools. Breckinridge, always an enthusiastic advocate of setting standards for social work education, was an appropriate standard-bearer for the AASSW's commitment to rigorous standards for professional education. Indeed, her election as president signaled social work educators' commitment to high scholarship. After dedicating a session of the 1934 annual meeting of the association to the theme of the Depression's effects on social work education, Breckinridge promptly initiated a study of all the professional social work schools in the nation to ascertain how closely each adhered to the prescribed curriculum.[69]

Breckinridge's advocacy of high standards for social work education evidently impressed Josephine Brown. Although Breckinridge's predecessor as the president of the AASSW, Jewish social work leader Maurice J. Karpf, had reportedly had an informal conversation with FERA director Harry Hopkins about some sort of training program the previous year, "nothing definite had come out of it," and the AASSW office files contained no records of the discussion.[70]

Immediately after the May 1934 conference, however, while aboard a train home, Josephine Brown penned a handwritten letter to Breckinridge to seek her counsel about a training program. "I hope you can endure this painful writing on a jerky train," she apologized, explaining that she was "most anxious to tell you my latest thoughts on the training program and learn your reaction." She closed: "I can't tell you how much I am enjoying working with you and how much I appreciate your help."[71]

Breckinridge also was impressed with Brown, whom she described as a person "who not only knows the content of professional equipment, but has respect for professional education in the field of Social Work." Breckinridge thus was enthusiastic about a collaboration between FERA and the AASSW on providing increased opportunities for professional training for relief workers.[72] "It is too wonderful that you think we can be of service!" Breckinridge exclaimed in a letter to Brown. She was keenly aware of the opportunity to advance her vision of social work education that the FERA training program offered. "It would be wonderful," she wrote, "if you could support the standards we are trying to establish and maintain."[73]

In fact, the FERA training initiative gave Breckinridge tremendous influence over the education of the first generation of public welfare workers. Breckinridge and Brown quickly agreed that FERA funding should be granted only to students who took courses in schools that conformed to the AASSW's "minimum curriculum"—or which received special approval from Brown in consultation with Breckinridge—to ensure that participating schools provided training that was "definitely professional."[74]

Breckinridge carried on an extensive correspondence with social work schools eager to obtain the necessary accreditation to be members in good standing with the AASSW and thus to participate in the FERA training program. It was essential, she believed, that only schools offering a comprehensive social work curriculum, rather than "random courses" in sociology departments, be included.[75] The "minimum curriculum" required of all AASSW schools fell into four groups:

medical and psychiatric case work; community organization and group work; public welfare administration; and research, statistics, and the law.[76] While the first two groups of requirements reflected the emphasis of the New York School of Social Work, the latter two sets of topics bore the imprint of the University of Chicago's School of Social Service Administration. The FERA training program thus ensured that the first generation of public welfare workers would be exposed to Breckinridge's cherished values of social scientific research and public-welfare administration. It also advanced Breckinridge's commitment to the professionalization of social work by providing "dignity and authority" to professional social workers and social work educators.[77]

Breckinridge was pleased that the program encouraged schools to conform to a standard curriculum—modeled on that offered at the University of Chicago—that included coursework, fieldwork, and "research that would command the respect of social scientists." Overlooking the coercive aspects of the program, she expressed satisfaction that there was "increasing agreement" on the necessity for professional preparation for social work as well as "substantial unanimity" that such preparation should include classroom instruction in community organization and public welfare as well as casework. The FERA experiment validated Breckinridge's well-established advocacy of high academic standards for social work and allowed her to put her passionate support for public welfare into practice.[78]

The FERA training program was, at least according to most official accounts, a tremendous success.[79] Breckinridge praised the program for its success in "recruiting an unusually well-qualified group of scholarship students from sections of the country where there has been a scarcity of trained workers." In 1935, 1,133 social workers in thirty-two states participated in a six-month program in twenty-one AASSW-approved schools through this program, roughly one-fifth of all social work students in that period.[80] Trainees praised the program for giving them more perspective, helping them develop a "professional attitude," and providing supervised field work, while their supervisors praised their "keener grasp of social problems," administrative potential, and "professional attitude." According to one state administrator, the trainees gained a "sounder interpretation of the spirit and purpose of the [federal emergency relief] administration"; another opined, "The training program has been a contribution to professional social work." The comments of students, supervisors, and administrators thus all suggested that the trainees absorbed Breckinridge's values in the course of their training, wherever they attended school.[81]

There were criticisms of the program, of course. The exclusion of some schools—particularly state schools in the west and the south, which had fewer dedicated social work programs—ensured that some educators would be resentful. Moreover, the schools that were included, many of them located in large metropolitan areas in the east and Midwest, gave short shrift to rural issues. While these matters probably would not have disturbed Breckinridge, they were definitely problems for Brown. Even had the end of FERA funding not necessitated the termination of this educational experiment, rising friction between Josephine Brown and Breckinridge's successor as AASSW president, Tulane University's Elizabeth Wisner, over Brown's plan to expand the program to include more land-grant universities and agricultural colleges would probably have been a death knell for the program. Nonetheless, the short-lived training program offered Breckinridge unparalleled opportunity for "leadership in the field of public welfare."[82]

The joint training program represented "new horizons" for social workers, Breckinridge explained in a 1936 address to the National Conference on Social Welfare. These new horizons greatly increased social workers' influence on public policy. During the Depression and New Deal, she explained, "the social worker has learned that public welfare is a field in which the social worker should not only be at home but should exercise great influence." In addition—and of equal importance in terms of exercising "great influence"—"many government officials have recognized the fact that the social worker should be included in the welfare organization and the influence and services of the social worker should be admitted as important factors in the sound development of public welfare."[83]

The FERA training program was terminated when FERA funding was discontinued in 1935. Breckinridge was no doubt disappointed by this development. However, the end of federal relief funding coincided with the adoption of the Social Security Act. Like the FERA training program, the Social Security Act offered "new horizons" for Breckinridge, giving her a fresh venue in which to exercise "great influence" over the emerging welfare state.

"A really sound and progressive national service"

In designing what would become the Social Security Act of 1935, President Roosevelt's Committee on Economic Security drew on two different streams of social legislation advocacy. The first was a "social insurance" tradition, deriving from male-dominated organizations such as the American Association for Labor Legislation, which focused on programs designed for predominantly male workers and aimed to replace breadwinners' wages in cases of unemployment, injury, or old age. The social insurance campaign already had achieved workmen's compensation laws at the state level; during the New Deal its proponents focused on programs such as unemployment insurance and old-age pensions. The second was a "social welfare" tradition, based in women's organizations such as the National Consumers' League, which focused on programs designed to assist mothers and children. By the 1930s these reformers had established state-level mothers' pensions programs and, by way of the Children's Bureau, experimented with a national program for maternal and infant healthcare. During the New Deal they hoped to obtain federal funding for similar programs. Although male and female reformers had worked for different aims and in separate organizations, they had often done so collaboratively. They now sought to incorporate their pioneering state-level programs into a federal plan for national economic security. The Committee on Economic Security designed a program that included both "social insurance" measures for (predominantly male) workers and "social welfare" measures for groups who were excluded from or disadvantaged in the workforce, such as mothers, children, and the disabled.[84]

Breckinridge, like most female social reformers, was primarily identified with the "social welfare" stream of social legislation in the Progressive era. Her work with the National Consumers' League, the Women's Trade Union League, and the Children's Bureau all reinforced her focus on programs designed for mothers and children, working women, and individuals with disabilities. However, she also served at least two terms as a member of the General Administrative Council of the American Association for Labor Legislation in the early twentieth century, and she had been an early supporter of the association's labor legislation proposals, including unemployment insurance. In the 1930s, like most social work professionals, she was a strong supporter of both "social welfare" and "social insurance" measures. The convergence of these two traditions helped create a "welfare consensus" during the New Deal, which fueled public support for the nascent welfare state and the Social Security Act of 1935.[85]

Breckinridge was an enthusiastic supporter of the work of the Committee on Economic Security and a strong proponent of its recommendations, which were eventually incorporated into the Social Security Act. Although she did not serve on the Committee on Economic Security, which was responsible for drafting the programs to be included in President Roosevelt's plan for federal welfare, she had strong ties to several of its members. The chair was Frances Perkins, whose appointment as secretary of labor Breckinridge had enthusiastically promoted; her FERA colleague, Harry Hopkins, also was a member. Her colleagues in the Children's Bureau also exercised strong influence: Katharine Lenroot and Grace Abbott drafted the child welfare sections of the bill, including what would become the most controversial program of the new welfare state, aid to dependent children (later Aid to Families with Dependent Children, or AFDC)—a program fashioned after the mothers' pension model that Breckinridge had pioneered. And Edith Abbott submitted written statements—perhaps with Breckinridge's input—to the committee.[86]

Preoccupied by what would turn out to be her brother Desha's final illness, with the help of the Abbott sisters Breckinridge nonetheless followed develop-

In the 1930s, Breckinridge worked closely with both Edith and Grace Abbott to promote first federal relief and then the Social Security Act. While Breckinridge often worked behind the scenes to influence social policy, the Abbott sisters took a more visible role by testifying on behalf of the Social Security Act. Together, the Abbott sisters were a formidable force, as suggested in this photograph.

Courtesy Special Collections Research Center, University of Chicago Library

ments closely. "Edith and Grace are both quite absorbed in the Committee on Economic Security," she informed Josephine Roche in November 1934.[87] The following spring, unable to attend the legislative hearings because she was called to her brother's deathbed in Kentucky, Breckinridge continued to monitor the bill's progress and to demand updates on the testimony of both Abbott sisters. "Grace back all right," Edith wired her absent partner. "Addressed joint legislative session yesterday and hopeful of results."[88]

While the Abbott sisters worked directly with the Committee on Economic Security and testified personally before Congress on behalf of the Social Security Act, Breckinridge worked behind the scenes to support their efforts. As she had done with earlier relief efforts, Breckinridge used her professional expertise and status to shape and promote the social welfare legislation that laid the groundwork for the welfare state—what Breckinridge called "a really sound and progressive national service."[89] Throughout the months of drafting and debate, Breckinridge rallied all the sources at her disposal to shape the provisions of what would become the Social Security Act and to ensure that the act would be adopted.

Breckinridge was concerned that the proposed Social Security Act provided no new relief program to replace FERA, scheduled to expire in 1935. Indeed, the Committee on Economic Security did not prioritize poor relief but rather promoted preventive measures; the assumption was that states and localities would resume responsibility for those Americans whose needs were not met by the provisions of the Social Security Act. Breckinridge, like most other social workers, believed that continued federal relief was necessary to adequately address the persistent problem of poverty. "An adequate national relief provision" was "absolutely essential" to "any program in the form of recovery," she opined. Urging one of Roosevelt's trusted advisors to persuade the president to support continued federal relief as part of a comprehensive plan for national recovery, Breckinridge used one of her stock arguments for federal welfare programs: "Services intended to remedy and prevent must be as wide in the range of their influence as the sources of misery with which they deal."[90] Unable to attend the special AASW conference that coincided with the legislative hearings on the bill, Breckinridge nonetheless supported the organization's efforts to extend FERA's work.[91]

Breckinridge was also a strong supporter of a national health program. In many ways the time seemed right for such a program to find a place in the new welfare state. The American Association for Labor Legislation had been a longtime supporter of compulsory healthcare insurance as well as old-age pensions and unemployment insurance.[92] Since the latter two Progressive-era proposals for "social insurance" had become part of the New Deal discussion of "social security," the idea of a federal healthcare program also was back on the agenda in the 1930s. Breckinridge was among the "leading and influential social workers of America" who signed a public statement in support of national healthcare. According to social worker Homer Folks, who orchestrated the statement, the open letter was "a very useful factor in support of public health in the economic security program," although the measure did not make it into the final version of the Social Security Act.[93]

Another of Breckinridge's interests was determining where responsibility would rest for administering the act's several provisions. The long-standing turf battle between the Children's Bureau and other government agencies ensured that there would be disagreement over where to house the new programs established by the act. During the lengthy process of maneuvering the bill through Congress,

Breckinridge lobbied influential politicians, urging them to assign responsibility for mothers' pensions to the Children's Bureau. "You know that the Bureau for more than twenty years has been helping to develop standards of administration in this field," she pressed Kentucky Senator Alban Barkley. "It seems a great waste not to utilize this wealth of experience and of contact." To reinforce her message, Breckinridge prevailed upon *Lexington Herald* managing editor Thomas Underwood to contact Barkley about this issue as well.[94]

While it is difficult, of course, to measure the effects of individual citizens' pressure on elected officials' decisions, Breckinridge's efforts seem to have had some impact, at least where her promotion of the Children's Bureau as a suitable home for new federal welfare programs was concerned. Kentucky Senator Fred Vinson—who once confided to Thomas Underwood that he was always favorably disposed to Breckinridge's suggestions—read a letter from Breckinridge about placing mothers' pensions under the authority of the Children's Bureau into the official record. After Breckinridge paid Senator Vinson a personal call in Washington, D.C., he informed her that her wishes had been answered—at least for programs involving maternal health and disabled children. "We have just finished the consideration of the Social Security bill and Maternal and Child Welfare, Crippled Children, etc., are all left with the Childrens' [*sic*] Bureau in the Department of Labor," he wrote.[95] Encouraged, Breckinridge confided to First Lady Eleanor Roosevelt that she was "very happy" at the thought that not only mothers' pensions but also old-age pensions were likely to be placed "into the skilled hands of the Labor Department and especially the Children's Bureau."[96]

Ultimately, however, Breckinridge's highest hopes went unrealized. The Social Security Act made no provisions for federal relief funding. In addition, due to "insurmountable opposition" from the medical establishment, the recommendation for national health insurance was dropped from the final version of the bill. Finally, most of the act's programs—including mothers' pensions—were assigned to a new federal agency, the Social Security Board. The only programs assigned to the Children's Bureau were healthcare for mothers and children, support for "crippled children," and services for "dependent" children.[97]

Breckinridge, as one of the framers of the original mothers' pensions, was disappointed in how this form of assistance was incorporated into the Social Security Act. Although Breckinridge was an advocate for mothers' pensions, she also knew from studies of state programs that they were not only chronically underfunded but also often poorly administered. For instance, in Illinois, where the responsibility for administering the program had been assigned to the courts, judges hostile to the program often denied assistance to would-be recipients. In other instances, perfunctory supervision by untrained probation officers resulted in benefits being dispensed to individuals who were legally disqualified for the program. Even when pensions were provided and supervision was skilled, however, the sums were "inadequate," in many cases "little more than doles."[98]

This unfortunate pattern persisted under the new federal program, now renamed "aid to dependent children." This was more than a simple name change. Breckinridge and other advocates of mothers' pensions had envisioned the program as similar in nature to soldiers' pensions. Mothers, like soldiers, rendered a valuable service to the nation and deserved financial compensation for their irreplaceable contribution. However, aid to dependent children was framed in terms of children's needs rather than in terms of mothers' rights. Indeed, the program failed to provide a subsidy for the caretaker, thereby making it virtually impossible for it to achieve the goal of enabling single mothers to stay out of the workforce to care for their children. Moreover, aid to dependent children—later aid to families with dependent children, or AFDC—was means-tested, meaning that only families falling below a certain income threshold were eligible for assistance. The programs designed for predominantly male workers, by contrast, were not. Finally, aid to dependent children, while federally funded, was a decentralized program that provided grants-in-aid to states, which were responsible for administration. As had been the case for both state mothers' aid programs and the Sheppard-Towner Act, this form of funding and administration permitted state and local administrators to impose their values on would-be recipients, using "morals testing" to determine which applicants were "worthy." Ultimately, these distinctions would lead to the development of a "two-tier" welfare state in which programs such as unemployment insurance and old-age pensions, which applied primarily to male workers, were regarded as "entitlements," while programs such as aid to dependent children, which benefited women and children, were stigmatized as "assistance."[99]

While the proposed welfare program did not include all of the measures Breckinridge had promoted, she nonetheless hailed the proposed legislation as "a great achievement." "It has been so long," she reflected, but "with all the hurdles still to overcome it is wonderful to have old age pensions, mothers pensions, maternity and infancy assistance, and blind & crippled [programs]—all reorganized as it were."[100] Breckinridge thus enthusiastically promoted the bill's adoption. As with federal relief, Breckinridge used her leadership in social work circles, her influence with powerful politicians, and behind-the-scenes campaigns to promote the Social Security Act.[101]

Through her leadership of the Chicago Chapter of the American Association of Social Workers and her close relationship with Walter West, the executive secretary of the national organization, Breckinridge attempted to ensure that the group would express public support in favor of the bill. However, disagreement within the AASW about whether to support the Wagner-Lewis Bill or the Lundeen Bill, which provided different methods for funding unemployment insurance, prevented the organization from taking a public stance on either bill. Breckinridge persisted, however, using her leadership in social work organizations to mobilize social workers' support for the Social Security Bill. Gertrude Wilson recalled that the Chicago Chapter of the AASW was "tremendously active" in support of the bill, holding a variety of fundraisers to send Edith Abbott and others to Washington, D.C., to testify on its behalf. Breckinridge later paid tribute to the importance of professional social work organizations' support by suggesting that the AASW and AASSW's role "in urging the Social Security Act" was "too completely a subject of our current thinking to need further elaboration."[102]

Perhaps Breckinridge had in mind a concerted push for the bill that occurred in spring 1935. As debate over the bill dragged on in the House Ways and Means Committee, Breckinridge and other supporters became concerned that their window of opportunity would close. Soliciting input from Breckinridge, Grace Abbott and Frank Bane collaborated on a statement, signed by "outstanding experts" in economics, business, labor, and social work and distributed to all members of Congress as well as the press, urging immediate adoption of the bill. Breckinridge, who not only signed the statement but also exhorted other influential social workers and social reformers to do so as well, explained that the bill was "not perfect," but although she and her colleagues had "been busy trying to secure some amendments," she feared that these efforts "might have done great damage to delaying its enactment." Breckinridge was now anxious to get to Congress and to the press a statement that it should be enacted promptly. After all, "This is an opportunity, the like of which may not come back again," she reflected. "Amendments can be taken care of later."[103]

Breckinridge also used her influence at the *Lexington Herald* to lobby for passage of the act. Because both committees that considered the bill—the House Ways and Means Committee and the Senate Finance Committee—were dominated by southerners, Breckinridge's Kentucky connections were especially useful. She not only urged Thomas Underwood to write editorials in support of the Social Security Bill but also served as his amanuensis, ghostwriting five editorials advocating passage of the bill. "I should like to have them unsigned just as though they were done in the office there," she explained to Underwood, and then use them to convince Kentucky legislators "to stand by sound proposals." Evidently, Breckinridge's idea was a good one. In June 1935 Underwood informed Breckinridge that two Kentucky politicians had publicly endorsed the Social Security Bill. "I think unquestionably the editorials in The Herald had a large part in this," he assured her.[104]

Although she previously had set aside her reservations about the details of the bill, Breckinridge reentered the discussion over amendments late in the game when, in July, Senator Bennett Champ Clark (D-MO) proposed an amendment that companies providing their own pension plans could opt out of the federal pension program. The Clark Amendment would have undermined the entire program because the most prosperous companies would opt out, leaving only the less financially secure employers in, thus making the contribution base narrower and less reliable and undermining the old-age insurance program's "universality and uniformity."[105] In addition, Breckinridge worried that the proposed amendment would encourage employment discrimination against senior citizens. She wrote on behalf of the faculty of the School of Social Service Administration to urge J. Hamilton Lewis, the senior senator from Illinois, "to resist with all your strength the Clark Amendment to Security Bill." In addition, she urged fellow social work educators, prominent city officials, and religious leaders to join her in opposition to the amendment.[106] After extended discussion and debate, the House and Senate finally agreed to remove the amendment from the bill. Breckinridge—and her fellow female politicos—believed her efforts had helped defeat the amendment. Calling attention to Breckinridge's behind-the-scenes work on the issue, Grace Abbott wrote: "I am grateful to you for helping on the Clark amendment."[107] And while Breckinridge routinely downplayed her own importance, in a private letter to Marion Talbot she confessed that if the amendment was defeated, "I'll think I had a little to do with it."[108]

After years of advocating for federal welfare programs and months of work on the Social Security Act, Breckinridge and her allies were relieved and happy when it finally passed in Congress and went to President Roosevelt for his signature. "It's wonderful the Security Bill is through," Grace Abbott cheered when the bill cleared Congress. "Very happy" that the bill had "really gone to the President," Katharine Lenroot delayed leaving Washington to visit Breckinridge and Edith Abbott until the outcome was certain. Breckinridge dubbed the day that the bill was signed, August 14, 1935, "the great date of the decade."[109]

"Constant guidance"

After the adoption of the Social Security Act, Breckinridge played an active, if usually behind-the-scenes, role in the administration—and expansion—of the New Deal welfare state. By serving on advisory committees, corresponding with policymakers, and promoting additional welfare legislation, Breckinridge maintained her long-established academic activism. She continued to exert influence on the developing welfare state throughout the 1930s. As she confided to Marion Talbot, "I like to think not so much that I help as that I have my hand a little in the New Deal things."[110]

The ink on Roosevelt's signature on the Social Security Act hardly had time to dry before Frances Perkins asked Breckinridge to serve on a new Advisory Committee on Community Child-Welfare Services. Breckinridge, of course, accepted with alacrity. When Martha Eliot, then acting chief of the Children's Bureau, asked her if she was willing to attend the inaugural meeting of the committee at her own expense, Breckinridge responded: "I think that I would crawl on hands and knees if it were necessary to try to be of service in connection with the Security Program!"[111]

The Advisory Committee on Community Child-Welfare Services was actually a subcommittee of the General Advisory Committee on Maternal and Child Welfare Services, which was designed to assist with the administration of maternal and child welfare programs placed under the Children's Bureau's authority by the Social Security Act. This was an important job, because the programs administered by the Children's Bureau were far more decentralized than those administered by the Social Security Board. Therefore, the oversight of advisory committees charged with making recommendations about coordinating national, state, and local efforts was essential to achieving any semblance of consistency from state to state. Breckinridge's committee was charged with supervising the work of local and state child-welfare agencies that received federal funding.[112]

Breckinridge's work on this committee drew on her experience with local service agencies as well as her expertise on training social work professionals. For instance, as discussed in chapter 5, one of the research projects she had supervised in the 1920s was a study of foster care for African American youth, who were often excluded from all-white orphanages and children's homes. Breckinridge's work with the child welfare advisory committee enabled her to put the knowledge she had gained from this program to use in assisting other localities to develop their own programs for underserved populations. Breckinridge's particular interest in professional training also was pertinent to her work on the child welfare advisory committee, for the Children's Bureau used much of its limited funding for the community child welfare program to provide professional training to social workers in charge of developing and overseeing local and state child welfare programs.[113]

Beginning in 1936, Breckinridge also served on a Special Committee on Training and Personnel that advised both the Children's Bureau and the Bureau of Public Assistance, which gave her the opportunity to continue the same sort of work she had done with the FERA training program on a greater scale. To Breckinridge's disappointment, the Social Security Act of 1935 had not required civil-service hiring standards for the administrators and staff charged with carrying out the programs created by the act. This was especially problematic for programs such as aid to dependent children, because local administrators had such wide discretion to determine eligibility for benefits. Without professional standards or oversight, discriminatory practices were commonplace. Breckinridge's work on the Special Committee on Training and Personnel helped to offset this deficiency until, in 1939, Breckinridge's former student and successor as AASSW president, Elizabeth Wisner, helped design amendments to the Social Security Act that implemented civil-service hiring throughout the new federal welfare system. Thereafter, Breckinridge's Special Committee on Training and Personnel helped child welfare programs at the state level to design civil-service rules.[114]

Breckinridge's work on advisory committees for New Deal programs ensured that public-welfare policy would be guided by professional scholarship and standards. Breckinridge described the important work of advisory committees in providing "constant guidance from experts and specialists in the various fields of service." Because of the complexity of issues arising in an enterprise that involved federal, state, and local jurisdictions and a diverse grouping of social service programs, she explained, "only by the use of such aids as well as sound organization and democratic appreciation of the part to be played can so gigantic an undertaking be hopefully approached."[115]

Breckinridge also kept tabs on the membership of the Social Security Board and offered the members informal counsel. Even before the Social Security Act had become law, Breckinridge confided to Talbot: "I am eager to learn who are appointed on the Security Board. If Miss Perkins has her way that will be a good Board, and Mothers' Pensions will be safe."[116] Once the bill was signed, Grace Abbott almost immediately began corresponding with Breckinridge about selections for the Social Security Board. "I think Jane Hoey may be made a member of the Social Security Board," she informed Breckinridge. "While she has no national acquaintance she has brains and will I think do a good job on the old age and mother's Pensions[;] I wish she knew more about Unemployment Insurance." Abbott anticipated that Breckinridge would advise and guide Hoey, a fellow social worker who was, in fact, appointed director of the Bureau of Public Assistance the following year. Indeed, through her work on the Special Committee on Training and Personnel, Breckinridge worked closely with Hoey—the only woman to hold a high-level post on the Social Security Board—to develop rigorous academic standards for employees of both the Social Security Board and the Children's Bureau.[117]

Breckinridge did not hesitate to share her opinions with other members of the Social Security Board as well. Although disappointed that the Children's Bureau did not administer Aid to Dependent Children, Breckinridge was pleased that the new federal guidelines resulted in changes in some state programs. She hoped that under the new guidelines it would be possible "to find some path toward uniformity, standardization, and equalization," and she promptly offered her services to Arthur Altmeyer, who had served on the Committee on Economic Security and had recently been appointed to the Social Security Board, noting that it would be "a source of great satisfaction if I could hope to be of even the slightest service to the members of the Board." Altmeyer was receptive to Breckinridge's overtures, assuring her: "We need your help and I trust that you will always feel free to write us giving us the benefit of your advice and judgment." Meanwhile, Breckinridge sent a copy of her letter to Katharine Lenroot, who incorporated her comments on the administration of mothers' pensions into a memo that she prepared for the Social Security Board.[118]

Not content to limit her "advice and judgment" to established programs, Breckinridge also promoted new social-welfare legislation throughout the 1930s. Almost immediately after the adoption of the Social Security Act, Breckinridge was pushing for amendments to expand the benefits of the existing programs as well as to add new programs, such as national health insurance.[119] The "reactionary" and "resistive" members of the American Medical Association continued to block plans for national health insurance.[120] However, Breckinridge had more success in her continued agitation for "general home relief"—federal relief administered by the Bureau of Public Assistance. Belying her modest demurral that she had "only microscopic influence, if any, in Kentucky," Breckinridge again used the pages of the *Lexington Herald* and her contacts in Kentucky to advocate for federal poor relief. In 1938 the Work Relief and Public Works Appropriation Act extended additional funding to the Works Progress Administration, thereby at least partially fulfilling Breckinridge's vision of federal poor relief.[121]

But at the top of Breckinridge's list was a federal ban on child labor. Breckinridge and her allies had tried—and failed—to abolish child labor for decades. In fact, Grace Abbott's original assignment at the U.S. Children's Bureau had been to enforce the nation's first ban on child labor, established by the Keating-Owen Act in 1916. However, the Supreme Court ruled the law unconstitutional in 1918. Child welfare advocates next attempted to adopt a Child Labor Amendment, which passed Congress in 1924 but did not gain the required number of ratifications from states to become law.[122]

Although she had been "cruelly disappointed" by previous failures, Breckinridge remained committed to efforts to regulate child labor. In the 1930s, with renewed attention to labor regulation of all kinds, the time seemed right for the Child Labor Amendment to make a comeback. Breckinridge joined a campaign to secure enough states to ratify the amendment. As was typical of her, she pondered how she might bring the influence of groups to which she belonged to bear on the issue. She also wrote to her elected representatives to urge them to help establish "a national minimum of protection" to American youth.[123]

The National Industrial Recovery Act of 1933 had placed limits on child labor and had established maximum-hour and minimum-wage legislation for both women and men. However, the act was a temporary measure, set to last for just two years. Although the president asked for authorization to extend the act in 1935, before he could get the measure through Congress the Supreme Court struck down the National Recovery Administration's labor guidelines as unconstitutional. In the meantime Breckinridge had joined statewide efforts to adopt a minimum-wage law as well as the campaign to have the state ratify the Child Labor Amendment. In 1933, when Illinois finally ratified the Child Labor Amendment and adopted a Minimum Wage Law, Breckinridge was thrilled, calling the two pieces of legislation "two bright spots on the record of Illinois."[124]

Although the Child Labor Amendment never gained enough state support to become law, both a ban on child labor and maximum-hour and minimum-wage legislation for all workers were incorporated into the Fair Labor Standards Act (FLSA) of 1938, which Breckinridge—along with her colleagues in the Children's Bureau, the Women's Bureau, and the National Consumers' League—vigorously promoted. Unlike the earlier NRA codes, which had permitted states to pay women a lower minimum wage than men—a policy Breckinridge had opposed—the FLSA established the same minimum wage rates for both men and women—at least in the industries covered by the act. Because the FLSA did not apply to agricultural, domestic, and service work, its provisions excluded many women workers, as well as many nonwhite workers. Nonetheless, it represented an important step forward for women's equality and for child welfare.[125]

While often invisible, Breckinridge's behind-the-scenes activities were effective in designing, adopting, and implementing the New Deal welfare state. As American Public Welfare Association founder and Social Security Board executive Frank Bane later remarked: "In setting up the various relief administrations and Social Security, it was Edith Abbott with Sophonisba and a few others ... who gave us the greatest help in organizing government for the administration of welfare programs. Edith and Sophonisba—as the University of Chicago called them, A and B.—what a pair!"[126]

Indeed, Breckinridge's long-term association with Abbott facilitated not only her professional achievements, as discussed in chapters 4 and 5, but also her political effectiveness, as discussed here. Chapter 10 turns to the personal dimensions of the two women's life partnership.

CHAPTER TEN

"A and B"

A Productive Partnership

"What women who share in life and work can mean to the world"

For more than forty years, Edith Abbott and Sophonisba Breckinridge—known as "A and B" on the University of Chicago campus—shared both their daily lives and their life work. Reflecting on their relationship in 1948, one mutual acquaintance wrote: "Your beautiful devoted friendship shines with a rare light, showing us what women who share in life and work can mean to the world."[1] Indeed, Breckinridge and Abbott's long-term relationship was a remarkable partnership, advancing both women's professional and political success as well as providing them with personal and practical support. This chapter explores the dynamics and the significance of this same-sex relationship from the women's first meeting in 1903 to Breckinridge's death in 1948.[2]

Edith Abbott, a former schoolteacher and brilliant statistician, came to the University of Chicago in 1903 to pursue a doctorate in political economy with Breckinridge's former professor, Laurence Laughlin. A graduate of the University of Nebraska, Abbott, like Breckinridge, was eager to pursue higher education and explore professional opportunities. Also like Breckinridge, Abbott was a member of a politically active family, although while W.C.P. Breckinridge had fought for the Confederacy before launching his law career, Abbott's father Othman A. Abbott, also an attorney, was a stalwart supporter of Lincoln. However, the similarities of the two women's backgrounds were more significant than their fathers' political differences. Both Breckinridge's and Abbott's lawyer-fathers had been supportive of their daughters' desire for higher education, but both women had to finance their own studies after college. Both also had inspiring women role models in their own families; whereas Breckinridge looked up to her schoolteacher aunt, Abbott followed the example of her suffragist mother. Perhaps most important for these two intellectually inclined women, however, they shared an interest in political economy and women's work. Thus, despite a ten-year age difference, Breckinridge and Abbott immediately forged what would prove to be an unbreakable bond.[3]

During the time Abbott attended the University of Chicago, she not only was a student in Breckinridge's class on the status of women, but she also was a resident of Green Hall, the women's graduate student residence for which Breckinridge served as head. Given the women's shared interests and close association during Abbott's years as a student, it is not surprising that Breckinridge took a special interest in the younger woman's professional prospects. After completing her PhD in 1905, Abbott—with Breckinridge's help—published a series of articles in the *Journal of Political Economy* as well as publishing her dissertation, a landmark study of women's wage labor. Breckinridge used Abbott's articles in her classes. "I am daily impressed with their value," she praised, adding, "I really am terribly proud of you." Also with Breckinridge's assistance, Abbott secured a series of prestigious research positions in Boston, Washington, D.C., and London before taking a teaching post at Breckinridge's alma mater, Wellesley College.[4]

Abbott and Breckinridge remained in close contact. "I have missed you sorely," Breckinridge confessed. "If you could have known all the times I have thought of you lately, you would have realized that you were greatly missed." For her part, Abbott admitted that letters from her sister Grace—who had followed in her older sister's footsteps by pursuing graduate study at the University of Chicago, enrolling in Breckinridge's course on women, and living at Green Hall—made her "homesick all the time" for Chicago. "I never expect to be so happy again anywhere as I was my first year at Chicago," she mourned.[5]

When Breckinridge offered her the chance to return to Chicago and work with her at the Chicago School of Civics and Philanthropy in 1908, Abbott accepted with alacrity. Breckinridge, who, according to a mutual acquaintance, "had not forgotten the student 'with the big brown eyes,'" was thrilled at the prospect of their reunion, signing one letter to Abbott, "very lovingly dear Heart—Nisba."[6]

For the next four decades, Abbott and Breckinridge were nearly inseparable. Although they did not share a residence until the 1940s (Breckinridge lived at Green Hall, and Abbott lived first at Hull House and then in rented quarters near campus), they were rarely apart. As previously discussed, they worked closely together on teaching, administration, and research first at the Chicago School of Civics and Philanthropy and then at the School of Social Service Administration as well as collaborating in promoting public welfare at local, state, and national levels. They also attended plays and dinner parties together, shared hotel rooms at conferences, and traveled abroad and vacationed together. And they gave each other unstinting affection and support. According to one mutual acquaintance, Breckinridge and Abbott enjoyed "the ideal friendship—an unselfish devotion which is rare."[7]

"Miss Breckinridge loved both of them"

Breckinridge and Abbott's close relationship in many ways resembled that between Breckinridge and Talbot in earlier years. Just as Talbot had done for her, Breckinridge sought opportunities for her one-time student. By 1909 she had convinced a publisher—who had originally met with her about co-authoring a book on home economics with Talbot—to publish Abbott's *Women in Industry*, for which Breckinridge wrote the introduction. While enthusiastic about Abbott's volume, the publisher remained keen on Breckinridge's original proposal. "I hope that your interest in economic studies at Hull House and elsewhere has not switched you entirely away from this Household book," he wrote. "Are you or Professor Talbot planning such a book?"[8]

Talbot also was concerned that she had been supplanted. Shortly after Breckinridge completed edits on Abbott's manuscript and sent it to the publisher in fall 1909, Abbott wrote to Talbot to apologize for the slight. By 1911 it was clear that Talbot felt threatened by Abbott personally as well as professionally. In October 1911 Talbot wrote to Abbott to demand an explanation for an unspecified "charge" Abbott laid on Talbot. In the same letter, Talbot indicated that she had offered Abbott her "hospitality" until Abbott "gave evidence that you did not wish my friendship." Despite her hurt feelings, Talbot explained, she sought a reconciliation for Breckinridge's sake: "I do it . . . that I may be guided in my method of helping make Nisba's life as happy and rich as it is in my power to do—an aim which has been constantly before me since the day when she came to me and let me lift her out from the shadow into the light, seventeen years ago."[9]

Although she refused to meet with Talbot, commenting that she was "sure that a discussion as you propose will not help any of us," after a series of tense exchanges, Abbott offered a full apology, giving as her reason the same one that Talbot gave: to avoid making Breckinridge unhappy. Indeed, Talbot and Abbott appeared to be locked in a battle to prove which of them loved Breckinridge the most! Abbott's belated apology simultaneously acknowledged Talbot's years of support and downgraded their number: "Of course I do not need to be reminded of the help you gave Nisba fourteen years ago." Abbott continued:

She will never lead one to forget any kindness that has been hers—the thing she forgets of course is that no one ever had the blessed privilege of doing anything for her who was not paid over and over again a thousand times full measure & then left in her debt. I feel quite unable to tell you how ashamed I am of the blunders I seem to have made. It seems very hard when I think I see what it has meant to have the joy of knowing and loving her—of trying to see how full of beauty she is with so much room for life and loving—it seems very hard that I should waste any of her precious strength. I can only say again that if I have been rude to you or to anyone that she loves I have not meant to be and I am ashamed of myself if I have so blundered and I heartily apologize.[10]

It is unclear what role, if any, Breckinridge played in this disagreement or its denouement. Later events would indicate that she did, indeed, have "so much room for life and loving" that she could—and did—maintain a close relationship with both Talbot and Abbott for the rest of her life. Breckinridge spent the majority of her time with Abbott, but she continued to vacation with Talbot at their shared summer home in Holderness, New Hampshire, where the two collaborated in 1912 on the long-awaited home economics volume, *The Modern Household*.[11] Although she spent her long days with Abbott, Breckinridge visited Talbot every evening. For their part, Abbott and Talbot established a chilly but cordial relationship. Decades later, a former student recalled:

> One of my memories is little Miss Breckinridge trudging along on a cold winter night over a few blocks to see Miss Talbot. She went every night to see her. On the other hand, Miss Talbot and Miss Abbott were not friends. I don't know what the cause was, but at any rate, Miss Breckinridge loved both of them.[12]

Talbot grudgingly accepted second place in Breckinridge's affections. In December 1912, while Breckinridge was in Lexington visiting family, Talbot wrote a long letter to her in which she remarked with understandable self-pity: "I must not tell you how I am going to miss you! You will perhaps be able to work out a less distracting and less fatiguing mode of life when I am not a constant factor in it."[13]

Although neither Breckinridge nor Talbot were willing to relinquish their friendship, by the mid-1910s, most people associated Breckinridge with Abbott rather than with Talbot. One University of Chicago graduate recalled the familiar sight of the two petite women, clad in Victorian fashion well into the twentieth century, walking together across campus, deep in conversation:

> I had seen Edith Abbott and Sophonisba Breckinridge walking from the Law Building to the Gothic turrets of their offices in Cobb Hall. Their preoccupation and leisurely pace gave them a pathway to themselves. Students walked around them on the grass. These diminutive Victorian ladies seemed larger because of their dress. Their skirts swept the sidewalk. Miss Abbott loomed larger in her black hat and dark dress. Miss Breckinridge's floppy Panama hat and voile dress set off a soft vivacious face and slender feminine figure.[14]

"I love you so!"

Because Abbott and Breckinridge were so rarely separated, they left few personal letters. Either Breckinridge did not keep Abbott's letters (which seems unlikely), or Abbott chose to exclude them from the collection of Breckinridge's papers she donated to the Library of Congress after Breckinridge's death, when she probably added the letters Breckinridge had written to her, and which she had preserved. Moreover, Abbott evidently preferred to make long-distance calls or telegraph rather than write letters. Therefore, there are only a few caches of personal, hand-written letters from Breckinridge to Abbott and only a scant handful of letters and telegrams from Abbott to Breckinridge. These letters reveal the women's intimate connection and show Breckinridge at her most vulnerable. Whereas in her professional correspondence Breckinridge always presented a competent and confident persona, in her letters to Abbott she admitted to fears and doubts and asked for love and reassurance.[15]

In 1928 Breckinridge traveled to Paris for the First International Conference on Social Work, part of a two-week series of social welfare gatherings. Because she traveled by steamship and made a side trip to Turkey en route to the conference and to New Hampshire on her return trip, she was separated from Abbott for nearly three months. In her earliest letter to Abbott during this extended excursion, written in mid-May, she confessed, "I don't see how I can go on tomorrow. . . . I can think only how good you are to me and how I am so foolish and uncertain and disagreeable. Dear—I think you understand—though—Dear—" Subsequent letters, while full of information about the places Breckinridge visited, the people she saw, and the sessions she attended, invariably opened and closed with expressions of affection, thanks for Abbott's "dear notes" (unfortunately not preserved), and outbursts of loneliness. "It seems to me I can hardly bear it any longer," Breckinridge wrote in early July. Part of Breckinridge's anxiety was due to Abbott's health problems. She repeatedly urged her to enjoy her vacation time in New York City and Colorado Springs, to "take a little care of yourself," and to ensure that "the blood pressure and blood count and everything that was not just right is at any rate better if not entirely well." Breckinridge also seemed to feel that she had been a burden to her partner, writing, "I'll try not to worry you anyway. I know a little of how I have troubled you—I'll try not to do so again." Whatever real or imagined difficulties Breckinridge referred to did not stop her from writing frequently with variations on the sentiment, "Dear—. . . I love you so!"[16]

Breckinridge and Abbott were not separated for any significant time again until late 1933, when Breckinridge traveled to South America for the Pan-American Conference, which resulted in a separation of approximately two months. "I feel dreadfully," she confessed. "I have never been so helpless before space and time. I think of you all the time. . . . I get little sleep—and I long for the sight of you." "I am really not fit any more—to do things alone," she concluded. "It is so long and so far." Referring to Abbott's encouragement to attend the conference, when she was preparing to return home, Breckinridge wrote hopefully: "I shall be seeing you soon—perhaps two weeks from today. You won't send me away again soon—please." For her part, in one of her rare preserved letters, Abbott wrote to Breckinridge: "Things going very well but very lonesome" and admitted that she was "thinking of you always." More frequently, Abbott sent "loving greetings" by telegram.[17]

In early 1935 Abbott and Breckinridge were separated once again while Breckinridge attended the deathbed of her favorite brother, Desha, in Lexington, Kentucky. Meanwhile, Abbott divided her time between Chicago, where she insisted on helping Breckinridge with her neglected correspondence and classroom teaching, and Washington, D.C., where she attended professional social work conferences and testified on behalf of the Social Security Act. Typically, the two exchanged lengthy handwritten letters (Breckinridge) and brief telegrams (Abbott) that revealed their constant care and concern. Breckinridge reassured Abbott that she was "perfectly well" and urged Abbott to "get some rest . . . and take care of your dear self." Abbott, although "terribly disappointed" at the separation, sent "my dear love always" from afar, asked how she could help, and assured Breckinridge, "I am with you and thinking of you . . . always." Thanking her partner for both her practical assistance and her emotional support, Breckinridge wrote: "I know how you are always with me—and how you would take it all if you could."[18]

Indeed, all of Abbott and Breckinridge's extant correspondence reveals their mutual devotion and their emotional dependence on one another. Abbott, like Breckinridge, evidently needed frequent reassurances. Writing from the train in July 1938, Breckinridge wrote: "Dear:—I have no message. You know how I am thinking of you. It was hard to leave you—you know that."[19] For her part, Breckinridge described herself as "foolishly upset" at even brief separations.[20]

Abbott and Breckinridge usually managed to avoid lengthy separations, largely by traveling and lodging together. When, in 1941, Abbott traveled to a conference in Atlantic City in advance of Breckinridge, she wired her to make arrangements for their reunion: "Hotel room number nine hundred one looking forward to tomorrow." The following year, when Breckinridge attended a conference in Washington, D.C., without Abbott, she called attention to the unusual circumstance: "I have a very comfortable room with two beds," Breckinridge assured Abbott, adding meaningfully, "one of which will be sadly vacant."[21]

Even during brief separations, Breckinridge and Abbott maintained nearly constant contact. In August 1943, when she went on a week-long vacation with her old friend (and Abbott's old rival), Marion Talbot, Breckinridge confessed, "a week seems a long time." Although none of Abbott's letters from this trip survive, she kept in touch by telegraph. "It was good of you to wire," Breckinridge wrote, explaining, "I wanted just to be reassured." Although the weather was fine, Talbot's health was good, and the trip was "very restful," Breckinridge was eager to return to Abbott. "It is a lovely day. I send my love. It will be wonderful to be back, I can never tell you!" she exclaimed, adding, "I am so sort of helpless away from you."[22]

The following fall, when Breckinridge again was on vacation with Talbot (and Abbott was visiting family in Nebraska), Breckinridge's need for her partner's reassurance was even more acute. "Dear," she began her first missive, "It was good of you to telegraph! I feel so far away!" Breckinridge also found Abbott's letters (not preserved) reassuring. "Dear:—It was so good to have your letter this morning," she opened one letter. Indeed, both women apparently expected—and received—frequent letters. Even when she had no news to share, Breckinridge wrote at least once a day, explaining, "I just send a hasty loving message—Dear—so grateful for everything. Always—." Despite the brevity of this trip (just over a week), Breckinridge chafed at the separation. "You are very constantly in my mind. . . . It seems a long time until next Friday," she mourned in one letter; in another, just two days later: "I miss you terribly. . . . It is wonderful to look forward to being with you again"; and two days later, "I really could not stand much more of this. It is all so huge and the distances are so great and we are so far away." By the end of the ten-day separation, Breckinridge insisted that the two women never again be apart. "Edith, when you get back and I get back, don't let me go again," she pleaded. "I can't get along without you." In her very next letter, she reiterated the sentiment: "Have I said that I had made up my mind that if I once got you back and got back myself, I'd never let you out of my sight again and I'd ask you never to let me go away." The next three letters, written over two days, repeated the message again and again: "If I get hold of you again—I'll never let go!" exclaimed Breckinridge. "You may be sure of that and reckon on it."[23] Indeed, it appears that the two women were never again parted until Breckinridge's death four years later.[24]

"A life-time of work together"

From the perspective of the twenty-first century historian, it is difficult to categorize Abbott and Breckinridge's relationship. The emotional intensity of their attachment—and Talbot's jealous possessiveness—suggest something other than a platonic relationship. In other words, for contemporary readers, it rings false to call them "just friends." In the time in which they formed their attachment, however, friendship was not automatically assumed to be less than or inferior to romance. Indeed, in some circles, same-sex friendships were considered superior to heterosexual marriage, which was marred by women's legal inferiority, political powerlessness, and economic dependence. In addition, for some, the presumption of female "passionlessness"—the belief that women did not experience sexual desire—furthered both the acceptance of women's same-sex relationship and the belief that these presumably purely spiritual relationships were superior to degraded sexual ones.[25]

During Breckinridge and Abbott's lifetime, however, ideas about female sexuality were in flux. The valorization of homosocial relationships, or "romantic friendships," persisted until the late nineteenth century, when women's increasing legal, economic, and political power enabled greater numbers of women to forego marriage and choose instead to establish life partnerships with other women. At about the same time that women's intimate relationships became common enough to have their own terminology, however—"smashes" for schoolgirl crushes and "Boston marriage" for long-term committed relationships—a new breed of "sexologists" on both sides of the Atlantic began to define—and stigmatize—both "homosexuality" and "lesbianism." Concern about sexuality was tied to anxieties about gender; between roughly 1880 and 1920, enthusiastic praise of the college-educated New Woman had been drowned out by anxious predictions about the "mythic mannish lesbian." By the early twentieth century, concerns about female independence and "deviant" behavior had reached such a fever-pitch that women's boarding schools and single-sex colleges had become suspect.[26]

Despite increased attention to and criticism of women's same-sex relationships in the early twentieth century, such relationships remained commonplace and, at least in some quarters, accepted. In particular, women engaged in higher education, social reform, and political activism routinely formed domestic partnerships with one another. While some of these women eventually fell prey to the rising tide of homophobia, others—including Abbott and Breckinridge—led what we might now think of as openly lesbian lives without negative consequences.[27]

However, increased acceptance of heterosexual sexual activity in modern America was accompanied by decreased tolerance of same-sex relationships of all kinds. By the 1940s, anxieties about lesbianism were intense enough that the positive image of the "maiden aunt" in a "Boston marriage" had been replaced by the frightening specter of the cross-dressing "prison lesbian." At the same time that public awareness of same-sex sexual attraction created a public outcry and sanctioned governmental repression, it also encouraged gay men and lesbians to adopt a self-consciously "homosexual" identity, develop a distinctive "gay" subculture, and launch a civil rights movement.[28]

The shifting definitions of sexuality pose a dilemma for scholars, especially for feminist biographers who struggle to avoid reinforcing "compulsory heterosexuality" by engaging in "the historical denial of lesbianism" while also recognizing that their own subjects did not—indeed, probably could not—identify as lesbians. Changing understandings of sexual attraction also posed challenges for the women whose lives and relationships spanned the very decades in which definitions of sexuality shifted under their feet. Some of Breckinridge and Abbott's contemporaries, wary of being "outed," concealed their relationships by burning their love letters. Others, apparently secure in the Victorian "female world of love and ritual," continued to understand their relationship as a nonsexual—although often a romantic or even an erotic—one. Still others, protected by their status as middle-class, white, educated professionals, may have differentiated between their own respectable "Boston marriages" and the allegedly deviant practices of working-class dykes, degraded prostitutes, and prison lesbians. A few, like Breckinridge's colleague and correspondent, prison director and social reformer Miriam Van Waters, defended lesbian women in prisons while also rejecting a lesbian identity for herself. And some simply refused to discuss the matter, certainly an understandable choice at a time when charges of lesbianism led to prompt dismissal, if not to prison.[29]

Because Breckinridge and Abbott fell into this last category—neither they nor their acquaintances broached the subject in their surviving correspondence—it is impossible to assign either of them a sexual identity after the fact. Nonetheless, their relationship merits close attention and critical analysis, for regardless of its "lesbianism" (or lack thereof), it was an extremely significant relationship. Whether platonic or passionate, Abbott and Breckinridge's relationship was a true partnership, one that helped both women achieve personal happiness, professional success, and political effectiveness.

Neither Breckinridge nor Abbott could have been entirely ignorant of the major shifts in definitions of sexuality that took place in their lifetime. As social scientists, they were conversant with all the most up-to-date scholarship. Although they resisted the "psychiatric persuasion" and emphasized social action, their disdain for psychology, including sexology, could not prevent them from being at least passingly aware of these developments. In a draft version of her review of Mary Beard's *Woman as a Force in History*, Breckinridge noted of the author: "She is fortunate . . . in having enjoyed normal family life, sharing it with an able and democratically minded husband who is a scholar of the first rank and a person of wide political and social experience."[30]

Whether she believed this herself or not—and the exclusion of this passage from the published version of the review could be interpreted either way—Breckinridge clearly understood that heterosexual marriage was regarded as "normal family life"; same-sex relationships, if not sexually deviant, were nonetheless viewed as "abnormal." This indicates at least some awareness of contemporary discussions of "normal" and "abnormal" sexuality. Moreover, it suggests that Breck-inridge and Abbott may have had more than one reason for rejecting the trend toward psychological analysis in social work. An emphasis on individual adjust-ment was, of course, inconsistent with the pair's commitment to public welfare and social justice; Breckinridge and Abbott may also have found the psychological profession's definition of same-sex intimacy as mental illness profoundly distaste-ful, even threatening.

Breckinridge and Abbott's well-known reluctance to engage with psychological scholarship and their possibly willful ignorance of psychoanalysis surely did not prevent them from knowing the professional cost to fellow academics in female partnerships. They must have known that their friend Mary Woolley, president of Mount Holyoke College, lost her post (and was replaced by a man) in 1936 largely due to negative attention to her long-term relationship with fellow profes-sor Jeannette Marks, although they did not explicitly address this issue in their passionate defense of Woolley.[31]

Breckinridge and Abbott, who in some ways closely resembled Woolley and Marks, escaped this fate despite steadily escalating anxiety about homosexual-ity. In the post–World War II era, the second "Red Scare" was accompanied by a "Lavender Scare": both alleged political radicals and suspected sexual devi-ants were subjected to scrutiny and repression. Although regularly charged with Communism, neither Abbott nor Breckinridge was ever accused of lesbianism. It may be that their advanced age and conservative appearance shielded them from suspicion, since "mannish" appearance was associated with lesbian sexuality, and all sexuality was associated with youth. Perhaps university students found it impossible to imagine the older women in their trademark large hats, long skirts, and upswept hairdos as sexual beings, much less homosexuals. Breckinridge and Abbott's class status also may have provided them with some protection from scrutiny. At any rate, the two women enjoyed a reputation as consummate profes-sionals with impressive credentials and impeccable characters. "To me, of course, you and she always remain 'The Ladies,'" one admirer wrote to Abbott.[32]

The closest students came to criticizing Breckinridge and Abbott's relation-ship was by complaining that they were so anxious for their female students to pursue professional careers that they discouraged them from marrying. Women students were so convinced of Abbott's opposition to marriage that those who married before completing their degrees delayed notifying her; some kept their marriages a secret entirely. Breckinridge shared Abbott's attitude: "Sophonisba was such a feminist that if any girl got married, she just wrote her off the books," one former student recalled. Natalie Walker Linderholm, formerly a star student, recalled that when she married, she was placed on "the Black List." Having come of age at a time when combining family life with a professional career was so difficult that Breckinridge and Abbott's own role models either abandoned their careers or remained single, they were deeply skeptical about the possibility of reconciling family responsibilities with professional demands—particularly for the students they saw as the future of the field.[33]

Breckinridge held out hope that the situation might be different for later generations, however. In the 1930s, while she was completing her magnum opus on women's role in American life, she fiercely opposed New Deal–era legislation that authorized gender discrimination in hiring and firing and vigorously upheld working wives' rights, urging the Cook County League of Women Voters to "stand ready to spring in behalf of preserving and increasing opportunities for women to do whatever they are personally qualified to do without reference to sex or to marital status."[34] In keeping with this stance, in her published review of Mary Beard's *Woman as Force in History*, she admiringly noted that Mary and Charles Beard "together shared the pursuit after knowledge," enabling the husband-and-wife team to attain both professional success and personal happiness.[35]

For Abbott and Breckinridge, however, this combination was more readily attained in the context of a same-sex relationship than within heterosexual marriage. By sharing what one admirer called "a life-time of work together," Abbott and Breckinridge were able to achieve professional success, wield political power, and enjoy personal happiness.[36]

In 1940, after stepping down as head of Green Hall, Breckinridge moved into the rented house that the Abbott sisters had shared between Grace Abbott's retirement from the Children's Bureau, in 1934, and her death, in 1939.[37] From this home base, Abbott and Breckinridge continued to collaborate on research and writing and kept in touch with their former students. They also both began work on their memoirs. One University of Chicago student who spent time at the women's residence vividly recalled the evidence of Breckinridge and Abbott's ongoing scholarship: "The ladies filled their desk drawers until they had to be taken out of the desks, then put papers on top of tables and everywhere they chose. Always intending to look over them but just never had time."[38]

Time was short not only because both women were growing older—by the time Breckinridge and Abbott combined households, they were in the mid-seventies and mid-sixties, respectively—but also because they continued to combine their academic pursuits with political activism. In particular, they worked together to defend the Children's Bureau against repeated attempts at governmental reorganization that threatened to reduce women's control over child welfare policy. As Breckinridge put it in a letter to Abbott's niece, Charlotte, in 1946: "Edith . . . has been working hard to resist the attack on the Children's Bureau. Once in so often one has an attack to resist." Abbott headed the Joint Emergency Committee to Save the Children's Bureau from 1946 until 1948, soliciting letters of support from public officials and social workers around the country. Breckinridge assisted Abbott behind the scenes by nudging Thomas Underwood to promote the Children's Bureau in the *Lexington Herald* and by urging elected officials in both her home state of Kentucky and her adopted state of Illinois to oppose either budget cuts or bureaucratic reorganization.[39]

"A shared devotion for all the best human strivings," as one mutual acquaintance put it, not only enabled the pair to achieve professional success and political power but also enriched Breckinridge and Abbott's personal relationship. As a former student observed in a letter to Abbott, it was "the combination of complete appreciation of you, personally and professionally," that made Breckinridge an ideal partner for Abbott. And Abbott was the ideal partner for Breckinridge; according to her correspondents, because she was "connected and concerned with all that was in her mind and heart," Abbott was "able to give Nisba so much love, companionship and help, in every way. You were what she most loved and needed."[40]

Breckinridge and Abbott's contemporaries recognized that their partnership allowed both women to thrive. University of Chicago colleague Kate Turabian, for instance, admired the women's ability to advance "the other's happiness without invasion of the personality."[41] Surely during their long relationship, Breckinridge and Abbott must have reflected upon the advantages of being partnered with another woman rather than being either married or unattached. After all, many of their contemporaries, colleagues, and close friends engaged in similar relationships.[42] Breckinridge hinted at her high opinion of same-sex relationships when she wrote to Abbott from her vacation home in New Hampshire, where she chaperoned several young women in the late 1920s. Breckinridge commented that her young charges were "very happy" and speculated, "I fancy each of them has 'my friend.'"[43] However, neither woman ever openly stated support for homosexuality or publicly identified as a lesbian.

Was their silence intentional? Did they understand their relationship as sexual and hide it, either out of shame or fear? Or did they simply draw no connection between their own intimacy and "sex deviance"? Frustratingly, the answers to these questions remain elusive. What is clear, however, is that Breckinridge and Abbott enjoyed a long and mutually fulfilling relationship. The fact of their personal relationship, if not its precise nature, was public knowledge. Without ever defining the relationship, Breckinridge and Abbott and their family members, close friends, professional colleagues, former students, and political allies all acknowledged its significance. Indeed, Abbott and Breckinridge both functioned as and were treated as a couple on the University of Chicago campus and at the many professional and political gatherings they attended. Students, friends, and colleagues all linked Abbott and Breckinridge in their correspondence, routinely closing letters to one with greetings and best wishes to the other.[44]

Breckinridge and Abbott also were fully incorporated into one another's families. Both women corresponded with the other's family members, keeping them informed about their welfare and rejoicing in their successes. They also shared information about both their own family members and the other woman's family members, treating members of both families as one extended family. For example, Grace Abbott wrote to Breckinridge about her brother, Desha, who had recently been in Washington, while Breckinridge gave Mr. and Mrs. Abbott updates on Charlotte Abbott, Grace and Edith's niece, who was then in Chicago. Members of both women's families inquired about the other woman's health and sometimes wrote directly to the partner rather than to their own family member. For instance, Arthur Abbott routinely inquired about Breckinridge's health in letters to his sister; occasionally, he wrote to Breckinridge herself. Family members also exchanged gifts and occasionally visits. In 1928, for example, Breckinridge determined to visit Grace Abbott, then in Colorado Springs for treatment for tuberculosis. Writing to the Abbotts to inform them of Grace's improved health, she suggested that she visit them in Nebraska on her return trip to Chicago. "It will make me so happy to see you and Judge Abbott," she wrote to Mrs. Abbott, "and you will be glad to hear about Grace and Edith." Finally, family members exchanged financial and legal advice; in the 1940s, Abbott's brother Arthur communicated with both Breckinridge and Abbott about the sale of the women's shared automobile and the details of Breckinridge's final will and testament.[45]

These entwined family relationships reached their peak in the 1930s, when both Breckinridge and Abbott assumed significant responsibility for their nieces. Both Charlotte Abbott and Nisba Desha Breckinridge, known as "Nim," lived in Chicago in the early 1930s. Nim spent a year at the University of Chicago settlement before attending college in Wisconsin, while Charlotte briefly attended the School of Social Service Administration before accompanying Grace Abbott to Washington, D.C., when she was appointed chief of the U.S. Children's Bureau. Nim and Charlotte continued to write and visit both Breckinridge and Abbott. Breckinridge and Charlotte developed an especially close relationship, often exchanging gifts and reading material. In 1933, when Charlotte was planning to visit Chicago and Abbott was out of town, Breckinridge insisted that she stay at Green Hall with her. "Come on home to Green Dear," she urged. "It is truly where you belong." Nim, meanwhile, pestered her aunt for information about Charlotte, whom she evidently regarded as a sort of honorary cousin.[46]

Friends, former students, and professional colleagues also treated Breckinridge and Abbott as a couple. Perhaps the most persistent, if rather humdrum, evidence of this dynamic is the sheer volume of letters requesting updates on Abbott's welfare from Breckinridge, and vice versa. To give just one example, in 1928, when Abbott was in an automobile accident, Breckinridge received numerous letters

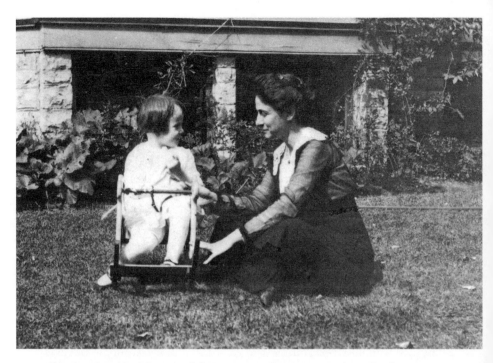

Abbott and Breckinridge were fully incorporated into one another's families, exchanging letters, visits, advice, and health updates. In the 1930s they also shared responsibility for their nieces' educations. Charlotte Abbott, shown here with her aunt Grace early in the twentieth century, became very close to Breckinridge, often exchanging gifts and reading material with her. In 1933, when Charlotte planned a trip to Chicago, Breckinridge insisted that she stay with her at Green Hall. "Come on home to Green Dear," she wrote.

Courtesy Special Collections Research Center, University of Chicago Library

from the women's circle of friends and from family members, commiserating with Breckinridge and sending best wishes to Abbott.[47]

Correspondence with family and friends further indicates that the two women did not merely keep tabs on one another's health and give updates to mutual acquaintances; they personally provided healthcare for each other. After Abbott's accident, her brother Arthur thanked Breckinridge for giving her "the best of care." In 1941 he again wrote to Breckinridge to thank her for her attentive care. "I am sorry that Edith is suffering from a cold but we are all relieved that you are there to do for her. It is so good of you," he wrote.[48] Abbott also cared for Breckinridge when she was sick; indeed, her attention was close enough that she fell prey to the same virus. "Thanks for the inquiry about Nisba," she responded to a letter from mutual friend and Children's Bureau chief Katharine Lenroot in 1947. "She got a bad cold about two weeks ago & I finally got it too so that I have been out for some days," she explained. "Nisba finds it hard to follow the Doctor's orders and I have got a nurse finally to help the cause along."[49]

"We were very close friends"

As it turned out, this "bad cold" ushered in Breckinridge's prolonged final illness. Breckinridge's weak heart and strong spirit struggled for dominance for many months. Native Lexingtonian and distant relative Robert Wickliffe Woolley's daughter, then living in International House on the University of Chicago campus, gave her father a detailed account of Breckinridge's last days. Even though Breckinridge's death was expected, she explained, "she rallied so often and would be so restless over inactivity, that although we were prepared, it was a shock when it occurred." Although her condition had declined enough by February 1948 that she required around-the-clock care, Breckinridge survived until late July. According to Woolley, Breckinridge died as quietly and composedly as she had lived, attended by Abbott, two nurses, and Abbott's successor as dean of the School of Social Service Administration, Wilma Walker, who came to "take care of arrangements" because "Miss A. just went to pieces." When Walker arrived, Woolley explained, "Nisba was calm but still living, in a few minutes she sighed and it was over."[50]

Breckinridge honored her life partner in her last will and testament. In addition to leaving her entire estate to "my dear friend, Miss Edith Abbott," she also named Abbott her executor, noting that "through her long and close association with me," Abbott was familiar with Breckinridge's wishes both for the distribution of personal items and the disposal of her physical remains.[51]

Breckinridge's directions caused some consternation. Her sister Ella had died in 1943, and her brother Robert had passed away in 1944, leaving Breckinridge "the last of the immediate family," as she expressed it in her memoirs. However, their children were the "heirs at law" and they were unhappy at their exclusion from the will. From Breckinridge's perspective, she already had dispensed with her family obligations. She had assumed financial responsibility for all of Robert's children—Nim, Bobby, and Clair—during the depths of the Great Depression, when her brother's marriage had ended in divorce and he became addicted to alcohol and gambling. Ella had never been close to Breckinridge, and her children—Lyssa and Lyman Jr.—had demonstrated little interest in their aunt's welfare, not even bothering to make contact during her last few months on earth. By the time of Breckinridge's death, all of her nieces and nephews had reached adulthood; moreover, according to both Woolley and Talbot, they were an un-grateful bunch. When she composed her memoirs in the mid-1940s, Breckinridge had reflected on "the very real weaknesses in my relations to my family" and pondered the reasons that they showed so little "real affection" for her. Finally, before her death, Breckinridge confided that "she feared the behavior of her rela-tives at the funeral in Lexington." Small wonder, then, that she chose to leave her entire estate, and her funeral arrangements, to the woman with whom she had shared her life for nearly half a century. Abbott insisted on holding services for Breckinridge in Chicago before allowing her body to be shipped to Lexington for a local funeral and burial in the family plot. "My feeling was that anything Miss Abbott wanted should be done," opined Woolley, since "she gave up everything to take care of Nisba."[52]

Ultimately, both Abbott's funeral arrangements and the disposal of Breck-inridge's estate served to underscore the importance of their relationship, even though nobody seemed quite sure what to call it. Asked during probate hearings to describe the nature of her relationship with Breckinridge, Abbott explained that the two women had been close associates for forty-five years and that Breckinridge had "lived with me" before she inquired, "Is that what you mean?" In response to follow-up questions, Abbott affirmed that she was "not a relative" at the same time that she asserted, "We were very close friends." While uncertain what label to attach to Abbott, the court upheld her legal claim to Breckinridge's estate. Although a lawyer attended the hearing on behalf of the "heirs at law," probate proceeded without incident, perhaps because the would-be claimants quickly realized that "so far as finances are concerned, there is nothing left." Indeed, while Breckinridge's estate amounted to more than $10,000 (mostly in the form of stock holdings), Abbott spent nearly half this amount on funeral expenses, estate taxes, and lawyers' fees. Moreover, during Breckinridge's final illness, she had paid at least a portion of Breckinridge's medical care over a period of several months. As Woolley put it, "two and then three nurses a day absorb a bank account."[53] Breckinridge's will may not have benefited Abbott financially, but it affirmed the primacy of their personal connection.

Friends and former students had little difficulty recognizing the importance of Breckinridge and Abbott's relationship. After Breckinridge's death, Abbott received a flood of condolence letters commenting on the women's mutual devo-tion. Frequently commenting on the ways in which Abbott and Breckinridge had shared both their daily lives and their life work, acquaintances described them as "devoted," "loyal friends" and applauded their "exceptionally beautiful friendship." Abbott and Breckinridge's mutual acquaintances knew that Abbott would sorely miss what Secretary of Labor Frances Perkins referred to as "the daily contact, the faithful loyalty, the shared experiences, [and] the tender friendship" that the two women had shared for so many years. Acknowledging that Breckinridge's death represented "a loss beyond words" for her life partner and that her absence would "leave a great void in your life," they urged Abbott to take comfort in the knowledge that the two women, together, had left a lasting legacy. "You and she have shared a common lot these many years," one letter read, "and your labors in behalf of human welfare have borne rich fruit."[54]

Breckinridge devoted her long life to social justice. Confronting challenges with what she called "passionate patience," she persevered in the face of repeated setbacks and stubborn resistance. Above all, she never gave up. As she explained, "the work of the world" did not get done by giving up when one was tired.

Courtesy Special Collections Research Center, University of Chicago Library

Epilogue

Passionate Patience

In 2017, the hashtag #ShePersisted went viral after Senator Elizabeth Warren (D-MA) refused to be silenced by House Majority Leader Mitch McConnell, transforming McConnell's justification for shutting down the popular Democratic leader—"Nonetheless, she persisted"—into a rallying cry for progressive politics.

Elizabeth Warren may have become the archetypal example of determined advocacy and female strength during the Trump presidency, but Sophonisba Breckinridge exemplified these characteristics throughout her entire life. After a lengthy struggle to achieve personal independence, Breckinridge dedicated her adult life to progressive reform. Over the course of decades, Breckinridge persisted in her commitment to social justice.

If not the patron saint of lost causes, Breckinridge was certainly a loyal supporter of unpopular ones. She endured repeated setbacks and defeats as she promoted progressive social policies throughout the Progressive era and the New Deal. After founding the Immigrants' Protective League in 1907, the same year that a new immigration law permitted the deportation of poor immigrants, she watched with horror as the federal government adopted ever more restrictive immigration laws. She supported a child-labor law, a measure that was enacted in 1917, only to be declared unconstitutional; subsequent efforts to adopt a child labor amendment failed repeatedly. After decades of agitation for minimum wage legislation for women workers, she witnessed the demise of such legislation in the aftermath of a 1923 Supreme Court decision upholding what fellow labor-legislation advocates called a "constitutional right to starve."[1] In 1929 she mourned the loss of funding for the Sheppard-Towner Act, the nation's first public health program, which provided healthcare for poor mothers and children in rural areas. Despite the achievement of woman suffrage in 1920, Breckinridge's efforts to reconcile equal rights for women with a recognition of their special circumstances were never fully successful and often resulted in bitter divisions. A founding member of the National Association for the Advancement of Colored People, she supported African American civil rights throughout the "nadir" of American race relations. Despite her unwavering support for a federal antilynching law, such a measure was not adopted in her lifetime. She opposed U.S. participation in both world wars, only to watch helplessly as the world was engulfed in devastating warfare twice in her lifetime.

Somehow, despite all these defeats, Breckinridge never lost her characteristically Progressive faith that social scientific research would lead to sound social policies. Breckinridge always believed that the way forward was public policy by the federal government. Her long-term goal remained constant: a national minimum standard of living, enshrined in national policy and funded by the federal government. As she explained in an attempt to gain a senator's support for New Deal policies: "My basis for appeal is simply a twenty-five year period of effort to secure in behalf of the public a reasonably competent and skilled service, and in behalf of the destitute, that measure of relief which I believe would be in accord with the purposes of the American people, and which, after a period of three hundred years, begins to acquire something of a reasonably adequate recognition as a national task."[2]

Although she often worked on the state level, Breckinridge ultimately put her faith in the State, with a capital S; that is, she believed that only the federal government could provide the type of policy she advocated. Attempting to create any sort of universal welfare program in diverse and divided state legislatures, she once remarked, made "the possibility of a truly national minimum seem very remote" indeed.[3]

However, she readily adopted many short-term strategies to achieve her long-term goals. While relying on what her closest companion, Edith Abbott, called "slow, laborious, and often discouraging piecemeal methods" to promote social justice, Breckinridge often reflected on the importance of being simultaneously passionate and patient.[4] Quoting the southern poet Sidney Lanier, she reflected: "If the progress seems often incredibly unendurably slow . . . the social worker must pray the prayer of the poet, to be filled with a 'passion of patience.'"[5]

Many of Breckinridge's most cherished goals were finally realized only near the end of her life, after a lifetime of unremitting effort. In the 1930s, the New Deal incorporated several of the social welfare programs she had helped design at the local and state levels into the federal welfare state, moving the nation decisively in the direction of ensuring her cherished goal of a national minimum. Breckinridge's determined advocacy of social justice at an international level at last achieved at least a formal endorsement in the form of the Universal Declaration of Human Rights, which the United Nations adopted in 1948, the year of her death.

However, even Breckinridge's most decisive victories were always qualified ones. Moreover, as she knew from sad experience, the battles were never over; laws and policies gained with great difficulty could be—and often were—overturned or reversed, especially in periods of economic difficulty. Her response to this reality was to rely on her network of female friends for emotional support and to turn to her political allies to redouble her efforts. For Breckinridge, "passionate patience" and political persistence went hand in hand.[6]

Political activists, policymakers, and concerned citizens may benefit from taking a page from Breckinridge's book, for many of the pressing social issues she grappled with throughout her long lifetime remain vitally important—and often divisive—in our own time.

For decades, Breckinridge lobbied on behalf of a federal antilynching bill. Her commitment to protecting African Americans' civil rights testifies to her belief that, as contemporary activists put it, "Black Lives Matter." In 1934, when Colorado Senator Edward Costigan asked Breckinridge for arguments to use in support of antilynching legislation, Breckinridge initially responded that the reasons for supporting legal safeguards for African Americans were so self-evident that they fell into the category of "truths too obviously true to demand demonstration." However, she went on to say that in addition to being necessary to protect black lives, antilynching legislation was necessary in order to protect "the very fabric and structure of our social and political order," which was threatened by acts of wanton violence. "My heart is filled with a great longing that your efforts may be successful," she concluded, and that "we may go toward a day when there may no longer be tragic victims, in the form of individuals lynched, persons who participate or communities which are degraded and demoralized by these indescribable occurrences." While her efforts to promote antilynching laws did not bear fruit in her lifetime, Breckinridge's words nonetheless serve as a reminder that all Americans—not just black Americans—have a stake in "the protection of lives." Her unremitting activism on behalf of African Americans also provides a reminder that the racial issues dividing the country today have a long history—and that efforts to improve race relations require steadfast commitment in the face of both fierce opposition and repeated failures. Indeed, only in late 2018 did the U.S. Senate finally approve antilynching legislation—still pending, at the time this book went to press in early 2019, in the U.S. House of Representatives.[7]

Throughout her lifetime, Breckinridge pressed for what she called "the claims of women" in all arenas—at home, at work, and in politics.[8] For Breckinridge, providing women "a fair chance" included defending their access to birth control.[9] As she explained in an unsigned editorial written during the Great Depression in response to critics of relief who complained about poor women who gave birth while receiving benefits, "the right to parenthood" was a fundamental right. However, she continued, unfortunately not all parenthood was freely chosen. Instead, responsible adults were, because of the Comstock Laws, denied access to information about contraceptives. The human cost of these legal restrictions on birth control, Breckinridge opined, was tremendous, measured both in the number of dangerous illegal abortions and in the number of poverty-stricken children. Breckinridge thus advocated an immediate repeal of anti-birth-control laws to "make possible a truly voluntary parenthood."[10] Today, as conservative politicians strive to limit women's ability to use contraceptives or procure abortions, Breckinridge's insights remain painfully relevant.

Breckinridge's insistence on promoting the welfare of immigrants also is instructive. Currently, federal immigration policies call for mass detainment and deportation of undocumented immigrants; Donald Trump assumed the presidency in part because of the popular appeal of his proposal to build a wall along the U.S.–Mexico border to prevent new arrivals. In this context, Breckinridge's opposition to deportations, her promotion of access to citizenship, and her determination to reform immigration policies to favor new arrivals and their family members all seem worthy of remembrance. In particular, Breckinridge's concern for Mexican migrants is instructive. As one of Breckinridge's correspondents pointed out, "These Mexicans have made a very real contribution to the development of the industries in the Southwest. . . . Furthermore in coming to this country at the call of industry they have broken their connection with Mexico and have cast in their lot with America. During the period of a dozen years they have established their homes in this country, sent their children to our public schools and have closely associated themselves with our social and economic life." But as competition for jobs increased, this contribution was "not being recognized" and instead Mexican migrants confronted "a great many injustices."[11] As a member of the Immigrants' Protective League, Breckinridge protested the inhumane treatment of Mexican immigrants during a deportation drive in 1931. Both documented and undocumented workers were "treated like cattle," rounded up without regard to their legal status, and detained for long periods without legal representation—before being ousted from their adopted homes. "Deportation is banishment," said one.[12] Because of these horrifying situations, Breckinridge maintained her commitment to immigrant rights and welfare for decades, even though her membership in the American Committee for the Protection of the Foreign Born, which a branch of the House Un-American Activities Committee (HUAC) dubbed "a Communist front for the protection of alien Communists," finally placed her on an official government list of suspicious individuals and "fellow-travelers" in 1948, the year of her death.[13]

Amid calls to "repeal and replace" the national healthcare program, Breck-inridge's lifelong campaign to ensure a "national minimum" also merits our at-tention. For Breckinridge, a national minimum included universal healthcare coverage for all Americans based on their need, not their ability to contribute to the costs of care. "What America wants in the way of security," she contended, "is *universal provision* of certain health services that will reach *everyone in need*, and not a system that reaches only the contributing group."[14] Breckinridge believed that the national government owed all its citizens a minimum standard of living, but she was especially concerned about the poor, the elderly, and the disabled— precisely the groups targeted by proposed cuts to Medicaid. Before we dismantle the federal system that Breckinridge and her fellow reformers so painstakingly built up and replace it with the private and local programs they found wanting, we may wish to revisit Breckinridge's beliefs about the federal government's re-sponsibility to its citizens.

The final stages of my work on this book have been punctuated by news reports of increasingly tense relations between the United States and North Korea. Read-ing these headlines, and noting the ways in which both nation's leaders subscribe to a definition of masculinity that equates manliness with militarism, I wonder if a renewed women's peace movement—animated by a desire for justice as well as a commitment to pacifism—might arise to counter the escalation of conflict and promote international mediation by neutral nations. Of course, participants in any such movement must be prepared for accusations of a lack of patriotism. Although Breckinridge avoided prosecution for her pacifism during her lifetime, in 1948, the year of her death, an official report from the California Senate's Fact-Finding Committee on Un-American Activities on "Communist Front Organiza-tions" warned that many "peace-loving Americans" were lured by "Communist double talk" into joining such organizations as the American League for Peace and Democracy. Moreover, the report asserted that Breckinridge's membership in this and related organizations—as well as her defense of civil liberties and opposition to HUAC's predecessor, the Dies Committee—indicated a "frenzied Communist-inspired" attitude.[15] Today, just as much as during Breckinridge's lifetime, Americans must grapple with the definition—and the demands—of patriotism.

Beyond the eerie echoes of the particular issues that concerned Breckinridge then—and still preoccupy Americans today—it is interesting to note that the wide range of Breckinridge's interests also characterizes today's "resistance." Moreover, the leadership of contemporary movements—whether the particular issue is the construction of pipelines across Native lands or the removal of Confederate statues on southern college campuses—is predominantly female. In other words, women's activism, then and now, represents a wide-ranging commitment to social justice that, while often led by women, is not narrowly or exclusively focused on women. In her 1933 study *Women in the Twentieth Century*, Breckinridge pointed out that from the antislavery movement forward, American women have been at the forefront of movements for "social advances," including efforts "to protect the underprivileged, to remedy inequalities, [and] to prevent distress." While "those measures suffer in days of spiritual depression and economic misery," she noted from the depths of the Great Depression, "the failure of such legislation, is, however, accepted by women as their failure, its continued advocacy as their responsibility." Today, just as much as in the 1930s, we need what Breckinridge called women's "energy, devotion and intelligence" as well as their "zeal" for social justice.[16]

Given the many parallels between Breckinridge's time and our own, it might be tempting to conclude that efforts to improve American society are doomed to failure. However, Breckinridge, I think, would have a different response. Throughout her life, she worked with what she called "passionate patience" to achieve social progress. Undeterred by either unwavering opposition or repeated setbacks, she fought long battles for even incremental gains, never losing faith that her efforts would eventually bear fruit.

While the political hot spots of today certainly indicate that persistence is called for, other developments suggest that Breckinridge's faith in civic engagement was not misplaced. Breckinridge never claimed a lesbian identity or demanded gay rights, but she did regard the law as the surest safeguard of social justice. The U.S. Supreme Court's decision to uphold the right of same-sex couples to marry—a decision that was delivered while I was conducting research for this book in the national capital—is (unless and until the full U.S. Congress adopts antilynching legislation) perhaps the most recent example of the national government providing what Breckinridge called a national minimum for its citizenry. With continued political activism on behalf of social justice, it will not be the last. As Edith Abbott wrote shortly after Breckinridge's death:

> She was not afraid of failure—"only of living in the gray twilight that knows neither victory nor defeat." The way was long and hard at times, and she often walked by faith. But she always had great confidence in the young—in their courage and their ability to right the old wrongs of the world.[17]

Breckinridge's unwavering confidence is a clarion call for contemporary activists. Her lifelong commitment to social justice offers an inspiring example for today's feminists. And her collaboration with other women suggests the importance of collective work for meaningful change. As a 1932 *Survey* article on the "Great Ladies of Chicago" explained, Breckinridge and other women had "awakened the social conscience of Chicago" and "created a center of social energy for a nation."

Thus, it was "women whose vision of social responsibility would set right a world now struggling in the results of its own lack of social responsibility."[18] As daily headlines illustrate, the world still struggles with a lack of social responsibility; we still need both an alert social conscience and an effective center of social energy to address social problems; and women still are at the forefront of the fight for social justice. Today, just as much as in Breckinridge's time, "a woman's work" is still "the work of the world."

Notes

Abbreviations

AALL Records	American Association of Labor Legislation Records, Kheel Center for Labor–Management Documentation and Archives, Cornell University Library, Ithaca, New York
Abbott Papers-NSHS	Abbott Family Papers, Nebraska State Historical Society, Lincoln, Nebraska
Abbott Papers-SCRC	Edith and Grace Abbott Papers, Special Collections Research Center, Regenstein Library, University of Chicago, Chicago, Illinois
Abbott Papers-UNL	Edith and Grace Abbott Papers, Archives and Special Collections, University of Nebraska-Lincoln Libraries, Lincoln, Nebraska
AF/AFP	Alice Freeman/Alice Freeman Palmer
Ballard Papers	Russell Ward Ballard Papers, Special Collections, Richard J. Daley Library, University of Illinois at Chicago, Chicago, Illinois
Barnhart Interview	Department of Sociology Interviews, Special Collections Research Center, Regenstein Library, University of Chicago, Chicago, Illinois
Bartlett Interview	Department of Sociology Interviews, Special Collections Research Center, Regenstein Library, University of Chicago, Chicago, Illinois
Blumer Interview	Herbert G. Blumer Interview, May 22, 1972, Department of Sociology Interviews, Special Collections Research Center, Regenstein Library, University of Chicago, Chicago, Illinois

Abbreviations

Bosworth Papers	Louise Bosworth Papers, Schlesinger Library, Radcliffe Institute, Harvard University, Cambridge, Massachusetts
Braden Memoirs	Reminiscences of Spruille Braden, Columbia Center for Oral History Archives, Rare Book and Manuscript Library, Columbia University, New York, New York
Breckinridge Biographical File	S. P. Breckinridge, 1888, Alumnae Biographical Files, Wellesley College Archives, Clapp Library, Wellesley College, Wellesley, Massachusetts
Breckinridge Estate Records	Will of Sophonisba Preston Breckinridge and Probate Records "In the Matter of Sophonisba P. Breckinridge" (No. 48-P-7605, docket no. 478, p. 46), Cook County Circuit Court Archives, Richard J. Daley Center, Chicago
Breckinridge Interview	Interview with Sophonisba Breckenridge [sic], February 21, 1920, Bureau of Vocational Information Records, 1914–1921. Box 3, folder 144: files on occupations: Law. Interviews; includes correspondence, 1918–1920. Schlesinger Library, Radcliffe Institute, Harvard University, Cambridge, Massachusetts
BTW	Booker T. Washington
Chalkley, "Magic Casements"	Eleanor Breckinridge Chalkley, "Magic Casements," Ms. Autobiography, ca. 1940s, Transcript by James C. Klotter, Kentucky Historical Society, Frankfort, 1982, copy in University Archives and Special Collections, Margaret King Library, University of Kentucky, Lexington, Kentucky
Class History	Marion Angelina Ely and Edith Louise Hall, "History of the Class of '88," Class of 1888 Records, Wellesley College Archives, Clapp Library, Wellesley College, Wellesley, Massachusetts
Class of 1888 Records	Class of 1888 Records, Wellesley College Archives, Clapp Library, Wellesley College, Wellesley, Massachusetts
Clay Papers	Laura Clay Papers, University Archives and Special Collections, Margaret King Library, University of Kentucky, Lexington, Kentucky
CSCP Records	Chicago School of Civics and Philanthropy Records, Special Collections Research Center, Regenstein Library, University of Chicago, Chicago, Illinois

Abbreviations

CSWE Papers	Papers of the Council for Social Work Education (formerly the American Association of Schools of Social Work), Social Welfare History Archives, University of Minnesota, Minneapolis, Minnesota
DB	Desha Breckinridge
DB Papers	Desha Breckinridge Papers, Breckinridge Family Papers, Library of Congress, Washington, D.C.
Dennett Papers	Mary Ware Dennett Papers, Schlesinger Library, Radcliffe Institute, Harvard University, Cambridge, Massachusetts
Department Records	Record Portfolios of Departments of the University, Special Collections Research Center, Regenstein Library, University of Chicago, Chicago, Illinois
Dressler Memoirs	Reminiscences of David Dressler, Columbia Center for Oral History Archives, Rare Book and Manuscript Library, Columbia University, New York, New York
DS	Doris Stevens
EA	Edith Abbott
EF	Ernst Freund
Elbert Scrapbook	Scrapbook of Ella Smith Elbert, Class of 1888 Records, Wellesley College Archives, Clapp Library, Wellesley College, Wellesley, Massachusetts
Ellery Scrapbook	Scrapbook of Florence Ellery, Class of 1888 Records, Wellesley College Archives, Clapp Library, Wellesley College, Wellesley, Massachusetts
ER	Eleanor Roosevelt
Faris Interview	Robert E. L. Faris Interview, May 24, 1972, Department of Sociology Interviews, Special Collections Research Center, Regenstein Library, University of Chicago, Chicago, Illinois
FDR	Franklin Delano Roosevelt
FP	Frances Perkins
Friday Scrapbook	Scrapbook of Lucy Florence Friday, Class of 1887, Class of 1887 Records, Wellesley College Archives, Clapp Library, Wellesley College, Wellesley, Massachusetts
GA	Grace Abbott
Hathway Papers	Marion Hathway Papers, Social Welfare History Archives, University of Minnesota, Minneapolis, Minnesota
HH	Hull House Collection, Special Collections, Richard J. Daley Library, University of Illinois at Chicago, Chicago, Illinois

HH-Oral Histories   Hull House Oral History Collection, Special Collections, Richard J. Daley Library, University of Illinois at Chicago, Chicago, Illinois

Hurll Papers   Estelle Hurll Papers, Wellesley College Archives, Clapp Library, Wellesley College, Wellesley, Massachusetts

Hutchinson Memoirs   Clark Bane Hutchinson Oral History Interview, July 18, 1997, www.socialsecurity.gov/history/fbane.html.

IDB   Issa Desha Breckinridge

IDB Papers   Issa Desha Breckinridge Papers, Breckinridge Family Papers, Library of Congress, Washington, D.C.

IL-LWV   League of Women Voters of Illinois Collection, Special Collections, Richard J. Daley Library, University of Illinois at Chicago, Chicago, Illinois

IPL-UIC   Records of the Immigrants, Protective League, Special Collections, Richard J. Daley Library, University of Illinois at Chicago, Chicago, Illinois

JA   Jane Addams

JAH   *Journal of American History*

JAPP   Jane Addams Papers Project (microfilm)

JL   Julia Lathrop

Johnson Memoirs   Oral Memoir of Arlien Johnson, National Association of Social Workers Oral History Project, Social Welfare History Archives, University of Minnesota, Minneapolis, Minnesota

JPE   *Journal of Political Economy*

JR   Julius Rosenwald

Kellogg Papers   Paul Kellogg Papers, Social Welfare History Archives, University of Minnesota, Minneapolis, Minnesota

Kendall Papers   Katherine Kendall Papers, Social Welfare History Archives, University of Minnesota, Minneapolis, Minnesota

Kincheloe Interview   Samuel C. Kincheloe Interview, June 27, 1972, Department of Sociology Interviews, Special Collections Research Center, Regenstein Library, University of Chicago, Chicago, Illinois

KL   Katharine Lenroot

LaFollette Papers   LaFollette Family Papers, Library of Congress, Washington, D.C.

Lenroot Memoirs   Reminiscences of Katharine F. Lenroot, Social Security Project, Columbia Center for Oral History Archives, Rare Book and Manuscript Library, Columbia University, New York, New York

Lenroot Papers	Katharine F. Lenroot Papers, Rare Book and Manuscript Library, Columbia University, New York, New York
Lewis Papers	Verl Lewis Papers, Social Welfare History Archives, University of Minnesota, Minneapolis, Minnesota
Linderholm Reminiscences	Natalie Walker Linderholm Reminiscences (1979), Natalie Walker Linderholm Papers, Schlesinger Library, Radcliffe Institute, Harvard University, Cambridge, Massachusetts
LOC	Library of Congress, Washington, D.C.
Lutz Papers	Bertha Lutz Papers, Brazilian National Archives
LWV Papers	Papers of the League of Women Voters, Library of Congress, Washington, D.C.
McCamant Scrapbook	Scrapbook of Catherine McCamant, Class of 1887 Records, Wellesley College Archives, Clapp Library, Wellesley College, Wellesley, Massachusetts
McCulloch Papers	Catharine Waugh McCulloch Papers, Schlesinger Library, Radcliffe Institute, Harvard University, Cambridge, Massachusetts
McKee Papers	Leila S. McKee Papers, Miami University, Oxford, Ohio
Merriam Memoirs	Interview with Ida Craven Merriam, Women in the Federal Government Project, Columbia Center for Oral History Archive, Rare Book and Manuscript Library, Columbia University, New York, New York
Miller Papers	Frieda S. Miller Papers, Schlesinger Library, Radcliffe Institute, Harvard University, Cambridge, Massachusetts
Mowrers Interview I and II	Dr. E. R. Mowrers Interview I and II, April 17, 1972, Department of Sociology Interviews, Special Collections Research Center, Regenstein Library, University of Chicago, Chicago, Illinois
MT	Marion Talbot
Mudgett Papers	Mildred Mudgett Papers, Social Welfare History Archives, University of Minnesota, Minneapolis, Minnesota
NASW Papers	Papers of the National Association of Social Workers (formerly the American Association of Social Workers), Social Welfare History Archives, University of Minnesota, Minneapolis, Minnesota

NAWSA Papers — Papers of the National American Woman Suffrage Association (microfilm), Library of Congress, Washington, D.C.

NWP Papers — Papers of the National Woman's Party, Library of Congress, Washington, D.C.

NYT — *New York Times*

Pederson Interview — Laura M. Pederson Interview, March 18, 1972, Department of Sociology Interviews, Special Collections Research Center, Regenstein Library, University of Chicago, Chicago, Illinois

Perlman Memoirs — Oral Memoirs of Helen Harris Perlman, National Association of Social Workers Oral History Project, Social Welfare History Archives, University of Minnesota, Minneapolis, Minnesota

Presidents' Papers — Presidents' Papers: Harper, Judson, and Burton Administration, Special Collections Research Center, Regenstein Library, University of Chicago, Chicago, Illinois

RG 43 — Records of International Conferences, Commissions, and Expositions, National Archives and Records Administration, College Park, Maryland

RG 59 — General Records of the Department of State, National Archives and Records Administration, College Park, Maryland

RG 174 — General Records of the Department of Labor, Office of the Secretary, Secretary Frances Perkins, General Subject File, 1933–1941, National Archives and Records Administration, College Park, Maryland

Rich Papers — Adena Miller Rich Papers, Special Collections, Richard J. Daley Library, University of Illinois at Chicago, Chicago, Illinois

Rosenwald Papers — Julius Rosenwald Papers, Special Collections Research Center, Regenstein Library, University of Chicago, Chicago, Illinois

Social Work Pamphlets — Pamphlets, Major, Social Welfare History Archives, University of Minnesota, Minneapolis, Minnesota

SPB — Sophonisba Preston Breckinridge

SPB Autobiography — Sophonisba Preston Breckinridge Autobiography, Sophonisba Preston Breckinridge Papers, Special Collections Research Center, Regenstein Library, University of Chicago, Chicago, Illinois

SPBP	Sophonisba Preston Breckinridge Papers (microfilm), Breckinridge Family Papers, Library of Congress, Washington, D.C.
SPB Papers-SCRC	Sophonisba P. Breckinridge Papers, Special Collections Research Center, Regenstein Library, University of Chicago, Chicago, Illinois
SPB Transcripts	Academic Transcripts for Sophonisba P. Breckinridge, Registrar's Office, University of Chicago, Chicago, Illinois
SPB-UIC	Sophonisba P. Breckinridge Collection, Special Collections, Richard J. Daley Library, University of Illinois at Chicago, Chicago, Illinois
SSA Records	University of Chicago School of Social Service Administration Records, Special Collections Research Center, Regenstein Library, University of Chicago, Chicago, Illinois
SSR	*Social Service Review*
Stevens Papers	Doris Stevens Papers, Schlesinger Library, Radcliffe Institute, Harvard University, Cambridge, Massachusetts
Swigert Divorce Records	Petition in Equity, Elizabeth M. Swigert v. Charles Swigert, February 13, 1897; Motion and Summons, Elizabeth M. Swigert v. Charles Swigert, February 13, 1897; Order, Elizabeth M. Swigert v. Charles Swigert, February 15, 1897; and Order, Elizabeth M. Swigert v. Charles Swigert, February 18, 1897, Kentucky Department for Libraries and Archives, Frankfort, Kentucky
Talbot Papers	Marion Talbot Papers, Special Collections Research Center, Regenstein Library, University of Chicago, Chicago, Illinois
Taylor Papers	William Graham Taylor Papers, Newberry Library, Chicago, Illinois
Thomas Papers	Papers of M. Carey Thomas in the Bryn Mawr College Archives, microfilm copy at Library of Congress, Washington, D.C.
Tousley Memoirs	Reminiscences of Clare M. Tousley, Community Service Society Project, Columbia Center for Oral History Archive, Rare Book and Manuscript Library, Columbia University, New York, New York
UK	University Archives and Special Collections, Margaret King Library, University of Kentucky, Lexington, Kentucky

Underwood Papers	Thomas Underwood Papers, University Archives and Special Collections, Margaret King Library, University of Kentucky, Lexington, Kentucky
Van Waters Papers	Miriam Van Waters Papers, Schlesinger Library, Radcliffe Institute, Harvard University, Cambridge, Massachusetts
Wald Papers	Lillian Wald Papers, Rare Book and Manuscript Library, Columbia University, New York, New York
Wald Papers-NYPL	Lillian D. Wald Papers, New York Public Library, New York, New York
Wallin Papers	Madeline Wallin Papers, Special Collections Research Center, Regenstein Library, University of Chicago, Chicago, Illinois
Washington Papers	Booker T. Washington Papers, Library of Congress, Washington, D.C.
WCC-CHM	Woman's City Club of Chicago Records, Research Center, Chicago History Museum, Chicago, Illinois
WCC-UIC	Woman's City Club of Chicago Records, Special Collections, Richard J. Daley Library, University of Illinois at Chicago, Chicago, Illinois
WCPB	William C. P. Breckinridge
WCPB Papers	William C. P. Breckinridge Papers, Breckinridge Family Papers, Library of Congress, Washington, D.C.
"Wellesley in 1884–85"	K. Gertrude Stevens, "Wellesley in 1884–85," Wellesley Annals, Wellesley College Archives, Clapp Library, Wellesley College, Wellesley, Massachusetts
"Wellesley in 1885–86"	Susie Wade Peabody, "Wellesley in 1885–86," Wellesley Annals, Wellesley College Archives, Clapp Library, Wellesley College, Wellesley, Massachusetts
"Wellesley in 1886–1887"	Marion A. Ely, "Wellesley in 1886–1887," Wellesley Annals, Wellesley College Archives, Clapp Library, Wellesley College, Wellesley, Massachusetts
"Wellesley in 1887–1888"	Maryette Goodwin, "Wellesley in 1887–1888," Wellesley Annals, Wellesley College Archives, Clapp Library, Wellesley College, Wellesley, Massachusetts
WH	William Harper
Wiley Papers	Anna Kelton Wiley Papers, Schlesinger Library, Radcliffe Institute, Harvard University, Cambridge, Massachusetts
WILPF-UCol	WILPF Papers, University of Colorado, Boulder, Colorado

WILPF-UIC   Women's International League of Peace and Freedom
                         Collection, Special Collections, Richard J. Daley
                         Library, University of Illinois at Chicago, Chicago,
                         Illinois
WILPF/WPP   Women's International League for Peace and Freedom
                         Collection (DG043), Part I: Woman's Peace Party,
                         1915–1920, Swarthmore College Peace Collection,
                         Swarthmore, Pennsylvania
Wilson Memoirs   Reminiscences of Gertrude Wilson, National Associa-
                         tion of Social Workers Oral History Project, Social
                         Welfare History Archives, University of Minnesota,
                         Minneapolis, Minnesota
Woolley Papers   Robert Wickliffe Woolley Papers, Library of Congress,
                         Washington, D.C.
WPP-UIC   Woman's Peace Party Collection, Special Collections,
                         Richard J. Daley Library, University of Illinois at Chi-
                         cago, Chicago, Illinois
WTUL Scrapbook   Women's Trade Union League of Chicago Scrapbook,
                         Special Collections, Richard J. Daley Library, Univer-
                         sity of Illinois at Chicago, Chicago, Illinois

Preface

1. SPB to Elisabeth Coit, July 3, 1933, SPBP.

2. Maxine Schwartz Seller, ed., *Women Educators in the United States, 1820–1922: A Bio-Biographical Sourcebook* (Westport, Conn.: Greenwood, 1994), 63–69. After completing her Bachelor of Science degree at Wellesley college in 1888, Breckinridge matriculated at the University of Chicago for graduate study. There, according to SPB Transcripts, she earned her PhD (1901) as well as her M.Phil. (1897) in political science, but she completed her dissertation with political economy professor Laurence Laughlin. She completed her JD in 1904. She listed her fields as Political Science, Economics, and Law. See Breckinridge Biographical File.

3. Beverly B. Cook, "Sophonisba P. Breckinridge," *Women and Politics* 3, no. 1 (April 1983): 95–102, esp. 97.

4. "A Woman Who Helps: The Story of a Southern Woman Who Is a Power in Chicago—Her Many-Sided Work—A Champion of the Championless," *Woman's Journal* (May 18, 1912): 160.

5. Some of the most in-depth studies are unpublished dissertations and theses. See Catherine Altany, "Power in the Midst of Powerlessness: The Contributions of Sophonisba P. Breckinridge to Social Work during the Formative Years of the Profession" (PhD diss., Mandel School of Applied Social Sciences, Case Western Reserve University, 1992); Nancy Ellen Barr, "A Profession for Women: Education, Social Service Administration, and Feminism in the Life of Sophonisba Preston Breckinridge, 1886–1948" (PhD diss., Department of History, Emory University, 1993); Catherine L. Coghlan, "An Examination of the Contributions of

Sophonisba Preston Breckinridge (1866–1948) to the Discipline of Sociology" (PhD diss., Department of Sociology, Texas Woman's University, May 2002); Margaret S. Vining, "Sophonisba Preston Breckinridge and the Graduate School of Public Welfare Administration at the University of Chicago" (MA thesis, George Washington University, 1982).

6. See notes and abbreviations for more detail on the research. For an edited and annotated version of Breckinridge's memoirs, see Anya Jabour, "Sophonisba Breckinridge (1866–1948): Memoirs of a Southern Feminist," in Giselle Roberts and Melissa Walker, eds., *Southern Women in the Progressive Era: A Reader* (Columbia: University of South Carolina Press, 2018), 9–43.

7. "Woman Who Helps."

Introduction

1. Memorials by Breckinridge's students as well as Breckinridge's own memoirs used the phrase "the work of the world." See Helen R. Wright, "Three against Time: Edith and Grace Abbott and Sophonisba P. Breckinridge," *SSR* 28, no. 1 (March 1954): 41–53 (quotation p. 43); and SPB Autobiography. For remaining quotations, see WCPB to SPB, October 22, 1884; and Gerald Stanley Lee to SPB, June 15, 1891, SPBP.

2. "Woman Who Helps."

3. Margot Lee Shetterly, *Hidden Figures: The American Dream and the Untold Story of the Black Women Mathematicians Who Helped Win the Space Race* (New York: Morrow, 2016); and Rebecca Skloot, *The Immortal Life of Henrietta Lacks* (Farmington Hills, Mich.: Gale, 2011).

4. James C. Klotter, *The Breckinridges of Kentucky* (Lexington: University Press of Kentucky, 1986), 379. See for instance Allen F. Davis, *American Heroine: The Life and Legend of Jane Addams* (New York: Oxford University Press, 1973); Jean Baker Elshtain, *Jane Addams and the Dream of American Democracy: A Life* (New York: Basic, 2001); and Louise W. Knight, *Jane Addams: Spirit in Action* (New York: Norton, 2010).

5. Sarah Hepola, "Gloria Steinem, a Woman Like No Other," *NYT*, March 16, 2012, http://www.nytimes.com/2012/03/18/fashion/in-the-womans-movement-who-will-replace-gloria-steinem.html.

6. Jill Conway, "Women Reformers and American Culture, 1870–1930," *Journal of Social History* 5, no. 2 (Winter 1971–72): 164–177 (quotations p. 168).

7. Christine Stansell, *The Feminist Promise: 1792 to the Present* (New York: Modern Library, 2011), chap. 7.

8. Nancy A. Hewitt, ed., *No Permanent Waves: Recasting Histories of U.S. Feminism* (New Brunswick, N.J.: Rutgers University Press, 2010).

9. Wendy Sarvasy, "Beyond the Difference versus Equality Policy Debate: Postsuffrage Feminism, Citizenship, and the Quest for a Feminist Welfare State," *Signs* 17 (1992): 329–63.

10. Mary K. Trigg, *Feminism as Life's Work: Four Modern American Women through Two World Wars* (New Brunswick, N.J.: Rutgers University Press, 2014).

11. Zona Gale, "Great Ladies of Chicago," *Survey*, February 1, 1932, 479–82 ("great ladies" quote pp. 480–81); "Strong-minded women" quote from Rebecca Hourwich Reyher Oral History, Search and Struggle for Equality and Independence, Suffragists Oral History Proj-

ect, Part II: Work with the Woman's Party, chap. 3, Early Suffrage Work, 1913–1915, Online Archive of California, https://oac.cdlib.org/view?docId=kt6xonb1ts&query=&brand=oac4. Other quotes from Raissa to EA, August 7, 1949; John M. Glenn to EA, April 23, 1949; and Ella K. Alschuler to EA, August 10, 1948, SPBP.

12. "University of Chicago: Amid Clashing Intellects It Forms a New Pattern for U.S. Education," *Life*, July 16, 1945, pp. 71–76 (quotation p. 72). Edith's brother commented that Abbott and Breckinridge were the only women in the picture. See Arthur Abbott to EA, July 16, 1945, Abbott Papers-UNL, box 18, folder 5.

13. "Woman Who Helps."

14. SPB to Mary Quinn, August 25, 1943, SPBP; and "Miss Breckinridge in East for Opening of Suffrage Exhibit," *Chicago Tribune*, August 26, 1943.

15. "Mrs. Catt Announces Committee Chairmen and Sponsors of Woman's Congress," *Washington Post*, March 10, 1940.

16. SPB to GA, November 28, 1933, SPBP.

17. SPB to MT, August 28, 1935, Talbot Papers.

18. SPB Autobiography; see also Anya Jabour, "Autobiography of an Activist: Sophonisba Breckinridge, 'Champion of the Championless,'" in Delphine Letort and Benaouda Lebdai, eds., *Women Activists and Civil Rights Leaders in Auto/Biographical Literature and Films* (Cham, Switzerland: Palgrave Macmillan, 2018), 45–63.

19. WCPB to SPB, March 30, 1885, SPBP.

20. Joyce Antler, "'After College, What?': New Graduates and the Family Claim," *American Quarterly* 32, No. 4 (Fall 1980): 409–34; see also Anya Jabour, "Duty and Destiny: A Progressive Reformer's Coming of Age in the Gilded Age," in James Marten, ed., *Children and Youth during the Gilded Age and Progressive Era* (New York: New York University Press, 2014), 230–51.

21. SPB to Neva Deardorff, March 4, 1932; and SPB to Mary Burnett, March 7 and 20, 1934, SPBP.

22. S. P. Breckinridge, "Family Budgets," *Standards of Child Welfare: A Report of the Children's Bureau Conferences, May and June, 1919* (Washington, D.C.: U.S. Department of Labor, 1919), 34–43 (quotation).

23. John S. Bradway to EA, May 30, 1949; and Elizabeth Bryan to EA, August 14, 1948, SPBP.

24. SPB to KL, October 27, 1933, Lenroot Papers.

25. Harriet Hyman Alonso, *Peace as a Women's Issue: A History of the U.S. Movement for World Peace and Women's Rights* (Syracuse, N.Y.: Syracuse University Press, 1993).

26. Katherine Marino, *Feminism for the Americas: The Making of an International Human Rights Movement* (Chapel Hill: University of North Carolina Press, 2019).

27. Raissa to EA, August 7, 1949; and Rose Sears to EA, June 8, 1949, SPBP.

Chapter 1. Becoming a Breckinridge

1. WCPB to SPB, March 30, 1885, SPBP; and SPB Autobiography.

2. Several scholars have devoted some attention to Breckinridge's childhood, education, and early career. See Ellen Fitzpatrick, *Endless Crusade: Women Social Scientists and Progres-*

sive Reform (New York: Oxford University Press, 1990); Melanie Beals Goan, "Establishing Their Place in the Dynasty: Sophonisba and Mary Breckinridge's Paths to Public Service," *Register of the Kentucky Historical Society* 101, nos. 1 and 2 (Winter/Spring 2003): 45–73; Joan Marie Johnson, *Southern Women at the Seven Sister Colleges: Feminist Values and Social Activism, 1875–1915* (Athens: University of Georgia Press, 2008); Klotter, *Breckinridges*, chap. 14; and Klotter, "Family Influences on a Progressive: The Early Years of Sophonisba P. Breckinridge," in Klotter and Peter J. Sehlinger, eds. *Kentucky Profiles: Biographical Essays in Honor of Holman Hamilton* (Frankfort: Kentucky Historical Society, 1982).

3. "My Ancestry," SPB Autobiography.

4. SPB Autobiography.

5. SPB Autobiography; Manuscript Census, Lexington, Fayette County, Kentucky, 1880; see also Jane Turner Censer, *North Carolina Planters and Their Children* (Baton Rouge: Louisiana State University Press, 1984), 56–58.

6. Lindsey Apple, *The Family Legacy of Henry Clay: In the Shadow of a Kentucky Patriarch* (Lexington: University Press of Kentucky, 2011), 180; Klotter, *Breckinridges*, 141–42.

7. WCPB to SPB, March 30, 1885, SPBP; and SPB Autobiography. On female reformers' relationships with their fathers, see for instance Victoria Bissell Brown, *The Education of Jane Addams* (Philadelphia: University of Pennsylvania Press, 2004), 13–15; and Kathryn Kish Sklar, *Florence Kelley and the Nation's Work: The Rise of Women's Political Culture, 1830–1900* (New Haven, Conn.: Yale University Press, 1995), 29–30; see also Susan Phinney Conrad, *Perish the Thought: Intellectual Women in Romantic America, 1830–1860* (New York: Oxford University Press, 1976), 12, 51–54, 187, 191, 195, 238; and Barbara Welter, *Dimity Convictions: The American Woman in the Nineteenth Century* (Athens: Ohio University Press, 1976), 6.

8. SPB Autobiography; see also SPB Autobiographical Notes, Miscellany: Speeches and Articles by and about Breckinridge Family, SPBP; and Chalkley, "Magic Casements."

9. SPB Autobiography.

10. SPB Autobiography.

11. SPB Autobiography.

12. "Now a Lawyer: A Former Washington School Teacher Admitted to the Bar," *Washington [D.C.] Evening Star*, January 28, 1897; see also Johnson, *Southern Women*, 109.

13. Chalkley, "Magic Casements," part 1, p. 21. For SPB's interest in Shakespeare, see *Wellesley Magazine*, November 9, 1895, book 29, p. 112, http://repository.wellesley.edu/mag/29.

14. SPB to IDB, April 21, n.d., IDB Papers; "Woman Who Helps"; Sophonisba P. Breckinridge, "Mary Desha," clipping from DAR publication, *New York State News Sheet*, SPB Papers-SCRC; and Chalkley, "Magic Casements," part 1, p. 30. Several of Breckinridge's relatives, including R. J. Breckinridge, were Presbyterian pastors, and the family attended Mt. Horeb Presbyterian Church. See SPB Autobiography; and "Breckinridge Suspended," *Washington, [D.C.] Evening Star,* October 13, 1894.

15. SPB Autobiography; Report of Nisba P. Breckinridge, January 24, 1873, Miscellany, 1873–1917, SPBP; and IDB to SPB, April 6, 1885, SPBP.

16. SPB Autobiography; see also *Annual Register of the State College of Kentucky* (Lexington: Transylvania, 1881), 8, 12; *Annual Register of the State College of Kentucky* (Frankfort: Major Johnston & Barrett, 1882), 8; *Annual Register of the State College of Kentucky* (Frankfort: Ma-

jor Johnston & Barrett, 1883), 8; *Annual Register of the State College of Kentucky* (Frankfort: Major, Johnston & Barrett, 1884), 7; and State of Kentucky Matriculators Book (1869–1889), 106, 122, 136, 156, all in UK.

17. SPB Autobiography.

18. SPB Autobiography.

19. Photo in Miscellany, 1873–1917, SPBP; see also Ida Husted Harper et al., *History of Woman Suffrage* (New York: National American Woman Suffrage Association, 1881–1922); and Kathleen L. Housley, *The Letter Kills but the Spirit Gives Life: The Smiths—Abolitionists, Suffragists, Bible Translators* (Glastonbury, Conn.: Historical Society of Glastonbury, Connecticut, 1993).

20. WCPB to SPB, March 30, 1885, WCPB Papers.

21. Jane Turner Censer, *The Reconstruction of Southern White Womanhood, 1865–1895* (Baton Rouge: Louisiana State University Press, 2003), especially 12–17, 153–83; and Anya Jabour, *Scarlett's Sisters: Young Women in the Old South* (Chapel Hill: University of North Carolina Press, 1997), chap. 8; see also Roberta Frankfort, *College Women: Domesticity and Career in Turn-of-the-Century America* (New York: New York University Press, 1977).

22. On Breckinridge's kinswomen, see Breckinridge, "Mary Desha"; Melanie Beals Goan, *Mary Breckinridge: The Frontier Nursing Service and Rural Health in Appalachia* (Chapel Hill: University of North Carolina Press, 1998); Melba Porter Hay, *Madeline McDowell Breckinridge and the Battle for a New South* (Lexington: University Press of Kentucky, 2009); and Anya Jabour, "'A Nurse's Duty': Mary Curry Desha Breckinridge and the Feminine Professional Ethic of Self-Sacrifice in Progressive-Era America," forthcoming in *Register of the Kentucky Historical Society,* 117, nos. 3–4 (Summer/Autumn 2019).

23. WCPB to SPB, March 30, 1885, SPBP.

24. Manuscript Census, Lexington, Fayette County, Kentucky, 1870, 1880; SPB Autobiography.

25. SPB Autobiography. See also Chalkley, "Magic Casements."

26. SPB to IDB, Thursday Eve., n.d.; and Sunday Aft., n.d. [Spring 1884], IDB Papers; May Estelle Cook, "Sophonisba Preston Breckinridge," Breckinridge Biographical File.

27. Irene Stevskal, "Three World Famous Women Honored Here This Week," *Chicago Tribune,* June 1946; see also WCPB to SPB, April 19, 1885, and May 10, 1885, SPBP.

28. SPB Autobiography. Elsewhere in her memoirs, Breckinridge contradicted her own claims of ignorance by remarking that when her aunt, Mary Desha, attempted to tell Issa and Nisba about W.C.P.'s affair, they refused to believe her and shunned her for several years.

29. SPB Autobiography. One of the men was Tom Morgan; the other was Tom Shackelford. Decades later, an acquaintance recalled that Tom Morgan had always carried Breckinridge's books for her and wondered why they never married. See Robert W. Woolley to EA, July 30, 1948, SPBP. Tom Shackelford continued to court Breckinridge after she left Kentucky to attend Wellesley College. See IDB to SPB, October 14, 1884, SPBP. She mentioned both men in her memoirs but identified them only as her classmates, not as her suitors.

30. Klotter, *Breckinridges,* ix, 317; and WCPB to SPB, March 30, 1885, SPBP.

31. IDB to SPB, January 22, 1885, SPBP.

32. Patricia A. Palmieri, "Patterns of Achievement of Single Academic Women at Welles-

ley College, 1880–1920," *Frontiers: A Journal of Women Studies* 5, no. 1 (Spring 1980): 63–67 (quotation p. 64).

33. SPB Autobiography.

34. SPB Autobiography.

35. SPB Autobiography. See also Amy Murrell Taylor, *The Divided Family in Civil War America* (Chapel Hill: University of North Carolina Press, 2005).

36. SPB Autobiography; see also Klotter, *Breckinridges*.

37. SPB Autobiography; see also Klotter, *Breckinridges*.

38. Mary Elizabeth Massey, *Women in the Civil War* (orig. pub. as *Bonnet Brigades*, 1966; rpt. Lincoln: University of Nebraska Press, 1994), 217–18, 297; Klotter, *Breckinridges*, 89; and Taylor, *Divided Family*, 28.

39. "Some Ways to Peace," January 24, 1936, Speech and Article Files, SPBP.

40. SPB Autobiography. See also Anya Jabour, *Topsy-Turvy: How the Civil War Turned the World Upside Down for Southern Children* (Chicago: Dee, 2010), chap. 6.

41. WCPB to SPB, May 10, 1885 (quotation); WCPB to SPB, June 1, September 4, 1891, SPBP; and W. C. P. Breckinridge, "Who Were the Confederate Dead?," address at the unveiling of the Confederate monument at Hopkinsville, Kentucky, May 19, 1887, copy in Miscellany: Speeches and Articles by and about Breckinridge Family, SPBP. See also Karen L. Cox, *Dixie's Daughters: The United Daughters of the Confederacy and the Preservation of Confederate Culture* (Gainesville: University Press of Florida, 2003).

42. See for instance, newspaper clipping, "Sophonisba Preston Breckinridge," April 16, 1911, Miscellany, 1873–1917, SPBP.

43. Qtd. in Klotter, *Breckinridges*, 147.

44. Clippings and transcripts, *Lexington Daily Press*, July 8, 1871; *Lexington Dollar Weekly*, July 22, 1871; *Kentucky Gazette*, February 15, 1873; *Courier Journal*, February 17, 1873; Council Proceedings, January 14, 1870; January 4, 1872; June 6, 1872; and W.C.P. Breckinridge, "Our Country," speech delivered at the Ninth Annual Festival of the New England Society of Pennsylvania, Philadelphia, December 23, 1880, all in Miscellany: Speeches and Articles by and about Breckinridge Family, SPBP.

45. Chalkley, "Magic Casements," part 1, pp. 12, 20, 33, 39–41, and 49.

46. Autobiographical Notes, Miscellany: Speeches and Articles by and about Breckinridge Family, SPBP. See also Jennifer Ritterhouse, *Growing Up Jim Crow: How Black and White Southern Children Learned Race* (Chapel Hill: University of North Carolina Press, 2006), especially chaps. 1 and 2.

47. W. C. P. Breckinridge, "Who Were the Confederate Dead?," quotations pp. 3, 16, and 28–29; and SPB Autobiography.

48. Ibid.

Chapter 2. Preparation for Citizenship

1. Katharine Coman, "Preparation for Citizenship at Wellesley College," *Education* 10, no. 6 (February 1890): 341–47, quotations 341–43; see also Helen Lefkowitz Horowitz, *Alma Mater: Design and Experience in the Women's Colleges from Their Nineteenth-Century Begin-*

nings to the 1930s (New York: Knopf, 1984); and Patricia Ann Palmieri, *In Adamless Eden: The Community of Women Faculty at Wellesley* (New Haven, Conn.: Yale University Press, 1995).

2. SPB Autobiography.

3. SPB to IDB, January 11, 1886, IDB Papers; Palmieri, *In Adamless Eden*.

4. IDB to SPB, February 18, 1885, SPBP.

5. See especially Ruth Bordin, *Women at Michigan: The "Dangerous Experiment"* (Ann Arbor: University of Michigan Press, 1999); and Charlotte W. Conable, *Women at Cornell: The Myth of Equal Education* (Ithaca, N.Y.: Cornell University Press, 1997).

6. The "Seven Sisters" include the single-sex schools Bryn Mawr, Mount Holyoke, Smith, Vassar, and Wellesley as well as the coordinate colleges Radcliffe and Barnard. Roughly one thousand southern women attended these schools between 1875 and 1915. On rules and religion at Wellesley and other women's colleges, see Horowitz, *Alma Mater*, 86–87; Johnson, *Southern Women*, 7–11, 54, and 83; and Palmieri, *In Adamless Eden*, 6–7. For quotation, see Alice Freeman, "A Review of the Higher Education of Women," *Forum*, September 1891, 30. On Wellesley's tuition, see Horowitz, *Alma Mater*, 85–86; and Virginia Sherwood, "American Universities and Colleges: XL—Wellesley College," *Frank Leslie's Popular Monthly*, p. 271, Elbert Scrapbook. On the Breckinridges' church membership, see "Breckinridge Suspended."

7. SPB to IDB, Friday Eve., n.d., IDB Papers.

8. SPB to IDB, February 21, 1886, IDB Papers; SPB to WCPB, June 10, 1887, WCPB Papers.

9. WCPB to SPB, May 10, 1885; IDB to SPB, January 22, 1885; WCPB to SPB, March 30, 1885; see also WCPB to SPB, April 19, 1885, all in SPBP.

10. SPB to IDB, June 10, 1886, IDB Papers.

11. SPB to IDB, Wednesday, n.d. [1884–1885], IDB Papers; Palmieri, *In Adamless Eden*, 31–33; and *Wellesley Courant* 1, no. 2 (September 28, 1888): 1, http://repository.wellesley.edu/courant/2.

12. SPB to WCPB, June 10, 1887, WCPB Papers; see also SPB to WCPB, March 9, 1887, WCPB Papers; and SPB to IDB, January 11, 1886, IDB Papers; SPB Autobiography.

13. On the "Special" teaching courses, see SPB to IDB, n.d., IDB Papers. On shorthand, see SPB to IDB, n.d., Monday Night; and SPB to WCPB, February 15, 1887, IDB Papers; SPB to WCPB, November 1, 1886; and SPB to WCPB, n.d., WCPB Papers.

14. SPB to Mary Snow, July 31, [1914], SPBP.

15. SPB to WCPB, February 15, 1887, IDB Papers.

16. SPB to Mary Snow, July 31, [1914], SPBP.

17. Horowitz, *Alma Mater*, 43, 54–55; *Wellesley Regulations*, rule 3, p. 2, Friday Scrapbook.

18. Ruth Bordin, *Alice Freeman Palmer: The Evolution of a New Woman* (Ann Arbor: University of Michigan Press, 1993), 94–95; and Palmieri, *In Adamless Eden*, 12.

19. Breckinridge Biographical File; SPB to Mary Snow, July 31, [1914], SPBP.

20. SPB to IDB, Thursday Morn., n.d.; SPB to IDB, November 4, 1886, IDB Papers; SPB to WCPB, January 22, 1886, WCPB Papers; "Wellesley in 1885–86," p. 3.

21. For quotation, see SPB to WCPB, March 20, 1887, WCPB Papers. Her Latin instructors included Sara Anna Emerson, Emily Clark, and Frances Ellen Lord. See SPB to IDB, Thursday Morn., n.d.; SPB to IDB, Wednesday, n.d. [1884–1885], IDB Papers; "Wellesley in 1885–86," p. 1; and "Wellesley in 1887–88," p. 2.

22. SPB to IDB, April 21, n.d., (quotation); n.d., and March 24, 1886, IDB Papers; see also Bordin, *Alice Freeman Palmer*, 94–95; and Palmieri, *In Adamless Eden*, 173–77.

23. SPB Autobiography.

24. SPB Autobiography; and SPB to IDB, Friday Morn., n.d. [1885–1886], IDB Papers; see also Palmieri, *In Adamless Eden*, 37–38.

25. SPB to WCPB, March 20, 1887, WCPB Papers.

26. SPB to IDB, April 21, n.d., IDB Papers; Palmieri, *In Adamless Eden*, 163.

27. "Wellesley in 1886–7," 13, and "Wellesley in 1887–88," 3; Palmieri, *In Adamless Eden*, 63.

28. Coman, "Education for Citizenship," 346; see also Breckinridge Biographical File; and SPB to WCPB, February 7, 1887, WCPB Papers.

29. SPB to IDB, Sunday, n.d., IDB Papers; Palmieri, *In Adamless Eden*, 39; and "Wellesley in 1887–88," p. 2.

30. SPB to WCPB, January 22, 1886, IDB Papers.

31. See for instance SPB to WCPB, November 1, 1886, January 9 and 31, 1887, February 7 and 13, 1887, February 12, 1888, WCPB Papers.

32. SPB to IDB, Wednesday night [1885–1886]; and SPB to IDB, May 7, 1886, IDB Papers.

33. Sherwood, "American Universities and Colleges."

34. List of Events, September 11–December 12, 1884, WCPB Papers. See also Wellesley College, "1942 Record Number of the Wellesley College Bulletin," *Wellesley College Bulletin*, vol. 32, no. 1 (1942): lil (http://repository.wellesley.edu/weslleysleyhistories/6) hereafter "Wellesley Bulletin."

35. "Wellesley in 1884–5," 3.

36. SPB to IDB, May 27, n.d., IDB Papers.

37. "Wellesley in 1886–7," 4–5; see also SPB to IDB, February 12, n.d.; [SPB to IDB] Fragment; and SPB to IDB, January 27, 1886, all in IDB Papers.

38. SPB to WCPB, January 31, 1887, WCPB Papers; see also "Wellesley in 1886–7," 5.

39. SPB to WCPB, n.d., WCPB Papers.

40. IDB to WCPB, August 22, 1886, WCPB Papers; and Horowitz, *Alma Mater*, 156–59.

41. Elizabeth Wallace to EA, June 5, 1949, SPBP.

42. "Wellesley College in 1887–88," 8.

43. Cook, "Sophonisba Preston Breckinridge"; Breckinridge Biographical File; Class of 1888 Book, 88; and "Wellesley in 1884–5."

44. Class History, 37; "Wellesley in 1884–5."

45. SPB to IDB, Sunday, n.d.; SPB to IDB, Monday, n.d.; SPB to IDB, March 10, n.d.; and SPB to IDB, Tuesday, n.d., [Jan-April 1885 folder], IDB Papers; Clipping, June 5, 1885, "Tree Day, May 29," McCamant Scrapbook, 137; Tree Day Program, 1885, Friday Scrapbook; "Wellesley in 1884–5," 5; Class History, 38; and Horowitz, *Alma Mater*, 172. Issa had the class seal made at Tiffany's jewelers; see IDB to SPB, March 18, 1885, SPBP. Hayes also was a suffragist and dress-reform advocate. See Palmieri, *In Adamless Eden*, 38–39.

46. "Wellesley in 1884–5," 2; Clipping, n.d., McCamant Scrapbook; and SPB to IDB, May 27, n.d., IDB Papers.

47. SPB to WCPB, November 1, 1886, January 31, 1887, and November 27, 1887, WCPB Papers; SPB to IDB, Thursday night, n.d., SPB to IDB, January 27, 1886, and SPB to WCPB,

March 13, 1887, IDB Papers; see also Josephine H. Batchelder, "A Wellesley Woman of Distinction," *Wellesley College News* 24, no. 15 (February 3, 1916): 7–8.

48. SPB to IDB, postcard, October 24, 1885; SPB to IDB, Sunday, n.d.; SPB to IDB, Thursday night, n.d.; SPB to IDB, May 27, [1886]; SPB to IDB, February 24, n.d.; SPB to WCPB, February 13, 1887; and SPB to IDB, February 23, 1887, all in IDB Papers. See also Clippings, November 17, 1887, and, n.d., McCamant Scrapbook; and "Wellesley in 1885–86," 5.

49. For quotations, see SPB to IDB, Tuesday Aft., n.d., Thursday Morn., n.d., and January 11, 1886, IDB Papers; and SPB to WCPB, November 1, 1886, WCPB Papers; and Josephine Simrall to SPB, February 21, 1936, SPBP. See also IDB to SPB, November 19, 1884, and January 19, 1885; and SPB to IDB, Saturday Morn., n.d., Tuesday Evening, n.d.; Thursday Eve., n.d., April 21, n.d., May 27, n.d., and May 7 and June 10, 1886, IDB Papers; Helen Clark to SPB, June 23, 1885, SPBP; Class of 1888 Book; and Johnson, *Southern Women*, 89. Ely was from Rockford, Cook from Oak Park. See *Register of the Wellesley College Alumnae Association, 1910–1911* (Boston: Wood, 1910), 60; and *Register of the Wellesley College Alumnae Association, 1912–1913* (Boston: Wood, 1912), 150. After graduating from Wellesley, Cook, who never married, returned to Chicago, where she taught high school English, engaged in political and civic reform, and published a book, *Little Oak Park*. See Douglas Deuchler, *Legendary Locals of Oak Park* (Charleston, S.C.: Arcadia, 2013), 20. 150. Ely also lived in Chicago after graduation, where she became president of the city's Wellesley Club. See *Wellesley Magazine* 1, no. 1 (October 15, 1892): 219. On Clark and Meddick, see "Wellesley Bulletin," 15, 29.

50. SPB to IDB, n.d. [Spring 1885], April 21, n.d.; May 27, n.d.; October 8, n.d., Monday, n.d., Tuesday Evening, n.d., Thursday evening, n.d.; January 14, 1886; n.d. [Winter 1884–1885]; April 12, 1886; all in IDB Papers; Jeannette A. Marks, "Outdoor Life at Wellesley College," 118; Outing 32 (May 1898): 117-124, quotation p. 118; Elbert Scrapbook; and *Wellesley Regulations*, rule 9, p. 4.

51. SPB to IDB, n.d., March 1, n.d., and February 1 and 23, 1887, IDB Papers. Caroline Soule, Class of 1880, taught Greek from 1885–1889. See "Wellesley Bulletin," lxi.

52. Clipping, "Wellesley College, May 22, 1885," McCamant Scrapbook, 134–35. See also Barbara Ehrenreich and Deirdre English, *For Her Own Good: Two Centuries of the Experts' Advice to Women* (New York: Random House, 1978), chap. 4; Carroll Smith-Rosenberg, "Puberty to Menopause: The Cycle of Femininity in Nineteenth-Century America"; and "The Hysterical Woman: Sex Roles and Role Conflict in Nineteenth-Century America," in *Disorderly Conduct: Visions of Gender in Victorian America* (New York: Knopf, 1985), 182–96 and 197–216.

53. IDB to SPB, March 26, 1885 [misdated 1884]; June [misdated] 24, 1884; September 15 and 17, 1884; October 10, 1884; and March 18, 1885; WCPB to SPB, September 24, 1884, January 16, 1885, all in SPBP.

54. IDB to SPB, September 26, October 18, and October 28, 1884, SPBP; see also IDB to SPB, January 3 and April 29, 1885, SPBP; and Smith-Rosenberg, "Hysterical Woman."

55. SPB to IDB, March 1, n.d., Monday Morn., n.d., March 15, 1886, and May 7, 1886, IDB Papers.

56. SPB to IDB, Thursday, n.d., and February 1, 1887, IDB Papers. The other woman, Miss Fine (or perhaps Miss Line) may have been May Margaret Fine, a member of the class of

1889 who later became the principal of Miss Fine's School. See "Wellesley Bulletin," 31. Math instructor Ellen Hayes also was a dress-reform advocate. See Palmieri, *In Adamless Eden*, 39.

57. SPB to IDB, Wednesday Eve., n.d., IDB Papers.

58. Stevskal, "Three World Famous Women"; and "Sophonisba P. Breckinridge, of U. of C., Dies," *Chicago Tribune*, July 31, 1948.

59. WCPB to SPB, October 8, 1884, and May 10, 1885, SPBP.

60. Palmieri, *In Adamless Eden*, 180.

61. Palmieri, *In Adamless Eden*, 181; on faculty-student relations, see chap. 11.

62. SPB to IDB, Wednesday, n.d., IDB Papers. According to the "Wellesley Bulletin," xxxiii, Emily Josephine Clark, class of 1882, taught Latin from 1884 to 1891; on Frances Ellen Lord, see Palmieri, *In Adamless Eden*, 41.

63. Nisba visited Shafer (SPB to IDB, January 11, 1886, IDB Papers), Morgan (SPB to IDB, February 21, 1886, IDB Papers) and Hayes (SPB to IDB, Sunday, n.d.) in their rooms; she not only visited Freeman but also went for walks and carriage rides with her (SPB to IDB, Tuesday Morn., n.d., IDB Papers; see also Alice Freeman to SPB, July 12, 1887, SPBP).

64. SPB Autobiography.

65. IDB to SPB, September 19, 20, and 24, October 7, 14, and 19, 1884; April 29 and May 17, 1885, SPBP.

66. SPB to WCPB, June 10, 1887, WCPB Papers; SPB to IDB, Tuesday morn., n.d., Wednesday night [1885–1886], Thursday night, n.d., and January 27, 1886, IDB Papers; Alice Freeman to SPB, July 12, 1887, and November 18, 1888, SPBP.

67. On Freeman's courtship and eventual marriage, see Bordin, *Alice Freeman Palmer*, 166–69, 173–82, and 208–11; Frankfort, *Collegiate Women*, chaps. 1 and 3; and Palmieri, *In Adamless Eden*, 35–37 and 96–100.

68. On Tom Shackelford, see SPB to IDB, Friday Eve., n.d., IDB Papers; and SPB Autobiography; see also IDB to SPB, October 14, 1884, SPBP. On Tom Morgan, see Robert W. Woolley to EA, July 30, 1948, SPBP.

69. For quotations, see AF to SPB, July 12, 1887, SPBP; and SPB Autobiography; see also AFP to SPB, December 30, 1887, November 18, 1888, SPBP.

70. SPB Autobiography; SPB to WCPB, November 27, 1887, WCPB Papers; Palmieri, *In Adamless Eden*, 37–38.

71. Palmieri, *In Adamless Eden*, 33.

72. Ibid., 99, 137–42; see also Horowitz, *Alma Mater*, 187–93. On "Boston marriages" (a phrase associated with, although not derived from, Henry James's 1886 novel *The Bostonians*), see Esther D. Rothblum and Kathleen A. Broheyn, eds., *Boston Marriages: Romantic but Asexual Relationships among Contemporary Lesbians* (Amherst: University of Massachusetts Press, 1993).

73. SPB to IDB, Thursday Morn., n.d., February 12, n.d., and February 21, 1886, IDB Papers. Estelle Hurll, who graduated from Wellesley in 1882 and earned her MA there in 1892, was instructor of ethics from 1884–1891. See "Wellesley in 1886–87," 2; Estelle Hurll letter to parents, October 4, 1885, Hurll Papers; and "Wellesley Bulletin," xlvi. On other faculty couples, see Judith Schwartz, "Yellow Clover: Katharine Lee Bates and Katharine Coman," *Frontiers* 4, no.

1 (Spring 1979): 59–67; Nan Bauer Maglin, "Vida to Florence: 'Comrade and Companion,'" *Frontiers* 4, no. 3 (Autumn 1979): 13–20; and Palmieri, *In Adamless Eden*, 78–81, 137–39.

74. Vida Scudder, *On Journey* (New York: Dutton, 1937), 219.

75. IDB to SPB, November 6, 1884, SPBP.

76. Coman, "Education for Citizenship," 344–45 (quotation); see also Breckinridge Biographical File.

77. SPB Autobiography. Wellesley's Southern Club was not established until 1900. See Johnson, *Southern Women*, 89–92.

78. See for example SPB to WCPB, February 7, 1887, WCPB Papers.

79. SPB to IDB, May 20, 1886, IDB Papers.

80. SPB Autobiography; see also Johnson, *Southern Women*, 98–99.

81. SPB Autobiography; IDB to SPB, September 19, 1884; and WCPB to SPB, October 3, 1884, SPBP.

82. SPB to IDB, n.d., IDB Papers.

83. IDB to SPB, September 26, 1884; WCPB to SPB, October 3, 1884, SPBP.

84. SPB Autobiography.

85. Johnson, *Southern Women*, 95–108.

86. For quotations, see SPB Autobiography; and SPB to IDB, February 23, 1887, IDB Papers; see also Bordin, *Alice Freeman Palmer*, 136; Johnson, *Southern Women*, 104; and Fitzpatrick, *Endless Crusade*, 8.

87. SPB to WCPB, February 13, 1887, and SPB to WCPB, March 13, 1887, IDB Papers; SPB to WCPB, June 10, 1887, WCPB Papers; Wellesley Annals, "Wellesley in 1884–5," p. 2; and Clipping, n.d., McCamant Scrapbook.

88. On the "semi-secular" atmosphere at Wellesley and President Freeman's views, see Bordin, *Alice Freeman Palmer*, 121–22, 134–36; and Horowitz, *Alma Mater*, 86–87. On the Christian Association and the Chapel Fund Association, see Wellesley Annals, "Wellesley in 1884–5," 2; Wellesley Annals, "Wellesley in 1886–7," 5; Wellesley Annals, "Wellesley in 1887–88," 3; Clipping, n.d., McCamant Scrapbook; and Clipping, "Wellesley College: Tenth Annual Commencement," Class of 1888 Records.

89. SPB to IDB, February 21, 1886, IDB Papers.

90. SPB to IDB, Thursday Eve., n.d., IDB Papers; WCPB to SPB, October 3 and 22, 1884; see also WCPB to SPB, December 12, 1884, February 15, 1885, March 2, 1885; and IDB to SPB, October 1, 1884, SPBP.

91. SPB to IDB, Thursday Eve., n.d. [1884–1885], (quotation); and SPB to IDB, Sunday, n.d., (prayer meetings), IDB Papers.

92. SPB to WCPB, June 10, 1887, WCPB Papers.

93. Wellesley College Tenth Annual Commencement Program, June 19, 1888, Ellery Scrapbook, Class of 1888 Records; SPB Transcripts.

94. Tree Day Program, June 5, 1888, Class of 1888 Book; and Class History, 16–21.

95. Clipping, "Wellesley College: Tenth Annual Commencement," Ellery Scrapbook.

96. Marion Angelina Ely, "Class Prophecy," Class History, 90, Class of 1888 Book.

97. "Wellesley in 1887–88," 8.

Chapter 3. Striving for the Ideal

1. Autographed letter signed by Sophonisba P. Breckinridge to "My dear Miss Bates," Easter Sunday [April 1] 1893, Special Collections, Wellesley College Library (hereafter SPB to Katharine Lee Bates, April 1, 1893).

2. Bates, "The Ideal"; and SPB to Katharine Lee Bates, April 1, 1893.

3. Antler, "After College, What?"

4. SPB Autobiography.

5. Jane Addams, "Filial Relations," in Addams, *Democracy and Social Ethics*, ed. by Anne Firor Scott (Cambridge, Mass.: Harvard University Press, 1964), 85–86; see also Antler, "After College, What?"

6. SPB to WCPB, June 10, 1887, WCPB Papers; SPB Autobiography; and Klotter, *Breckinridges*, chap. 12.

7. SPB Autobiography; see also Bordin, *Women at Michigan: The "Dangerous Experiment."*

8. Breckinridge Interview, https://iiif.lib.harvard.edu/manifests/view/drs:2582661$413i.

9. Joan Marie Johnson, "Job Market or Marriage Market? Life Choices for Southern Women Educated at Northern Colleges, 1875–1915," *History of Education Quarterly* 47, no. 2 (May 2007): 149–72.

10. SPB Autobiography.

11. See especially Censer, *Reconstruction*, 156–58, 170–71, and 177–78; and Mary E. Cookingham, "Bluestockings, Spinsters, and Pedagogues: Women College Graduates, 1865–1910," *Population Studies* 38, no. 3 (November 1984): 349–64, especially 355–58.

12. SPB Autobiography.

13. SPB Autobiography; AFP to SPB, November 18, 1888; and Kate M. Jaquette to EA, July 31, 1948, SPBP.

14. SPB Autobiography.

15. SPB Autobiography; Censer, *Reconstruction*, 179–80.

16. Antler, "After Marriage, What?"; Christine Carter Jacobson, *Southern Single Blessedness: Unmarried Women in the Urban South, 1800–1865* (Urbana: University of Illinois Press, 2006); Johnson, "Job Market or Marriage Market?"; and Palmieri, "Patterns of Achievement," 63–67.

17. SPB Autobiography; Nancy Bristow, *American Pandemic: The Lost Worlds of the 1918 Influenza Epidemic* (New York: Oxford University Press, 2012).

18. Class Letters, 1890–1891, Class of 1888 Records.

19. SPB Autobiography.

20. SPB Autobiography; "Ready for the Bar," *New York Times*, November 29, 1892.

21. SPB Autobiography; see also IDB to SPB, June 26, 1891, WCPB Papers; WCPB to SPB, May 14, July 4, 19, 26, August 25, September 4, October 13, November 19, 27, 1891, and January 27, 1892; IDB to SPB, May 17, June 14, [June n.d.], July 22 1891, January 31, 1892, SPBP.

22. Brown, *Education of Jane Addams*, chap. 8; and Helen Lefkowitz Horowitz, *The Power and Passion of M. Carey Thomas* (New York: Knopf, 1994), chap. 6.

23. IDB to SPB, May 11, 1892; see also WCPB to SPB, April 26, 1892; IDB to SPB, June 4, July 14, 1892; DB to SPB, [ca. 1891], SPBP.

24. Gerald Stanley Lee to SPB, January 10, 1892; "Ready for the Bar"; Antler, "After College, What?," 413–17; and Horowitz, *Power and Passion*, chap. 6.

25. WCPB to SPB, January 5, 1892; IDB to SPB, May 11, 1892, SPBP; and SPB to IDB, May 24, 1892, WCPB Papers.

26. Gerald Stanley Lee to SPB, June 1, 15 (quotations), 1891, SPBP.

27. SPB Autobiography.

28. IDB to SPB, June 26, October 25, 1891, WCPB Papers; and IDB to SPB, January 28, 1892, SPBP.

29. Stella Riordan to SPB, March 29, 1891; Claire McDonald to SPB, August 20, 1891; May Estelle Cook to SPB, n.d., 1891; and May [Estelle Cook] to SPB, [August 11, 1891], SPBP.

30. Curry Breckinridge to WCPB Breckinridge, June 12, 1892, WCPB Papers; see also Paschal (Ann Arbor, Michigan) to SPB, February 22, 1892, SPBP.

31. WCPB to SPB, June 27, 1892, SPBP; and Klotter, *Breckinridges*, 163.

32. DB to SPB, July 22, 1892, SPBP.

33. Vida Scudder to SPB, August 9, 1892, SPBP; SPB Autobiography.

34. "Ready for the Bar"; and *Constitution, By-Laws, Roll of Members and Proceedings of the Kentucky State Bar Association at its Organizational Meetings held in Louisville, Kentucky, November the Nineteenth, Nineteen Hundred and One* (Louisville: Kentucky State Bar Association, 1910), 20.

35. Louise Breckinridge, Statement, July 3, [1894]; and John Lancaster to WCPB, May 23, 1894, WCPB Papers; and Klotter, *Breckinridges*, 161–63. Klotter, *Breckinridges*, 352n27, dates the marriage to April 29, 1893. See also Patricia Miller, *Bringing Down the Colonel: A Sex Scandal of the Gilded Age, and the "Powerless" Woman Who Took On Washington* (New York: Crichton /Farrar, Straus and Giroux, 2018).

36. William Rose to M. Totten, December 7, 1893; William Rose, "Report," January 18, 1894; and WCPB to Charles Meng, January 18, 1894, WCPB Papers; "Breckinridge Suspended"; and Klotter, *Breckinridges*, 163–69.

37. WCPB to George O. Graves, April 24, 1894; see also DB to WCPB, September 12, 13, 1893; Mollie Shingleblower to WCPB, November 25, 1893; SPB to WCPB, August 28, 1893, January 8, June 2, July 21, 1894; WCPB to DB, January 22, 1894; C. H. Steele to WCPB, February 3, 1894; Nannie White to WCPB, March 5, 1894; and WCPB to Myall, April 30, 1894, WCPB Papers.

38. SPB Autobiography.

39. SPB Autobiography; SPB to WCPB, August 28, September 25, and December 30, 1893; DB to WCPB, September 12, 1893; and SPB to WCPB, January 27, 1894, WCPB Papers.

40. SPB to WCPB, January 27, 1894, WCPB Papers.

41. For quotations, see WCPB to Mr. Mitchell, May 10, 1894; and SPB to WCPB, May 4, 1894, WCPB Papers. See also SPB to WCPB, January 8, May 5, 7, [July 20], July 21, 1894; WCPB to DB, July 11, 1894; and WCPB to SPB, March 7, 1894, all in WCPB Papers.

42. SPB to WCPB, September 8 and November 20, 1894, WCPB Papers; and Class Letters, 1894–1895, Class of 1888 Records.

43. SPB Autobiography.

44. Marion Talbot to SPB, January 3, 1892, SPBP; SPB Autobiography; and Bordin, *Alice*

Freeman Palmer, 232–35. The ACA later became the American Association of University Women. See Susan Levine, *Degrees of Equality: The American Association of University Women and the Challenge of Twentieth-Century Feminism* (Philadelphia: Temple University Press, 1995).

45. SPB Autobiography; see also Fitzpatrick, *Endless Crusade*, 12–13.

46. In her autobiography, Breckinridge mistakenly dated her first year at UC as 1894–95; her transcripts, however, indicate that she enrolled in Autumn 1895. See SPB Autobiography; and SPB Transcripts. See also Felice Batlan, "Law and the Fabric of the Everyday: The Settlement Houses, Sociological Jurisprudence, and the Gendering of Urban Legal Culture," *Southern California Interdisciplinary Law Journal* 17, no. 2 (Spring 2006): 235–81; and Fitzpatrick, *Endless Crusade*, 44–46.

47. Freund Papers, box 20, folders 2, 4, 5, and 7; and Freund, *The Police Power, Public Policy, and Constitutional Rights* (Chicago: Callahan, 1904). See also Michael Willrich, *City of Courts: Socializing Justice in Progressive Era Chicago* (Cambridge: Cambridge University Press, 2003).

48. SPB Autobiography.

49. SPB Autobiography; WCPB to Curry Breckinridge, December 15, 1896; WCPB to SPB, December 28, 1896, SPBP.

50. SPB Autobiography; SPB Transcripts.

51. SPB, "The Administration of Justice in Kentucky," Master's thesis, University of Chicago, 1897, quotations pp. 1 and 42, Speeches and Articles Files, SPBP; SPB Autobiography; and SPB Transcripts.

52. SPB Autobiography; Handwritten Affidavit Signed by Judges of the Kentucky Court of Appeals, January 22, 1897, SPB Papers-SCRC; Certificate, Notary Public, January 22, 1897, Miscellany, SPBP; and "A Kentucky Portia," *Texas Daily-Herald*, February 3, 1897.

53. SPB Autobiography; "Sophonisba's First Case: Col. Breckinridge's Lawyer Daughter Files Model Papers in a Divorce Case," *Kansas City Journal*, February 15, 1897; "Miss Breckinridge Successful in the First Step of Her Maiden Case," *Maysville [Ky.] Daily Public Ledger*, February 19, 1897; and Swigert Divorce Records. See also Peter Bardaglio, *Reconstructing the Household: Families, Sex, and the Law in the Nineteenth-Century South* (Chapel Hill: University of North Carolina Press, 2000); David Peterson Del Mar, *The American Family: From Obligation to Freedom* (Palgrave Macmillan, 2011); and Michael Grossberg, *Governing the Hearth: Law and the Family in Nineteenth-Century America* (Chapel Hill: University of North Carolina Press, 1985).

54. "Miss Florence Barlow at the Tennessee Centennial," *Richmond [Ky.] Climax*, October 13, 1897; Breckinridge Interview; and SPB Autobiography.

55. SPB Autobiography. Breckinridge dated her return to 1898, but SPB Transcripts and her correspondence indicate that she returned to Chicago in time for the Fall 1897 term.

56. Fitzpatrick, *Endless Crusade*, 34–38 (quotation p. 37). See also Maureen A. Flanagan, *Seeing with Their Hearts: Chicago Women and the Vision of the Good City, 1871–1933* (Princeton, N.J.: Princeton University Press, 2002).

57. See especially Fitzpatrick, *Endless Crusade*, chaps. 2 and 3; see also Steven J. Diner, *A City and Its Universities: Public Policy in Chicago, 1892–1919* (Chapel Hill: University of North Caro-

lina Press, 1980); Thomas Haskell, *The Emergence of Professional Social Science: The American Social Science Association and the Nineteenth-Century Crisis of Authority* (Urbana: University of Illinois Press, 1977); and Monica Mercado and Katherine Turk, *"On Equal Terms": Educating Women at the University of Chicago* (Chicago: University of Chicago Library, 2009).

58. SPB Autobiography.

59. Madeline Wallin to Mother, January 15, 1893, folder 4; Madeline Wallin to Mother, March 20, 1894, folder 5, Wallin Papers; see also Madeline Wallin to Father, November 13, 1892; January 15, 1893, folder 4; Madeline Wallin to Mother, December 12, 1892, folder 4; and "Faculty Aid," May 7, 1894, folder 12, all in Wallin Papers.

60. SPB Transcripts; Freund Papers, box 1, folders 2, 4, 5, 10, and 12.

61. Madeline Wallin to Father, October 23, 1892, folder 4, Wallin Papers; Fitzpatrick, *Endless Crusade*, 46.

62. SPB Autobiography; SPB Transcripts; Fitzpatrick, *Endless Crusade*, 46; and Madeline Wallin to Father, November 13, 1892, folder 4, Wallin Papers.

63. Fitzpatrick, *Endless Crusade*, 47–49; and Alfred Bornemann, *J. Laurence Laughlin* (Washington, D.C.: American Council on Public Affairs, 1940), 23–24.

64. SPB Autobiography; S. P. Breckinridge, *Legal Tender: A Study in American and English Monetary History* (Chicago: University of Chicago Press, 1903).

65. James Parker Hall, "Review," *JPE* 12, no. 1 (December 1903): 131–35 (quotations, 132).

66. SPB Autobiography.

67. SPB to Mr. Gurney, June 20, 1903, SPBP; SPB Transcripts.

68. Breckinridge Interview; and SPB to Margaret B. Bennett, April 27, 1933, SPBP; see also Virginia G. Drachtman, *Sisters in Law: Women Lawyers in Modern American History* (Cambridge, Mass.: Harvard University Press, 2001); and Tracy A. Thomas and Tracey Jean Boisseau, eds., *Feminist Legal History: Essays on Women and the Law* (New York: New York University Press, 2011).

69. In 1903 Talbot predicted that Breckinridge would go into law practice after completing her JD. See Susan Peabody to Leila S. McKee, November 23, 1903, McKee Papers, box 2, folder 22.

70. Quoted in Klotter, *Breckinridges*, 194–95.

71. Bates, "The Ideal."

Chapter 4. Academic Activism

1. "1,500 Idle Riot around Hull House"; "Women Help Slug Police; Bullets Fly: Haymarket Widow and 20 Others Locked Up after Parade Is Stopped"; "Riot Views of Different Sides"; and "The Weather," *Chicago Tribune*, January 18, 1915; and "Chicago Unemployed Riot: Shots Fired and a Number Cut and Bruised—Miss Addams to the Rescue," *NYT*, January 18, 1915.

2. [Miss Sophinisba Breckenridge, arrested during protest at Hull House,] *Chicago Daily News*, [January 18, 1915], Chicago History Museum, http://chsmedia.org/media /dn/06/0639/DN-0063953.jpg. Despite the caption, which was supplied by the cataloger, no other source indicates that Breckinridge was arrested for her role in the protest.

3. Russell Ballard, "The Years at Hull House," *SSR* 22, no. 4 (December 1948): 432.

4. SPB, "Family Budgets," 43.

5. SPB Autobiography; Ellen Fitzpatrick, "For the 'Women of the University': Marion Talbot, 1858–1948," in Geraldine Joncich Clifford, ed., *Lone Voyagers: Academic Women in Coeducational Universities, 1870–1937* (New York: Feminist, 1989), 87–124; Lynn Gordon, *Gender and Higher Education in the Progressive Era* (New Haven, Conn.: Yale University Press, 1990), chap. 3; and Jana Nidiffer, *Pioneering Deans of Women: More than Wise and Pious Matrons* (New York: Teachers College Press, 2000), chap. 4.

6. MT to WH, October 24, 1898, and MT to Judson, August 27, [1907], President's Papers, box 41, folder 7; MT to Judson, September 8, 1906, Presidents' Papers, box 38, folder 16; Emily Talbot to SPB, April 13, 1898; E. Kellogg to MT, September 21, 1899, SPBP.

7. WCPB to SPB, September 5, 1901, June 6, 1903, and November 1, 11, 1904; and DB to SPB, January 1, 1904, SPBP; Warranty Deed, Henry Russell and Mary M. Talbot to MT and SPB, October 23, 1912, Talbot Papers, box 9, folder 8.

8. See for example Louise Stanley to MT, May 4, 1916; Louise Green to MT, [April 29, 1925]; and Ruth Lindquist to MT, May 21, 1925, Talbot Papers, box 2, folder 1.

9. For quotation, see MT to WH, December 20, 1901; see also MT to WH, December 1, 1900, January 23, 1902, November 16, 1903, and April 20, 1904; WH to MT, February 16, 20, 1901, January 28, 1902; and April 23, 1904, all in President's Papers, box 38, folder 16.

10. SPB Autobiography.

11. WH to MT, April 23, 1904, President's Papers, box 38, folder 16; Nidiffer, *Pioneering Deans of Women*, 43–44; and Gordon, *Gender and Higher Education*, 115–17.

12. Gordon, *Gender and Higher Education*, chap. 3; and Anya Jabour, "Separatism and Equality: Women at the University of Chicago, 1895–1945," Societa Italiana Per Lo Studio Della Storia Contemporanea, "Universities, Institutions, and Society (1914–1968)," September 6, 2014, Pisa, Italy, https://www.youtube.com/watch?v=osLol6cXXow.

13. Fitzpatrick, *Endless Crusade*; and Robyn Muncy, *Creating a Female Dominion in American Reform, 1890–1935* (Oxford: Oxford University Press, 1994).

14. SPB Autobiography. Breckinridge received job offers from the Western College for Women in Oxford, Ohio (later incorporated into Miami University), as well as from Oberlin College. See SPB to Leila S. McKee, November 26, 1903, McKee Papers, box 2, folder 22; and Mary to SPB, April 24, 1904, SPBP.

15. MT to WH, January 23, 1902, Presidents' Papers, box 28, folder 16.

16. See especially Megan J. Elias, *Stir It Up: Home Economics in American Culture* (Philadelphia: University of Pennsylvania Press, 2008); and Sarah Stage and Virginia B. Vincenti, eds., *Rethinking Home Economics: Women and the History of a Profession* (Ithaca, N.Y.: Cornell University Press, 1997)

17. MT, "Sanitary Science and Its Place in the University," *University Record*, December 4, 1896 (quotation); "First Draft of a Plan for a Department of Household Technology," February 1902; and MT to WH, February 18, 1904, Presidents' Papers, box 50, folder 17; and Sarah Stage, "Home Economics, What's in a Name?" in Stage and Vincenti, eds., *Rethinking Home Economics*, 1–14.

18. MT to WH, March 11 and 24, 1904; WH to MT, March 28, 1904, President's Papers, box 50, folder 17; WH to MT, March 17, 1905, Talbot Papers, box 2, folder 5; undated memo on the History of the Department of Household Administration, ca. 1920, Talbot Papers, box 5, folder 6; and SPB Autobiography.

19. SPB Autobiography.

20. SPB Autobiography. See also Lela B. Costin, *Two Sisters for Social Justice: A Biography of Grace and Edith Abbott* (Urbana: University of Illinois Press, 1983); and Wright, "Three against Time." Abbott initially came to the university for a summer course in 1902; she enrolled as a full-time student in autumn 1903. She lived at Green Hall, over which Breckinridge and Talbot presided.

21. Edith Abbott, *Women in Industry: A Study in American Economic History* (New York: Appleton, 1909); and Charles Nutter to SPB, July 14, August 2 and 13, 1909, SPBP.

22. EA and SPB, "Employment of Women in Industries: Twelfth Census Statistics," *Journal of Political Economy* 14, no. 1 (January 1906): 14–40 (quotation p. 14).

23. SPB to EA, March 3, June 28, and July 15, 1907; February 10, April 13, and May 6, 1908; and Carroll D. Wright to SPB, August 12, 1905, SPBP; and Fitzpatrick, *Endless Crusade*, 87–90.

24. "University Girl Upholds Toilers," *Chicago Tribune*, October 17, 1906; Fitzpatrick, *Endless Crusade*, 169; and Louise C. Wade, "The Heritage from Chicago's Early Settlement Houses," *Journal of the Illinois State Historical Society* 60, no. 4 (Winter 1967): 411–41, esp. 419–20.

25. Charles J. Bushnell, "Some Social Aspects of the Chicago Stock Yards: Chapter 1—Industry at the Chicago Stock Yards," *American Journal of Sociology* 7, no. 2 (September 1901): 145–70; and EA and SPB, "Women in Industry: The Chicago Stockyards," *JPE* 19, no. 8 (October 1911): 632–54.

26. "Conditions in Stockyards Described in the Neill-Reynolds Report," *Chicago Tribune*, June 5, 1906; Richard G. Arms, "From Dis-Assembly to Assembly: Cincinnati, the Birthplace of Mass Production," *Bulletin of the Historical and Philosophical Society of Ohio* 17 (1959): 195–203; and Upton Sinclair, *The Jungle* (New York: Doubleday, 1906).

27. SPB to JA, [April 2, 1906], JAPP; EA and SPB, "Women in Industry," 652; and "Conditions in Stockyards Described."

28. "Woman Puts O.K. on Neill Report," *Chicago Tribune*, June 11, 1906; Fitzpatrick, *Endless Crusade*, 169; and Wade, "Heritage."

29. "'Industry Worse than War': University of Chicago Woman Says Trade Is Militarized," *Chicago Tribune*, November 12, 1908.

30. SPB, "Legislative Control of Women's Work," *JPE* 14, no. 2 (February 1906): 107–9 (quotation p. 107).

31. Judith A. Baer, *The Chains of Protection: The Judicial Response to Women's Labor Legislation* (New York: Praeger, 1978); Vivien Hart, *Bound by Our Constitution: Women, Workers, and the Minimum Wage* (Princeton, N.J.: Princeton University Press, 1994); Julia Novkov, *Constituting Workers, Protecting Women: Gender, Law and Labor in the Progressive Era and New Deal Years* (Ann Arbor: University of Michigan Press, 2001); Elizabeth Anne Payne, *Reform, Labor, and Feminism: Margaret Dreier Robins and the Women's Trade Union League*

(Urbana: University of Illinois Press, 1988), chaps. 3 and 4; Sklar, *Florence Kelley*; and Nancy Woloch, *A Class by Herself: Protective Laws for Women Workers, 1890s–1990s* (Princeton, N.J.: Princeton University Press, 2015), chaps. 1–4;

32. SPB, "The Illinois Ten-Hour Law," *JPE* 18, no. 6 (June 1910): 465–70.

33. Woloch, *Class by Herself*, 48–51.

34. SPB, "Two Decisions Relating to Organized Labor," *JPE* 13, no. 4 (September 1905): 593–97.

35. [Sophonisba Preston Breckinridge,] "Concerning the Garment Workers Strike: Report of the Sub-Committee to the Citizens' Committee, November 5, 1910," n.p., Schlesinger Library, microfilm in History of Women no. 8605 (Research Publications, 1977); Susan Roth Breitzer, "Hull House, the Garment Workers Strikers, and the Jews of Chicago," *Indiana Magazine of History* 106, no. 1 (March 2010): 40–70; and Flanagan, *Seeing with their Hearts*, 109–10 and 112–13.

36. SPB, "Legislative Control of Women's Work," 107, 109.

37. Woloch, *Class by Herself*, chap. 3.

38. SPB, "Illinois Ten-Hour Law."

39. "Will Ask Parties for Living Wage," *Chicago Tribune*, June 14, 1912.

40. Frances Kellor to SPB, n.d. [ca. 1912], and September 6, 1912, SPBP; and Costin, *Two Sisters*, 47–48.

41. SPB to Chairman, State Senate Investigating Committee, March 8, 1913; "Will You Help in the Consumers' League Minimum Wage Campaign?" (with handwritten emendations); "A Bill for an Act Relating to the Wages and Minors Employed in Industry," SPBP.

42. See especially Woloch, *Class by Herself*, 18–25; and Landon R. Y. Storrs, *Civilizing Capitalism: The National Consumers' League, Women's Activism, and Labor Standards in the New Deal Era* (Chapel Hill: University of North Carolina Press, 2000), chap. 2.

43. SPB, "Illinois Ten-Hour Law," 468–69; see also Frances Olsen, "From False Paternalism to False Equality: Judicial Assault on Feminist Community, 1869–1895," *Michigan Law Review* 84 (June 1986): 1518–41.

44. SPB, "Legislative Control of Women's Work," 107.

45. Ballard, "Years at Hull House," 432; John Sorensen, ed., *A Sister's Memories: The Life and Work of Grace Abbott, from the Writings of Her Sister, Edith Abbott* (Chicago: University of Chicago Press, 2015), 118; and *Hull House Year Books* and List of Hull House Residents, HH, box 32, folder 294.

46. Babette Munson Interview with Alex Elson, box 2, folder 27; and Romonolo Nuncius Interview with Evelyn Crawford Smith, February 25, 1982, box 4, folder 54, both in HH-Oral Histories; see also Mary Jo Deegan, *Jane Addams and the Men of the Chicago School, 1892–1918* (New Brunswick, N.J.: Transaction, 1990); Rima Lunin Schwartz, ed., *Hull-House Maps and Papers* (Urbana: University of Illinois Press, 2007).

47. Edwin Rothschild Interview by Evelyn Crawford Smith, April 2, 1982, HH-Oral Histories, box 4, folder 65. See also Virginia K. Fish, "The Hull House Circle: Women's Friendships and Achivements," in J. Sharistanian, ed., *Gender, Ideology, and Action* (New York: Greenwood, 1986), 185–227; R. L. Sherrick, "Private Visions, Public Lives: The Hull-House Women in the Progressive Era" (PhD diss., Northwestern University, 1980); Kathryn Kish

Sklar, "Hull House in the 1890s: A Community of Women Reformers," *Signs* 10 (1985): 658–77; E. J. Stebner, *The Women of Hull House: A Study in Spirituality, Vocation, and Friendship* (Albany: State University of New York Press, 1997).

48. Russell, "Years at Hull House," 342.

49. "Memorandum for Miss Addams, suggesting a plan to be proposed by the Relief Committee for the care of tramps who ask for food at Hull House," [March 1911], SPBP.

50. Barbara Sicherman, *Alice Hamilton: A Life in Letters* (Urbana: University Illinois Press, 1984, 2001), 115.

51. SPB to "Dear" [EA], March 3 (quotation) and June 28, 1907, SPBP. The phrase "settlement spirit" comes from Muncy, *Creating a Female Dominion*, 14.

52. "Historical Sketch of the Development of the Course of Instruction in the Chicago School of Civics and Philanthropy, 1903–1913," Taylor Papers, box 62, folder 2537.

53. Ibid.; Presidents' Statement for Trustees," May 18, 1911; Presidents' Report, 1912–1913; and CSCP Registrar's Reports, 1910–11, 1911–1912, 1912–1913, 1913–1914, box 61, folder 2521; and "Recommendations of the President and the Dean," April 27, 1914, box 61, folder 2522, all in Taylor Papers; CSCP *Announcements*, 1909–1920, CSCP Records, box 1, folders 2–12; and Memorandum Concerning the Future of the Chicago School of Civics and Philanthropy, 1919–1920, box 20, folder 10, Abbott Papers-SCRC (hereafter "CSCP Memo").

54. See especially Anya Jabour, "Relationship and Leadership: Sophonisba Breckinridge and Women in Social Work," *Affilia: Journal of Women and Social Work* 27, no. 1 (Spring 2012): 22–37; and Robyn Muncy, "Gender and Professionalization in the Origins of the U.S. Welfare State: The Careers of Sophonisba Breckinridge and Edith Abbott," *Journal of Policy History* 2, no. 3 (July 1990): 290–315.

55. "The New Profession and Preparation for It," CSCP Bulletin 1, no. 6, October 1910, CSCP Records.

56. Previously, a high school degree had been required for admission, and the CSCP offered only a one-year course of study. See "Recommendations of the President and the Dean," April 27, 1914, Taylor Papers, box 61, folder 2522; and CSCP *Announcements*, 1909–1920, CSCP Records, box 1, folders 2–12.

57. President's Statement for Trustees, May 18, 1911, box 61, folder 2521, Taylor Papers.

58. Louise Marion Bosworth to Eleanora W. Bosworth, January 15, 1912, Bosworth Papers.

59. EA, "Sophonisba Preston Breckinridge over the Years," *SSR* 22, no. 4 (December 1948): 417–23 (quotation pp. 418–19).

60. Wright, "Three against Time," 47.

61. MT to Julius Rosenwald, penciled handwritten draft, September 16, 1916, Talbot Papers, box 2, folder 8.

62. *Chicago News*, 1946, clipping in Class of 1888 Records. Abbott initially was hired as the assistant director of research in the Department of Social Investigation. She was subsequently promoted to associate director and then became co-director. When Breckinridge advanced to dean, Abbott became director of research. See "First Meeting of the Incorporators and Trustees," April 27, 1908, and "Minutes of the Autumn Meeting of the Trustees," October 27, 1908, Taylor Papers, box 61, folder 2520; and CSCP Bulletins, CSCP Records.

63. Wright, "Three against Time," 44.

64. David Naguib Pellow, *Garbage Wars: The Struggle for Environmental Justice in Chicago* (Cambridge, Mass.: MIT Press, 2002), 21–31.

65. Flanagan, *Seeing with Their Hearts*, 90–91; Harold L. Platt, "Jane Addams and the Ward Boss Revisited: Class, Politics, and Public Health in Chicago, 1890–1930," *Environmental History* 5, no. 2 (April 2000): 194–222.

66. Charles Ball to SPB, November 4, 1909, SPBP.

67. For quotations, see Charles Ball to SPB, November 8, 1909; and SPB to Leroy T. Stewart, February 11, 1910; see also SPB to Julia Lathrop, December 23, 1909; SPB to Kate Holliday Claghorn, March 24, 1910; Charles Ball to Edith Abbott, October 4, 1909; Charles Ball to SPB, October 6, 1909, SPB to Charles Ball, November 1, 1909, and SPB to Dora Allen, April 22, 1910, SPBP; and Linderholm Reminiscences, 6–7.

68. SPB to Charles Ball, November 1, 1909, SPBP.

69. Richard Hofstadter, *The Age of Reform* (New York: Vintage, 1955), 186–97. SPB and EA, eds., *The Housing Problem in Chicago* (Chicago: University of Chicago Press, 1910–1915), is available online at https://catalog.hathitrust.org/Record/008869222.

70. On social science and social reform, see especially Diner, *City and Its Universities*; Fitzpatrick, *Endless Crusade*; and Haskell, *Emergence of Professional Social Science*.

71. CSCP Bulletin 1, no. 3, January 1910, 71, CSCP Records.

72. Caroline Bedford to SPB, May 17, 1910, and SPB to Charles Ball, November 1, 1909, SPBP.

73. SPB to W. A. Evans, February 11, 1910, and W. A. Evans to SPB, February 14, 1910, SPBP.

74. Lawrence Veiler to SPB, October 28, 1910; Pauline Goldhurst to SPB, February 28, 1911; Emily W. Dinwiddie to SPB, March 2, 1911; E. Harman to SPB, May 1, 1911; Mary L. Birtwell to SPB, May 2, 1911; Mary Forbes to SPB, May 9, 1911; R. H. Norton to SPB, December 4, 1914; W. Law Shannon to SPB, December 18, 1915; SPB to Alfred Baker, December 22, 1915; and E. M. McMahon to SPB, July 6, 1916, all in SPBP.

75. "Women and Housing Reform," *National Housing Association: Housing Problems in America Proceedings* (1912), 265–69 (quotations pp. 265–66), box 1, folder 3, SPB-UIC.

76. Bernard Flexner to JA, May 23, 1911; Bernard Flexner to Lillian Wald, May 23, 1911; clipping in Oswald Garrison Villard to JA, May 24, 1911; and JA to SPB, May 26, 1911, SPBP; see also Mary Jo Deegan, "W. E. B. DuBois and the Women of Hull-House, 1895–1899," *American Sociologist* 19, no. 4 (Winter 1988): 301–11.

77. Sophonisba Breckinridge, "The Color Line in the Housing Problem," *The Survey* 29 (February 1, 1913): 575–76.

78. See for instance SPB to Ida Wells Barnett, July 13, 1914; SPB to W. E. B. Du Bois, August 6, 1914; and W. E. B. Du Bois to SPB, August 14, 1914, SPBP; SPB to BTW, March 1, 1909; BTW to SPB, March 5, 1909; SPB to BTW, September 16, 1911; BTW to SPB, October 24, 1914; SPB to BTW, October 25, 1915, Washington Papers, Special Correspondence, "Breckinridge, Sophonisba."

79. SPB, review of *Half a Man: The Status of the Negro in New York*, in *American Journal of Sociology* 17, no. 3 (November 1911): 414–17 (first quotation p. 414); and SPB, "Interpreter for His Race," *Chicago Defender*, November 20, 1915, 4 (second quotation).

80. Breckinridge, "Color Line."

81. Celia Parker Woolley to SPB, November 16, 1913, SPBP; Breckinridge, "Color Line," 575.

82. Oswald Garrison Villard to JA, August 18, 1913, with handwritten note from JA to SPB, August 18, 1913; and JA to SPB, September 9, 1913, SPBP.

83. James Potter to MT, January 6, [1915]; C. C. Surber to MT, Ella Flagg Young, and Fannie Smith, January 7, 1915; Thomas Wilkinson to MT, January 9, 1915; W. Higham to MT, January 11, 1915; Elizabeth Lindsay Davis and Jessie L. Johnson to MT, January 14, 1915, all in Talbot Papers, box 5, folder 16; and Peter Mortensen to SPB, October 22, 1918, SPBP.

84. Toure F. Reed, *Not Alms but Opportunity: The Urban League and the Politics of Racial Uplift, 1910–1950* (Chapel Hill: University of North Carolina Press, 2008), 18.

85. In addition to Willrich, *City of Courts*, see Victoria Getis, *The Juvenile Court and the Progressives* (Urbana: University of Illinois Press, 2000); Anne Meis Knupfer, *Reform and Resistance: Gender, Delinquency, and America's First Juvenile Court* (New York: Routledge, 2001); and Steven S. Schlossman, *Love and the American Delinquent: The Theory and Practice of "Progressive" Juvenile Justice, 1825–1920* (Chicago: University of Chicago Press, 1977).

86. SPB and EA, *The Delinquent Child and the Home* (New York: Russell Sage, 1912, 1917), 70.

87. CSCP Report, July 1912, Taylor Papers, box 61, folder 2521. See also Harvey Baker to SPB, September 7, 1912; Joseph M. Deuel to Mr. Glenn, September 19, 1912 (copy); James McInerney to Russell Sage Foundation, October 7, 1912 (copy); and Isaac Franklin Russell to J. M. Glenn, October 3, 1912 (copy), SPBP.

88. SPB, "Neglected Widowhood in the Juvenile Court," *American Journal of Sociology* 16, no. 1 (July 1910), 53–87 (quotation p. 67).

89. Joanne L. Goodwin, *Gender and the Politics of Welfare Reform: Mothers' Pensions in Chicago* (Chicago: University of Chicago Press, 1997).

90. SPB, "Child Labor Legislation," *Elementary School Teacher* 9, no. 10 (June 1909): 511–16 (quotation p. 513).

91. SPB and EA, "The School and the Working-Child: A Plea for Employment Supervision in City Schools," in *Finding Employment for Children Who Leave the Grade Schools to Go to Work* (Chicago: Manz Engraving / Hollister, 1911), 5–18.

92. Anna Nichols to SPB, February 13, 1906, SPBP.

93. SPB, "Child Labor Legislation," *Elementary School Teacher* 9, no. 10 (June 1909): 511–16 (quotation p. 516).

94. SPB to Chairman, State Senate Investigating Committee, March 8, 1913; "Will You Help in the Consumers' League Minimum Wage Campaign" (with handwritten emendations), SPBP.

95. W. L. Bodine to SPB, February 14, 1910, with enclosed note on "817 Galt St.," January 17, 1910, SPBP.

96. SPB to T. T. Claxton, July 22, 1914, SPBP.

97. See for example Lillian Wald to SPB and EA, February 7, 1917; and Gertrude English to SPB, March 23, 1917, SPBP.

98. EA and SPB, *Truancy and Non-Attendance in the Chicago Schools: A Study of the Social Aspects of the Compulsory Education and Child Labor Legislation of Illinois* (Chicago: University of Chicago Press, 1917), 353.

99. Sophonisba P. Breckinridge, "The Community and the Child," *The Survey*, February 4, 1911, 782–786 (quotation p. 782).

100. Sorensen, *Sister's Memories*, 135.

101. Ibid., 135–36; Bozena Pavlik to SPB, October 9, 1919, and February 20, 1920, SPBP; see also SPB to Bozena Pavlik, September 4 and October 7, 1919, February 19 and 23, 1920, SPBP.

102. Sorensen, *Sister's Memories*, 128, 135. See also Robert L. Buroker, "From Voluntary Association to Welfare State: The Illinois Immigrants' Protective League, 1908–1926," *JAH* 58, no. 3 (December 1971): 643–60; Suronda Gonzalez, "Complicating Citizenship: Grace Abbott and the Immigrants' Protective League, 1908–1921," *Michigan Historical Review* 24, no. 2 (Fall 1998): 56–75; and Henry B. Leonard, "The Immigrants' Protective League of Chicago, 1908–1921," *Journal of the Illinois State Historical Society* 66, no. 3 (Autumn 1973): 271–84.

103. Sorensen, *Sister's Memories*, 114.

104. Ibid., 128–30, and 135; "Urge Home for Immigrants," *Chicago Tribune*, March 19, 1911; and Fourth Annual Report, 1913, 10, supplement II, box 4, folder 59A, IPL-UIC.

105. Fourth Annual Report, 1913, 7; Ninth Annual Report, 1917, 30, supplement II, box 4, folder 60A; and Plan of Organization and Work to Be Undertaken by the Immigrants' Commission and Annual Budget Adopted by Commission, October 18, 1920, supplement II, box 4, folder 58; all in IPL-UIC; SPB to Sen. Johnson Camden, July 24, 1914; Grace Abbott to SPB, [July 26 or 28, 1919], SPBP; *Reports of the Department of Labor, 1916* (Washington, D.C.: GPO, 1917), 105–7; John Higham, *Strangers in the Land: Patterns of American Nativism, 1860–1925* (New Brunswick, N.J.: Rutgers University Press, 1955), chaps. 7 and 8; and Mae M. Ngai, *Impossible Subjects: Illegal Aliens and the Making of Modern America* (Princeton, N.J.: Princeton University Press, 2004).

106. "Eleven Years of Community Service," [January, 1920], supplement II, box 4, folder 60A (quotations); Annual Report, 1911–1912; and Fourth Annual Report, 1913, 13, supplement II, box 4, folder 59A, IPL-UIC; Legal Aid Society of Chicago to Subscribers, [1914]; and SPB to Mrs. William E. Boyes, July 14, 1914, SPBP.

107. Annual Report, 1911–1912; Fourth Annual Report, 1913, 13–15; and Sixth Annual Report, 1915, 12, supplement II, box 4, folder 59A, IPL-UIC.

108. Annual Report, 1909–1910, supplement II, box 4, folder 59A, IPL-UIC.

109. Sorensen, *Sister's Memories*, 127.

110. Linderholm Reminiscences, 8–12.

111. SPB, *New Homes for Old* (New York: Harper and Brothers, 1921), 8, 76.

112. SPB, "Education for the Americanization of the Foreign Family," *Journal of Home Economics* 11, no. 5 (May 1919): 107; on "foreign visitors," see for instance Katherine Van Wyck to SPB, March 21, 1919; Edmund Lynde to SPB, March 26, 1919; and Mary Henson to SPB, July 25, 1919, SPBP.

113. SPB, *New Homes for Old,* 8; and SPB, "Education for the Americanization of the Foreign Family."

114. Wilson Memoirs, 32.

115. See for example M. E. Blackburn to JA, May 20, 1911; Ivy Jackson Welling to SPB, [November 13, 1913]; Faye Myers to SPB, July 13, 1914; Lidas Aubrey to "My dear Sirs," July 22, 1914; Ann MacPherson to SPB, July 24, 1914; Evelyn Stoddart to SPB, July 25, 1914; Laura Drake Gill to SPB, August 1, 1914; SPB to Laura Drake Gill, August 5, 1914; SPB to Miss Wallace, August 5, 1914; SPB to May Cheney, July 18, 1914; SPB to Jessica Piexotto, July 18, 1914; SPB to Faye Myers, July 18, 1914; SPB to T. T. Claxton, July 20, 1914; Clara Milspaugh to SPB, July 20, 1914; SPB to Clara Millspaugh, July 22, 1914; and Sara Jacobs to SPB, July 21, 1914, SPBP.

116. See especially SPB to JR, March 5, June 1, 1912; and Secretary to Julius Rosenwald to SPB, July 16, 1913, Rosenwald Papers, box 7, folder 16; and SPB to B. L. Haynes, July 22, 1914, SPBP; see also Irene Carlton-LaNey, "The Career of Birdye Henrietta Haynes, a Pioneer Settlement House Worker," *SSR,* 68, no. 2 (1994): 254–73.

117. SPB to C. M. Douglas, July 24, 1914, SPBP.

118. Nancy to SPB, n.d. [April 13, 1948]; Mary Jane Tilley to Edith Abbott, August 1, 1948, SPBP.

119. Wright, "Three against Time," 450. See also University of Chicago Press Release, July 30, 1948, SPB-SCRC.

120. JA to SPB, October 1, 1912, and July 31, 1913, SPBP; JA to SPB, April 30, 1912, JAPP, reel 6; and SPB to JA, February 3, [1906], JAPP, reel 4.

121. Donald Bean to SPB, August 10, 1917; Mary Wheeler to SPB, July 25, 1914; Adelaide Mary Walsh to SPB, July 18, 1914; and SPB to Mrs. William Boyes, May 30, 1917, SPBP.

122. By 1915, Breckinridge was earning $3,000 per year for her work at the University of Chicago (both administration and teaching). She was supposed to draw an annual salary of $2,000 at the CSCP but often did not receive paychecks there. On the University of Chicago, see President Judson to President Harris (Northwestern University), September 4, 1915, President's Papers, box 38, folder 16; on the CSCP see "Comparison of the Financial Statements of the New York School of Philanthropy and the Chicago School of Civics and Philanthropy," Rosenwald Papers, box 7, folder 18 (hereafter "Financial Statements").

123. SPB to Madeline Breckinridge, July 25, 1914; see also SPB to GT, July 18, 1914; and SPB to C. M. Douglass, July 24, 1914, SPBP.

124. SPB to EA, September 17, 1917, SPBP.

125. University of Chicago press release, July 30, 1948, SPB-SCRC.

126. H.P. Judson to MT, May 2, 1913, Talbot Papers, box 2, folder 7; see also MT to JR, September 16, 1916, box 2, folder 1, Talbot Papers.

127. "CSCP Memo."

128. David Kinley to GT, February 26, 1906; "Report of the President of the Board of Trustees," October 27, 1908, box 61, folder 2520; "Statement to the Trustees of the CSCP by Committee Appointed May 5, 1916"; and President's Report for the Year Ending August 31, 1916, box 61, folder 2522, Taylor Papers; and Jane Addams, David Kinley, Julian Mack, Gra-

ham Taylor, and SPB to the President of the Board of Trustees, February 3, 1916, Rosenwald Papers, box 7, folder 17; and "Financial Statements."

129. On settlement houses and the "social justice" orientation to social work, see J. L. Andrews and Michael Reisch, *The Road Not Taken: A History of Radical Social Work in the United States* (Ann Arbor, Mich.: Sheridan, 2001); Clarke A. Chambers, *Seedtime of Reform: American Social Service and Social Action, 1918–1933* (Minneapolis: University of Minnesota Press, 1963); Allan F. Davis, *Spearheads for Reform: The Social Settlements and the Progressive Movement, 1890–1914* (New York: Oxford University Press, 1967); on scientific philanthropy and individual casework, see Elizabeth N. Agnew, *From Charity to Social Work: Mary E. Richmond and the Creation of an American Profession* (Urbana: University of Illinois Press, 2004); H. Specht and M. E. Courtney, *Unfaithful Angels: How Social Work Has Abandoned Its Mission* (New York: Free Press, 1994); Regina Kunzel, *Fallen Women, Problem Girls: Unmarried Mothers and the Professionalization of Social Work, 1890–1945* (New Haven, Conn.: Yale University Press, 1993); Leslie Margolin, *Under the Cover of Kindness: The Invention of Social Work* (Charlottesville: University Press of Virginia, 1997); Karen W. Tice, *Tales of Wayward Girls and Immoral Women: Case Records and the Professionalization of Social Work* (Urbana: University of Illinois Press, 1998); and Stanley Wenocur and Michael Reisch, *From Charity to Enterprise: The Development of American Social Work in a Market Economy* (Urbana: University of Illinois Press, 1989); and on the competing schools of thought, see John Ehrenreich, *The Altruistic Imagination: A History of Social Work and Social Policy in the United States* (Ithaca, N.Y.: Cornell University Press, 1985); James Leiby, *History of Social Welfare and Social Work in the United States* (New York: Columbia University Press, 1978); Leslie Leighninger, *Social Work: Search for Identity* (Westport, Conn.: Greenwood Press, 1987); Roy Lubove, *The Professional Altruist: The Emergence of Social Work as a Career, 1880–1930* (Cambridge, Mass.: Harvard University Press, 1965); Linda M. Shoemaker, "Early Conflicts in Social Work Education," *Social Service Review* 72 (1998): 182–91; and Linda M. Shoemaker, "'Charity and Justice': Gender and the Mission of Social Work: Social Work Education in Boston, New York, and Chicago, 1898–1930" (PhD diss., State University of New York, 2001).

130. Course Notes, "Survey of the Field" and "Survey of the Field and Function of Religious Social Work," box 62, folder 3536; Examination Notes, "Local Government and the Church," Spring 1913, box 62, folder 2534; and Notes, "Introduction to the Study of Social and Philanthropic Work," Taylor Papers, box 62, folder 2532; CSCP Bulletin 1, no. 1 (July 1909): 7, CSCP Bulletin no. 12, July 1911, 6, CSCP Records; Linderholm Memoirs, 1–2.

131. Tousley Memoirs, 73.

132. For other treatments of the conflicts at the CSCP, see Fitzpatrick, *Endless Crusade*, chap. 7; Muncy, *Female Dominion*, chap. 3; and Shoemaker, "Charity and Justice," chaps. 2 and 5.

133. Linderholm Memoirs, 1–2.

134. President's Statement for Trustees, May 18, 1911, box 61, folder 2521; and "Recommendations of the President and the Dean," April 27, 1914, box 61, folder 2522, Taylor Papers.

135. According to CSCP alumna Natalie Walker Linderholm, Breckinridge and Abbott "felt that no man was going to push these things through to the goal that *they* saw ahead." Linderholm Memoirs. 4–5.

136. "Statement to the Trustees of the CSCP by Committee Appointed May 5, 1916," box 61, folder 2522; and Minutes, Executive Committee Meeting, October 30, 1918, box 61, folder 2523, Taylor Papers; Jane Addams, David Kinley, Julian Mack, Graham Taylor, and SPB to the President of the Board of Trustees, February 3, 1916, Rosenwald Papers, box 7, folder 17; and GT to William Graves, June 21, 1918, Rosenwald Papers, box 7, folder 18.

137. For quotation, see GT to Julian Mack, March 4, 1920, Rosenwald Papers, box 7, folder 19. See also Million Dollar Endowment Fund form letter, March 29, 1919, box 61, folder 2523; and "Meeting of the CSCP at the Fortnightly Club, Chicago, February 13, 1920," box 61, folder 2525, Taylor Papers.

138. SPB to GT, July 1 and 3, 1920, box 12, folder 566; and Statement of Liabilities and Receipts for the Balance of the Year Ending August 31, 1920, box 61, folder 2525, Taylor Papers.

139. SPB to Charles Crane, December 8, 1920 (quotations); SPB to GT, July 7, 1920; SPB to JL, July 15, 1920; and SPB to JR, July 29, 1920, box 20, folder 10, Abbott Papers-SCRC.

140. For quotations, see SPB to Charles Crane, December 8, 1920; and SPB to JL, July 15, 1920, box 20, folder 10, Abbott Papers-SCRC; Extract from the Minutes of School of Civics Trustees' Meeting Held July 9, 1920; and GT to "My dear Ken," July 29, 1920 Taylor Papers, box 61, folder 2525.

141. JL to EA, August 10, 1920, box 20, folder 10, Abbott Papers-UNL.

Chapter 5. The *Other* Chicago School

1. Martin Bulmer, *The Chicago School of Sociology: Institutionalization, Diversity, and the Rise of Sociological Research* (Chicago: University of Chicago Press, 1984); and Hasia R. Diner, *Service and Scholarship: Seventy-Five Years of the School of Social Service Administration of the University of Chicago, 1908–1983* (Chicago: University of Chicago, 1985).

2. See especially Lela B. Costin, "Edith Abbott and the Chicago Influence on Social Work Education," *SSR* 57, no. 1 (March 1983): 94–111; Fitzpatrick, *Endless Crusade*, chap. 7; Muncy, "Gender and Professionalization"; and Muncy, *Creating a Female Dominion*, chap. 3; Shoemaker, "Early Conflicts"; and Shoemaker, "Charity and Justice," chap. 5.

3. JL to EA, August 10, 1920, box 20, folder 10, Abbott Papers-UNL.

4. See Minutes of a Meeting of the Board of Trustees, July 21, 1921; Check, SPB to Schwartz Brothers, and Statement of Liabilities and Receipts for the Balance of the Year Ending August 31, 1920; and SPB to Ralph Norton, July 13, 1920, Taylor Papers, box 61, folder 2525.

5. Mary Jane Tilley to EA, August 1, 1948, SPBP.

6. Taylor Diary, July 21, 1921, box 4, Taylor Papers.

7. See for example Marjorie Robinson Eckels, Class of 1943, in *Reflections, 2008–2009: Chicago/SSA/Centennial* (Chicago: UC School of Social Service Administration, 2009), 15.

8. Elizabeth Bryan to EA, August 14, 1948, SPBP.

9. SPB to William Graves, January 21, 1924, and February 24, 1924, Rosenwald Papers, box 9, folder 6.

10. EF to JR, November 21, 1923, and JR to Ernest Judson, December 12, 1923, Rosenwald Papers, box 9, folder 7.

11. SPB to GA, January 14, 1924, SPBP; see also SSA Memorandum, Winter Quarter, 1924,

box 20, folder 5, Abbott Papers-SCRC; and SPB to President Burton, December 12, 1923, President's Papers, box 77, folder 23.

12. MT to Dean Tufts, May 28, November 17, November 29, and December 5, 1924; MT to J. Spender Dickerson, August 14, 1924, Presidents' Papers, box 80, folder 9.

13. MT to Board of Trustees, June 12, 1924, box 2, folder 9; and Edith Flint, Marion Talbot, and Elizabeth Wallace to the President of the University and the President of the Board of Trustees at the University of Chicago, December 1924, box 5, folder 11, Talbot Papers. Breckinridge's salary increased from $5,000 in 1922–23 ($2,000 as associate professor in the SSA; $1,000 as assistant dean of women; and $2,000 as instructor in Household Administration) to $6,000 as professor of social economy in the SSA in 1926–27 and $8,000 in 1931–32; Abbott's salary increased from $4,000 annually in 1922–23 to $5,000 the following year and $7,000 the year after that. By 1931–32 she earned $9,000 annually ($7,000 as professor and $2,000 as dean). See Individual Record of Edith Abbott; and Individual Record of Sophonisba Preston Breckinridge, SSA, Department Records, box 1, folder 9.

14. John S. Bradway to EA, May 30, 1949, SPBP.

15. Unknown to EA, n.d., [ca. August 2, 1948], SPBP.

16. Margaret Leal to EA, August 2, 1948, SPBP.

17. Hutchinson Memoirs; SPB to GA, March 9, 1925; and SPB to GA, August 22, [1931], SPBP.

18. See for instance Helen Myrick to SPB, October 10, 1919; and Mona to SPB, July 9, 1927, SPBP.

19. "How Social Work Became a Profession," Mudgett Papers, box 1, folder 9.

20. Wright, "Three against Time," 41.

21. "Memorandum in Support of a Request for a Contribution to the Endowment of the Graduate School of Social Service Administration of the University of Chicago," 1929, box 19, folder 1 (quotation), Abbott Papers-SCRC; see also Number and Classification of Courses Given, GSSA, Department Records, box 1, folder 9; President's Reports and Course Announcements, 1920–1929, box 1, folders 1–4, and box 2, folders 1–3, SSA Records.

22. "University of Chicago-School of Social Service Administration (1925–1926)," box 20, folder 1 (quotation); "Report of the Work of the Graduate School of Social Service Administration Prepared for the Trustees of the School of Civics and the Friends Who Contributed to the Budget of the School from 1920 to 1925," [1926]; and "Memorandum in Support of a Request for a Contribution to the Endowment of the Graduate School of Social Service Administration at the University of Chicago," 1929, box 19, folder 1; and "A Message to the Alumni," 1929, box 14, folder 1, all in Abbott Papers-SCRC; and University of Chicago President's Reports, 1920–1930, SSA, box 1, folder 4; and box 2, folder 1, SSA Records. See also Irene Carlton-LaNey and S. C. Alexander, "Early African American Social Welfare Pioneer Women," *Journal of Ethnic and Cultural Diversity in Social Work* 10 (2001): 67–84; Steven J. Diner, "Chicago Social Workers and Blacks in the Progressive Era," *SSR* 44 (1970): 393–410; and Sandra M. Stehno, "Public Responsibility for Dependent Black Children: The Advocacy of Edith Abbott and Sophonisba Breckinridge," *SSR* 62, no. 3 (September 1988): 485–503.

23. "Report of the Work of the Graduate School of Social Service Administration Prepared for the Trustees of the School of Civics and the Friends Who Contributed to the Budget of

the School from 1920 to 1925," [1926], box 19, folder 1; and "Memorandum from the Dean of the School of Social Service to the President of the University of Chicago with a Review of the Work of the School under the Rockefeller Foundation Grant 1926–1931," box 19, folder 2, both in Abbott Papers-SCRC; President's Reports, 1925–1929, box 2, folder 1; and Report of the Dean of the School of Social Service Administration, 1930–31, box 2, folder 3, both in SSA Records.

24. See President's Reports, 1920–1927, box 2, folder 1; Report of the Dean of the School of Social Service Administration, 1931–1931, box 2, folder 3, both in SSA Records; "Memorandum from the Dean of the School of Social Service to the President of the University of Chicago with a Review of the Work of the School under the Rockefeller Foundation Grant 1926–1931," box 19, folder 2; and "Memorandum to the President of the University Regarding the Income, Registration, and Certain Increased Expenditures in the School of Social Service Administration Since the Renewal of the Rockefeller Grant in July, 1931," 1933, box 19, folder 3; and "Report to Mr. Woodward about the Use of the Deutsch Foundation during the Year 1929–1930," box 20, folder 1, all in Abbott Papers-SCRC.

25. Sophonisba P. Breckinridge, *Family Welfare Work in a Metropolitan Community: Selected Case Records* (Chicago: University of Chicago Press, 1927), 3–4, 13–14 (quotations); *The Family and the State: Select Documents* (1934); and *Social Work and the Courts: Select Statutes and Judicial Decisions* (1934); Edith Abbott, *Immigration: Select Documents and Case Records* (Chicago: University of Chicago Press, 1924); *Some American Pioneers in Social Welfare* (1938); and *Public Assistance: American Principles and Policies* (1940); and G. Laing to William Graves, March 21 and May 13, 1924, Rosenwald Papers, box 9, folder 8.

26. Wayne McMillen, "The First Twenty-Six Years of the Social Service Review," *SSR* 27, no. 1 (March 1953), 1–14 (quotations pp. 2 and 3); and Arthur Abbott to EA, July 5, 1943, box 1, folder 3, Abbott Papers-UNL.

27. Esther Immer to EA, August 1, 1948, SPBP.

28. For the couple's nickname, see Frank Bane to Arlien Johnson, copy enclosed in Frank Bane to Wilma Walker, October 24, 1957, Abbott Papers-SCRC; for their adjoining offices, see Leonard White to SPB, November 1, 1928, SPBP; for examples of their shared correspondence, see William Hodson to SPB, May 21, 1928 (marked in pencil, "Did E.A. see this?"); Selba Eldridge to SPB, April 6, 1936, (marked, "E.A."); Archibald Sutherland to EA, January 15, 1934 (marked "Miss Breckinridge"); and William J. Ellis to "Dr. Edith Breckinridge," May 8, 1935, SPBP.

29. SPB to EA, July 23, 1938, box 18, folder 4, Abbott Papers-UNL; SPB to EA, July 6 and 26, 1928; September 17, 1942; September 5 and 9, 1944; and EA to SPB, December 15, [1933], SPBP.

30. Arthur P. M[iles] to EA, February 22, 1949; Mereb E. Mossman to EA, March 26, 1949; and Ben Meeker to EA, April 12, 1949, SPBP; and Eleanor K. Taylor, "The Edith Abbott I Knew," *Journal of the Illinois State Historical Society* 70, no. 3 (August 1977): 178–84 (quotation p. 179).

31. Elizabeth Bryan to EA, August 14, 1948 (quotation); see also Elizabeth Wisner to EA, September 29, 1948; Dorothy Burke to EA, May 1, 1949, SPBP; Taylor, "Edith Abbott"; Dressler Memoirs. 4, 8–9; Arlien Johnson to Marion Hathway, November 22, 1939, January

10, 1945, box 7, folder 48, Hathway Papers; Wilson Memoirs, 31–34, 54, 82; Johnson Memoirs, 52, 55–65; Helen Perlman to Katherine Kendall, June 26, 1984 (quotation); October 31, 1989, August [1991]; September 15, 1992, box 13, folder 1; Katherine Kendall to Susan Purdie Dixon, March 19, 1993; and Donald Beless to Susan Purdie Dixon, April 6, 1993, box 14, folder 7, Kendall Papers.

32. Student Notes, July 23, 1935, SSA 350, box 29, folder 2, SSA Records; JA to EA, June 6, 1923, JAPP; and EA Class Materials, box 3, folders 6 and 9, Abbott Papers-UNL.

33. EA Class Materials, boxes 2–7, Abbott Papers-UNL; Russell Ballard Class Notes, supplement II, box 1, folders 6 and 7; and box 3, folders 29, 31, and 34, Ballard Papers; Verl Lewis Class Materials, box 3, Lewis Papers; and SSA 350 Course Materials, box 29, folder 2, SSA Records.

34. EA Class Materials, box 3, folder 5; box 7; and box 11, folder 15, Abbott Papers-UNL; and Mrs. Hortense Wade Wilson to SPB, December 6, 1933, SPBP.

35. EA Class Materials, box 3, folder 2, Abbott Papers-UNL; see also Helen R. Wright, "The Debt of the School of Social Service Administration," *SSR* 22, no. 4 (December 1948): 448–50.

36. EA Class Materials, box 2, folder 9; and Student Papers, box 7, Abbott Papers-UNL; SSA 350 Class Materials, box 29, folder 2, SSA Records; Ruth Colby to EA, July 30, 1948, SPBP.

37. EA Class Materials, box 6, folder 7, Abbott Papers-UNL; Student Notes, July 23, 1935, SSA 350, box 29, folder 2, SSA Records.

38. "Federal Grants-in-Aid," Abbott Papers-UNL, box 2, folder 8; and SPB to Frances Perkins, June 11, 1935, SPBP.

39. "Federal Grants-in-Aid," Abbott Papers-UNL, box 2, folder 8; Student Notes, June 27, 1935, SSA 350, box 29, folder 2, SSA Records.

40. EA Class Materials, box 3, folders 2 and 4, Abbott Papers-UNL.

41. Georgia Bell Travis to EA, August 3, 1948, SPBP.

42. Arthur P. M[iles] to EA, February 22, 1949, SPBP.

43. Frank. T. Flynn Jr., "A Summary of Legislation Concerning Care of the Feeble-Minded in Indiana," SSA 350, July 2, 1935, with SPB's handwritten comments, SSA Records, box 29, folder 2.

44. Edith Finlay to SPB, [February 13, 1948], SPBP.

45. Johnson Memoir, 59–62.

46. Thomas Goebel, *The Children of Athena: Chicago Professionals and the Creation of a Credentialed Society, 1870–1920* (Hamburg: LIT, 1996); see also Diner, *City and Its Universities*; Haskell, *Emergence of Professional Social Science*; Thomas L. Haskell, ed., *The Authority of Experts: Studies in History and Theory* (Bloomington: Indiana University Press, 1984); and Don S. Kirschner, *The Paradox of Professionalism: Reform and Public Service in Urban America, 1900–1940* (Westport, Conn.: Greenwood, 1986). On Breckinridge and Abbott's involvement in the AASW (later the National Association of Social Workers), see AASW Membership, Publicity, Leaflets and Pamphlets, 1919–1955, NASW Records, folder 59; and R. L. Stotzer and J. E. Tropman, "Professionalizing Social Work at the National Level: Women Social Work Leaders, 1910–1982," *Affilia* 21, no. 1 (March 2006): 9–27.

47. Penina Migdal Glazer and Miriam Slater, *Unequal Colleagues: The Entrance of Women into the Professions* (New Brunswick, N.J.: Rutgers University Press, 1987); see also Mary Ann Dzuback, "Gender, Professional Knowledge, and Institutional Power: Women Social Scientists and the Research University," in Ann Mari May, ed., *The 'Woman Question' and Higher Education: Perspectives on Gender and Knowledge Production in America* (Cheltenham: Elgar, 2008), 52–76; Patricia M. Hummer, *The Decade of Elusive Promise: Professional Women in the United States, 1920–1930* (Ann Arbor: UMI Research, 1979); Muncy, "Gender and Professionalization"; Margaret W. Rossiter, *Women Scientists in America: Struggles and Strategies to 1940* (Baltimore, Md.: Johns Hopkins University Press, 1982); and David Walkowitz, "The Making of a Feminine Professional Identity: Social Workers in the 1920s," *American Historical Review* 95 (1990): 1051–76.

48. On changing standards for social science nationally, in addition to Haskell, *Emergence of Professional Social Science*, see Mary O. Furner, *Advocacy and Objectivity: A Crisis in the Professionalization of American Social Science, 1865–1905* (Lexington: University Press of Kentucky, 1975); and Dorothy Ross, *The Origins of American Social Science* (Cambridge: Cambridge University Press, 1991). On Chicago sociologists in particular, see Deegan, *Jane Addams*, and Steven J. Diner, "Department and Discipline: The Department of Sociology at the University of Chicago," *Minerva* 13, no. 4 (1975): 514–33.

49. Deegan, *Jane Addams*, 23, 136.

50. Pederson interview, 8; and Kincheloe interview, 4.

51. Deegen, *Jane Addams*, 316; Mowrers interview, I:20–21, and Mowrers interview, II:4. For more on the gendered dimensions of these conflicts, see James D. Orcutt, "Teaching in the Social Laboratory and the Mission of SSSP [Society for the Study of Social Problems]: Some Lessons from the Chicago School," *Social Problems* 43, no. 3 (August 1996): 235–45; and D. Sibley, "Invisible Women? The Contribution of the Chicago School of Social Service Administration to Urban Analysis," *Environment and Planning* 22 (1990): 733–45.

52. SPB to Kathryn McHale, December 29, 1932, SPBP.

53. Undated fragment, box 20, folder 8; and EA to J. Laurence Laughlin, March 18, 1924, box 1, folder 1, Abbott Papers-SCRC. See also Rosalind Rosenberg, *Beyond Separate Spheres: The Intellectual Roots of Modern Feminism* (New Haven, Conn.: Yale University Press, 1982), 50. Abbott had taught statistics part time in the Sociology Department before joining the SSA. See Individual Record of Edith Abbott, SSA, Department Records, box 1, folder 9.

54. Pederson interview, 8; see also Barnhart interview, 13–14; and Mowrers interview, II:3–4; and Mereb E. Mossman to EA, March 26, 1949, SPBP.

55. Department Records, box 1, folders 8 and 9; "Local Community Research Projects on which Research Assistants Are Working, Fall Quarter, 1925"; and "Wieboldt Thesis Subjects," n.d., box 20, folder 11, Abbott Papers-SCRC.

56. Blumer interview, 8; and Barnhart interview, 13–14.

57. Bartlett interview, 3, 12; see also Barnhart interview, 13–14; and Faris interview, I:18–19; Dressler Memoirs, 3–4, 7, 9; and Bruere Memoirs, 7, 17.

58. Dee Garrison, *Apostles of Culture: The Public Librarian and American Society, 1876–1920* (New York: Macmillan, 1977); Barbara Melosh, *"The Physician's Hand": Work Culture and Conflict in American Nursing* (Philadelphia: Temple University Press, 1982); Joel Perlmann

and Robert A. Margo, *Women's Work? American Schoolteachers, 1650–1920* (Chicago: University of Chicago Press, 2001); and Susan M. Reverby, *Ordered to Care: The Dilemma of American Nursing, 1850–1945* (Cambridge: Cambridge University Press, 1987).

59. Katherine Kendall, "Women at the Helm: Three Extraordinary Leaders," *Affilia* 4 (1989): 23–32 (quotation p. 23); see also Costin, "Edith Abbott"; Muncy, *Creating a Female Dominion*, chap. 3; and Shoemaker, "Charity and Justice," chap. 5.

60. "Report to the President of the University of Chicago from the Dean of the School of Social Service Administration for the Years from 1930 to 1937," box 19, folder 4; and "Report of the Work of the Graduate School of Social Service Administration Prepared for the Trustees of the School of Civics and the Friends Who Contributed to the Budget of the School from 1920 to 1925," (1926), box 19, folder 1, Abbott Papers-SCRC.

61. Wilson Memoirs, 118–19; Tousley Memoirs, 73–74; see also Perlman Memoirs, 226–27; and Agnew, *From Charity to Social Work*.

62. Johnson Memoirs, 50.

63. Arlien Johnson, "Her Contribution to the Professional School of Social Work," *SSR* 22 (1948): 442–47 (quotation p. 442).

64. President's Report, 1924–1925, 20, SSA Records, box 1, folder 3; "Memorandum to the President of the University Regarding the Income, Registration, and Certain Increased Expenditures in the School of Social Service Administration Since the Renewal of the Rockefeller Grant in July, 1931"; and "University of Chicago-School of Social Service Administration (1925–1926)," box 20, folder 1, Abbott Papers-SCRC.

65. SPB, "New Horizons of Professional Education for Social Work," *National Conference on Social Welfare, Official Proceedings of the Annual Meeting 1936*, 124; and "Report of the Dean to the Alumni, June 1934," box 19, folder 4; and "A Message to the Alumni," 1929, 7 and 12, box 14, folder 1, Abbott Papers-SCRC.

66. Wright, "Three against Time," 48.

67. Bulmer, *Chicago School of Sociology*, chap. 8.

68. See for instance LCRC Reports, 1925, box 20, folder 10, Abbott Papers-SCRC; and SPB to Anita Blaine, March 1, 1928; SPB to L. D. White, March 17 and October 15, 1928; and Memorandum to Mr. White and Members of the Sub-Committee on Research Projects for 1929–30, February 28, 1929, SPBP.

69. Stehno, "Public Responsibility."

70. SPB to Jacob Kepecs, May 4, 1929; SPB to Leonard White, November 23, 1928, and March 29, 1929, SPBP.

71. Stehno, "Public Responsibility."

72. "Memorandum in Support of a Request for a Contribution to the Endowment of the Graduate School of Social Service Administration of the University of Chicago" 1929, box 19, folder 1, Abbott Papers-SCRC.

73. "Report of the Work of the Graduate School . . . 1920 to 1925"; see also Muncy, *Female Dominion*, 85–86; and Jennifer Cote, "'The West Point of the Philanthropic Service': Reconsidering Social Work's Welcome to Women in the Early Twentieth Century," *SSR* (March 2013): 131–57.

74. See for instance "Doctors of Philosophy, 1926–1931" [list of graduates and their jobs], box 19, folder 2; "Message to the Alumni," 1929, box 14, folder 1; and "List of Students Who

Have Received Higher Degrees since the 1931 Report to the Rockefeller Foundation," box 20, folder 3, Abbott Papers-SCRC.

75. Johnson, "Her Contribution," 442; see also J. L. Andrews, "Female Social Workers in the Second Generation," *Affilia* 5 (1990): 46–59.

76. KL to EA, August 3, 1948, SPBP.

77. Bessie Louise Pierce to EA, July 30, 1948, SPBP.

78. Wright, "Debt of the School," 450.

Chapter 6. Defining Equality

1. *Woman's Journal*, May 1931, p. 25.

2. SPB to Belle Sherwin, March 16, 1931, Legal Status of Women, Sophonisba Breckenridge [*sic*] Folder, LWV Papers, part III, series A, National Office Subject Files, 1920–1932.

3. See especially Nancy F. Cott, *The Grounding of Modern Feminism* (New Haven, Conn.: Yale University Press, 1987); Kathryn Kish Sklar, "Why Were Most Politically Active Women Opposed to the ERA in the 1920s?" in Joan Hoff-Wilson, ed., *Rights of Passage: The Past and Future of the ERA* (Bloomington: Indiana University Press, 1986); and Kathryn Kish Sklar, Anja Shuler, and Susan Strasser, eds., *Social Justice Feminists in the United States and Germany: A Dialogue in Documents, 1885–1933* (Ithaca, N.Y.: Cornell University Press, 1998).

4. SPB to KL, October 27, 1933, Lenroot Papers.

5. JA to SPB, July 31, 1907, JAPP, Reel 5; and Edith Rider to MT, January 6, 1907, Presidents' Papers, box 31, folder 3.

6. See for example "Women's Varied Interests," which appears next to "Charming Toilettes for Old Ladies" and beneath advice "For 'Embonpoint,'" *Minneapolis Journal*, February 18, 1906, part VI, Woman's Section. See also "Learned Women Will Be Luncheon Guests," *San Francisco Call*, July 10, 1910.

7. "Woman Superior Industrially: Dr. Breckinridge Says She Is of More Material Value to World Than Man," *San Francisco Call*, June 23, 1910; see also "Heavy Enrollment for Summer Session," *San Francisco Call*, June 17, 1910.

8. EA and SPB, *The Wage-Earning Woman and the State: A Reply to Miss Minnie Bronson* (Boston: Boston Equal Suffrage Association for Good Government, [191–]), 5, retrieved on August 5, 2013 at http://pds.lib.harvard.edu/pds/view/2580907?n=1&s=4&printThumbnails=no.

9. SPB, "Political Equality for Women and Women's Wages," *Women in Public Life*, Annals of the American Academy of Political and Social Science 56 (November 1914): 122–33 (quotations).

10. Lee Ann Banaszak, *Why Movements Succeed or Fail: Opportunity, Culture, and the Struggle for Woman Suffrage* (Princeton, N.J.: Princeton University Press, 1996), 11; see also table 3.1, p. 45.

11. "Suffrage Jubilee: Less Agreeable Business Will Follow Rejoicings," *New York Daily Tribune*, September 24, 1911.

12. Aileen S. Kraditor, *The Ideas of the Woman Suffrage Movement, 1890–1920* (New York: Columbia University Press, 1965).

13. "Urges Suffrage," *Chicago Tribune*, February 26, 1912.

14. See for instance "W.C.T.U. Notes: Eminent People Declare for Equal Suffrage," *Williston (N.D.) Graphic*, March 19, 1914.

15. Kraditor, *Ideas*.

16. On literacy tests, see JA and GA to Oscar Underwood, January 23, 1911, JAPP; on lynching, see Bernard Flexner to JA, May 23, 1911, and Oswald Garrison Villard to JA, May 24, 1911, enclosed in JA to SPB, May 26, 1911, SPBP; and on public schools, see SPB and EA, "The School and the Working-Child."

17. Christine Lunardini, *From Equal Suffrage to Equal Rights: Alice Paul and the National Woman's Party, 1910–1928* (New York: New York University, 1986, 2000).

18. Fuller, *Laura Clay*, 114–25; Harper, *History of Woman Suffrage*, 5:319; "Chicago to Lead Suffrage Fight?" *Chicago Tribune*, October 20, 1911. See also Trisha Franzen, *Anna Howard Shaw: The Work of Woman Suffrage* (Urbana: University of Illinois Press, 2014); and Joan Marie Johnson, *Funding Feminism: Monied Women, Philanthropy, and the Women's Movement, 1870–1967* (Chapel Hill: University of North Carolina Press, 2017).

19. SPB to Catharine McCulloch, October 24, 1911, McCulloch Papers; Harper, *History of Woman Suffrage*, 5:324.

20. Catharine McCulloch to SPB, October 28, 1911, McCulloch Papers.

21. M. Carey Thomas to Mary Garnett, November 9, 1912, Thomas Papers, reel 25; Fuller, *Laura Clay*, 123–27; Harper, *History of Woman Suffrage*, 5:324; Mary Isabel Brush, "Nevada, Oregon, Kansas and Wisconsin to Vote on Woman's Suffrage at Next Election," *Chicago Tribune*, November 19, 1911.

22. Catharine McCulloch to SPB, October 28, 1911, McCulloch Papers.

23. Laura Clay to SPB, November 1, 1911, Clay Papers.

24. SPB to JA, April 17, 1912, JAPP.

25. For quotation, see JA to [SPB], September 14, 1912. See also Belle La Follette to JA, January 2, 1912; Anna Howard Shaw to JA, August 16, 1912; JA to [Catharine Waugh McCulloch], August 24, 1912, [M. Carey Thomas] to Marjorie Dow Johnson, July 23, 1912, Copy to JA; [M. Carey Thomas] to JA, July 23, 1912; and JA to Jessie Ashley, October 19, 1912, all in JAPP; JA to SPB, December 11, 1911; SPB to JA, February 26, 1912; Mary Ware Dennett to JA, October 15, 1912; Jessie Ashley to JA, October 17, 1912; Clara Landsberg to SPB, October 19, 1912, enclosing Jessie Ashley to JA, October 17, 1912; JA to Jessie Ashley, October 19, 1912, Copy to SPB; and JA to SPB, October 20, 1912, all in SPBP; Knight, *Jane Addams*, 184; and Mary Isabel Brush, "Nevada, Oregon, Kansas and Wisconsin to Vote on Woman's Suffrage at Next Election," *Chicago Tribune*, November 19, 1911.

26. Mary Isabel Brush, "Society Leaders Will Promote Suffrage Cause in Chicago's Fashionable Circles: National Association to Open Branch," *Chicago Tribune*, December 24, 1911.

27. JA to SPB, [May 7, 1912], (quotation); and SPB to JA, April 17, 1912, JAPP; SPB to Mrs. Stanley McCormick, April 2, 1912; SPB to Catharine McCulloch, May 4, 1912; SPB to Anna Howard Shaw, May 4, 1912; and Anna Howard Shaw to Members of the Official Board, May 4, 1912, McCulloch Papers; "National Not Wanted at Suffrage Convention Here," *Chicago Tribune*, April 18, 1912.

28. M. Carey Thomas to Marjorie Dowell Johnson, July 23, 1912; see also M. Carey Thomas to JA, July 23, 1912, JAPP.

29. SPB to Belle La Follette, January 25, 1912, Belle Case La Follette Special Correspondence, La Follette Papers, series D, box 11; and SPB to Catharine McCulloch, September 12, 1912, McCulloch Papers.

30. SPB to Mary Ware Dennett, August 9, 1912, Dennett Papers; "Warns Women of Illinois: Dr. Anna H. Shaw Advises Suffragists to Avoid Party Ties," *Chicago Daily Tribune*, September 25, 1912; "Meet of Suffrage Chiefs: Chicago Women to Attend Executive Committee Session Today; Officers Will Be Chosen; Members Enthusiastic in Praise of the Progressive Party," *Chicago Tribune*, October 1, 1912; Jane Addams, "Woman's Suffrage and the Progressive Party," *Chicago Tribune*, October 28, 1912; Lunardini, *From Equal Suffrage*, 55, 72; Harper, *History of Woman Suffrage*, 5:424.

31. Lunardini, *From Equal Suffrage*.

32. Knight, *Jane Addams*, 84; Lunardini, *From Equal Suffrage to Equal Rights*, 97; Harper, *History of Woman Suffrage*, 5:518; Anna Howard Shaw to JA, August 16, 1912, JAPP; "Policewomen Eye Pankhurst Visit," *Chicago Tribune*, November 1, 1913; "Chicago Women Protest against Mrs. Pankhurst's Deportation," *Chicago Tribune*, October 19, 1913; and "Mrs. Pankhurst to Attend Ball of Trade League," October 28, 1913, clipping, WTUL Scrapbook.

33. Lunardini, *From Equal Suffrage*; Harper, *History of Woman Suffrage*, 5:594.

34. Untitled Suffrage Speech [ca. 1919–1920], Miscellany, 1918–1924, SPBP.

35. Jan Doolittle Wilson, *The Women's Joint Congressional Committee and the Politics of Maternalism, 1920–30* (Urbana: University of Illinois Press, 2007), Introduction, chap. 1, and appendix A (175–76).

36. Cott, *Grounding of Modern Feminism*, 88.

37. Wilson, *Women's Joint Congressional Committee*, chap. 2.

38. Candice Lewis Bredbenner, *A Nationality of Her Own: Women, Marriage, and the Law of Citizenship* (Berkeley: University of California Press, 1998), esp. chap. 3.

39. Cott, *Grounding of Modern Feminism*, 125.

40. Wilson, *Women's Joint Congressional Committee*, chap. 4.

41. See for example Alice Paul to Florence Kelley, December 9, 1920; Director of Memorial Ceremonies to Mabel Cratty, January 4, 1921; Margaret Crook to Emma Wald, January 14, 31, 1921; and Margaret Crook to Marie Moore Forrest and Hazel Mackaye, February 4, 1921, NWP Papers, part II, series 1, section C.

42. Mabel Kittredge to Alice Paul, February 5, 21, 1921, NWP Papers, part I: 1913–1974, series 1: Correspondence, section A: 1877–1933; Jessie W. Hughan, Roger Baldwin, A. J. Muste, J. B. C. Woods, and Paul Jones to Alice Paul, January 4, 1921, NWP Papers, part II, series 1, section C.

43. Sophonisba P. Breckinridge, "The Equal Wage," *Proceedings of the Women's Industrial Conference, Called by the Women's Bureau of the United States Department of Labor, Washington, D.C., January 11, 12, and 13, 1923*, Bulletin of the Women's Bureau 33 (Washington: GPO, 1923), 85–91.

44. "Proposed Amendment to the Constitution of the United States," enclosed in Agnes Nestor to EF, August 22, 1921; Clara Mortenson Beyer to EF, December 19, 1922; and Ethel M. Smith to EF, August 3, 1923, all with Freund's handwritten comments, Freund Papers, box 1, folders 6 and 7.

45. Program of National Convention, Washington, D.C., February 15–18, [1921], NWP Papers, part I: 1913–1974, series 1: Correspondence, section A: 1877–1933 , Sklar, "Why."

46. League of Women Voters Education Fund, *Changed Forever: The League of Women Voters and the Equal Rights Amendment* (Washington, D.C.: National League of Women Voters, 1988), 7. Breckinridge chaired the Illinois branch's Committee on Uniform Laws Concerning Women in 1923–1924. See Board Lists, box 77, folder 650, IL-LWV.

47. Kathryn H. Stone, *25 Years of a Great Idea: A History of the National League of Women Voters* (Washington, D.C.: National League of Women Voters, 1946), quotations pp. 11, 12, 15; see also Louise M. Young, *In the Public Interest: The League of Women Voters, 1920–1970* (Westport, Conn.: Greenwood, 1989).

48. Untitled Suffrage Speech [1919–1920], Miscellany, 1918–1924, SPBP.

49. 1930 Convention Transcripts, p. 326, LWV Papers, 1918–1974, part II, series A: Transcripts and Records of National Conventions, 1919–1944.

50. S. P. Breckinridge, "The Home Responsibilities of Women Workers and the 'Equal Wage,'" *JPE* 31, no. 4 (August 1923): 521–43.

51. Joan G. Zimmerman, "The Jurisprudence of Equality: The Women's Minimum Wage, the First Equal Rights Amendment, and *Adkins v. Children's Hospital*, 1905–1923," *JAH* 78, no. 1 (June 1991): 188–225.

52. On the NWP and citizenship, see National League of Women Voters press release, December 3, 1929, enclosed in Gladys Harrison (LWV) to Sara Grogan (NWP), February 15, 1930; on section 213(a), see Maude Younger to Alice L. W. Movius, December 8, 1932, and "Sample Copy to 'Opposed' or 'Doubtful,'" December 15, 1932; and on jury duty, see Unsigned to M. Carey Thomas, April 8, 1925, with enclosures, all in NWP Papers, part I: 1913–1974, series 1: Correspondence, section A, 1877–1933. On the LWV and jury duty and employment of married women, see "An Explanation of the Program of the Legal Status of Women Committee Adopted by the 1926 Convention of the National League of Women Voters"; and "Legal Status Activities in the States," December 5, 1930, both in Legal Status of Women Committee Files, 1930–1932, LWV Papers, part III, series A, National Office Subject Files, 1920–1932.

53. Unsigned to M. Carey Thomas, April 8, 1925, with enclosures, NWP Papers, part I: 1913–1974, series 1: Correspondence, section A, 1877–1933.

54. Indeed, some of Breckinridge's contacts with the NWP suggested the possibility that she might have been able to forge an alliance between the two groups, had she been so inclined. While conducting research on women's status for the President's Committee on Social Trends in 1932, she contacted members of the New York Woman's Party to inquire about "the struggle of the New York teachers for equal pay," and a member of the branch's executive board, Jane Norman Smith, responded with a "courteous" note promising to send information. See Jane Norman Smith to Mrs. Matthews, May 27, 1932; Jane Norman Smith to SPB, May 31, 1932, NWP Papers, part I: 1933–1974, series I: Correspondence, section A: 1877–1933.

55. Sophronisba [sic] P. Breckinridge, "The Problem of Women in Industry," in *Handbook: Chicago Industrial Exhibit* (Chicago: Kirchner, Meckert, 1907), 55.

56. Sophonisba P. Breckenridge [sic], "The Child and Society," in Elisha M. Friedman,

ed., *America and the New Era: A Symposium on Social Reconstruction*, chap. 19 (New York: Dutton, 1920), quotation p. 318.

57. SPB, "The Changing Role of the State in Child Welfare," ca. 1940, draft, Miscellany, 1940–1941, SPBP.

58. Breckinridge, "Neglected Widowhood," 60.

59. Ethel Smith to SPB, February 19, 1924, SPBP.

60. [National Woman's Party], "The Equal Rights Amendment and Protective Legislation," [1929], box 1, folder 6, Wiley Papers.

61. "Could 'Mothers' Pensions' Operate under Equal Rights Amendment?" *Congressional Digest* (March 1, 1924): 202.

62. Davis, *American Heroine*, 266; Kim E. Nielsen, *Un-American Womanhood: Antiradicalism, Antifeminism, and the First Red Scare* (Columbus: Ohio State University Press, 2001); Issues of the *Woman Patriot* in Abbott Papers-UNL, box 40, folder 5.

63. Ethel M. Smith, *Toward Equal Rights for Men and Women* (Washington, D.C.: Committee on the Legal Status of Women, National League of Women Voters, 1929), 3–4.

64. 1930 Convention Transcripts, 336–41, 375, LWV Papers 1918–1974, part II, series A: Transcripts and Records of National Conventions, 1919–1944; see also Sklar, "Why."

65. See Margaret Hicks to SPB, October 7, 1929, with enclosure, "The Story of the Committee on the Legal Status of Women," October 1929, Legal Status of Women Committee, Dr. Sophonisba Breckinridge, 1928–1930, LWV Papers, part III, series A, National Office Subject Files, 1920–1932; see also LWV Papers, part III, series A: National Office Subject Files, 1920–1932, Committee on the Legal Status of Women, especially S. P. Breckinridge, "Draft of Explanation of Legal Status of Women Program," January 1931; and Edith Valet Cook, "History of Government and the Legal Status of Women," [1940].

66. 1930 Convention Transcripts, 310, LWV Papers, 1918–1974, part II, series A: Transcripts and Records of National Conventions, 1919–1944.

67. Transcript of the Eighth National Convention of the National League of Women Voters, April 23–28, 1928, 51–52, LWV Papers, 1918–1974, part II, series A: Transcripts and Records of National Conventions, 1919–1944.

68. Committee on Legal Status of Women, Reports of State Chairmen, 1927–1928; Legal Status of Women Committee, Dr. Sophonisba Breckinridge, 1928–1930; Legal Status of Women Committee, 1930–1932, especially "An Explanation of the Program of the Legal Status of Women Committee Adopted by the 1926 Convention of the National League of Women Voters"; "Report of the Activities of the Legal Status Committees in the States," January 7, 1931; Committee on the Legal Status of Women, Semi-Annual Report, April 1, 1931–October 1, 1931; *Legal Status News*, February 10, 1930; Naturalization and Citizenship of Women, Cable Act, 1930–1932; and Committee on the Legal Status of Women Questionnaires, 1930, all in LWV Papers, part III, series A, National Office Subject Files, 1920–1932.

69. Anya Jabour, "Prostitution Politics and Feminist Activism in Modern America: Sophonisba Breckinridge and the Morals Court in Prohibition-Era Chicago," *Journal of Women's History* 25, no. 3 (Fall 2013): 143–66; and "Women Learn Duties as Jurors," *Chicago Tribune*, February 7, 1931.

70. S. P. Breckinridge, "Draft of Explanation of Legal Status of Women Program," January

1931, Breckinridge Correspondence, Legal Status of Women, LWV Papers, part III, series A, National Office Subject Files, 1920–1932.

71. Sophonisba P. Breckinridge, *Survey of the Legal Status of Women in the Forty-Eight States: Following the Program of the Committee on the Legal Status of Women National League of Women Voters* (Washington, D.C.: National League of Women Voters, 1930).

72. Edith Valet Cook, "History of Government and the Legal Status of Women," [1940], LWV Papers, part III, series A, National Office Subject Files, 1920–1932.

73. Goodwin, *Gender and the Politics of Welfare Reform*, 91–104, 112–15; SPB to Julia Margaret Hicks, March 13, 1928 ("immoral conduct" quotation), Legal Status of Women Committee, Dr. Sophonisba Breckinridge, 1928–1930, LWV Papers, part III, series A, National Office Subject Files, 1920–1932; and Julia Margaret Hicks to SPB, October 24, 1928, with enclosure (other quotations), SPBP.

74. See for example Mary E. McDowell and Adena Miller Rich to SPB, March 1, 1928; Illinois Joint Committee to SPB, June 18, 1928; Julia Margaret Hicks to SPB, October 24, 1928, with enclosure; Adena Miller Rich to SPB, October 30, 1928, March 7, 1931, and August 5, 1931; United Charities of Chicago, various branches, to SPB, July 1929, with enclosed "Schedule of Independent Citizenship of Married Women," all in SPBP.

75. "Schedule of Independent Citizenship of Married Women," n. d. (ca. June 1928), SPBP.

76. Fred Schlotfeldt to SPB, April 15, 1931, SPBP; see also Bredbenner, *Nationality of Her Own*, 158–63.

77. "Statement of Changes Recommended by the National League of Women Voters in the Cable Act 'Relative to the Naturalization and Citizenship of Married Women,'" December 2, 1929, Naturalization of Citizenship of Women: Cable Act, 1930–1932, LWV Papers, part III, series A: National Office Subject Files, 1920–1932 (hereafter "Recommended Changes to Cable Act.")

78. Julia Margaret Hicks to SPB, October 9, 1929, Legal Status of Women Committee, Dr. Sophonisba Breckinridge, 1928–1930, LWV Papers, part III, series A, National Office Subject Files, 1920–1932, with enclosure, "Changes to be Supported in the Cable and Immigration Acts to Make Them Non-Discriminatory" (hereafter "Cable Act Changes").

79. SPB to Gladys Harrison, November 4, 1929, Legal Status of Women Committee, Dr. Sophonisba Breckinridge, 1928–1930, LWV Papers, part III, series A, National Office Subject Files, 1920–1932.

80. Julia Margaret Hicks to SPB, October 9, 1929; SPB to Gladys Harrison, October 12, 1929, and November 4, 1929, Legal Status of Women Committee, Dr. Sophonisba Breckinridge, 1928–1930, LWV Papers, part III, series A, National Office Subject Files, 1920–1932.

81. "Cable Act Changes."

82. Ibid.

83. Ibid.

84. "Memorandum with reference to the Cable Act," Statement rec'd from Miss Breckinridge, November 4, 1929, LWV Papers, part III, series A, National Office Subject Files, 1920–1932.

85. "Recommended Changes to Cable Act."

86. Gladys Harrison to Idella Swisher, December 15, 1930, in Committee on the Legal Sta-

tus of Women, Department of Independent Citizenship—Cable Act, January 1–December 31, 1930, LWV Papers, part II, series A. See also Bredbenner, *Nationality of Her Own*, 155–56 (quotation p. 155).

87. Martha Gardner, *The Qualities of a Citizen: Women, Immigration, and Citizenship, 1870–1965* (Princeton, N.J.: Princeton University Press, 2005), chap. 8; and Bredbenner, *Nationality of Her Own*, chaps. 3, 4, and 5.

Chapter 7. Women against War

1. Jane Addams, Emily G. Balch, and Alice Hamilton, *Women at the Hague: The International Congress of Women and Its Results* (New York: Macmillan, 1915), 3, 4, and 6; SPB to EA, April 23, 1915, and April 24, 1915, SPBP; and James B. McCreary to Unknown, re: Jane Addams and Sophonisba Preston Breckinridge, April 7, 1915, JAPP, reel 8. See also APB [Alice Peloubet Norton] to SPB, April 26, 1916, WILPF/WPP Collection, series B, 1: Correspondence, National Office, Chicago, 1915–1919, box 1 (microfilm reel 12:9).

2. Grace Abbott to SPB, May 17, [1915]; Dr. Aletta Jacobs to SPB and EA, January 6, 1916, SPBP; and Alice Hamilton to Mary Rozet Smith, April 22, 1915; see also S. A. Byles to JA, May 10, [1915], and Alice Page to JA, May 12, [1915], all in JAPP, reel 8; and "Report of the International Congress of Women, April 28–May 1, 1915," WPP-UIC, box 1, folder 2. Delegates came from the Netherlands (1,000); the United States (47); Germany (28); Sweden (12); Norway (12); Hungary (9); Denmark (6); Austria (6); Belgium (5); Great Britain (3); Canada (2); and Italy (1). See Lela B. Costin, "Feminism, Pacifism, Internationalism, and the 1915 International Congress of Women," *Women's Studies International Forum* 5, no. 3–4 (1982): 300–315.

3. "Report of the International Congress of Women"; and Addams, Balch, and Hamilton, *Women at the Hague*, 9, 150–59.

4. Harriet Hyman Alonso, *Peace as a Women's Issue: A History of the U.S. Movement for World Peace and Women's Rights* (Syracuse, N.Y.: Syracuse University Press, 1993); and Harriet Hyman Alonso, *The Women's Peace Union and the Outlawry of War, 1921–1942* (Knoxville: University of Tennessee, 1989); Marie Louise Degen, *The History of the Woman's Peace Party* (Baltimore, Md.: Johns Hopkins University Press, 1939); Carrie A. Foster, *The Women and the Warriors: The U.S. Section of the Women's International League for Peace and Freedom, 1915–1946* (Syracuse, N.Y.: Syracuse University Press, 1995); Erika A. Kuhlman, *Petticoats and White Feathers: Gender Conformity, Race, the Progressive Peace Movement, and the Debate Over War, 1895–1919* (Westport, Conn.: Greenwood, 1997); Kuhlman, "'Women's Ways in War': The Feminist Pacifism of the New York City Woman's Peace Party," *Frontiers* 18, no. 1 (1997): 80–100; Leila J. Rupp, *Worlds of Women: The Making of an International Women's Movement* (Princeton, N.J.: Princeton University Press, 1997); Linda K. Schott, *Reconstructing Women's Thoughts: The Women's International League for Peace and Freedom before World War II* (Stanford, Calif.: Stanford University Press, 1997); Ingrid Sharp and Matthew Stibbe, "Women's International Activism during the Inter-War Period, 1919–1939," *Women's History Review* 26, no. 2 (April 2017): 163–72 (introduction to special theme issue); Christy Jo Snider, "Patriotism and Peace: Gender and the Politics of Transnational Nongovernmental Organi-

zations, 1920–1945" (PhD diss., Purdue University, 2000); Christy Jo Snider, "The Influence of Transnational Peace Groups on U.S. Foreign Policy Decision-Makers during the 1930s: Incorporating NGOs into the UN," *Diplomatic History* 27, no. 3 (June 2003): 377–404; and Christy Jo Snider, "Planning for Peace: Virginia Gildersleeve at the United Nations Conference on International Organization," *Peace and Change* 32, no. 2 (April 2007): 168–85.

5. "Some Ways to Peace," January 24, 1936, Speech and Article Files, SPBP; see also Mineke Bosch with Annemarie Kloosterman, *Politics and Friendship: Letters from the International Woman Suffrage Alliance, 1902–1942* (Columbus: Ohio State University Press, 1990); Rebecca L. Hegar, "Translatlantic Transfers in Social Work: Contributions of Three Pioneers," *British Journal of Social Work* 38 (2008): 716–33; Leila J. Rupp and Verta Taylor, "Forging Feminist Identity in an International Movement: A Collective Identity Approach to Twentieth-Century Feminism," *Signs* 24, no. 2 (Winter 1999): 363–86; Davide Rodogno, Bernhard Struck, and Jakob Vogel, eds., *Shaping the Transnational Sphere: Experts, Networks and Issues from the 1840s to the 1930s* (New York: Berghahn, 2015); Anja Schuler, *The Women's Movement and Social Reform: Jane Addams and Alice Salomon in Transatlantic Dialog, 1889–1933* (Stuttgart: Steiner, 2004); Kathryn Kish Sklar, "'Some of Us Who Deal with the Social Fabric': Jane Addams Blends Peace and Social Justice, 1907–1919," *Journal of the Gilded Age and Progressive Era* 2, no. 1 (January 2003): 80–96; and Sklar, Schuler, and Strasser, *Social Justice Feminists.*

6. "Some Ways to Peace."

7. SPB to DB, Wednesday, [April 1898]; SPB to DB, July 22, 1898, DB Papers; and Hay, *Madeline McDowell Breckinridge,* 50–51.

8. See especially Kristin L. Hoganson, *Fighting for American Manhood: How Gender Politics Provoked the Spanish-American and Philippine-American Wars* (New Haven, Conn.: Yale University Press, 1998).

9. "Some Ways to Peace."

10. See especially Alonso, *Peace as a Women's Issue,* chaps. 2 and 3; Foster, *Women and the Warriors,* chap. 2; and Schott, *Reconstructing Women's Thoughts,* chap. 2.

11. "History of the Woman's City Club," July 1937, WCC-CHM; Woman's City Club of Chicago Year Book, 1910–1911; and Woman's City Club Bulletins, 1914, 1915, and 1916, WCC-UIC; "Sixth Woman Enters the Aldermanic Race," *Chicago Tribune,* January 14, 1914; "Woman Voters in Suffrage Rally at Auditorium," *Chicago Tribune,* February 2, 1914; Alice Greenacre, *A Handbook for the Women Voters of Illinois,* edited by Sophonisba P. Breckinridge (Chicago: Chicago School of Civics and Philanthropy, 1913).

12. SPB to Madeline McDowell Breckinridge, August 1, 1914, SPBP. Italy, Japan, and the United States later joined the Allies, while the Ottoman Empire and Bulgaria joined the Central Powers.

13. WCC Bulletin 3, no. 5, October 1914, 2, WCC-UIC.

14. WCC Bulletin 3, no. 7, December 1914, 2, WCC-UIC.

15. "Outline History of the Woman's Peace Party," WILPF/WPP Collection, series A: Historical Records, box 1 (microfilm reel 12:1); see also Alonso, *Peace as a Women's Issue,* 57–58; and Schott, *Reconstructing Women's Thoughts,* 38–46.

16. Woman's Peace Party Preamble and Platform Adopted at Washington, D.C., January 10, 1915, and Amended January 11, 1916, folder 4, WPP-UIC (hereafter WPP P&P); see also

Alonso, *Peace as a Woman's Issue*; Jill Conway, "The Woman's Peace Party and the First World War," in J. L. Granatstein and R. D. Cuff, eds., *War and Society in North America* (Toronto: Nelson, 1971), 52–65; Linda Schott, "The Woman's Peace Party and the Moral Basis for Women's Pacifism," *Frontiers* 8, no. 2 (1985): 18–24; and Barbara J. Steinson, "'The Mother Half of Humanity': American Women in the Peace and Preparedness Movements in World War One," in Carol R. Berkin and Clara M. Lovett, eds., *Women, War, and Revolution* (New York: Holmes and Meier, 1980), 259–81.

17. "Some Ways to Peace."

18. "We Women of the United States," n.d. [1915], WILPF/WPP Collection, series A, box 1, (microfilm reel 12:1); see also Schott, "Woman's Peace Party," 20–21.

19. "RESOLUTIONS adopted by the International Congress of Women at The Hague, May 1, 1915," Miscellany, 1873–1917, SPBP; see also Degen, *History of the Woman's Peace Party*, 86.

20. See especially Addams, *Women at the Hague*; Alonso, *Peace as a Women's Issue*, 58–69; and Costin, "Feminism, Pacifism, Internationalism."

21. *Advocate of Peace* 77, no. 7 (July 1915): 167–68; SPB to JA, December 4, 1917; and [JA] to SPB, October 8, 1917, JAPP, reel 11.

22. Costin, "Feminism, Pacifism, Internationalism."

23. Degen, *History of the Woman's Peace Party*, 156–57 (quotation p. 156).

24. Alonso, *Peace as a Women's Issue*, 63; and Schott, *Reconstructing Women's Thoughts*, 56–61.

25. Report, First Annual Meeting of Woman's Peace Party, Washington, D.C., January 8–10, 1916, box 1, folder 4, WPP-UIC.

26. WPP P&P.

27. "Minutes of the Conference of the Executive Board of the Woman's Peace Party with the Delegates to the International Congress of Women after the War, June 10th, 1916 at the Home of Mrs. Joseph T. Bowen, 1430 Astor St., Chicago, Illinois," Wald Papers, box 35, folder 4.1 (WILPF International, 1918–1922).

28. Alonso, *Peace as a Women's Issue*, 64–45.

29. Louis P. Lochner to JA, July 30, 1915, with enclosures: "Minutes of the Committee Appointed to Consider Steps to be Taken with Reference to the Resolutions Submitted by Norman Angell and the New York Committee"; "INTERNATION[AL] COMMITTEE: Memorandum for executive committee on American nation in line with Miss Addams suggestions," [July 30, 1915]; and [Louis P. Lochner] to SPB, July 30, 1915 (quotation), carbon copy; and "Letter proposed to be sent to the people whose names appear on the sheet attached," all in JAPP, reel 8. The male members were Henry Morris, George Mead, and Louis Lochner, secretary of the Chicago Peace Society. Addams later appointed additional members from New York organizations, including Lillian Wald.

30. David S. Patterson, *The Search for a Negotiated Peace: Women's Activism and Citizen Diplomacy in World War I* (New York: Routledge, 2008).

31. Patterson, *Search for a Negotiated Peace*, 183.

32. SPB to JA, August 30, 1916, and SPB to JA, September 4, [1917], JAPP, reel 9; Roger Baldwin to Paul Kellogg, July 26, 1917 (SPB on letterhead of AUAM), Kellogg Papers, box 32,

unnumbered folder, "American Union Against Militarism, 1915–1917"; and Blanche Wiesen Cook, "Democracy in Wartime: Antimilitarism in England and the United States, 1914–1918," *American Studies* 13, no. 1 (Spring 1972): 51–68.

33. Jane Addams, Lucia Mead, Anna Garlin Spencer, Alice Thacher Post, and Sophonisba P. Breckinridge to Woodrow Wilson, October 29, 1915, quoted in Patterson, *Search for Negotiated Peace*, 187.

34. Rhodi Jeffreys-Jones, *Changing Differences: Women and the Shaping of American Foreign Policy, 1917–1994* (New Brunswick, N.J.: Rutgers University Press, 1995), 28.

35. *Commission for Enduring Peace: Hearing before the Committee on Foreign Affairs, House of Representatives, Sixty-Fourth Congress, First Session, on H.R. 6921 and H.J. Res. 32, Statement of Miss Jane Addams and Others, January 11, 1916* (Washington, D.C.: GPO, 1916), 10–12.

36. *United States and the Orient: Hearings before the Committee on Foreign Affairs, House of Representatives, Sixty-Fourth Congress, Second Session, on H.R. 1661, Statement of Miss Jane Addams and Others, December 12, 1916* (Washington, D.C.: GPO, 1916), 3, 6, 12.

37. See especially Robert W. Tucker, "A Benediction on the Past: Woodrow Wilson's War Address," *World Policy Journal* 17, no. 2 (Summer 2000): 77–93.

38. "Some Ways to Peace."

39. SPB to Robert La Follette, March 2, 1917 (telegram), and March 5, 1917, Robert La Follette Special Correspondence, La Follette Papers, series B, box 80. See also *Commission for Enduring Peace*, 12–13.

40. Kuhlman, *Petticoats and White Feathers*, 57–61, 94–96; and Schott, *Reconstructing Women's Thoughts*, 56–68.

41. [Harriet P. Thomas] to JA, March 24, 1917, JAPP, reel 11; see also Alonso, *Peace as a Women's Issue*, 74–76; Kuhlman, *Petticoats and White Feathers*, 94–96; and Anna Howard Shaw to MT, April 13, 1918, folder 8, box 2, Talbot Papers.

42. Kuhlman, "'Women's Ways in War,'" 90; and Kuhlman, *Petticoats and White Feathers*, 94–96.

43. "Suggestions for Work in War Time, submitted by the Chicago Branch of the Woman's Peace Party," n.d., folder 5, box 1, WPP-UIC; and Barbara J. Steinson, *American Women's Activism in World War I* (New York: Garland, 1982), 259–60.

44. SPB to JA, September 4, [1917]; and September 14, 1917, JAPP; and Alonso, *Peace as a Women's Issue*, 77.

45. Alonso, *Peace as a Women's Issue*, 77–78.

46. Ibid., 72–81, quotation p. 78; Allen F. Davis, *American Heroine: The Life and Legend of Jane Addams* (1973; reprint, Chicago: Dee, 2000), chap. 14; and Schott, *Reconstructing Women's Thoughts*, 68–72; see also Kathleen Kennedy, *Disloyal Mothers and Scurrilous Citizens: Women and Subversion During World War I* (Bloomington: Indiana University Press, 1999).

47. Special Announcement, Spring Quarter, 1918: Courses Bearing on the War and in Preparation for War Service, folder 10, box 5, Talbot Papers; Minutes, Annual Meeting of the Board of Trustees of the Chicago School of Civics and Philanthropy, October 17, 1918; Organization of Courses at the School of Civics and Philanthropy [1918]; Registration Summary, Elizabeth Dixon to JR, July 23, 1918; and GT to W. C. Graves, June 21, 1918, folder 18, box 7, all in Rosenwald Papers.

48. Flyer, "Work and Fight: Together We Win," n.d.; and Flyer, "The Woman Student Training Corps at the University of Chicago," n.d., folder 10, box 5, Talbot Papers; Margaret Vining, "War and Peace 101: The University of Chicago, Sophonisba Breckinridge and Applied Sociology in the Great War," *Icon: Journal of the International Committee for the History of Technology* 14 (2008), 106–22 (quotation p. 111); and Merle Curti, "The American Scholar in Three Wars," *Journal of the History of Ideas* 3, no. 3 (June 1942): 241–64.

49. MT to President Judson, August 21, 1917, folder 10, box 5, Talbot Papers.

50. Undated memo; "Proposals presented on April 16, 1917, by Dean Marion Talbot," (printed pamphlet with handwritten notations), folder 10, box 5, Talbot Papers.

51. JL to MT, April 18, 1917, folder 8, box 2, Talbot Papers.

52. Pauline Goldmark to Members of the National Committee on Women in Industry, November 2, 1917; Ashley Hughes to Members of the National Committee on Women in Industry, November 19, 1917; Ashley Hughes to GA, December 6, 1917; M. Edith Campbell to SPB, December 17, 1917, with enclosures ("To the Members of the General Committee on Women in Industry" and "Plan for Woman's Division"); M. Edith Campbell to SPB, December 18, 1917, with enclosed reports; and Ashley Hughes to EA, January 19, 1918, with enclosed reports, all in SPBP.

53. Special Announcement, Spring Quarter, 1918: Courses Bearing on the War and in Preparation for War Service, folder 10, box 5, Talbot Papers.

54. "Suggestions for Work in War Time"; see also Christy Jo Snider, "Patriots and Pacifists: The Rhetorical Debate about Peace, Patriotism, and Internationalism, 1914–1930," *Rhetoric and Public Affairs* 8, no. 1 (Spring 2005): 59–83.

55. "War Work Takes the Life of Miss Breckinridge," *Chicago Tribune*, June 24, 1918; and Jabour, "'A Nurse's Duty.'"

56. Watercolor by E. Carrance, original in Mary Curry Desha Breckinridge Papers, Breckinridge Family Papers, box 845, published in Sheridan Harvey et al., *American Women: A Library of Congress Guide for the Study of Women's History and Culture in the United States* (Washington, D.C.: Library of Congress, 2001), 162. Thanks to Ione Crummy, Jane Edgar, and Elizabeth Hubble for translation assistance.

57. Samuel Walker, *In Defense of American Liberties: A History of the ACLU* (Carbondale: Southern Illinois University Press, 1990).

58. Frances H. Early, "Feminism, Peace, and Civil Liberties: Women's Role in the Origins of the World War I Civil Liberties Movement," *Women's Studies* 18 (1990): 95–115; Frances H. Early, *A World without War: How U.S. Feminists and Pacifists Resisted World War I* (Syracuse, N.Y.: Syracuse University Press, 1997), 226n50; and Vining, "War and Peace 101," 115 and 121n22.

59. "The Immigrant and the War," Being the Ninth Annual Report of the Immigrants' Protective League for the Year Ending December 31st, 1917, Supplement II, box 4, folder 60A, IPL-UIC; see also Early, *World without War*.

60. JA to Anna Garlin Spencer, December 2, 1919; and Anna Garlin Spencer to JA, February 23, 1920, quoted in Foster, *Women and the Warriors*, 36; see also Degen, *History of the Woman's Peace Party*, 222–23.

61. "What Kind of Peace Do Women Want?"; see also *Pictorial Review* to SPBP, December 3, 1918 [telegram], SPBP.

62. "Some Ways to Peace."

63. Ibid.

64. *Commission for Enduring Peace*, 12–13.

65. "What Kind of Peace Do Women Want?"

66. Sandi E. Cooper, "Peace as a Human Right: The Invasion of Women into the World of High International Politics," *Journal of Women's History* 14, no. 2 (Summer 2002): 9–25; and Jo Vellacott, "Feminism As If All People Mattered: Working to Remove the Causes of War, 1919–1929," *Contemporary European History* 10, no. 3 (2001): 375–94.

67. "Program for Constructive Peace"; "We Women of the United States"; "Program For International Action at the Close of the War"; "Program for World Action, after the War," n.d. [1915]; and "Woman's Peace Party Program for Constructive Peace," January 10, 1915, all in WILPF/WPP Collection, series A: Historical Records, box 1 (microfilm reel 12:1).

68. "What Kind of Peace Do Women Want?"; and GA to SPB, February 7, 1919, SPBP.

69. *Report of the International Congress of Women, Zurich, May 12 to 17, 1919* (Geneva: Women's International League for Peace and Freedom, [1919]), 243–46 (quotation). See also Kuhlman, *Reconstructing Patriarchy*, 111–17; Sklar, et al., *Social Justice Feminism*, 229–42; Steinson, *American Women's Activism*, 350, 360n14; and Vellacott, "Feminism," 377–83.

70. Alonso, *Peace as a Women's Issue*, 81–82; Kuhlman, *Reconstructing Patriarchy*, 116–17; and Vellacott, "Feminism," 380–84.

71. Anna Garlin Spencer to JA, April 5, 1920, JAPP.

72. Degen, *History of the Woman's Peace Party*, 241, quoting from "Constructive Pacifism," *Survey* 43(1920): 387.

73. C. H. Dennis (*Chicago Daily News*) to Jane Addams, October 24, 1923 [with handwritten note from JA to SPB] and enclosed "American Peace Award Plan," SPBP; see also Charles DeBenedetti, "The $100,000 American Peace Award of 1924," *Pennsylvania Magazine of History and Biography* 98, no. 2 (April 1974): 224–29; and Sally Marks, *The Illusion of Peace: International Relations in Europe, 1918–1933* (London: Macmillan, 1976).

74. Kuhlman, *Reconstructing Patriarchy*, 127–34.

75. Vellacott, "Feminism," 386.

76. Seth Koven and Sonya Michel, *Mothers of a New World: Maternalist Politics and the Origins of Welfare States* (New York: Routledge, 1993); Alisa Klaus, *Every Child a Lion: The Origins of Maternal and Infant Health Policy in the United States and France, 1890–1920* (Ithaca, N.Y.: Cornell University Press, 1993); and Ann Orloff, *The Politics of Pensions: A Comparative Analysis of Britain, Canada, the United States, 1880–1940* (Madison: University of Wisconsin Press, 1993).

77. Ken Maynard to "Miss Breckinridge and Miss Abbott," March 4, 1923, SPBP.

78. Martha Branscombe, "A Friend of International Welfare," *SSR* 22, no. 4 (December 1948): 436–41; Ogden Chisolm, *Brief Report of the Proceedings of the Ninth International Prison Congress* (New York: International Prison Commission, 1925); *First General Congress on Child Welfare: Reports* (Geneva: Save the Children Fund, 1925), document 63, p. 1; Alberti, *Beyond Suffrage*, 87; and Kenneth F. Rich to Etienne Clouset, July 1, 1927, SPBP.

79. SPB to EA, July 1, 6, 8, 1928, SPBP; see also Anette Kniephoff-Knebel and Friedrich W. Seibel, "Establishing International Cooperation in Social Work Education: The First Decade of the International Committee of Schools for Social Work," *International Social*

Work 51, no. 6 (2008): 790–812; and Kerstin Eilders, "Social Policy and Social Work in 1928: The First International Conference of Social Work in Paris Takes Stock," in Sabine Hering and Berteke Waaldijk, eds., *History of Social Work in Europe (1900–1960): Female Pioneers and Their Influence on the Development of International Social Organizations* (Opladen: Leske and Budrich, 2003), 119–28.

80. *First International Conference of Social Work: Paris, July 8th–13th 1928* (Paris, 1929), vol. 1, p. 852, and vol. 2, p. 235; and "Programme of the International Conference of Social Work" (Paris, July 8–13, 1928), Social Work Pamphlets, box 95: International Conference of Social Work.

81. Adena Miller Rich to Etienne Clouset, July 1, 1927, SPBP.

82. *Commission for Enduring Peace*, 12.

83. "Cases Handled by Immigrants' Protective League in Cooperation with the International Migration Service during First Ten Months of 1926," Miscellany, 1925–1927, SPBP.

84. See for example Mary E. McDowell and Adena Miller Rich to SPB, March 1 and October 30, 1928; Illinois Joint Committee to SPB, June 18, 1928; and Fred Schlotfeldt to SPB, April 15, 1931, SPBP.

85. "Functions of Immigrants' Protective League in Connection with Deportation Cases," n.d., Series 1, box 6, folder 66; and "Chicago's Deportation Drive of 1926"; "The June Deportation Drive in Chicago," July 2, 1930; Adena Miller Rich to Anita Jones, June 3, 1930; and "Memorandum on the United States Deportation Drive of October, November 1931 in Chicago," December 12, 1931, supplement II, box 4, folder 54A, IPL-UIC.

86. Immigrants' Protective League, "Twenty Ways in Which the League Assisted in the Passage of the Adult Education Bill," July 20, 1927, Miscellany, SPBP.

87. Breckinridge, *New Homes for Old*, lxii.

88. "College Women Meet in Holland," *New York Times*, July 25, 1926; "Downtown Clubs," *Chicago Tribune*, November 27, 1929; Christy Jo Snider, "Creating a Transnational Identity: The International Federation of University Women Confronts Racial and Religious Membership Restrictions in the 1930s," in Jensen and Kuhlman, *Women and Transnational Activism*, 193–218; and Megan Threlkeld, "The Pan-American Conference of Women, 1922: Successful Suffragists Turn to International Relations," *Diplomatic History* 31, no. 5 (November 2007): 801–28 (quotations p. 801).

89. Program, "International Summer School in Connection with the Fourth Congress of the Women's International League for Peace and Freedom," May 17–May 31, 1924, WILPF-UCol, 1st Accession, series 1, box 23, folder 2; JA to James Tufts, December 16, 1923, JAPP, reel 15; and Foster, *Women and the Warriors*, 50.

90. "A Statement of Foreign Policy," April 24–27, 1929; and WILPF-U.S. program 1930–31, folder 4.3, box 35, Wald Papers; see also Foster, *Women and the Warriors*; see also Harriet Hyman Alonso, "Suffragists for Peace during the Interwar Years, 1919–1941," *Peace and Change* 14, no. 3 (July 1989): 243–62; and Anne Marie Pois, "The U.S. Women's International League for Peace and Freedom and American Neutrality, 1935–1939," *Peace and Change* 14, no. 3 (July 1989): 263–84.

91. SPB to Virginia Wieland, March 25, 1942, SPBP; see also Alonso, *Peace as a Women's Issue*, chap. 4; and Alonso, *Women's Peace Union*.

92. Hannah Clothier Hull to JA, with enclosed clippings, [January 23, 1925], JAPP; "List

of Delegates from National Women's Trade Union League of America to Conference on Cause and Cure of War, Chicago, Ill., January 26–29, 1937, at Palmer House," January 8, 1937, Miscellany, SPBP; see also Linda Schott, "'Middle-of-the-Road' Activists: Carrie Chapman Catt and the National Committee on the Cause and Cure of War," *Peace and Change* 21, no. 1 (January 1996): 1–21; Threlkeld, "Pan-American Conference of Women"; and Susan Zeiger, "Finding a Cure for War: Women's Politics and the Peace Movement in the 1920s," *Journal of Social History* 24, no. 1 (Fall 1990): 69–86.

93. Lucia Maxwell, "Spider Web Chart: The Socialist-Pacifist Movement in America Is an Absolutely Fundamental and Integral Part of International Socialism," *Dearborn Independent*, 22 March 1924, http://womhist.alexanderstreet.com/wilpf/doc3.htm#spiderweb.

94. Davis, *American Heroine*, 263–65.

95. Quoted in Davis, *American Heroine*, 266; see also Molly Ladd-Taylor, "Hull House Goes to Washington: Women and the Children's Bureau," in Noralee Frankel and Nancy S. Dye, eds., *Gender, Class, Race, and Reform in the Progressive Era* (Lexington: University Press of Kentucky, 1991), 110–26; and Muncy, *Creating a Female Dominion*, especially chap. 3.

96. For Breckinridge's later reflections, see SPB to Ellen Starr Brinton, July 19, 1938, SPBP; on the 1920s, see SPB to JA, January 26, 1924 (misdated; actually 1925); and Hannah Clothier Hull to JA, with enclosed clippings, [January 23, 1925], JAPP; Florence Kelley to SPB, June 5, 1927, SPBP; and Kim E. Nielsen, *Un-American Womanhood: Antiradicalism, Antifeminism, and the First Red Scare* (Columbus: Ohio State University Press, 2001), 124–30; appendix B, p. 147.

97. See for example "U. of C. 'Red Peril' Cited 23 Yrs. Ago by Prof. Shorey," *Chicago Tribune*, April 15, 1935; and "U. of C. 'Red' Quiz Hits New High in Uproar," *Chicago Tribune*, June 8, 1935.

98. Elizabeth Dilling, *The Red Network: A Who's Who" and Handbook of Radicalism for Patriots* (Chicago: privately published, 1934).

99. SPB to Ida Curry, November 26, 1934, SPBP.

100. "Some Ways to Peace."

101. List compiled from correspondence, membership cards, receipts for pledges, and Breckinridge's handwritten lists of donations, 1930s–1940s, SPBP; see also Alonso, *Women's Peace Union*, appendix 1, pp. 181–86.

102. S. P. Breckinridge, Review of Mary Louise Degen, *The History of the Woman's Peace Party*, SSR. 14, no. 2 (June 1940): 383; see also "People's Peace Group Formed," *Chicago Tribune*, October 12, 1939.

103. For examples of Breckinridge's wartime interests and activities, see James T. Nicholson to SPB, April 17, 1941 (regarding European refugees); Emily Davison to SPB, May 2, 1941 (regarding the London Blitz); SPB to Hon. Breckinridge Long, July 18, 1941 (regarding German Jewish refugees); Bill Jr. [a cousin] to SPB, February 12, 1942 (member of the military); SPB to Virgil Chapman, February 27, 1942 (regarding legal defense of a soldier accused of theft); SPB to Hon. Francis Biddle, Department of Justice, April 21, 1942 (regarding civil rights of immigrants and subversives); Elizabeth B. MacLatchie for Martha A. Chickering to SPB, November 4, 1942 (regarding internment of Japanese Americans); SPB to Henry L. Stimson, Secretary of War, April 20, 1943, and SPB to Franklin D. Roosevelt, April 20, 1943

(regarding African American soldiers); SPB to Virgil Chapman, June 17, 1943, and SPB to Ed. Gossett, June 17, 1943 (regarding Chinese exclusion); SPB to Lt. Harold Feldman, June 17, 1943 (former student enrolled in military); SPB to Senator Scott W. Lucas, November 13, 1943 (regarding aid to European children); SPB to Hon. Breckinridge Long, December 15, 1943 (regarding Jewish refugees); SPB to Hon. Virgil Chapman, August 16, 1944 (regarding GI Bill of Rights); Stanley Nowak, American Committee for Protection of Foreign Born, n.d. [ca. 1945] with enclosure, "An Open Letter to President Truman" (regarding deportation of immigrants because of political opinions), all in SPBP.

104. "Some Ways to Peace"; and "Proposed Statement by S. P. Breckinridge," Statement for the Radio November [19]36, Speech and Article Files, SPBP.

Chapter 8. The Potential and Pitfalls of Pan-American Feminism

1. "U.S. 'Big Four' at Pan-American Parley," clipping, Miscellany, December 1933, SPBP.

2. Paul Mallon, "News behind the News," *Reno Evening Gazette*, December 26, 1933.

3. "Woman Adds Luster to Breckinridge Fame," clipping, Breckinridge Biographical file; "Name First Woman Delegate to Pan-American Congress," *Kingsport [Tenn.] Times*, Friday, November 3; "Dems Hail Appointment of Miss Breckinridge," *Steubenville [Ohio] Herald-Star*, October 30, 1933.

4. "A Woman of Mind and Heart," clipping, Miscellany, December 1933, SPBP.

5. "Another Woman to Represent Nation at Foreign Conference: Dr. Breckinridge Sails for Montevideo with Lots to Do for Women's Cause," *Christian Science Monitor*, November 15, 1933, clipping, Miscellany, December 1933, SPBP.

6. "Some Social Work Problems of International Scope," [1933; marked in pencil, "Paper by SPB read at Montevideo"], Speeches and Articles file, SPBP (quotations pp. 3, 4, 13, and 16); see also Foster, *Women and the Warriors*, chap. 5.

7. "A Woman Delegate in a Pan-American Conference," [1934], Speeches and Articles file, SPBP (quotations p. 1).

8. Katherine M. Marino, "La Vanguardia Feminista: Pan-American Feminism and the Rise of International Women's Rights, 1915–1946" (PhD diss., Stanford University, 2013); Megan Threlkeld, *Pan American Women: U.S. Internationalists and Revolutionary Mexico* (University of Pennsylvania Press, 2014); and Esther Sue Wamsley, "A Hemisphere of Women: Latin American and U.S. Feminists in the IACW, 1915–1939" (PhD diss., Ohio State University, 1998).

9. Breckinridge and Stevens were active in international and transnational groups alike, but as this chapter deals with them as official representatives in proceedings authorized by nation-states, I refer to them as international feminists or feminist internationalists. On the distinction between international and transnational, see Jocelyn Olcott, "A Happier Marriage? Feminist History Takes the Transnational Turn," in Virginia M. Bouvier, ed., *The Globalization of U.S.-Latin American Relations: Democracy, Intervention, and Human Rights* (Westport, Conn.: Praeger, 2002), 237–58.

10. Esther Sue Wamsley, "Constructing Feminism across Borders: The Pan American Women's Movement and the Founding of the Inter-American Commission of Women,"

in *Crossing Boundaries: Women's Organizing in Europe and the Americas, 1880s-1940s*, ed. by Pernilla Jonsson, Silke Neunsinger, and Joan Sangster (Uppsala University, Sweden, 2007), 51–72; and Wamsley, "Hemisphere of Women," chap. 3.

11. See for example "Factional Antagonism Seen," *NYT*, December 18, 1933; Harold B. Hinton, "Rights of Women Bring Parley Rift," *NYT*, December 12, 1933; "2 Feminist Leaders Go to Rights Parley," *Omaha [Neb.] Evening World-Herald*, November 13, 1933; "Our Attitude Is Explained," *NYT*, December 20, 1933; "Feminists Assail Our Stand on Pact," *NYT*, December 19, 1933; Paul Mallon, "News Behind the News," *Reno Evening Gazette*, December 26, 1933.

12. SPB, "Memorandum with Reference to My Participation in the Seventh International Conference of American States, Montevideo," December 27, 1933, Miscellany, 1933, SPBP (hereafter SPB, "Montevideo Memorandum.")

13. For debates on nationality, see especially Diane Elizabeth Hill, "International Law for Women's Rights: The Equality Treaties Campaign of the National Woman's Party and Reactions of the U.S. State Department and the National League of Women Voters (1928–1938)" (Ph.D. diss., University of California-Berkeley, 1999); Beatrice McKenzie, "The Power of International Positioning: The National Woman's Party, International Law and Diplomacy, 1928–34," *Gender and History* 23, no. 1 (April 2011): 130–46; and Megan Threlkeld, "How to 'Make This Pan-American Thing Go?': Interwar Debates on U.S. Women's Activism in the Western Hemisphere," in Kimberly Jensen and Erika Kuhlman, eds., *Women and Transnational Activism in Historical Perspective* (Netherlands: Dordrecht, 2010), 173–91. For speculations as to the reasons for Breckinridge's appointment, see especially "Hull Names Woman Delegate to Pan-American Congress," *Washington Post*, October 28, 1933; and "Dr. S. P. Breckinridge Is Active at Parley: Woman Delegate Is Expected to Expound Our Viewpoint on Equal Rights Treaty," *NYT*, December 11, 1933.

14. Braden Memoirs, 717 (Stevens quote), 720, 722. For Stevens's alleged document tampering and Breckinridge quote, see Alexander Weddell and S. Breckinridge, "Strictly Confidential Memorandum Re: Attitudes and Conduct of Inter-American Commission of Women," December 28, 1933, RG 59 Decimal file 710: G Women's Rights, box 3772 (hereafter "Strictly Confidential Memorandum"). For Stevens's accusation that Breckinridge was the one doing the tampering, see DS, memorandum, December 23, 1933, box 78, folder 9, Stevens Papers.

15. "Aid for Women Held Big Need at Montevideo," *Washington Post*, December 10, 1933.

16. Paul Mallon, "Behind the News in Washington and Wall Street," *Steubenville [Ohio] Herald-Star*, December 26, 1933.

17. "2 Feminist Leaders Go to Rights Parley," *Omaha [Neb.] Evening World-Herald*, November 13, 1933.

18. SPB to KL, October 27, 1933, Lenroot Papers.

19. Harold B. Hinton, "Women Ask Pacts Equalizing Rights," *NYT*, December 9, 1933.

20. Untitled draft article, ca. 1918, Miscellany, SPBP.

21. "Factional Antagonism Seen," *NYT*, December 18, 1933.

22. Ellen Carol DuBois, "Internationalizing Married Women's Nationality: The Hague Campaign of 1930," in Karen Offen, ed., *Globalizing Feminisms, 1789–1945* (London: Rout-

ledge, 2010), 204–16; Bredbenner, *Nationality of Her Own*, chap. 3; Gardner, *Qualities of a Citizen*, chap. 8; and Hill, "International Law."

23. Carol Miller, "'Geneva—The Key to Equality': Inter-war Feminists and the League of Nations," *Women's History Review* 3, no. 2 (1994): 219–45; and Paula Pfeffer, "'A Whisper in the Assembly of Nations': United States' Participation in the International Movement for Women's Rights from the League of Nations to the United Nations," *Women's Studies International Forum* 8, no. 5 (1985): 459–71.

24. Mildred Adams, "Again Controversy Arises over Equality for Women: Two Philosophies That Clash at the Pan-American Conference Have Divided Women's Groups Here since Pre-Suffrage Days," *NYT*, December 24, 1933.

25. Asunción Lavrin, *Women, Feminism, and Social Change in Argentina, Chile, and Uruguay, 1890–1940* (Lincoln: University of Nebraska Press, 1995), chap. 1; see also Christine Ehrick, "*Madrinas* and Missionaries: Uruguay and the Pan-American Women's Movement," *Gender and History* 10, no. 3 (November 1998): 406–24; Karen Mead, "Beneficent Maternalism: Argentine Motherhood in Comparative Perspective, 1880–1920," *Journal of Women's History* 12, no. 3 (Autumn 2000): 120–45; and Francesca Miller, *Latin American Women and the Search for Social Justice* (Hanover, N.H.: University Press of New England, 1991).

26. K. Lynn Stoner, "In Four Languages but with One Voice: Division and Solidarity within Pan-American Feminism, 1923–1933," in David Sheinin, ed., *Beyond the Ideal: Pan-Americanism in Inter-American Affairs* (Westport, Conn.: Praeger, 2000), 79–94.

27. GA to EA, October 8, 1933, SPBP; see also Francesca Miller, "The International Relations of Women of the Americas 1890–1928," *Americas* 43, no. 2 (October 1986): 171–82; Corinne A. Pernet, "Chilean Feminists, The International Women's Movement, and Suffrage, 1915–1950," *Pacific Historical Review* 69, no. 4 (November 2000): 663–88; and Wamsley, "Constructing Feminism."

28. Ehrick, "*Madrinas* and Missionaries," 417; Pernet, "Chilean Feminists," 672–73; and Darcy Rendon, "Contesting U.S. Feminist Imperialism: The Transnational Activism of Mexican Feminist Elena Arizmendi, 1911–1938" (BA thesis, Smith College, 2011), chap. 3.

29. Christine Ehrick, *The Shield of the Weak: Feminism and the State in Uruguay, 1903–1933* (Albuquerque: University of New Mexico Press, 2005).

30. Donna J. Guy, "The Politics of Pan-American Cooperation: Maternalist Feminism and the Child Rights Movement, 1913–1960," *Gender and History* 10, no. 3 (November 1998): 449–69 (quotation 451); and Guy, "The Pan-American Child Congresses, 1916 to 1942: Pan-Americanism, Child Reform, and the Welfare State in Latin America," *Journal of Family History* 23, no. 3 (July 1988): 272–92.

31. See especially Seth Koven and Sonya Michel, "Womanly Duties: Maternalist Politics and the Origins of Welfare States in France, Germany, Great Britain, and The United States, 1880–1920," *American Historical Review* 95 (1990): 1076–108.

32. Guy, "Pan-American Child Congresses"; and Katharine F. Lenroot, *The Sixth Pan-American Child Congress* (Washington, D.C.: Pan-American Union, 1930).

33. Katharine F. Lenroot, *Sixth Pan-American Child Congress, Lima, July 4–11, 1930: Report of the Delegates of the United States of America* (Washington, D.C.: GPO, 1931), 55.

34. Neva Deardorff to Lillian Wald, January 12, 1931; Minutes of the Meeting of the United

States Committee on Cooperation in Pan American Child Welfare Work, June 17, [1931]; Constitution of the United States Committee on Cooperation in Pan-American Child Welfare Work; and "United States Committee on Cooperation in Pan-American Child Welfare Work," box 41, folder 5, Wald Papers.

35. "Recommendations as to the Pan-American Conference at Montevideo," November 1933, Miscellany, SPBP; "Envoys Ready for Trip to South," *San Diego Evening Tribune*, November 10, 1933; "Montevideo Talks May Cover Debts," *NYT*, December 1, 1933; Harold B. Hinton, "Montevideo Pacts Face Fights Here," *NYT*, December 26, 1933.

36. Press release, November 9, 1933; and Cordell Hull to FP, October 25, 1933, RG 174, box 50, folder labeled "Conference-Pan American at Montevideo, Uruguay, Dec. 1933" (hereafter RG 174, box 50, Montevideo folder).

37. Jonathan Mitchell, "'Intra-Nationalism' at Montevideo: The Long-Range Results of the Roosevelt Doctrine May Be Better Relations in the Western Hemisphere," *New York Literary Digest*, December 2, 1933, copy in Miscellany, December 1–15, 1933, SPBP.

38. DS, "I Meet Miss Breckinridge," draft manuscript (quotation p. 12), Stevens Papers, box 126, folder 13.

39. SPB, "Montevideo Memorandum." See also FP to Cordell Hull, October 12, 1933; and Cordell Hull to FP, October 25, 1933, RG 174, box 50, Montevideo folder.

40. GA to EA, October 8, 1933, SPBP; and GA to FP, September 30, 1933, with handwritten response, in RG 174, box 50, Montevideo folder.

41. Susan Ware, *Beyond Suffrage: Women in the New Deal* (Cambridge, Mass.: Harvard University Press, 1961), especially chap. 1; FP to Cordell Hull, October 12, 1933; and Cordell Hull to FP, October 25, 1933, RG 174, box 50, Montevideo folder.

42. SPB to KL, October 28, 1933, SPBP.

43. See especially materials in RG 174, box 50, Montevideo folder. See also Hill, "International Law," 279.

44. SPB to KL, November 2, 1933, SPBP.

45. SPB to KL, October 27, 1933, Lenroot Papers; and SPB to KL, November 2, 1933, SPBP.

46. See especially Cordell Hull to FP, October 25, 1933; FP to Cordell Hull, October 27, 1933; KL to FP, October 27, 1933, RG 174, box 50, Montevideo folder.

47. SPB, "Montevideo Memorandum"; passenger list, USMS *American Legion*, Miscellany, December 1933, SPBP. See also *Final Act: Seventh International Conference of American States, Montevideo, Uruguay, December 3–26, 1933*, copy in Miscellany, December 1933, SPBP (hereafter *Final Act*); and press release, November 9, 1933, RG 174, box 50, Montevideo folder.

48. Braden Memoirs, 708, 711, 719.

49. SPB, "Montevideo Memorandum."

50. "Women and the Seventh Conference, Prepared by S.P.B. for the Delegation," Miscellany, December 1933, SPBP (quotations pp. 6, 9, 15, 16). See also Hill, "International Law for Women's Rights," 282.

51. DS, "I Meet Miss Breckinridge," 5–6, Stevens Papers, box 126, folder 13.

52. Hill, "International Law for Women's Rights," 284–86.

53. IACW log, November 28, 1933, box 96, folder 8, Stevens Papers.

54. See for example "Guests at Doña Mesquita's Tea," November 24, 1933, box 96, folder 3; see also IACW log, box 96, folder 8; "Montevideo," June 2, 1964, box 126, folder 13; and records in box 78, folders 6–9; and box 96, folders 12 and 13, Stevens Papers.

55. SPB, "Montevideo Memorandum." See also *Final Act*; and "Women in the International Conferences of American States," filed after SPB to Leo S. Rowe, October 22, 1938, SPBP.

56. SPB to Belle Sherwin, December 8, 1933, SPBP.

57. Margarita Mendoza to DS, October 4, 1933, box 77, folder 8, Stevens Papers.

58. *Final Act*, 9–16.

59. DS, "I Meet Miss Breckinridge," 7 (quotations); see also "Guests at Doña Mesquita's Tea," and DS to Bertha Lutz, November 12, 1930, box 62, folder 11, Stevens Papers.

60. DS, "I Meet Miss Breckinridge," 8.

61. June E. Hahner, *Emancipating the Female Sex: The Struggle for Women's Rights in Brazil, 1850–1940* (Durham, N.C.: Duke University Press, 1990), chap. 4, esp. pp. 134–46, 168, 173–74; Katherine Marino, "Transnational Pan-American Feminism: The Friendship of Bertha Lutz and Mary Wilhelmine Williams, 1926–1944," *Journal of Women's History* 26, no. 2 (Summer 2014): 63–87, esp. 68–73; and Teresa Cristina Marques de Novaes, "Entro o igualitarismo e a reforma dos direitos das mulheres: Bertha Lutz na Conferencia Interamericana de Montevideu, 1933" (Between the Equalitarism and Women's Rights Reformation: Bertha Lutz at Montevideo Interamerican Conference, 1933), *Revisto Estudios Feministas* 21, no. 3 (2013): 927–44.

62. Sarah Anne Buck, "Activists and Mothers: Feminist and Maternalist Politics in Mexico, 1923–1953" (PhD diss., Rutgers University, 2002), 317–20, 552–53, and 564–66; and DuBois, "Internationalizing Married Women's Nationality," 209.

63. Lavrin, *Women, Feminism, and Social Change*, 345–48.

64. William Belmont Parker, *Paraguayans of To-Day* (New York: Hispanic Society of America, 1921), 19–20; and Juan Speratti, *Feminismo* (Asunción: Author, 1989).

65. Wamsley, "Hemisphere of Women," 221.

66. SPB to Belle Sherwin, December 8, 1933, SPBP; and Seventh International Conference of American States, *Third Committee, Civil and Political Rights of Women, Minutes and Antecedents* (Montevideo, 1933), 8 (hereafter *Third Committee*). See also Lavrin, "International Feminism," 521; and Wamsley, "Hemisphere of Women," 238–41.

67. See especially Besse, *Restructuring Patriarchy*, 168–71; Marino, "Transnational Pan-American Feminism," 69, 72–73; and Maria Lucia Mott, "Maternal and Child Welfare, State Policy and Women's Philanthropic Activities in Brazil, 1930–45," in Marian van der Klein, Rebecca Jo Plant, Nichole Sanders, and Lori R. Weintrob, eds., *Maternalism Reconsidered: Motherhood, Welfare and Social Policy in the Twentieth Century* (New York: Berghahn, 2012), 168–89.

68. Committee III—Civil and Political Rights of Women, Plenary Session—December 19, 1933, Miscellany, 1933, SPBP. See also *Third Committee*, 19, 25–26 (quotation p. 25).

69. SPB to Belle Sherwin, January 31, 1934, SPBP.

70. Untitled document, Stevens Papers, box 26, folder 8, p. 16.

71. Commission III—Political and Civil Rights of Women, Meeting No. 3—December 15, 1933, Miscellany, 1933, SPBP; *Third Committee*, 8–9, 13.

72. Third Committee, "Whereas: It Has Been Approved by the Committee on Civil and Political Rights of Women That the Office of Its Chairman Be Rotatory," n.d., Third Committee—Political and Civil Rights of Women, box 5, MLR entry 23, RG 43; see also Hill, "International Law for Women's Rights," 310.

73. Committee III—Civil and Political Rights of Women, Plenary Session—December 19, 1933, December 16–31, 1933, SPBP; *Third Committee*, 15; and Seventh International Conference of American States, *First, Second, and Eighth Committees, Minutes and Antecedents* (Montevideo, 1933), 189 (hereafter *First, Second, and Eighth Committees*).

74. *Third Committee*, 26; see also Hill, "International Law for Women's Rights," 310–11.

75. IACW Log, December 15, box 96, folder 8; and "Mr. Weddell's Speech on Women's Rights"; "Miss Minerva Bernardino (Dominican Republic)," box 79, folder 1, Stevens Papers. See also Ellen DuBois and Lauren Derby, "The Strange Case of Minerva Bernardino: Pan-American and United Nations Women's Rights Activist," *Women's Studies International Forum* 32 (2009): 43–50.

76. Seventeen nations voted for the continuation of the IACW. The U.S. abstained, and Argentina voted against continuation. See "Third Commission: Continuation of Inter-American Commission of Women," box 79, folder 4, Stevens Papers.

77. "Equal Nationality Treaty Hailed as Women's Victory," *Washington Post*, December 19, 1933; "Hull Praises Miss Stevens on Her Victory over Him," *NYT*, December 25, 1933; see also Stevens Papers, clipping box 2. See also DS to Maurtua, December 13, 16, and 20, 1933; DS to President Olaya, Bogota, Colombia, December 23, 1933; Angel Giraudy to Presidente Grausanmartin, Havana, Cuba, December 26, 1933; and DS to [IACW Executive Secretary Fanny Bunand-Sevastos (Buenos Aires)], December 31, 1933, box 77, folder 11, Stevens Papers.

78. "Suggestions for Memorandum on Instructions, Items 6, 8, 18, 19 of the Agenda, Submitted by the Secretary of Labor"; Cordell Hull to FP, October 25, 1933; and FP to Cordell Hull, October 27, 1933, RG 174, box 50, Montevideo folder.

79. SPB to Belle Sherwin, January 31, 1934, SPBP.

80. Ibid.

81. Memorandum with Reference to Proposal Introduced to Committee VIII—December 21, 1933 (quotations pp. 2, 3, 4); and SPB, "Montevideo Memorandum," SPBP. See also *First, Second, and Eighth Committees*, 192.

82. *First, Second, and Eighth Committees*, 192; see also Hill, "International Law for Women's Rights," 311–12.

83. "Breckinridge Tries Another Channel," p. 1, and "Breckinridge Proposal—VIII Committee (International Conferences)," box 126, folder 13, Stevens Papers.

84. SPB to EA, December 22, 1933, SPBP.

85. Stevens believed that Breckinridge concocted this plan with Lutz's input, which may well have been the case. See "I Meet Miss Breckinridge," p. 11; and "Montevideo: Supplement to Ripper-Bill Memo, Christmas Eve," box 126, folder 13, Stevens Papers.

86. Seventh International Conference of American States, Minutes and Antecedents, vol. 6, *Plenary Sessions* (Montevideo, 1933), p. 108 (hereafter *Plenary Sessions*).

87. Braden Memoirs, 719–21.

88. Ibid., 721; see also "Rift in Women's Commission," *NYT*, December 25, 1933.

89. "Conference Saves Women's Board: Final Working Session Rejects Plan to Abolish Inter-American Commission," *NYT*, December 25, 1933.

90. *Third Committee*, 28–29.

91. Committee III—Political and Civil Rights of Women, Meeting No. 4—December 16, 1933, Miscellany, December 1933, SPBP.

92. Memorandum by the Secretary of Labor on Topic 18 of the Agenda of the Seventh International Conference of American States, November 6, 1933, Miscellany, SPBP; SPB to FP, December 4, 1933; and KL to FP, October 27, 1933, RG 174, box 50, Montevideo folder.

93. Memorandum by Benjamin Muse, Committee 5—Social Problems, Subcommittee No. 1—Inter American Bureau of Labor, Meeting of Wednesday, December 13, [1933], and accompanying proposals, Miscellany, 1933, SPBP.

94. SPB, "Women in the International Conferences of American States," filed after SPB to Leo S. Rowe, October 22, 1938, SPBP (quotation p. 4).

95. Chapter V—Sub-Committee 1—Bureau of Labor, undated memo with handwritten comments, Miscellany, December 1–15, 1933, SPBP; and Committee V—Social Problems, Plenary Session-December 18, 1933, Miscellany, December 16–31, 1933, SPBP.

96. Bertha Lutz to SPB, January 1, 1934, SPBP. Breckinridge returned to the United States by plane, which garnered some attention in the press. See "Sophonisba Breckinridge," clipping, Breckinridge Biographical File.

97. Bertha Lutz to C. C. Catt, February 12, 1934, Lutz Papers; see also Bertha Lutz to SPB, January 1, 1934; SPB to Bertha Lutz, March 10, 1934; and SPB to Ruth Shipley, February 4 and 6, 1934, SPBP; and Ilan Rachum, "Feminism, Woman Suffrage, and National Politics in Brazil: 1922–1937," *Luso-Brazilian Review* 14, no. 1 (Summer 1977): 118–34.

98. Bertha Lutz to C. C. Catt, August 25, 1934, Lutz Papers.

99. SPB to Bertha Lutz, March 10, 1934, SPBP; and Bertha Lutz to C. C. Catt, February 12, 1934, Lutz Papers.

100. Bertha Lutz to Carrie Chapman Catt, July 7 (quotations) and July 15, 1936, NAWSA Papers.

101. "Some Ways to Peace," [handmarked in pencil, Natl Conf Cause & Cure of War, 1/24/36, Final Draft], Miscellany, SPBP.

102. SPB to Frieda Miller, March 10, 1936, SPBP. See also Anna O'Neill to SPB, April 11, 1936; Ernest Gruening to SPB, May 2, 1936; and SPB to Cordell Hull, March 10, 1936; and June 17, 1936, SPBP.

103. Braden Memoirs, 721 (second quotation); "'Good Neighbor Policy' Lauded by Only Woman in Hull Group: Mrs. Musser Here on Way to Peace Parley at Buenos Aires," clipping (first quotation); Frieda Miller to Bertha Lutz, July 28, 1936; Mary Anderson to FP, September 4, 1936; FP to Frieda Miller, October 24, 1936; and Frieda Miller to FP, October 27, 1936, all in RG 174, box 47, folder labeled "Inter-American Peace Conference, Buenos Aires, Argentina, 1936"; SPB to Frieda Miller, March 10, 1936, SPBP; and "Frieda S. Miller," SPB to Editor, University of Chicago Magazine, November 1938, Miller Papers, series 1, box 1, folder 1. See also Pernet, "Chilean Feminists," 682n71; and Ware, *Beyond Suffrage*, 78–79.

104. SPB to Frieda Miller, March 2, 1936; and Frieda Miller to SPB, March 7, 1936, SPBP.

105. Katherine M. Marino, "Marta Vergara, Popular-Front Pan-American Feminism and the Transnational Struggle for Working Women's Rights in the 1930s," *Gender and History* 26, no. 3 (November 2014): 642–60.

106. Frieda Miller, "Personal and Confidential Report to the Secretary of Labor on the First Pan-American Labor Conference of the International Labor Organization, Santiago, Chile, 2–14 January 1936," RG 174, box 47, folder labeled "International Labor Office-Santiago Conference."

107. Miller, "Geneva," 224–38.

108. Marino, "Popular-Front Pan-American Feminism," 650–54 (quotation p. 653).

109. Ibid., 654–55.

110. SPB to Cordell Hull, January 13, 1939, SPBP; untitled manuscript, box 26, folder 8, Stevens Papers; Wamsley, "Hemisphere of Women," 240–41 and 247–48; and Hill, "International Law for Women's Rights," 314–16. Winslow's name had previously been proposed as a delegate to the Peace Conference by Breckinridge's allies in the Roosevelt administration, although not, so far as these materials indicate, by Breckinridge herself. See materials in RG 174, box 47, folder labeled "Inter-American Peace Conference, Buenos Aires, Argentina, 1936."

111. Pfeffer, "Whisper," especially pp. 466–67.

112. "Ill-Timed Woman's Quarrel," *NYT*, December 20, 1933, Stevens Papers, clippings box 2.

113. Marino, *Feminism for the Americas.*

Chapter 9. Toward a National Minimum

1. Katharine F. Lenroot, "Friend of Children and of the Children's Bureau," *SSR* 22, no. 4 (December 1948): 427–430.

2. Kriste Lindenmeyer, *"A Right to Childhood": The U.S. Children's Bureau and Child Welfare, 1912–1946* (Urbana: University of Illinois Press, 1997), 21–22.

3. *Standards of Child Welfare*, 431, 433–35, 440.

4. SPB, "Family Budgets," *Standards of Child Welfare*, 43; see also Lenroot, "Friend of Children," 428.

5. Lenroot, "Friend of Children," 428. See also Molly Ladd-Taylor, "Hull House Goes to Washington: Women and the Children's Bureau," in Noralee Frankel and Nancy S. Dye, eds., *Gender, Class, Race and Reform in the Progressive Era* (Lexington: University of Kentucky Press, 1991), 110-126.

6. SPB to Sen. Hiram Bingham, March 15, 1932; and SPB to Marguerite Owen, January 13, 1932, SPBP.

7. JL to SPB, July 30, 1921; and SPB to GA, August 27, 1921; SPB to GA, October 23, 1921; GA to SPB, February 3, 1927; SPB to GA, March 3, 1931; and SPB to Hester Browne, June 24, 1931, SPBP; EA and SPB, *The Administration of the Aid-to-Mothers Law in Illinois* (Washington, D.C.: GPO, 1921); Muncy, *Creating a Female Dominion*, 86–87, 91; and Lindenmeyer, *Right to Childhood*, esp. chap. 1.

8. Molly Ladd-Taylor, *Mother-Work: Women, Child Welfare, and the State, 1890–1930* (Urbana: University of Illinois Press, 1994), chap. 6.

9. SPB Autobiography.

10. GA to SPB, November 17, 1921, box 1, folder 4, Abbott Papers-UNL; SPB to GA, October 11 and 24, 1921, SPBP; Lindenmeyer, *Right to Childhood*, chaps. 3 and 4; and Wilson, *Women's Joint Congressional Committee*, chap. 2.

11. SPB to Frank Bane, May 19, 1934; and "The Changing Role of the State in Child Welfare," ca. 1940, draft, Miscellany, 1940–1941, SPBP. See also Ladd-Taylor, *Mother-Work*, 180–84.

12. Ladd-Taylor, *Mother-Work*, chap. 6; Lindenmeyer, "A Right to Childhood," chap. 4; and Skocpol, *Protecting Soldiers and Mothers*, chap. 9.

13. Lindenmeyer, "A Right to Childhood," 100–103; 184–90; and SPB to Sen. William E. Borah, November 19, 1934, SPBP.

14. SPB to GA, March 18, 1932 (quotation); see also SPB to GA, March 28, 1930; John C. Cooper (R-OH) to Thomas Underwood, March 24, 1930; SPB to Hon. Morton Hull, January 7, February 5, and March 8, 1932; SPB to Walter West, January 14, 1932; and SPB to Hon. Virgil Chapman, January 16, 1932, SPBP; GA to SPB, February 4, 1931, box 15, folder 1, Abbott Papers-UNL; and Wilson, *Women's Joint Congressional Committee*, chap. 7.

15. *Nineteenth Annual Report of the Chief of the Children's Bureau* (Washington, D.C., GPO, 1931), 62; see also Lenroot, "Friend of Children," 429; SPB to Georgia Osborne, January 22, 1930; and SPB to Jane Chandler, April 7, 1930, SPBP; and Lindenmeyer, "A Right to Childhood," 164–70.

16. "Foreword," n.d. [filed in February 1933], SPBP; *White House Conference, 1930: Addresses and Abstracts of Committee Reports* (New York: Century, 1931), 45–47; and Lindenmeyer, "A Right to Childhood," chap. 7.

17. SPB to Sen. Hiram Bingham, March 15, 1932, SPBP; see also Lindenmeyer, "A Right to Childhood," 171.

18. KL to SPB, March 10, 1932, SPB to Prentice Murphy, March 11, 1932; DB to SPB, February 16, 1933; SPB to Sen. Hiram Bingham, March 15, 18, and 21, 1932; and GA to SPB, [1933], SPBP.

19. Georgia Bell Travis to EA, August 3, 1948, SPBP.

20. SPB to Edward Costigan, March 28, 1932, SPBP; and Edith Abbott and Katherine Kiesling, "Evictions during the Chicago Rent Moratorium Established by the Relief Agencies, 1931–33," *SSR* 9, no. 1 (March 1935): 34–57.

21. "Report on Cases from Renter's Court 4/27 to 5/14," [1932], Miscellany, 1932, SPBP.

22. "Renters' Court Report for Week of April 25 to 30 inc.," [1932], Miscellany, 1932, SPBP.

23. "Renters' Court Report, Week of April 18 to 23 inclusive," [1932], Miscellany, 1932, SPBP.

24. "Renters' Court Report for Week of April 25 to 30 inc.," [1932], Miscellany, 1932, SPBP.

25. "Renters' Court Report for Week of April 11 to 16 inc.," [1932], Miscellany, 1932, SPBP.

26. "Grace Abbott" typescript, pp. 55–56, Abbott Papers-NSHS, series 2, folder 3; Sorensen, *Sister's Memories*, 363; SPB to Edward Costigan, March 28, 1932, SPBP; and *Federal Aid for Unemployment Relief: Hearings Before a Subcommittee of the Committee on Manufactures, United States Senate, Seventy-Second Congress, Second Session, on S. 5125, a Bill to Provide for Cooperation by the Federal Government with the Several States in Relieving the Hardship and Suffering Caused by Unemployment, and for Other Purposes. January 3 to 17, 1933* (Washington, D.C.: GPO, 1933), 547.

27. SPB to Edwin Cooley, May 26, 1930; and G. E. Benjamin to SPB, June 21, 1931, SPBP.

28. In addition to Koven and Michel, *Mothers of a New World*, see Michele Landis Dauber, *The Sympathetic State: Disaster Relief and the Origins of the American Welfare State* (Chicago: University of Chicago Press, 2012); and Daniel T. Rodgers, *Atlantic Crossings: Social Politics in a Progressive Age* (Cambridge, Mass.: Harvard University Press, 2000).

29. "National Funds for a National Crisis," *SSR* 5, no. 4 (December 1931), 652–54. Although Breckinridge and Abbott shared responsibility for editing the *SSR*, Breckinridge's correspondents assumed Breckinridge wrote this editorial. See Frank Bane to SPB, December 22, 1931; and Fred Hall to SPB, December 28, 1931, SPBP.

30. Muncy, *Creating a Female Dominion*; and Ware, *Beyond Suffrage*, chap. 1.

31. SPB to FDR, January 13, 1933, SPBP. Both Grace Abbott and Mary Dewson urged Breckinridge to write to Roosevelt on Perkins's behalf. See GA to SPB, [December 7, 1932]; Mary W. Dewson to SPB, January 9, 1933, SPBP.

32. SPB to KL, March 7, 1933, SPBP.

33. SPB to FP, March 7, 1933, SPBP.

34. [SPB], "Memorandum on the Minimum Wage," n.d., filed after Hazel Kyrk to SPB, Mr. Douglas, and Mr. Ogburn, June 27, 1933, SPBP. Breckinridge subsequently worked with the state committee to design the Illinois Minimum Wage Bill and then lobbied lawmakers to support it. See Gertrude Wilson to SPB, May 10, 1933; SPB to Josephine Perry, June 21, 1933; SPB to Roy S. Woods, June 22, 1933, SPBP.

35. Ware, *Beyond Suffrage*; and Ware, *Partner and I: Molly Dewson, Feminism, and New Deal Politics* (New Haven, Conn.: Yale University Press, 1989).

36. SPB to Josephine Roche, November 19, 1934, SPBP. See also Robyn Muncy, *Relentless Reformer: Josephine Roche and Progressivism in Twentieth-Century America* (Princeton, N.J.: Princeton University Press, 2014).

37. SPB to Mary Dewson, May 7, 1934, SPBP.

38. SPB to Charles Johnson, October 1, 1931; see also Walter West to SPB, November 30, 1931; SPB to Frederick Siedenberg, January 5, 1932; SPB to Edward Ryerson, January 28, 1932; and SPB to Mrs. Sydney B. Snow, January 30, 1932, SPBP.

39. Fred Hall to SPB, December 28, 1931; and Frank Bane to SPB, December 22, 1931, SPBP.

40. Edward Costigan to SPB, December 19, 1931; and Marguerite Owen to SPB, January 12, 1932, SPBP.

41. Sorensen, *Sister's Memories*, 365.

42. SPB to Marguerite Owen, January 13, 1932; and Marguerite Owen to SPB, January 16, 1932, SPBP.

43. Marguerite Owen to SPB, January 6, 1932; and GA to SPB, [March 2, 1932]; see also SPB to Marguerite Owen, January 13, 1932; and Committee on Federal Action on Unemployment, Memo to Members of the Consultant Group, [June 22, 1933], all in SPBP. The Committee on Unemployment, originally established in 1931, was renamed the Committee on Federal Action on Unemployment in 1932 and, in 1933, renamed the Committee on Federal Action on Social Welfare. See Jacob Fisher, *The Response of Social Work to the Depression* (Cambridge, Mass.: Schenkman, 1980), 40–41, 43, 71–73.

44. SPB to Wayne McMillen, January 9, 1932; and Marguerite Owen to SPB, February 19, 1932, SPBP.

45. See especially Doolittle, *Women's Joint Congressional Committee*; Muncy, *Creating a Female Dominion*; and Ware, *Beyond Suffrage*.

46. "Memorandum from S. P. Breckinridge to the members of the American Association of Social Workers who have not found it worthwhile to join the Chicago Chapter," March 12, 1932 [hereafter AASW Memo, 1932]; and SPB to Walter West, March 4, 1932, SPBP.

47. Walter West to SPB, April 14, 1932; and Committee on Federal Action on Unemployment, Memo to Members of the Consultant Group, [June 22, 1933], SPBP.

48. For quotation, see AASW Memo, 1932. For her election to this office in 1933, see press release, June 28, 1933, Miscellany, 1933, SPBP.

49. Wilson Memoirs, 128.

50. SPB to Charles Miner, July 1, 1932, SPBP.

51. *The Nation* quoted in [SPB,] "To Members of the Chicago Chapter," [1934], Miscellany, 1934; SPB to Morton Hull, March 2, 1931 [probably misdated and actually 1932], and "The Promotion by Social Workers of State and National Legislative Programs," [marked in pencil: AASW, 1934], Speech and Article Files, SPBP.

52. SPB, *Public Welfare Administration in the United States: Select Documents* (Chicago: University of Chicago Press, 1927), 3.

53. See for instance SPB to Morton Hull, March 2, 1931 [probably misdated and actually 1932]; SPB to Frank Bane, July 25, 1933 [marked in pencil, "Comments on Report of A.A.S.W. Com[mittee] 7/23/33"]; and SPB to Harry L. Hopkins, June 29, 1933, SPBP.

54. SPB to Philip Klein, December 19, 1939, SPBP.

55. SPB to FDR, January 27, 1933; SPB to Harry L. Hopkins, June 29, 1933; Minutes, American Association of Social Workers, Chicago Chapter, July 18, 1933; SPB to Walter West, July 29, 1933; and SPB to Ellen C. Potter, August 25, 1933, SPBP; see also "Statement with reference to Federal Relief Administration," [1933], Speeches and Article file, SPBP.

56. SPB to Frank Bane, April 28, 1934, and enclosure, "What Is Relief?"; SPB to Mary Anderson, August 24, 1933; SPB to Walter West, March 22, 1934; and AASW Memo, 1932; Jane Addams and Raymond Sanford to SPB, June 1, 1933; John B. Andrews to SPB, October 28, 1933; "Memorandum on the Minimum Wage," following Hazel Kyrk to SPB, Mr. Douglas, and Mr. Ogburn, June 27, 1933, SPBP.

57. AASW Memo, 1932, SPBP.

58. SPB to Josephine Roche, July 1, 1935, SPBP.

59. SPB to Frank Bane, July 25, 1933 [marked in pencil, "Comments on Report of A.A.S.W. Com[mittee] 7/23/33"], April 28, 1934, and enclosure, "What Is Relief?"; and May 19, 1934; SPB to Walter West, October 17, 1933, and February 10, 1934; SPB to Mary Anderson, August 24, 1933; Joseph Kepecs to SPB, August 8, 1933; "American Association of Social Workers, Chicago Chapter, Question 4"; and "Tentative Program, American Association of Social Workers, Conference on Governmental Objectives for Social Work, February 16 and 17, 1934," SPBP.

60. Committee on Federal Action on Unemployment, Memo to Members of the Consultant Group, [June 22, 1933], SPBP; Fisher, *Response of Social Work to the Depression*, 43, 71–74.

61. SPB to Ellen C. Potter, August 1, 1933, SPBP.

62. GA to SPB, May 27, 1933, with handwritten notation by SPB, SPBP.

63. Mary W. Dewson to SPB, February 7, 1934, SPBP.

64. SPB to Walter West, July 19, 1933; and Minutes, American Association of Social Workers, Chicago Chapter, July 18, 1933, SPBP.

65. American Association of Social Workers, Chicago Chapter, Question 7, n.d. [filed February 1934]; and American Association of Social Workers, Conference on Governmental Objectives for Social Work, February 16 and 17, 1934, "Tentative Program," SPBP.

66. Mary W. Dewson to SPB, March 5, 1934, SPBP.

67. Mildred D. Mudgett to SPB, January 3, 1934; and SPB to Elizabeth Wisner, May 5, 1934, SPBP; and Emilia E. Martinez-Brawley, "From Countrywoman to Federal Emergency Relief Administrator: Josephine Chapin Brown, a Biographical Study," *Journal of Sociology and Social Welfare* 14, no. 2 (May 1987): 153–85, available online at http://scholarworks.wmich .edu/cgi/viewcontent.cgi?article=1814&context=jssw. On Lundberg and Lenroot, see Muncy, *Creating a Female Dominion*, 51–52; and KL to SPB, July 3, 1948, SPBP.

68. Mildred Mudgett Memoirs, "Four Seasons" (typescript) (quotation p. 225), Mudgett Papers, folder 4. On Breckinridge's service on the AASW Committee on Standards and Personnel in Public Service, see "Draft of the Minutes of the Annual Meeting of the American Association of Social Workers, Monday, May 16, 1927," p. 9, NASW Papers, box 1, folder labeled "NASW: AASW Annual Meetings, 1918–1928." On Breckinridge's service on the Committee on Developing and Protecting Professional Standards in Public Welfare Work for the American Public Welfare Association, see Joseph Moss to SPB, May 15, 1933, SPBP. On the AASW standards as of 1933, see Fisher, *Response*, 20–21.

69. "How Social Work Became a Profession: Recollections of the 1935 Study of Schools of Social Work," Mudgett Papers, folder 9; Mrs. M. C. Burnett to Mildred Mudgett, April 19, 1934; SPB to Mildred Mudgett, April 21, 1934; and "Report to the Executive Committee of the Secretary of the American Association of Schools of Social Work," n.d. [ca. 1935]; CSWE Papers, box 1, Folder labeled "Breckinridge"; and "Minimum Curriculum as Adopted at the December 1932 Meeting of the American Association of Schools of Social Work," Miscellany, 1934, SPBP.

70. Elizabeth Wisner to SPB, April 30, 1934; SPB to Elizabeth Wisner, May 5, 1934; SPB to Mary Burnett, May 5, 1934; SPB to Mildred Mudgett, May 7, 1934; and Mary Burnett to SPB, May 9, 1934 ("nothing definite"), SPBP.

71. Josephine Brown to SPB, May 2, [1934], SPBP.

72. SPB to Josephine Brown, May 13, 1934, SPBP. See also SPB to Directors of the Schools of Social Work, May 13, 1934, SPBP.

73. SPB to Josephine Brown, May 28, 1934, CSWE Papers, box 1, Breckinridge folder.

74. While there was an advisory committee, its members consistently upheld Breckinridge's judgments, and Brown herself relied exclusively on Breckinridge for advice. See "Memorandum from the Advisory Committee Appointed by the Association of Schools of Social Work at the Request of Miss Josephine Brown, Special Assistant to the Federal Relief Administration, Regarding Training of Personnel for Federal Relief Services," n.d. [ca. 1934], CSWE Papers, box 1, Breckinridge folder.

75. Elizabeth Wisner to SPB, March 19, 1934; and Mildred Mudgett to SPB, n.d. [filed March 1934], SPBP.

76. Sophonisba P. Breckinridge, "New Horizons of Professional Education for Social Work," *National Conference on Social Welfare, Official Proceedings of the Annual Meeting, 1936,* pp. 119–32, esp. p. 125.

77. Sophonisba P. Breckinridge, "What We Have Learned about Emergency Training for Public Relief Administration," *National Conference on Social Welfare, Official Proceedings of the Annual Meeting, 1935,* pp. 246–58 (quotation p. 252).

78. SPB, "What We Have Learned about Emergency Training for Public Welfare Administration," [marked in pencil, "Natl Conf, 1935, SPB"], Speech and Article Files, SPBP.

79. See for instance "Evaluation of FERA Training Program," *Compass* 17, no. 1 (September 1935): 6–7.

80. Breckinridge, "New Horizons," 131. Of the participants, 253 were male and 880 were female. See "The Professional Schools," *SSR* 10, no. 2 (June 1936): 352–54 (quotation p. 353).

81. Josephine C. Brown, "What We Have Learned about Emergency Training for Public Relief Administration," *National Conference on Social Welfare, Official Proceedings of the Annual Meeting, 1935,* pp. 237–45 (quotations pp. 241–42).

82. Breckinridge, "What We Have Learned," 253; and Martinez-Brawley, "From Country-woman," 168–72.

83. "The New Horizons of Professional Education for Social Work," [marked by hand, "Paper read Nat'l Conf. Atlantic City May 1936"], Speech and Article Files, SPBP.

84. Kathryn Kish Sklar, "Two Political Cultures in the Progressive Era: The National Consumers' League and the American Association for Labor Legislation," in Linda K. Kerber, Alice Kessler-Harris, and Kathryn Kish Sklar, eds., *U.S. History as Women's History: New Feminist Essays* (Chapel Hill: University of North Carolina Press, 1991), 36–62; David A. Moss, *Socializing Security: Progressive-Era Economists and the Origins of American Social Policy* (Cambridge, Mass.: Harvard University Press, 1996); Landon R. Y. Storrs, *Civilizing Capitalism: The National Consumers' League, Women's Activism, and Labor Standards in the New Deal Era* (Chapel Hill: University of North Carolina Press, 2003); and Suzanne Mettler, *Dividing Citizens: Gender and Federalism in New Deal Public Policy* (Ithaca, N.Y.: Cornell University Press, 1998).

85. Clarke A. Chambers, "Social Security: The Welfare Consensus of the New Deal," in Wilbur J. Cohen, ed., *The Roosevelt New Deal: A Program Assessment Fifty Years After* (Austin: Lyndin B. Johnson School of Public Affairs, University of Texas, 1986), 145–59 (quotation p. 152). On Breckinridge's work with the NCL and the WTUL, see chap. 4. For Breckinridge and the AALL, see John B. Andrews to SPB, January 20, 24, 27, 29; February 18, 1911 (box 3, folders 27, 28, 29, and 35), and January 2, 1912 (box 4, folder 69); SPB to John B. Andrews, January 20 and 27, 1911 (box 3, folders 25 and 28), and January 2, 1912 (box 4, folder 74); and SPB to Irene Osgood Andrews, March 4, 1908 (box 1, folder 7) and May 17, 1913 (box 6, folder 81), AALL Records.

86. Lindenmeyer, *"A Right to Childhood,"* 179–98; Mettler, *Dividing Citizens,* 128–33 and 128n44.

87. SPB to Josephine Roche, November 19, 1934, SPBP.

88. EA to SPB, February 13, 1935, SPBP; "Breckinridge, Dixie Editor, Is Dead at 67," *Washington Post,* February 19, 1935; and Mettler, *Dividing Citizens,* 128n44. Abbott's testimony is

reprinted as "The Beginnings of the Social Security Act" in Grace Abbott, *From Relief to Social Security: The Development of the New Public Welfare Services and Their Administration* (Chicago: University of Chicago Press, 1941; rpt., New York: Russell and Russell, 1966), 199–225.

89. SPB to Sen. Alban Barkley, May 7, 1935, SPBP.

90. SPB to Hon. Louis McHenry Howe, December 11, 1934, SPBP.

91. SPB to EA, February 12, 1935; Walter West to Chapter Chairmen, February 26, 1935; and "1935 Conference: American Association of Social Workers" [February 1935], SPBP; Welfare Workers to Open Session: 3-Day Discussion of U.S. Problems Set Here," *Washington Post*, February 14, 1935; and Fisher, *Response*, 73.

92. Daniel S. Hirschfield, *The Lost Reform: The Campaign for Compulsory Health Insurance in the United States from 1932 to 1943* (Cambridge, Mass.: Harvard University Press, 1970).

93. Homer Folks to SPB, December 17, 1934, SPBP.

94. SPB to Sen. Alban Barkley, May 7, 1935; see also SPB to Hon. Robert M. LaFollette, January 28, 1935; SPB to Hon. Marvel M. Logan, January 28, 1935; Edward Costigan to SPB, January 30, 1935; Thomas Underwood to Alben W. Barkley, n.d. [1935]; and Thomas Underwood to SPB, n.d. [1935], SPBP.

95. SPB to Hon. Fred M. Vinson, February 1, 1935; Fred M. Vinson to Thomas Underwood, February 28, 1935, and March 25, 1936, and Fred M. Vinson to SPB, April 3, 1935 (quotation), SPBP; *Economic Security Act: Hearings Before the Committee on Ways and Means House of Representatives, Seventy-Fourth Congress First Session, on H.R. 4120, A Bill to Alleviate the Hazards of Old Age, Unemployment, Illness, Labor, and Dependency, to Establish a Social Insurance Board in the Department of Labor, to Raise Revenue, and for Other Purposes* (Washington, D.C.: GPO, 1935), 1069, available online at https://www.ssa.gov/history/35house.html.

96. SPB to Eleanor Roosevelt, June 3, 1935; see also KL to SPB, n.d. [1935], SPBP.

97. Chambers, "Social Security," 152; and Lindenmeyer, "A Right to Childhood," 193.

98. EA and SPB, *Administration of the Aid-to-Mothers Law in Illinois*, 159.

99. See especially Barbara Nelson, "The Origins of the Two-Channel Welfare State: Workmen's Compensation and Mothers' Aid," in *Women, the State, and Welfare*, ed. Linda Gordon (Madison: University of Wisconsin Press, 199), 123–51; and Mettler, *Dividing Citizens*, 128–33, 137–41, 158–75.

100. SPB to MT, August 9 and 11, 1935, Talbot Papers.

101. On Breckinridge's relationship with Frank Bane and Walter West, see SPB to MT, August 11 and 22, 1935, Talbot Papers.

102. Wilson Memoirs, 128; SPB, "The Profession of Social Work," [marked by hand: AASSW Adv. Comm on Training, 1937], 22, Speech and Article Files, SPBP; and Fisher, *Response*, 64–65.

103. SPB to Mrs. Emmons Blaine, March 9, 1935; SPB to Rev. Frederick Siedenberg, March 9, 1935; "To the President and Congress of the United States," with handwritten note from GA to SPB, n.d. [1935]; and press release, "Back Official Security Bill," March 22, 1935, SPBP.

104. SPB to Thomas Underwood, April 14 (first quotation), April 18; and Thomas Underwood to SPB, April 15, May 12, and June 7 (second quotation), 1935, SPBP. On the dominance

of southerners, see Edwin E. Witte, *The Development of the Social Security Act* (Madison: University of Wisconsin Press, 1962), 100.

105. Nancy J. Altman, *The Battle for Social Security: From FDR's Vision to Bush's Gamble* (Wiley, 2005), 75–80 (quotation p. 75).

106. SPB to Hon. J. Hamilton Lewis, July 17, 1935 (quotation); SPB to Thomas Egan, July 18, 1935; SPB to Joseph L. Gill, 1935; and Rev. D. J. Frawley to Hon. J. Hamilton Lewis, July 19, 1935, SPBP. The amendment was passed in the Senate, but the House objected. Legislative staffers conducted research into a modified version of the amendment, but they reported that it would take months of additional work to craft an acceptable amendment. The amendment then went back to both the House and Senate, which finally agreed to remove it from the act. Breckinridge intervened before the amendment returned to Congress.

107. GA to SPB, n.d. [filed in 1933 but probably 1935], SPBP.

108. SPB to MT, August 9, 1935, Talbot Papers.

109. GA to SPB, n.d. [filed in 1933 but probably 1935]; KL to SPB, August 12, 1935; and SPB, "The Changing Role of the State in Child Welfare" [draft copy marked "Annals, September 1940"], p. 15, Speech and Article Files, SPBP.

110. SPB to MT, August 30, 1935, Talbot Papers.

111. FP to SPB, August 16, 1935; and SPB to Frances Perkins, August 21, 1935; Martha M. Eliot to SPB, November 25, 1935; and SPB to Martha Eliot, November 29, 1935 (quotation), SPBP.

112. *The Children's Bureau: Yesterday, Today and Tomorrow* (Washington, D.C.: GPO, 1937), 42–43, 52–53.

113. *Report of the Chief of the Children's Bureau, Fiscal Year Ended June 30, 1940* (Washington, D.C.: GPO, 1941), 159, 177–81.

114. SPB to Sen. Alban W. Barkley, May 7, 1935; and Report on the Meeting of the Advisory Committee on Training and Personnel, January 27, 1938, SPBP; *Report of the Chief of the Children's Bureau . . . 1940*, 181–82; Lathrop, "Friend to Children," 428; Mettler, *Dividing Citizens*, 138 and 158–75; Alice Kessler-Harris, "Designing Women and Old Foods: The Construction of the Social Security Amendments of 1939," in Linda K. Kerber, Alice Kessler-Harris, and Kathryn Kish Sklar, eds., *U.S. History as Women's History: New Feminist Essays* (Chapel Hill: University of North Carolina Press, 1995), 87–106 (Wisner's involvement at p. 93); and Stanley Wenocur and Michael Reisch, *From Charity to Enterprise: The Development of American Social Work in a Market Economy* (University of Illinois Press, 2001), 179.

115. SPB, "The Changing Role of the State."

116. SPB to MT, August 9, 1935, Talbot Papers.

117. GA to SPB, n.d. [filed in 1933 but actually 1935], SPBP. Breckinridge probably knew Hoey, a New Yorker, through their mutual involvement on the National Conference of Social Work. Hoey served on the professional organization's editorial committee from 1929 to 1932. See "Report of the Editorial Committee to the Executive Committee of the National Conference of Social Work," n.d. [June 1929], SPBP. On Breckinridge and Hoey's work together establishing education and training standards for social workers, see especially "Report on the Meeting of the Advisory Committee on Training and Personnel," January 27,

1938, SPBP; and Lathrop, "Friend to Children," 428. See also "Jane M. Hoey (1892–1968)—
Social Worker, Welfare Administrator, Government Official," *Social Welfare History Project*.
Retrieved August 22, 2017, from http://socialwelfare.library.vcu.edu/people/hoey-jane-m/.

118. SPB to Arthur J. Altmeyer, December 13, 1935; Arthur J. Altmeyer to SPB, December
16, 1935; and KL to SPB, December 21, 1935, SPBP.

119. "Amendments to the Social Security Act," *SSA* 10, no. 4 (December 1936): 664–65.

120. Ellen C. Potter to SPB, July 22, 1938 (quotations); and SPB to Sen. Alben W. Barkley,
February 6, 1939, SPBP.

121. See SPB to Thomas Underwood, March 7 (first quotation), March 15, and March 25,
1938; SPB to Alben W. Barkley (second quotation), March 25, 1938; SPB to Frank Bane, March
25, 1938; Alben Barkley to SPB, March 31, 1938; and Public Resolution 122, 75th Congress
(H.J. Res 679), SPBP.

122. Lindenmeyer, *"A Right to Childhood,"* chap. 5; and Wilson, *Women's Joint Congressional
Committee*, chaps. 4–6.

123. SPB to GA, February 24, 1923; and SPB to Sen. N. W. Mason, May 6, 1933; see also
Bess Smenner to SPB, September 18, 1925; J. E. Hagerty to SPB, January 30, 1925; SPB to GA,
March 11 [?], 1925; SPB to Roy S. Woods, June 22, 1933; SPB to Gov. Henry Horner, July 1,
1933; SPB to KL, January 14, 1933; KL to SPB, January 16, 1933; and SPB to KL, January 20,
1933, SPBP. See also Lindenmeyer, *"A Right to Childhood,"* 195–98.

124. SPB to Anne S. Davis, July 2, 1933, SPBP.

125. Mary Dublin to SPB, March 10, 1938; and SPB to Mary Dublin, March 12, 1938, SPBP.
See also Lindenmeyer, *"A Right to Childhood,"* 197–98; Mettler, *Dividing Citizens*, chaps. 7
and 8; and Storrs, *Civilizing Capitalism*, chaps. 7 and 8. On Breckinridge's opposition to differential pay scales, see "The Problem of Unequal Wages," *Chicago Daily News*, [January 1,
1933], clipping in Miscellany, December 1933, SPBP.

126. Frank Bane to Arlien Johnson, copy enclosed in Frank Bane to Wilma Walker, October 24, 1957, Abbott Papers-SCRC.

Chapter 10. "A and B"

1. M. E. Humphrey to EA, August 5, 1948, Abbott Papers-SCRC.

2. Although Abbott first came to the university in 1902 for a summer course, she dated her
acquaintance with Breckinridge to 1903. See Wright, "Three against Time," 43; and Abbott's
testimony in Breckinridge Estate Records.

3. Costin, *Two Sisters*, chap. 1. Breckinridge was ten years older than Abbott.

4. SPB to EA, March 3, 1907, SPBP; and Costin, *Two Sisters*, 28–37.

5. SPB to EA, June 28, 1907, SPBP; GA to EA, [April 16, 1906]; and [Summer 1906], Abbott Papers-UNL; and Costin, *Two Sisters*, 38–39.

6. Wright, "Three against Time," 43; SPB to EA, October 23, 1907, box 1, folder 10, Abbott
Papers-SCRC.

7. Bessie Louise Pierce to EA, July 30, 1948; SPBP; SPB to Howard Knight, December
2, 1927; SPB to Hotel Benjamin Franklin, November 2, 1931; EA to SPB, telegram, ca. 1940;
EA to Jeannette Rankin, February 18, 1924; SPB to GA, February 21, 1928, Grace E. B. to

SPB, March 17, 1932; SPB to Mr. Ogburn, August 30, 1932; and SPB to A. L. Bowen, August 28, 1937, SPBP; EA to Mother, May 17, 1914; and EA to O. A. Abbott, n.d. [ca. 1915], box 83, folder 2, Abbott Papers-SCRC; GA to Parents, Easter Sunday, [1935]; GA to Mother, December 31, [1931]; SPB to GA, September 18, 1935, box 15, folder 1, Abbott Papers-UNL.

8. Charles Nutter to SPB, July 14, August 2, August 13, SPBP.

9. EA to MT, September 23, 1909; MT to EA, October 30, 1911, Talbot Papers, box 2, folder 1.

10. MT to EA, November 12, [1911], November 14, 1911; EA to MT, November 12, 1911 and n.d., 1911, Talbot Papers, box 2, folder 1.

11. MT to President Judson, July 1912; and EA to MT, February 23, 1913, Talbot Papers, box 2, folder 1; see also M. J. Deegan, "'Dear Love, Dear Love': Feminist Pragmatism and the Chicago World of Love and Ritual," *Gender and Society* 10 (1996): 590–607.

12. Johnson Memoirs, 57.

13. MT to SPB, [December 25, 1912], SPBP.

14. Taylor, "Edith Abbott," 178–79.

15. On Abbott's donation of SPB's papers to the LOC, see Lewis Coffin to EA, November 10, 1948; and EA to Lewis Coffin, November 17, 1948, and January 31, 1949, box 1, folder 6, Abbott Papers-SCRC.

16. SPB to EA, May 17, June 7, 10, July 1, 6, 8, 10, 26, 30, 31, August 1, 7, 1928, SPBP.

17. SPB to EA, November 19, December 22, 1933; EA to SPB, November 13, 1933; and January 4 and 6, 1934 (telegrams), SPBP.

18. SPB to EA, n.d. [marked ca. 1935, filed after December 1935 correspondence]; SPB to EA, February 12 and 16, 1935; EA to SPB, February 13, 14, 15, and 18, 1935 (telegrams); see also SPB to EA, February 13, 15, and 20, 1935, all in SPBP.

19. SPB to EA, July 23, 1938, box 18, folder 4, Abbott Papers-UNL.

20. SPB to EA, March 4, 1940, SPBP.

21. EA to SPB, telegram, [June 2, 1941]; SPB to EA, November 2, 1942, SPBP.

22. SPB to EA, August 1, 3, 4 (with postscript from August 5), 6, 1943, SPBP.

23. SPB to EA, September 3, 4, 5 [two letters], 6, 8 [two letters], 9, 10, n.d. ["Thursday afternoon"], 14, 15, 16 [two letters], 1944, SPBP.

24. Breckinridge confided to Abbott's niece that she did not want to leave Abbott at home alone. See SPB to Charlotte Abbott, November 15, 1944, box 95, folder 8, Abbott Papers-SCRC.

25. Nancy F. Cott, "Passionlessness: An Interpretation of Victorian Sexual Ideology, 1790–1850," in Nancy F. Cott and Elizabeth H. Pleck, eds., *A Heritage of Her Own: Toward a New Social History of American Women* (New York: Simon and Schuster, 1979), 162–81; Carroll Smith-Rosenberg, "The Female World of Love and Ritual: Relations between Women in Nineteenth-Century America," *Signs* 1, no. 1 (1975): 1–29; Lillian Faderman, *Surpassing the Love of Men: Romantic Friendship between Women from the Renaissance to the Present* (New York: Morrow, 1981).

26. Esther Newton, "The Mythic Mannish Lesbian: Radclyffe Hall and the New Woman," *Signs* 9, no. 4 (1984), 557–75; Nancy Sahli, "Smashing: Women's Relationships before the Fall," *Chrysalis* 8 (Summer 1979): 17–27; Carroll Smith-Rosenberg, "The New Woman as

Androgyne: Social Disorder and Gender Crisis, 1870–1936," in *Disorderly Conduct: Visions of Gender in Victorian America* (New York: Oxford University Press, 1985), 245–96.

27. See especially Faderman, *To Believe in Women*; Franzen, *Spinsters and Lesbians*; Palmieri, *In Adamless Eden*; and Ware, *Beyond Suffrage*, 8–10, 24–26.

28. Lillian Faderman, *Odd Girls and Twilight Lovers: A History of Lesbian Life in Twentieth-Century America* (New York: Columbia University Press, 1991); Estelle B. Freedman, "The Prison Lesbian: Race, Class, and the Construction of the Aggressive Female Homosexual, 1915–1965," *Feminist Studies* 22, no. 2 (1996): 397–423; Madeline Davis and Elizabeth Lapovsky Kennedy, *Boots of Leather, Slippers of Gold: The History of a Lesbian Community* (New York: Routledge, 1993); Christina Simmons, "Companionate Marriage and the Lesbian Threat," in *Women and Power in American History: A Reader, Vol. II: From 1870*, ed. Kathryn Kish Sklar and Thomas Dublin (Englewood Cliffs, N.J.: Prentice Hall, 1991), 183–94; George Chauncey, *Gay New York: Gender, Urban Culture, and the Makings of the Gay Male World, 1890–1940* (New York: Basic, 1994); and John D'Emilio, *Sexual Politics, Sexual Communities: The Making of a Homosexual Minority in the United States, 1940–1970* (Chicago: University of Chicago Press, 1983).

29. Blanche Wiesen Cook, "The Historical Denial of Lesbianism," *Radical History Review* 20 (Spring/Summer 1979): 60–65; Adrienne Rich, "Compulsory Heterosexuality and Lesbian Existence," *Signs* 5 (Summer 1980): 631–60; Estelle B. Freedman, "'The Burning of Letters Continues': Elusive Identities and the Historical Construction of Sexuality," *Journal of Women's History* 9, no. 4 (Winter 1998): 181–200; Freedman, *Maternal Justice: Miriam Van Waters and the Female Reform Tradition* (Chicago: University of Chicago Press, 1996); Elizabeth Lapovsky Kennedy, "'But We Would Never Talk about It': The Structures of Lesbian Discretion in South Dakota, 1928–1933," in Ellen Lewis, ed., *Inventing Lesbian Cultures in America* (Boston: Beacon, 1996), 15–39; Leila J. Rupp, "Imagine My Surprise: Women's Relationships in Historical Perspective," *Frontiers* 5, no. 3 (1980): 61–70; Susan Ware, "Unlocking the Porter-Dewson Partnership: A Challenge for the Feminist Biographer," in Sara Alpern et al., eds., *The Challenge of Feminist Biography* (Urbana: University of Illinois Press, 1992); Katy Coyle and Nadiene Van Dyke, "Sex, Smashing, and Storyville in Turn-of-the-Century New Orleans: Reexamining the Continuum of Lesbian Sexuality," in John Howard, ed., *Carryin' On in the Lesbian and Gay South* (New York: NYU Press, 1997), 54–72. On Breckinridge's correspondence with Van Waters, see for instance SPB to Mrs. McFarland, July 15, 1928 (letter of recommendation for Van Waters); SPB to Miriam Van Waters, March 6, 1941, and Miriam Van Waters to SPB, September 27, 1940 and March 14, 1941, Van Waters Papers.

30. Draft Review, [ca. April 4. 1946], SPBP; see also Elizabeth Lunbeck, *The Psychiatric Persuasion: Knowledge, Gender, and Power in Modern America* (Princeton University Press, 1994); and Muncy, *Female Dominion*, 83.

31. Ethel B. Dietrich to SPB, July 8, 22, 1936; SPB to Mrs. Thompson, August 3, 1936, SPBP; see also Anna Mary Wells, *Miss Marks and Miss Woolley* (Boston: Houghton Mifflin, 1987).

32. Dorothy Burke to EA, May 1, 1949, SPBP. See also Megan Elias, "'Model Mamas': The Domestic Partnership of Home Economics Pioneers Flora Rose and Martha Van Rensselaer," *Journal of the History of Sexuality* 15, no. 1 (January 2006): (p. 71 on class); and Franzen, *Spinsters and Lesbians*, 69–71 (on dress); and Kennedy, "But We Would Never Talk

about It,"15–39 (on class). On government repression, see David K. Johnson, *The Lavender Scare: The Cold War Persecution of Gays and Lesbians in the Federal Government* (Chicago: University of Chicago Press, 2004); and Julia M. Allen, *Passionate Commitments: The Lives of Anna Rochester and Grace Hutchins* (New York: SUNY Press, 2013).

33. Merriam Memoirs, 11; Linderholm Memoirs, 13; and Costin, *Two Sisters*, 181.

34. SPB to Lotta Ringer, October 7, 1933, SPBP; see also SPB, *Women in the Twentieth Century: A Study of Their Political, Social and Economic Activities* (New York: McGraw-Hill, 1933); and "The Problem of Unequal Wages," *Chicago Daily News*, [January 1, 1933], clipping in Miscellany, SPBP.

35. SPB, Review, *SSR* 20, no. 2 (June 1946): 277–78 (quotation p. 277).

36. Anne Breckinridge to EA, August 12, 1948, SPBP.

37. On SPB's retirement, see George A. Works to SPB, October 10, 1940 and June 24, 1941, SPBP; on the Abbott-Breckinridge residence at 5544 Woodlawn see materials in box 1, folder 3, Abbott Papers-SCRC.

38. Daughter to Robert Woolley, August 2, 1948, Woolley Papers, box 2; see also Sara M. Southall to EA and SPB, [May 30, 1948]; Mary Stanton to SPB, [June 18, 1948], SPBP; and Elizabeth Wisner to EA, October 18, 1945, box 27, folder 2, Lenroot Papers. On the women's memoirs, see Sorensen, ed., *Sister's Memories*; and Jabour, "Sophonisa Breckinridge (1866–1948): Memoirs of a Southern Feminist."

39. SPB to Charlotte Abbott, June 18, 1946, box 95, folder 8, Abbott Paper-SCRC; on Abbott and the Emergency Committee to Save the Children's Bureau, see Lenroot Papers, series II.2 (box 18, folders 9, 10, and 11). On Breckinridge's activities, see SPB to KL, June 11, 1946, Lenroot Papers, box 18, folder 11; and SPB to KL, May 8, 1946, with enclosed clipping, "Save the Children's Bureau," box 27, folder 2, Lenroot Papers.

40. Anne Breckinridge to EA, August 12, 1948; Agnes van Driel to EA, July 30, 1948; Mary C. Preston to EA, August 5, [1948] and March 6, [1949], SPBP.

41. Kate Turabian to EA, August 11, 1948, SPBP.

42. For instance, Katharine Lenroot had a long-term relationship with another woman, Emma Lundberg. See KL to SPB, July 3, 1948; and KL to EA, August 3, 1948, SPBP. So too did Jane Addams, Miriam Van Waters, Mary W. Dewson, and many other Progressive-era and New Deal women. See especially Faderman, *To Believe in Women*; Freedman, "'The Burning of Letters' Continues"; Ware, *Partner and I*; and Ware, *Beyond Suffrage*.

43. SPB to EA, July 30, [1928], SPBP.

44. JA to EA, July 18, 1911, box 1, folder 1, Abbott Papers-UNL; Florence Kelley to SPB, June 5, 1927; Edna Zimmerman to SPB, January 4, 1928; Rachel Eaton to SPB, January 24, 1928; Elizabeth Macadam to SPB, January 4, 1932; Theodora Bosanquet to SPB, January 16, 1931; Nicholas Kelley to SPB, March 7, 1932; L. Walker Linderholm to SPB, May 18, 1946; Virginia Cates to SPB, June 2, 1946; Mary Stanton to SPB, [June 18, 1948]; and KL to SPB, July 3, 1948, SPBP.

45. SPB to Mrs. Abbott, January 10, 1924, March 20, 1928 (quotation); SPB to GA, August 19, 1922, February 18, 24, 1923, May 30, 1931, October 19, 1932, January 8, 1934, October 8, 1933; GA to SPB, July 20, 1931, [December 1931]; Mr. and Mrs. Abbott to SPB, [ca. 1927]; SPB to Mrs. Abbott, March 20, 1928; Desha Breckinridge to EA, December 12, 22, 1933, SPBP;

Arthur Abbott to EA, November 4, 1908, box 18, folder 4; Arthur Abbott to EA, July 10, November 7, 12, December 18, 31, 1945; March 25, 1946, folder 5; and Arthur Abbott to SPB, June 9, 1937, folder 6; GA to EA, August 31, [1924], box 15, folder 1; Arthur Abbott to SPB, July 17, November 26, 1941, folder 2; Arthur Abbott to EA, January 19, April 1, December 6, 24, 1943, October 27, December 2, 4, 11, 14, 1944, box 1, folder 3; GA to SPB, February 4, 1931, box 15, folder 1, Abbott Papers-UNL.

46. SPB to Charlotte Abbott, September 3, 1931, July 5, 1933 (quotation), October 24, 1933, June 3, 1939, January 14, June 16, 1940, June 10, 1943, May 27, 1944, January 7, 1945, box 95, folder 8, Abbott Papers-SCRC; SPB to EA, September 27, 1931; Nisba Desha Breckinridge to SPB, January 6 and 11, 1932; SPB to GA, October 19, 1932, SPBP; and SPB to MT, August 30, 1935, box 3, folder 5, Talbot Papers.

47. Martha Speakman Wood to SPB, [October 1, 1928]; JL to SPB, October 6, 1928; Lewis Merriam to SPB, October 8, 1928; Florence Kelley to SPB, October 13, 1928, SPBP; clipping, September 28, 1928, "Edith Abbott, Educator, Is Hurt by Auto," Rich Papers, box 1, folder 75.

48. Arthur Abbott to SPB, October 3, 1928, box 83, folder 3, Abbott Papers-SCRC; Arthur Abbott to SPB, July 17, 1941, box 1, folder 2, Abbott Papers-UNL.

49. EA to KL, n.d. (ca. 1947), box 27, folder 2, Lenroot Papers.

50. Daughter to Robert Woolley, August 2, 1948, Woolley Papers. According to testimony from the probate records, she had in-home nurses beginning in February 1948. She died shortly after midnight on July 30, 1948, of an unspecified heart complaint. See Breckinridge Estate Records and "Miss Breckinridge Dies in Chicago, 82," NYT, July 31, 1948.

51. Breckinridge Estate Records.

52. SPB Autobiography; Breckinridge Estate Records; Daughter to Robert Woolley, August 2, 1948, Woolley Papers; and MT to Nisba Desha Breckinridge, May 16, 1946 (penciled draft), box 3, folder 9, Talbot Papers. On SPB's support for Robert's children, see especially Clair Breckinridge to SPB, August 8, 1937: DB to SPB, August 24, 27, 1927, July 25 and 27, 1932, and July 8, 1933; Mary D. Sharpe to SPB, August 15, 1931; Account of Nisba Breckinridge, April 28, 1932; Nisba Desha Breckinridge to SPB, January 6, 11, 1932; Elsie Smithies to SPB, May 16, 1932; SPB to Dr. W. J. Monilaw, July 25, 1932; Dr. W. J. Monilaw to SPB, July 27, August 4, 1932; S. Satterfield to SPB, September 7, 1934; SPB Secretary to Murray Drug Company, September 22, 1934; and Charles L. Street to SPB, October 12, 1934, SPBP.

53. Breckinridge Estate Records.

54. Robert Woolley to EA, July 30, 1948; Marie Plamandon and Mary Amberg to EA, July 31, 1948; Walter Pettit to EA, August 1, 1948; Frances Perkins to EA, August 19, 1948; Anne Breckinridge to EA, August 12, 1948; and Edna Zimmerman to EA, August 4, 1948, SPBP.

Epilogue

1. Alice Kessler Harris, "Law and a Living: The Gendered Content of 'Free Labor,'" in Frankel and Dye, eds., Gender, Class, Race, 87–109 (quotation p. 87).

2. SPB to Sen. William E. Borah, November 19, 1934, SPBP.

3. SPB, Public Welfare Administration, 10.

4. EA, "Sophonisba P. Breckinridge Over the Years," 420.

5. Quoted in Katharine F. Lenroot, "Sophonisba Preston Breckinridge, Social Pioneer," *SSR* 23, no. 1 (March 1949): 88–92 (quotation p. 90).

6. "Some Ways to Peace."

7. SPB to Edward Costigan, February 19, 1934, SPBP. See also Louis P. Masur, "Why It Took a Century to Pass an Anti-Lynching Law," *Washington Post*, December 28, 2018; and Emmett Till Antilynching Act, https://www.congress.gov/bill/116th-congress/house-bill/35/text.

8. SPB to William Cooper, April 2, 1932, SPBP.

9. SPB to Elisabeth Coit, July 23, 1933, SPBP.

10. "The Emergency Relief and the Birth Control Movement," enclosed in SPB to Thomas Underwood, April 18, 1935, SPBP.

11. Robert McLean to SPB, October 28, 1931, SPBP.

12. "Persons Arrested," October–November 1931, IPL-UIC, supplement II, box 4, folder 54A.

13. California Legislature, *Fourth Report of the Senate Fact-Finding Committee on Un-American Activities, 1948: Communist Front Organizations* (Sacramento: California Senate), 114, 350.

14. "Social Insurance and/or Social Security," *SSR* 8, no. 3 (September 1934): 537–40 (quotation p. 539).

15. California Legislature, *Fourth Report*, 150–51 and 350–51.

16. SPB, *Women in the Twentieth Century: A Study of Their Political, Social and Economic Activities* (New York: McGraw-Hill, 1933), 269 and 272.

17. EA, "SPB Over the Years," 420.

18. Gale, "Great Ladies of Chicago," 479–482 (first and second quotations p. 479; last quotation 482).

Index

Pan-American Union: IACW in, 227; revitalization of, 202
Panic of 1837, 13
Pankhurst, Christabel, 148
Pankhurst, Emmeline, 148, 152
Paris Peace Conference (Versailles), 190–91
Park, Robert, 132, 134
Parsons, Lucy, 81
Paul, Alice, 148, 152; on ERA, 205; hunger strike by, 153
peace movements: international, 171; woman suffrage and, 173–74; women's, 2, 169–200, 283. See also pacifism
pension plans, companies', 256. See also mothers' pensions
Perkins, Frances, 211, 219, 223; on Breckinridge-Abbott partnership, 276–77; Breckinridge and, 238, 257, 348n21; on Committee on Economic Security, 250; on Pan-American labor bureau, 222; and Social Security Board, 258
personal lives, historical context of, vii
Pethick-Lawrence, Emmeline, 174
philanthropy, scientific, 114–15, 136
political economy, Breckinridge's study of, 78
politics, party, 152; Breckinridge on, 244; social work's freedom from, 243
Pollard, Madeline, 69
Popular-Front Pan-American feminism, 225. See also Pan-American feminism
Popular Peace Conference (Buenos Aires, 1936), 226–27
Pound, Roscoe, 72, 157
poverty, Breckinridge's advocacy concerning, 21, 24, 39, 107
President's Committee on Social Trends, Breckinridge's work for, 328n54
professionalization: disassociation from advocacy, 132; gender dynamics of, 135; objectivity in, 132; problems of, 131–32; in Progressive era, 87; reform and, 136; of social work, 113, 117, 126, 128, 135–36, 241
professionalization, women's, vii; Breckinridge's influence on, 99–100; role of research in, 115. See also women, professional
Progressive era: belief in information, 104; Breckinridge's participation in, 2; professionalization in, 87; social welfare pro-

grams of, 237; at University of Chicago, 76, 117; urban planning in, 103
Progressive Party: Breckinridge's support for, 151; Platform of Industrial Minimums, 94, 151
prostitutes: accused, 163; recruitment of, 109
protectionism, debates about, 216
protective legislation, 154; advocates for, 210; Breckinridge's advocacy of, 3–4, 92–95, 103, 157, 159, 204, 222–23, 225; Equal Rights Amendment and, 154, 203; Lutz's proposal for, 222–23; NWP on, 216; opposition to, 204; Progressive Party support for, 151. See also labor legislation; women workers
psychology, Breckinridge on, 269, 270
public money, public administration of, 245
public policy, versus private charity, 129, 130, 238

race relations: Breckinridge on, 26, 50–53, 103–5; nineteenth-century, 27–28, 103–5
Reconstruction: Breckinridge family during, 20–21, 26, 51; enfranchisement of African Americans, 147; legislation of, 26–27; "Radical," 51
Red Cross: during Great Depression, 236; at University of Chicago, 185
Red Scare (1920s), 160; Breckinridge during, 188, 197–200; University of Chicago during, 199
reform, Progressive: Breckinridge's advocacy for, viii, ix, 7–8, 83. See also Progressive era
reform, social: Chicago movements for, 4, 76, 77, 88, 96; interrelatedness of, 5; research and, 4, 76, 102–3, 135, 138; urban, 76
reformers, women, 2; Chicago group, 4; at Hull House, 96–100; as role models, 129; in Roosevelt administration, 238; in SSA curriculum, 129. See also activism, women's
"resistance," twenty-first century: female participants in, 283
Rich, Adena Miller, 166
Richmond, Mary, 114–15, 136
Riley family, before Chicago Renters' Court, 236
Roche, Josephine, 251; in Roosevelt administration, 239
Roosevelt, Eleanor, 217, 223, 225, 245; Breckinridge and, 253

women, professional, vii; barriers to, 60; in
social work, 98–99; teachers, 61. *See also*
professionalization
women, unmarried: family claims on, 60;
year in Europe, 65
women's clubs: Breckinridge's work with,
109; pacifism of, 174
women's colleges: elite, 32; in loco parentis, 32; postgraduate experiences, 56, 58;
preparation for service, 30. *See also* higher
education, women's; Wellesley College
Women's Confederation for American Peace,
224
Women's Consultative Committee on Nationality, 226
Women's Industrial Conference, 154
Women's International League for Peace and
Freedom (WILPF), 2, 177, 191; foreign-
policy feminism of, 197; Fourth Inter-
national Congress (Washington, 1924),
196; on Spider's Web chart, 198. *See also*
International Committee of Women for
Permanent Peace
Women's International League for Peace and
Freedom, Section for the United States
(WILPF-U.S.), 177; aid to Europe, 193;
Breckinridge in, 191–92, 199, 202, 210. *See
also* Woman's Peace Party
Women's Joint Congressional Committee
(WJCC), 153
Women's Peace Union, 197
Women's Political Union, suffragism of, 174
women's rights: fascist threat to, 228; federal
role in, 162; feminist differences over, 5, 8,
146, 158, 168, 205; feminist pacifism and,
175, 178, 182; international movement for,
171; labor legislation and, 151–52; League

of Women Voters on, 162; Pan-American,
203; at Seventh Pan-American Conference, 210; at Wellesley, 36–37; to work, 223.
See also citizenship, women's; equal rights;
suffrage
women's rights demonstration (Radcliffe
College, 1943), 5
Women's Trade Union League, 156; Breckinridge's work with, 250
women workers: Abbott's study of, 89;
Breckinridge's advocacy for, 109, 222–23;
industrial, 89, 154; labor legislation for,
223; legislative control of, 95; minimum
wage for, 94, 103, 279; right to marry, 223;
social justice for, 109; ten-hour laws for, 93,
94, 95, 103, 109; trade unions and, 93, 156,
250; working conditions of, 92. *See also* labor legislation; protective legislation
Woolley, Mary, 270
Woolley, Robert Wickliffe: daughter of, 275,
276
World War I: antipreparedness movement,
179–80; Breckinridge's internationalism
during, 189–90; Breckinridge's opposition
to, 171; civic engagement concerning, 174;
conscientious objectors in, 188; debts to
U.S. following, 193; defense industries of,
186; "nonresister" stance toward, 182–83;
outbreak of, 174; preparedness for, 182; refugees from, 195–96; University of Chicago
support for, 184–86; U.S. participation in,
116, 181–89; Woman's Peace Party in, 173,
182, 183, 186; women's responsibility in, 187
World War II: Breckinridge's pacifism during,
200; feminist internationalism in, 204
Wright, Helen, 122, 137–38
Wright, J. Butler, 212

ANYA JABOUR is Regents Professor of History at the University of Montana. Her books include *Topsy-Turvy: How the Civil War Turned the World Upside Down for Southern Children* and *Scarlett's Sisters: Young Women in the Old South.*

The University of Illinois Press
is a founding member of the
Association of University Presses.

Composed in 10.75/13 Arno Pro
with Scala Sans display
by Jim Proefrock
at the University of Illinois Press
Cover designed by Jennifer S. Fisher
Cover illustration: Sophonisba Breckinridge, ca. 1880s
(Wellesley College Archives). Background: Women
delegates to the Progressive Party National Convention
in Chicago, 1912 (State Library of New South Wales).
Manufactured by Sheridan Books, Inc.

University of Illinois Press
1325 South Oak Street
Champaign, IL 61820-6903
www.press.uillinois.edu